Business Risk Management

Business Risk Management

Bob Ritchie

Staffordshire University Business School
UK

and

David Marshall

Staffordshire University
UK

CHAPMAN & HALL
University and Professional Division

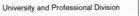 London · Glasgow · New York · Tokyo · Melbourne · Madras

Published by Chapman & Hall, 2–6 Boundary Row, London SE1 8HN

Chapman & Hall, 2–6 Boundary Row, London SE1 8HN, UK

Blackie Academic & Professional, Wester Cleddens Road,Bishopbriggs, Glasgow G64 2NZ, UK

Chapman & Hall Inc., 29 West 35th Street, New York NY10001, USA

Chapman & Hall Japan, Thomson Publishing Japan, Hirakawacho Nemoto Building, 6F, 1-7-11 Hirakawa-cho, Chiyoda-ku, Tokyo 102, Japan

Chapman & Hall Australia, Thomas Nelson Australia, 102 Dodds Street, South Melbourne, Victoria 3205, Australia

Chapman & Hall India, R. Seshadri, 32 Second Main Road, CIT East, Madras 600 035, India

First edition 1993

© 1993 Bob Ritchie and David Marshall

Typeset in Times by Falcon Graphic Art, Wallington, Surrey

Printed in Great Britain at the Alden Press, Oxford

ISBN 0 412 43100 9

∞ Printed on permanent acid-free text paper, manufactured in accordance with the proposed ANSI/NISO Z 39.48–199X and ANSI Z 39.48–1984

Contents

An introduction to risk $\boxed{1}$

1.1 PRELIMINARY ISSUES

As authors, we ought to find it very easy to write a book about risk. After all, we all know when we take risks, whether it be crossing the road, slicing vegetables in the kitchen or setting up a new business. In fact, because of the many dangers that surround us, every event that we survive represents a continuous learning opportunity to gain information on how to avoid or reduce the threat of the unwanted consequence; so most of the things that we plan and do each day are dominated by the experiences that we had in the past. If we look at the way in which the human species has managed to survive through the centuries, it should be obvious that we have necessarily been aware of risk as a factor in everyday life. Indeed, whether we go back to the primitive days when the first signs of intelligence were emerging or examine the intellectual demands required by the complexity of our lives in the twentieth century, the whole process of risk analysis and evaluation has been accepted and approved as a significant contributing element to the way in which both individuals and organizations will take and implement decisions. In primitive times, a hunter might routinely be required to confront a dangerous animal in order to get and keep food – a decision based on expediency. As our culture has become more modern and richer, an increasing number have demanded that the more obvious risks be eliminated from our society – a decision to use community wealth for socially altruistic purposes.

But even though many different risks are now recognized and governments attempt to regulate or control the causes of danger, there is also a trend to pursue risk actively. It is a paradox that as cars have become safer, we feel the need to drive them more quickly and with less regard for the speed limits. Many now engage in 'risk recreations' such as hang-gliding, mountaineering, caving, skiing etc, and the risk element is considered an essential part of the experience. Crowds flock to the new adventure parks where 'white-knuckle' rides scare and entertain. Thus, from these two opening paragraphs, we should recognize that risk may have both positive and negative characteristics – it may be desirable to some and unwanted by others.

The main theme of this book is to begin the process of answering the question, 'Is there a best way to manage risk in business?' Common sense may tell us that no one way will ever be the best for every different situation, but we may be able to identify principles that may help every organization to optimize its performance. This will involve a focus on the theory and practice of decision-making when confronted by uncertainty, and we shall be looking at those situations in which there is a need for the managers to balance the often conflicting demands of the different possible strategies believed to produce both short- and long-term performance as measured by the organization. But because business is an integral part of the social and economic environment that we call the market, we will also be examining how the environment works and affects the operation of the business.

Experience shows that the most effective managers are those who take time to think about present needs and future trends. The difficulty is that trying to analyse the future always poses more questions than it offers answers. But a manager who is more aware of possible developments and outcomes, both internal to the organization and in its markets, and who acts proactively rather than reactively, is more likely to be successful. The thought invested by such a manager is the equivalent of capital. It is the investment of intelligence and creativity, and it is equally as important to the modern business as the acquisition of financial and physical production resources. Indeed, an organization's goals can be seriously prejudiced by uninformed decision-making. At worst, the survival of the business may be placed at risk because management fail to appreciate the significance of potential loss exposure (Figure 1.1). One recent and dramatic example was provided by the American corporation, A. H. Robins Inc., which was bankrupted as a result of claims arising from the marketing of its Dalkon Shield. The moral for managers is as stated by Tuffey (1991), namely,

> We are at all times surrounded by potential solutions to our problems . . . We have only to be alert to the possibilities and make effective use of them. (p. 39)

This alertness has not always been considered a beneficial characteristic. At certain periods in history, society has made very different judgments about the trustworthiness of those who have demonstrated powers of

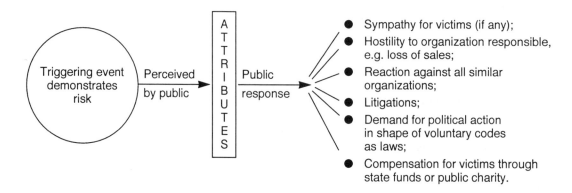

Figure 1.1 Public responses to risk events.

foresight. In classical times, those endowed with superior predictive abilities might have been considered to have had magical qualities as oracles or soothsayers. Their wisdom, often associated with old age and valued experience, might have guided statesmen and changed the destiny of ancient worlds. In the Middle Ages, others might have been considered witches or warlocks, imposing superstitious fear. Their characterization as being old, and being attended by cats as 'familiars', converted the everyday into something threatening, and detection in heresy by a Church militant would have often lead to execution by burning.

As we have moved into the modern ages of scientific rationalism, the more obvious mythologies and superstitions have been replaced by more pragmatic concerns in the commercial world. If we ignore the fringe sciences of graphology (handwriting analysis) and dowsing (detection generally using metal rods), both of which have been used for personnel recruitment, the majority of business people now accept the need to develop more scientific powers of foresight. So whereas early man might 'point the bone' and sacrifice animals to examine their entrails, we may now command software packages to give us an insight into 'truth'. The modern process of automated consultation is, of course, intended to be more reliable than the gory exploration of intestines by a good home cook with a fortune-telling business to run. But one of the modern problems is that the expectations of users may sometimes exceed the powers of the machine. Advertising agencies often make extravagant claims as to the predictive abilities of their clients' wares, and lead users to place unjustified faith in the machine's output. One of the issues to be explored in this book will therefore be the extent to which any information system can produce material for safe use in decision-making.

A further issue is that as human knowledge has grown, so our appreciation of risks has changed. In a medical context, there has been a significant shift in the public's perception as scientific measurement has become more refined. When scientists could only measure carcinogens at the level of parts per million, the response from the public was less alarmed than when carcinogens could be detected at the level of parts per billion. Whether rationally or not, the public were more concerned because the tests had become more sensitive. Now even the smallest particle detected is unacceptable to some. There has also been a risk transition, i.e. we have moved from risks associated with an agricultural society of great poverty, to the more modern risks associated with urban living and industrialization. Such is the complexity and significance of many new technologies and the concentration of production and transportation facilities, that a single mistake can now cause a major disaster, e.g. a pilot may fail to observe proper procedures and crash an airliner into the heart of a city or a nuclear power plant may melt down and release radiation over a large area.

As a result, there is a remarkable new paradox emerging. We have become aware of so many factors that could be considered in decision-making, whether at an individual or at a global level. We know so much more about pollution and the ecosystem, about genetic engineering and food production, and so on. Yet the honest specialist will also humbly admit how much we do not know. Indeed, so rapid is the growth of information that we actually live in a time of unprecedented uncertainty. In an ideal world, we would have stability of information so that we could allow proper debates to shape our values before allowing the next input of information. But each month sees a new issue in the mass media, whether it be salmonella in eggs, the greenhouse effect or acid rain; and the population is becoming ever more risk-conscious without firm information upon which to evaluate those risks.

The problem is made more acute by the capacity of the news media to produce instantaneous coverage of any event. If this capacity was used only to give an instant alert in the case of imminent danger, it would be highly beneficial. But sometimes the sensationalist response of the media has been excessive when later weighed against the reality of the risk. This raises the difficult question of when it is proper to withhold information from the public. There is a natural tendency in a free society to argue against any form of censorship. But if wild scare stories appear before the scientists have completed their detailed work, the endless crying of wolf in the media may undermine public confidence in both the science and the communications media.

1.2 THE NATURE OF AN ORGANIZATION

1.2.1 Society as an organization distinguished

As a preliminary step to understanding risk, we need to understand a little about the social and commercial contexts within which we live and work. At one extreme, we tend to think of the global society which is trying to provide a safe environment for people to live in and to deal with the big problems of pollution, poverty, famine, etc. This society has to be capable of supporting many different cultures and it survives by finding the common denominators between all the diverse interests. At the other end of the spectrum, we find the more controlled form of organization that we call business. Business organizations are fundamentally different from social organizations. The following are typical of the distinctions that can be made:

- Within the limits of social (and, consequently, legal acceptability) all the people can do what they like, when they like it, but a business is usually specialized, undertaking only a limited number of activities;
- Once people are born into the world, they have various human rights to live, to be educated and to work without discrimination – a civilized society cannot exile its citizens but a business has the power both to hire and fire the members of the organization, and it will also have a discretion whether to educate or train those who work there;
- Ignoring the duty not to compete with the employing organization, what an employee does when not at work is irrelevant to the operation

of the business, whereas a society cannot stop being 'interested' in the activities of all the people, all the time;

- The nature of the business operation is to control the activities of those who work, while the aim of a society should be to support the activites who live in the community;
- Because of the need to keep bankers and investors happy, a business will have to balance its books on a regular basis, whereas global societies may take the decision to run a deficit for many years.

1.2.2 The concept of the business organization

The taking of certain classes of risk is fundamental to the development of commercial organizations. We must therefore propose a concept of the organization as a business enterprise. The history of the modern state has been an evolution from an agricultural to an industrial base of activity. Many factors were at work, but one of the social and economic features that helped to make this transformation less disruptive was the emergence of the notion of a business and its acceptance as a legitimate means of assuming power over people and property. In philosophical terms, the characterization of business has always been a reflection of the prevailing codes of morality and rationality. As the Industrial Revolution passed through its early stages, thinkers such as Beccaria and Jeremy Bentham began to formulate the concept of Utilitarianism as a new reformation to justify not only the abolition of slavery but the dismantling of the penal state. It flowed from questions such as that asked of the death penalty for crime,

> Is it really useful or necessary for the safety and good order of society? (Beccaria, 1785, p. 42)

Today, such questions would be considered doctrinaire and simplistic, and not capable of answer in absolute terms. But the then prevailing quality of thinking and analysis was more mechanical and pedantic in its evaluation of social phenomena and psychology. A similar example emerges through the work of Newton whereby the world came to be viewed as a form of mechanism, operating with a regularity determined by its internal structure and the laws of nature.

It should therefore come as no surprise that the concept of business and the means of its strategic control reflected a perception of it as a form of machine, created by its owner to serve the owner's purpose which was the extraction of a profit from the market.[1] Indeed, because of the prevailing political doctrine of *laissez faire*, the new captains of industry were allowed almost total omnipotence, with Parliament and the courts prepared to protect the right of owners to a return of their investment.

To survive, this concept requires a strictly hierarchical society with the working class tightly controlled and available for exploitation in conditions that we would consider unfit for any human being to have to endure. However, as the workers were barely literate and bombarded on all sides by the discourse of submissiveness, they were acquiescent with low levels of aspiration to improve their lot. Indeed, with the ever-present threats of death, disease and destitution, concepts of human dignity were of little interest in the struggle to survive. But following the introduction of compulsory education, the loss of manpower through disease and war, and the increasing costs of training workers to operate the more sophisticated machinery, the concept of the organization as a machine began to change.

Fuelled by an expansion in the world markets, business found that it did not have the capital to grow in line with demand. The only way to fund the necessary expansion was by diluting private ownership through the public subscription of shares. Thus, the private owner was no longer godlike and communication with the owners of the equity became a more diffuse process. From the workers' point of view, the management became a form of agent or intermediary between the shopfloor and the now absent owners. One of the benefits of unionization was that it allowed representation from outside the organization to meet on more equal terms with the providers of capital such as banks, insurance companies and pension fund managers and, within the social environment, the introduction of state benefits and the welfare state meant that workers were not pressured to the same extent by the threat of destitution to accept poor working conditions.

The conceptual change was from the organization as a machine to the organization as a biological entity. This represents a major shift of emphasis for whereas a machine can have no purpose of its own, i.e. it is simply a tool in the hands of its owner(s), an organism is capable of having its own needs and desires. It is true that such needs may be primitive and instinctual, e.g. to survive, grow and replicate itself, but the effect is to force a reappraisal of the fundamental assumptions about profit. If a human is deprived of oxygen, death results. Similarly, if a commercial organization fails to make a profit, it ceases to exist. Thus, by analogy, profits are necessary for the continued existence of an organization and so the need for profit is converted from an end to a means to the end of survival.

This has now led us to consider business in terms of social systems and subsystems (some of which may be non-living, e.g. a manufacturing process), each of which may be subsumed within the organization and may have its own purposes which are not wholly consistent with those of the organization at large. The effectiveness of modern management must now be assessed in terms of its ability to produce reconciliations of the divergences that may exist between the social subsystems, and to adjust satisfactorily to the needs of the non-living subsystems to ensure a stable and acceptably safe working environment. If there are defects in the interface between the human and the non-living subsystems, this may cause accidents. Hence, an accident may be caused because of machine failures or malfunctions, or because the information flow from the process did not alert the human monitors to the emerging problem.

Management must also organize to meet the new threats to business autonomy from organized interest groups within the external environment. Thus, social organizations such as Friends of the Earth monitor the businesses which pollute the ecosphere and bring pressure to bear for change, and state agencies such as the Health and Safety Executive and the National Rivers Authority have coercive powers to require change. Such changes will usually affect profitability and represent a major shift in terms of the accountability of business to those injured by its activities. According to Cartland (1991), American shareholders are becoming more militant in claiming injury, and they are now responsible for half the claims against officers and directors of American companies. These claims are usually associated with mergers and acquisitions where the share values are prejudiced, e.g. prematurely cutting off an auction, the fairness of a merger price, the value of an acquisition, leaving poison pills, etc. may give rise to actions alleging breach of fiduciary duties. More controversially, because takeovers inflate share prices, directors have been sued for trying to defend against an aggressive takeover, or for spending too much of the organization's money to defend their own interests.[2] Although these trends have yet to cross the Atlantic, they may be an indication of risk exposure to come. Laws have also changed to introduce remedies for workers who are injured through lack of care on the part of factory and office managers. This represents the elevation of the status of a worker from simple cog in the machine to a human being entitled to the same care and respect as all other parts of the organizational body politic.

A modern organization must therefore be seen as a social system in which there is division of labour. This reflects the reality that once two or more people are involved, their separate efforts must be co-ordinated if the best is to be made of their efforts. This requires the proper allocation of responsibility between those involved – the horizontal plane within the traditional organization – and the definition of authority within the system – the vertical plane within the traditional organization. There are three ways in which to divide the labour:

1. by input or function;
2. by output or service;
3. by market or receivers of service.

The last way is important in that modern concepts such as Total Quality Management see each part of the organization which is separated by input or output as a potential customer to the services of the other parts. Thus, instead of perceiving the organization as a centrally controlled economy comparable to that of a communist state, its internal state is considered as a market economy in its own right, matching the market economy in the external environment. Theory says that to optimize performance, an organization must try to provide the best service to all its customers, whether those customers are internal or external.

One of the most effective ways of enhancing performance is to encourage specialization. Thus, the modern manager may produce a decision support system which depends on batteries of experts whose services are always on call. Computer programmers may generate new models upon which to judge the performance of the market, better market research may produce more reliable statistical data, better statistical techniques may produce more accurate analyses. A different result of this narrow specialization is the increasing unlikeliness that any one manager now has the expertise to supervise the work of the others in the organization. Gone are the days of the traditional manager who rose through the ranks, learning the jobs at each level of progression. The task of the modern manager is now to lead the fellow employees, providing a supportive environment in which each may contribute effectively to the well-being of the organization. Indeed, it would now be proper to value an organization in terms of its future potential to manage its workers. This recognizes that those workers who are well motivated in support of their organization will contribute more to its future than those more distant investors. Indeed, this may be forcing a reappraisal of the concept of ownership.

European shareholders are rarely concerned with the practicality of management, being content to take their dividends at the end of each financial year and treating the annual general meetings as mere formalities. Although the larger institutional investors may have a more direct influence, e.g. through board membership, there is increasing separation between the concepts of investor and owner, with consequent resistance to the exercise of power by the shareholder. Against such a background, it may not be unreasonable to consider that any organization is owned by and for the benefit of those who are employed by it. Organizations now plan staff development, i.e. to increase the competence of staff and to enable them to realize their legitimate desires. This means, among other things, improving the quality of life within the organization. This is not an economic concept, yet it is becoming an indispensable part of a manager's portfolio as we move into an increasingly aesthetic appraisal of what it means to be employed by an organization. (The nature of an organization is considered in more detail in Chapter 10.)

1.3 RISK IN SOCIETY

1.3.1 Risks taken by individuals

Within a government framework of acceptability, people may wager on the outcome of sporting contests or the occurrence of chance events. They are allowed to use any reasonable means, including those of alleged scientific precision such as computer databases, to predict the future performance of animals or players on the basis of past form. It is entirely consistent with public policy to encourage such activities since the money derived from betting levies and taxation helps to offset the national debt. Some states more directly tap this human obsession to achieve great returns from minimal stakes through local and national lotteries, syphoning off a proportion of the funds of speculation for the subsidy of more altruistic services such as hospitals, the relief of poverty or the promotion of the arts. People in other states may succumb to the blandishments of television or other advertising campaigns and invest in shares and other securities, for example trusting that 'junk bonds' are a safe means of increasing wealth or that newly privatized industries will make a safe return on capital invested.

Nothing said so far should detract from the importance attributed to the risk/gain factor in the present business environment. It is reflected in common expressions such as 'speculate to accumulate', and there is implicit confirmation of this acceptance and the value attributed to it in the contemporary rituals of social or commercial gambling. Even in modest and conventional business situations, it is now recognized that real economic progress is impossible without the taking of some risks. Indeed, depending on the prevailing economic conditions, it is possible that even survival as a business or just the maintenance of the status quo may be impossible without taking risks. Thus, people come to associate risk-taking with success and progress, and there are rewards in terms of salary and/or promotion given to those who make good decisions in risky situations.

Other people may be more positive and participate in the speculations of confident business managers, or seek to become the managers of their own businesses. It is interesting to note how modern organizations try to encourage a positive attitude towards risk-taking. Many companies now adopt performance-related criteria and structure the salary and bonus systems with the intention of shifting the culture of the organization towards greater entrepreneurial activity. Bonuses may be set both for the individual and the team. For the individual employee, minimum targets may be agreed with percentage bonuses, usually up to an agreed maximum, for achieving greater performance. Sometimes, this may be tied into a share option scheme which will give the individual a dividend if the organization's performance is good. Team building is encouraged by a different tier of bonuses tied into performance targets set by reference to groups of different sizes within the organization. Each employee may then be allowed to gamble the bonus(es) or a percentage of the minimum salary – the most usual limit is up to 20 per cent of salary. If the agreed targets are not met, the employee will lose the entitlement to the bonus(es) and the agreed percentage of salary. But if the targets are met, the bonus(es) and salary element will be increased. The amount of this increase will usually be determined by the extent of the money risked. The hope is that employees at all levels of the organization will be encouraged to take a more positive role in promoting the organization's activities. However, remember that in the UK the way in which these schemes are written down must take account of the Wages Act which forbids fines and deductions from salaries unless various conditions are met.

1.3.2 Risks at a national level

Although each potential or actual entrepreneur will measure success in individual material terms, the long-term wealth of the state relies upon the accumulated success of its residents. The modern capitalist state must therefore always be positive in its support of the infrastructure of commerce, providing a reasonably fraud-free environment in which wealth may be acquired fairly and in free competition. We should also remember that the tax system has been designed so as to allow losses to be set against profits. This aspect of the tax system gives encouragement to business because the potential reduction in tax liability helps to reduce the overall risk. This entitlement to relief does, of course, depend upon making sufficient profits from the other projects to get the full benefit from the losses.

It has been interesting to observe that as capitalism emerged as the victorious system in the international cold war of the doctrines, entrepreneurship has become increasingly important in the global context. There will be a powerful pressure in many countries towards a *laissez faire* approach, hoping that business will relieve poverty and encourage economic growth. In America, presidents Reagan and Bush moved towards 'less government' while consecutive Conservative governments in the United Kingdom move increasingly towards the reduction or elimination of public expenditure in support of the growing private sector. In the new Commonwealth of Independent States, the political problem in converting the old 'black economy' into the legitimate economy is that too many of the Nomenclatura (the old Communist Party bosses) were involved in the creation of private wealth and cannot now be seen to be running the new industries and enterprises. In all countries, old and new, business has new roles to play and new responsibilities to consider.

1.3.3 Risks at an international level

At an international level, the process of risk appraisal by the United Nations and other groupings of states is now seen as fundamental to the survival of the human species and the existence of life in determining how societies should feed, clothe, house and transport themselves so as to minimize ozone depletion, maintain the present ecosystem, reduce environmental pollution, etc. Although many of the macro issues might have appeared to be external to the individual or to the organization, they are nevertheless contributing factors to the general level of uncertainty within our global society. As such, they should not be overlooked at any level. At the very least they should be discussed if not positively confronted by organizations that can make some difference, say, through their buying policies of raw materials or production processes. Equally, the political process, both local and national, should shape the values and policies within which businesses operate and people live their lives.

Until the 1970s, the political focus tended to be retrospective, i.e. society looked at the damage that had been caused to the environment and discussed how to begin cleaning up the mess. Today, the view is both retrospective and prospective, i.e. the expectation is that while the clean-up continues, both industry and individuals will act to reduce damage in the future, e.g. by producing less waste or recycling it, by modifying industrial processes, by legislating to control emissions and dumping, etc. The challenge for both industry and the regulators is always to identify the best solution for each problem, i.e. it should never be assumed that any one solution will actually resolve all difficulties. Thus, to prevent the discharge of waste chemicals, an organization might build holding tanks, but then cause air discharges through evaporation or loss into the water-table through leaching.

1.3.4 Regulatory frameworks and methods

In the UK, the Health and Safety Executive has cautiously expressed the view that the use of quantified risk assessment might become a useful part of the process to control industrial risks.[3] However, although a part of the functions of risk assessment are contained within a regulatory framework of notification and consultation, the British approach is somewhat limited. In Europe, there are two good examples of risk assessment legislation. The first example is to be found in Norway. In 1981 the Norwegian Petroleum Directorate issued the *Guidelines for Safety Evaluation of Platform Conceptual Design*. The initial design of all offshore oil and gas platforms must now go through a quantitative risk evaluation process designed to establish whether the concept of the proposal is acceptable. The aim is to ensure that all the risks are identified and considered before any installation is constructed. Once the design is complete, the building and operation of the platform is monitored, verifying whether the initial assumptions were correct and, where appropriate modifying the design or the operating procedures to reduce the now identified risks. Thus, risk assessment and design are seen as a single procedure to optimize safety. The second example is to be found in Holland where, in 1985, the Dutch government introduced a stringent scheme involving criteria of both individual and social risk to protect the environment (Versteeg, 1988).

Indeed, as a general proposition, we believe that this form of risk assessment is inevitably linked to reliability engineering where the frequency analysis of the failure of components and equipment is of vital relevance. In this, the failure of a component is not merely a question of the quality of design and manufacture, but also of the environment in which the component is expected to function. The major problem is the insufficiency of data as to failure rates for each component in different environments. Until governments begin the more systematic collection of this data, the verification of design safety will continue to be problematic.

But no matter what the level of decision-making, whether municipal or inter-governmental, at its most simplistic level, the basic process of deciding whether the taking of any risk is acceptable will always be determined by the stakes and the odds, i.e. by identifying what is hazarded and assessing the level of probability that the outcome will be favourable. This will necessitate some form of information gathering exercise – a form of audit of industry, supplemented by the reporting of incidents by monitoring bodies and the public. Only when a substantial body of reliable information has been collected and collated can proper standards be produced and guidelines be written.

1.3.5 The drafting of regulations

The key to the writing of effective official documents is the use of easily understood language, so that those who are expected to comply may know exactly what is required of them. It has been interesting to observe the shift in the terminology used by NATO since July 1990. At that time, the heads of state recognized that changes were taking place in Central and Eastern Europe. In 1992, we can now see that the former enemies of the West have dismantled their political and military framework of co-operation and have rejected the concept of ideological hostility to the West. This has necessitated a significant reappraisal of the challenges to the security of the West. In November 1991, NATO issued a new document entitled *The Alliance's Strategic Concept*. The importance of the adaptation of perspectives was highlighted by the abandonment of the use of the concept of 'threat'.

> In contrast with the predominant threat of the past, the risks to Allied security that remain are multi-faceted in nature and multi-directional, which makes them hard to predict and assess . . . Risks to Allied security are less likely to result from calculated aggression against the territory of the Allies, but rather from the adverse consequences of instabilities that may arise from the serious economic, social and political difficulties, including ethnic rivalries and territorial disputes, which are faced by many countries in central and eastern Europe.
> (paras 9 and 10)

Whereas a threat is seen as a direct issue arising from the confrontation between two polarized and opposed groups of states, all that remains are the less easily identifiable risks to peace. Threats are therefore seen as more tangible and immediately predictable, and they require positive responses by deploying troops and equipment in strategically important locations. Risks, on the other hand, are less immediately quantifiable but no less real and must be met by carefully structured planning efforts such as a flexible rapid response force, and new political initiatives to enhance civilian control over military forces and budgets, to reduce the spread of nuclear weapons etc. We may draw the general rule that a threat is something clearly identified and sufficiently probable that it must be met by positive and focused counter-measures. A risk is something less easily identified and more difficult to assess in terms of probability. But if it is considered sufficiently real, it must be the subject of a planning exercise.

1.3.6 The practice of risk management

The practicality of risk management at all levels of human activity (more often than not on a wing and a prayer of intuition, educated guesswork or political expediency) is now being matched by the development of conceptual models and empirical research strategies into the phenomenon of risk by many discipline areas including economics, accountancy/finance and the behavioural sciences. More recently, the research programs of the larger hardware and software producers have been focusing millions of dollars and pounds sterling towards the commercially risky market of providing comprehensive information systems and analytical tools to aid decision-makers within organizations, e.g. capital asset pricing model developments and computerized decision support systems. The problem with many of these eminently worthy efforts is that the approach is frequently somewhat mechanical in nature, striving to produce certainty in an otherwise uncertain world. But as already indicated, much of the advertising hype would have the potential user believe that output from these systems is highly reliable. Indeed, there is considerable evidence to suggest that the way in which quantitative data is presented to users can have a significant effect on outcomes and often users do not perform any analysis on output to normalize it or to establish its credibility (Hester *et al.*, 1990).

1.3.7 Risk management and insurance distinguished

Returning directly to the theme of this book, the management of risk in the business environment, a historical review will show that managers tended to deal with the phenomenon of risk as a matter for insurance, and risks were assessed only in terms of possible costs. In a sense, this misunderstands the nature of insurance. If you believe that the various probabilities attaching to future sources of loss can be accurately assessed, the payment of insurance premiums is a transfer of resources against known contingencies. We prefer the modern interpretation adopted by McGuire *et al.* (1991), that

> the essence of the transaction is to pay a sum to change the probabilities for the better. (p. 330)

Thus, insurance premiums are a form of loss prevention or self-protection. Now, the topic of risk management is considered fair game for a wide variety of specialists including statisticians and economists, doctors and psychologists, lawyers and accountants, sociologists and political scientists, environmental health groups etc. This diversity of input recognizes that all otherwise specialized disciplines may have something interesting and useful to contribute to the debate on what is a risk and when is it acceptable to take that risk.

1.3.8 Risk and the other academic disciplines

The difficulty is that each discipline by virtue of its specialization, is only addressing a part of the risk spectrum. The contribution that each discipline may make to the overall debate is therefore limited. We have the task of trying to break down some of the institutionalized barriers between the different disciplines, borrowing and combining ideas whenever a synergy produces a good result. One of the other components of this book is to explore the possibility of developing normative models, whether in general decision-making or in individual decision-making where relatively constrained decision scenarios are in operation. The purpose would be to give managers a better opportunity to understand what they do and thereby improve their performance. The aim is therefore not simply to restate the present range of tools, techniques and approaches which relate to risk and uncertainty, but rather to challenge many of the assumptions upon which these have been based and to question their validity in solving real business problems.

However, we must introduce a note of caution. The analysis and evaluation of risk depends upon our capacity to manipulate information. The modern hardware and software developments in our 'high-tech' society appear to be giving us ever more sophisticated powers and calculations of enormous complexity can now be undertaken at high speed. We have to recognize that the only consequence of this computing power may simply be to show up deficiencies in the models we have been creating and using. Indeed, there is something of a dilemma for those who design models. Given the advances in the technology to provide significantly more raw computing power, we are offered the apparent potential for the handling of bigger and more complex models. But it may be better to invest our effort in verifying and validating the smaller models first. Once we are assured of the accuracy and reliability of the simple models, we may then more safely move on to the more complicated versions. When designing models, we should therefore be aiming for:

- creating the ability to deal with both static and dynamic situations;
- complete transparency in the structure of the model and in the mathematical basis of all calculations so that the reliability of the model can be assessed and its quality measured through comparisons with other models of similar situations;
- compatibility with mathematical and statistical methods for the analysis of uncertainty and sensitivity.

Until better models are available, the best that we may be able to hope for is a more practical set of conclusions. Since we cannot devise rules and techniques for eliminating risks from our lives, perhaps all that we should be aiming for is a few simple rules for coping in an environment in which future events may cause unwanted consequences.

1.4 RISK AND STRATEGIC MANAGEMENT

Having clarified the terminology of the context within which the art of management is to be practised, the first major issue is to study the handling of risk at a strategic management level. The subject of 'strategic management' as a recognizable and definitive field of study and research has a much shorter history than other discipline areas which impinge on business decision-making. Although research has been conducted into the nature and the processes of strategic decision-making, few substantive models of risk within this process have been developed or researched. Bettis (1982) while recognizing the contribution of financial, economic and corporate strategy theory in emphasizing the importance of risk in the performance of a firm, concluded that

> practice in the area of strategy formulation usually incorporates risk analysis. In spite of this risk has received only limited attention in the strategy research literature. There is a critical need to begin examining risk in both empirical and clinical strategy research. (p. 25)

He argued that there should be more clinical research studies to examine the managerial perceptions of risk and to determine how these perceptions influence the process of strategic decision-making. The problem is to match the research to the reality of decision-making. Although the strategic management field has developed a separate identity from other academic fields including economics, finance and organizational studies, the approaches to risk in these other fields is often considered inappropriate to the practical strategic decision processes. For example, many studies have sought to make use of primarily normative models which:

1. employ restricted alternative/outcome decision situations; and
2. assume perfect information availability and rational decision-taking behaviour.

Such models and assumptions are far removed from the descriptive reality of strategic decision-making in a high pressure commercial environment. As the degree of complexity and the dynamism of the total decision-making environment accelerates more rapidly, organizations and their managers frequently face decisions for which they are singularly ill-equipped. This is not to say that the decision-makers have not had some form of training. The problem lies in the decision-making methodologies, tools and techniques in which the managers have been trained. Often, these tools and techniques have performed reasonably well in the past and most of the managers are able to use them with some degree of comfort. But, with the passage of time, these methods may gradually lose their value and may even be counter-productive to achieving the organization's objectives. Best practice therefore requires organizations to monitor the changing nature of the decision-making environment and the suitability of the older methods. This becomes more important given the speed and severity with which the consequences of incorrect decisions may impact upon the organization. Should deficiencies be detected, managers should consider urgently whether there should be corresponding changes in the manner in which the risk parameter is handled. We try to reflect this practical need through an evaluation of the contribution of risk research in these fields to the field of strategic management, and by trying to develop an appropriate model of strategic decision-making incorporating risk. Astley *et al.* (1982) suggested that the study of strategic decision-making remains of paramount importance in the field of organization theory and management. (p. 357)

1.4.1 Total systems intervention

Most recent contributions to this debate have been made by R. L. Flood and M. C. Jackson (1991) who propose a meta-methodology called total systems intervention (TSI). They distance themselves from the more pragmatic view that management science is about building up a better toolkit of techniques that 'work', and seek to create a comprehensive theory that will help management science to develop as an intellectual discipline. They reject the isolationist approach of always applying the same, tried-and-tested technique or group of techniques because this will always threaten the need to distort the facts to fit the given technique. Instead, they argue that the aim of management should always be the emancipation of all individuals employed within the organization, offering them the opportunity for the maximum development of their potential.

If we reject the idea of the 'quick fix', organizations should be explored by using a range of different techniques, selecting the most appropriate technique for each aspect of the exploration. For this purpose, the three phases of TSI are:

- creativity;
- choice;
- implementation.

The creative phase requires the managers to think about their organization in terms of systems metaphors, e.g. the organization as a machine, an organism, a team, a culture, etc. The point of this stage is to decide which metaphors best capture the spirit of the organization. The managers must then choose which methodologies best suit the characteristics of the organization as now disclosed. The task during the implementation stage is to use the appropriate methodologies to transform the dominant perceptions of the organization, its structures and purposes into specific proposals for change.

But whatever theoretical models are adopted to guide managers, the process of management should be seen as iterative in the pursuit of constructive change with risks within acceptable limits. This begs the question as to the purpose of change. Some managers aim to set policy by identifying defects in the existing systems and then trying to remove those deficiencies. Unfortunately, this approach does not guarantee to improve performance because the replacement methods may be as bad or worse than those replaced. The true aim of change should therefore be to get what we want and not merely to dispose of what we do not want.

1.4.2 Information at a strategic level

The second major issue explored within the book is the interaction between risk perception and information processing within the strategic decision-making situation. The impact that increasing levels of risk perception have on the nature of the data/information search and processing activities both

1. quantitative in terms of time and volume of data; and
2. qualitative in terms of the type of information sought and used,

is to be examined. The influence that the availability of both data and information have on the perception of risk is likewise examined to:

- gauge the reactions of decision-makers to information messages (from blind panic to controlled responses where there is a genuine willingness to reappraise options and to change direction);
- assess the extent of any changes in the perception of relevant risks; and
- evaluate the consequent decisions taken.

Information can represent a significant contributing input into the operations and decisions of an organization. It can also be an embarrassment to be discounted or concealed, or through its dissemination, a means for democratizing the decision-making process. In terms of extreme possibilities, organizations have therefore had to decide whether to invest heavily in the capital and human resources to produce information systems based on developments in information technology, or to retain an essentially autocractic management hierarchy with power based upon limited access to information sources. This book is, in part, designed to evaluate the contribution that information may make to the strategic level of decision-making.

A further underlying theme of the book is the evaluation and development of earlier work by other authors on a contingency framework for management decision-making, with particular emphasis on the strategic level of decisions. In addition to formulating a contingency model, the book also seeks to examine certain key contingency variables.

To help explore and explain the issues in the later stages of the book, the authors have adopted a simulation/case study approach. Simulation has been a fairly standard approach to the teaching of strategic management, particularly in the form of case studies and business simulations. Developments in information technology have facilitated the development of organizational models on which decision-makers may simulate the effects of particular strategic options (e.g. Strategic Management Associates' PIMS (Profit Impact of Marketing Stategies). The experience gained through the use of the simulation/case study approach should provide a basis on which the issues may be explored and more fully comprehended. The aim is to examine the micro or individual level of decision processing. Previous empirical research in this area has focused mainly on the structures and content of strategy-making as opposed to the processes involved. Where the process has been the purpose of the research this has usually been interpreted in terms of the macro or organizational processes, as opposed to the micro or individual-oriented decision processes. In focusing on the decision processes, it has proved necessary to draw on research studies from a number of other related fields of study, and to integrate these into the framework and context of strategic decision-making. The book does not seek to explore all facets of the decision-making processes, but to concentrate primarily on the dimensions of risk and information, and their consequent interactions.

1.5 CONTINGENCY THEORY OF MANAGEMENT

The book embraces the Contingency Theory of Management, particularly in relation to the decision-making processes. The alternative approaches are evaluated and contrasted with the Contingency approach and, while recognizing the potential advantages of the former, it is recognized that the Contingency Model provides a more powerful and representative description of the practical decision-making processes. The penalties of adopting a contingency stance on strategic decision-making are identified and evaluated, and this, in turn, provides a contribution to the Contingency Theory debate.

1.6 OBJECTIVES OF THE BOOK

The book has been designed to achieve the following objectives within the context of the strategic management decision processes in business organizations:

1. an evaluation and distinction between the terms 'risk' and 'uncertainty' in decision-making;
2. the development of a contingency model of the strategic decision-making processes;
3. empirical research and evaluation of the risk construct, and the primary factors contributing towards the differences in risk perceived in different strategic situations;
4. an examination of the influence that the information variable has on the perception of risk;
5. an assessment of the influence that risk perceived has on the quantitative and qualitative dimensions of the information search and processing activities within the decision formulation process;
6. an understanding of the relationship between the perception of risk in the alternative solutions to a decision and the choice of a particular alternative; and
7. the evaluation of simulation as an appropriate research methodology for empirical research in management decision processes.

In meeting these objectives, we will be drawing ideas from a variety of different disciplines, including:

- general management theory and practice;
- decision theory and practice;
- quality assurance methodology and practice;
- financial risk management and practice;

- insurance – a system that helps to share out the cost of loss;
- statistics and the actuarial methodologies that underpin the assessment of probabilities;
- psychology – helping us to understand the cognitive processes underlying the perception and the taking of risks;
- education and training – remember that technological progress is often a bottom-up system, i.e. until there are trained personnel employed, the new techniques cannot be implemented; managers must therefore wait for the teachers, lecturers and trainers to be trained so that the schools, colleges, universities and in-house courses can produce the right level of understanding in the next generation of students and employees. (Remember that if the public are to have confidence in the government, relevant departments must also acquire the relevant knowledge and expertise. Should the public also learn something about the problem, their help and support to solve that problem may be more forthcoming.)

Naturally, this list is only a sample of relevant disciplines. The intention in producing this list is to emphasize the need to take an increasingly holistic approach to problem and solution identification. It may be very comfortable to establish credibility in a narrow specialization. We would advocate the more systematic approach of trying to find relationships between concepts and techniques in the various disciplines, reflecting the increasingly complex environment in which we are to live and develop, and the multiplicity of different values and cultures that our species has developed.

For managers, actual or prospective, we would hope to provide a number of practical guidelines to answer the following 'simple' questions:

- Which risks should be considered? It is tempting only to consider those risks perceived as acute or highly probable.
- Should consideration only be given to risks affecting limited classes of prospective victims? An organization might have a policy only to consider risks to the capital subscribed by the shareholders rather than to consider the risks of injury sustained by those employed by the organization.
- If a wide range of possible victims is to be considered, should we only consider those who are particularly at risk, or include those of average sensitivity? It might, for example, be more cost-effective to target control or security measures on those most at risk, rather than to spread the resources too thinly.
- Should there be any geographical limits imposed? It is tempting only to consider local problems and to ignore the national or international dimensions as being too remote from the organization's interests.
- What sort of timescale limitations should be imposed? Even at short timescales, uncertainty may be a real problem. The longer the timescale of decision-making, the greater the difficulty in producing reliable estimates of risk.
- How far down the line of causation should we go? It is easier to stop at

first-order consequences and to ignore secondary effects.

1.7 STRUCTURE OF THE BOOK

In discussing the role of risk in strategic decision-making, the first step in Chapter 2 is to consider how people think and talk about risk. Once we have a view of the broad concept of risk, we can move on in Chapter 3 to a consideration of the nature of a decision and the role of risk perceptions in decision-making. In Chapter 4 we will develop an operational definition of strategic management, and provide a synopsis and broad evaluation of the research conducted within this field. Chapters 5, 6 and 7 review, evaluate and develop the terms uncertainty and risk, and seek to develop a working definition for the term risk as a basis for the creation of a model for decision-making. A contingency theory or model of the strategic management processes is developed in Chapter 8, following a review and evaluation of the developments in management theory and the parallel developments in contingency theory.

Chapter 9 continues the contingency theme while focusing on the body of research into decision-making processes, with specific emphasis on the use of information within such processes. Chapter 10 considers the nature of an organization in more detail and Chapter 11 returns to a more practical view of risk management as a preliminary to the case study section of the book.

1.8 CONCLUSIONS

There will always be elements of risk in what we do. That our society is safer today than it used to be is due to our growing awareness of the causes of danger and the increasing willingness of states to take action to reduce the level of perceived threats. Because of this new proactiveness, modern business must always consider the needs of the community. In part, this will be self-interested, i.e. there will be greater profit in producing safer, greener products. In part, the state requires this greater sensitivity through the use of regulations. We have therefore moved from the Newtonian world of the organization as an uncaring machine serving the needs of its owner, to the organization as a living organism which needs a supportive environment to ensure survival. Thus, just as an animal needs appropriate food and a safe place to live, so the organization has to maintain the morale of those who work for it while satisfying the external market with a good product or service.

Remember that the flow of interaction between a state and the organization is two-way. Although the state may use its power to intervene whenever it perceives a threat, too active a policy may so disrupt business that it cannot survive. Just think what would happen if new regulations to eliminate sources of risk made dramatic changes every week. There would be chaos as business constantly tried to reorganize to meet the new requirements and costs would rise sharply. The rate of change must therefore be set following discussion between the interested parties. If this means that some of the known risks must be allowed to remain, the decision-makers must agree priorities, hoping to target the more acute dangers first. But given the considerable uncertainty attached to the risk assessment process, this balancing of risks may sometimes lead to arbitrariness and incorrect decisions.

Finally, never forget that risks may have both positive and negative qualities. There are circumstances that some people would find highly dangerous, whether physically or emotionally, that others would actively enjoy. Thus, in the sporting and social part of our lives, some will actively pursue dangerous activities. In the business world, some entrepreneurs will take tremendous risks, finding the experience highly enjoyable, while other more conservative managers will avoid situations of risk wherever possible. Risk is not just a set of natural, physical phenomena that may cause injury to people, e.g. like lightning in a thunder storm. It is also a part of human psychology in what we perceive as being dangerous and what we consider acceptable.

QUESTIONS

1. At a broad general level, make two lists of five activities or phenomena that would be considered risks for an individual. Let the first list show undesirable activities and the second list show activities and events that are considered acceptable.
2. Make a list of five activities or phenomena that would represent risks for a business.
3. Make a list of five activities or phenomena that would represent a risk for a state.
4. What do you think is the difference between a threat and a risk?
5. Under what circumstances should a government interfere with the way in which the business environment is functioning?

Notes

1. Until the Married Women's Property Acts produced in the latter part of the nineteenth century, it was not legally possible for women to own and exploit property. Indeed, women had to wait until 1925 before their general right to own land was confirmed. It is therefore proper to limit early business purposes to the male imagination.
2. Just to give two of the many recent cases, the directors of SmithKline faced a claim that they had failed to seek additional potential buyers and therefore did not get the best price when acquired by Beecham Group plc, while the over-optimistic directors in the case of *Blackman* v. *Polaroid Corp* were censured because they failed to correct a glowing quarterly financial report and so artificially supported the

share price even though they had become aware of problems with the Polavision videocamera.

3. This view was expressed in *Quantified Risk Assessment: Its Input to Decision Making* (HSE, HMSO, 1989) and it forms the basis of the methodology used by the Major Hazard Assessment Unit to take decisions about petrochemical installations and pipelines.

Risk, language and discourse $\boxed{2}$

INTRODUCTION

Concise dictionaries frequently offer simple definitions for all the words they contain. But, no matter how simple the meaning attributed to each word, the way we use the written or spoken word is capable of creating sophisticated levels of meanings. Whether or not listeners or readers can detect all of the possible interpretations will depend upon their access to information about what is being said, the person saying it and the purposes for which it appears to be said. Given that the word 'risk' is used in many different contexts with an equally wide variety of definitions, we have to look at the way in which people talk about risk. This will allow us to explore some of the more interesting ideas about language and power within our society. The aims of this chapter are to begin the process of:

- clarifying the range and scope of 'risk' as a word in our language;
- investigating the composition of risk as a philosophical concept; and
- evaluating its role within the modern organization.

For example, one of the first questions that you might like to consider is whether the concept of risk reflects only negative or the hazard type of outcome, or whether it can incorporate more positive dimensions such as failing to meet target returns on capital but still making a profit.

2.1 RISK AND LANGUAGE

Our task is to explore the way in which people perceive and describe risk. As an example of the sort of exercise that we must engage in, let us take two situations in which we should plan a response to a possible outcome and look at the way in which we use words to describe the decision-making process.

1. Let us consider why a driver might decide to carry a spare tyre in the boot of the car. Stating the obvious, the reason is that should one of the tyres fitted to the vehicle burst, the wheel may be replaced by the spare. Carrying the spare requires the driver to make a commitment of capital against an event that may never arise during the period of ownership. A person may drive thousands of miles a year and never have the bad luck to run over an object sharp enough to burst the

tyre, so why spend the money on carrying a spare and the equipment necessary to change the wheels over? It would be reasonable to assert that most drivers would not think about this issue on a regular basis. The spare tyre is a natural component in the purchase of the car and it will sit in the boot with little attention being paid to it although the issue may be reviewed from time to time as manufacturers raise awareness, e.g. by including a temporary spare sufficient only to travel to a garage for a proper repair or replacement.

If we were to ask the driver to explain or evaluate this decision to carry a spare, would the driver use language suggesting that the process is a reaction based on foresight of risk (rather like an insurance policy) or is it basing a decision upon an assumption? If we decide to invest funds against a particular contingency and approach the matter on the basis of foresight, all that happens is that we acquire data as to possible outcome and costs. When we have that data, we may then analyse likelihoods and probabilities and decide whether it is expedient to take precautionary measures. Thus, foresight alone is not enough. It is the equivalent to a fact-finding exercise which may then be processed and evaluated to help decide future action. But if we were to assume that a tyre will burst at some time during the vehicle's life span and that the consequences of being stranded without a spare are severe, then the cost of that spare will be borne willingly.

We therefore propose the general rule that to make decisions based upon foresight of risk alone is not sensible. To plan upon the basis of positive assumptions about future events and their costs is a better approach. Thus, having made the issues more explicit by talking about them, we take better quality decisions by moving through the evaluation process before taking the decision. To react merely to foresight is to produce 'knee-jerk' responses, i.e. unthinking and mechanical reflexes to a given stimulus.

2. Similarly, it is often said that, when managers plan for change, there is a risk that their efforts will be frustrated by the resistance of those employed in the organization. We would wish to challenge the bland use of the word 'risk' in such situations and to look critically at the way in which the concept of risk is misunderstood and misinterpreted. Hence, in any situation of change we would accept that some of those employed will resist the proposed changes. But we would argue that the resistance of those to be affected by the changes should be viewed positively and not negatively. Their views should be seen as a constructive contribution to what should be the continuing dialogue between planners and users on how to improve the functioning of the organization.

Although any practical resistance may slow down change, it is a part of the way in which a social system adapts itself over a period of time. Indeed, time is often vital in transforming the unfamiliar into the familiar and thereby gaining acceptance. The fact of resistance is a start to a feedback process which is capable of modifying innovation before and during its diffusion throughout the organization. Those who are to implement these changes may be able to point to unintended consequences on the part of planners and to identify ways in which the proposals may be enhanced for the benefit of all involved. Seen in such a light, resistance and opposition are not risks to be feared but useful contributions to the planning exercise which should reduce the risk of a poor outcome from the planning process.

2.1.1 The development of management styles

As a general proposition, we take the view that if the working manager's performance is genuinely to be improved, there must be new, flexible and more innovative approaches to identifying, measuring, analysing and evaluating risks in real decision-making situations. Risk management should not be thought of as solely a strategic management issue. It should be seen as a part of every manager's general function of planning for the future. Thus, instead of formally dividing risk up into convenient but separated functions, e.g. of financial risk or health and safety risks, all managers should try to plan satisfactory outcomes from current decisions.

According to Rosabeth Moss Kanter,[1] a management consultant and editor of the Harvard Business Review, organizations will evolve away from the present more structured hierarchies into a matrix form. In such an environment, the new manager will have to acquire the skills of an all-rounder. The present form of business organization tends to encourage people to specialize. She argues that the successful managers of the future will be able to anticipate the need for change and to cut across the different management functions to gain the necessary support to make the changes effectively. Although specialization will have its place, strength will come from coalitions and partnerships within the organization. The power will therefore accrue to those who:

- are prepared to take responsibility for controlling costs and risks; and
- can communicate the right messages to the right people at the right time.

To maximize the chance of making the communication effective, the manager should get to know the audience, understanding what is important to them and how their needs can be addressed.

2.2 HOW DO PEOPLE THINK ABOUT RISK?

Sometimes people express their uncertainty as to the outcome of future events through the use of words such as probable, possible, expected, likely etc. This literary approach is only useful if those who use it agree on the values or meanings to be given to the words used. Thus, concepts like risk are an abstraction. They cannot be seen and touched as such. So people tend to relate risks to specific situations where there are particular stimuli considered to be dangerous. When we give meaning to words, we do so within the context of the sentences we speak or write. If we do not have a particular context in mind when asking people about risk, people will make up their own contexts based on their own experiences, beliefs, habits etc., adding in other dimensions such as fairness, comprehensibility and the degree to which the situation appears to be controllable. These contexts will be as varied as each person's own experiences and concerns. So if we ask people the general question of what risks they worry about, their answers will be immensely varied. If we ask what risks they worry about in connection with the local waste-incinerating plant, this gives a positive focus to their answer and will recall to their immediate consciousness all of those issues that informed their reaction to the plant over the years.

A further problem is that unlike experts, ordinary people do not think in terms of statistical or mathematical probabilities. They prefer to express ideas in terms of sensations, emotions and other intangibles. This can leave a big communication gap between the expert and the lay person. The expert tends to think of the public as ill-informed because they do not respond favourably to highly technical language, while the public thinks the expert too divorced from everyday reality because of this dependence on abstract data. This is not necessarily a situation requiring correction. It simply needs to be understood when experts try to conduct a dialogue with non-experts, e.g. in consulting with the public through the mechanism of a public inquiry as to the siting of a toxic waste disposal site.

2.2.1 Words of absolute and relative meaning

If we talk of something as being a danger or relatively safe, the unspoken questions are: 'how dangerous is dangerous?' and 'how safe is safe?' Yet it is still common for the mass media to carry the public pronouncements of experts as they attempt to reduce our worries by assuring us that a 'margin of safety' or a 'safety factor' has been built into potentially dangerous projects. There are two main problems in this use of the concept of safety:

1. The way in which different groups of people discuss safety issues often clouds the question of whether the matter should be dealt with as a risk assessment or a risk management exercise. This can be of fundamental importance in fixing individuals with responsibility for taking action in the future or for not taking action when it was required.
2. We would also suggest that this is an inappropriate use of language and that it would be more meaningful to describe the process as building in a 'margin of protection' for the public. At a conceptual level, safety is often thought of as an absolute, i.e. the absence of danger or risk. Thus, if we continue to use the word safety we may create unrealistic expectations in the mind of the public as to the degree of protection that is actually offered. Protection is a word of more relative meaning. Hence, we understand that the use of a seat

belt in the car is for our protection and that it does not create an immunity from injury.

When groups of people, both expert and non-expert, attempt to measure the degrees of protection or safety alleged to be achievable in a particular project, it can lead to challenging technical, economic or political debates. We should remember that the directors of companies involved, politicians representing constituencies at risk, scientists, economists, accountants, lawyers etc. tend only to be expert in one area of activity, yet all these specialists may have to pool their expertise to determine whether a particular project should be allowed to go ahead. Thus, to a greater or lesser extent, each contributor to the decision will have to depend on the others to make themselves clear when they use their own forms of measurement and language (i.e. jargon). In some areas of knowledge, the lay public has been trained to understand scientific scales of measurement, e.g. most people know that the Richter scale for measuring earthquake intensity is logarithmic. But, for our immediate purposes, the semiotic points as to the weakness of our language to provide unambiguous meanings underlines the more general need for an agreed scale for the measurement and description of risk and uncertainty if managers are to take better quality decisions. The more usual techniques are based upon probabilities and odds.

> By putting the degree of certainty in the form of odds, the assessor is given a different psychological viewpoint to judge it. The bet specifies a definite act implied by his assessment, and he is often thereby more able to judge whether he would have been willing to act that way. (Moore, 1983, p. 38)

But simply stating probabilities is more passive and many executives are unhappy with the implication that business decision-making is little more than gambling. Much research has indicated, however, that most people have great difficulty in manipulating probability according to the norms of probability theory (Fischoff and Beyth-Marom, 1983). The inference must be that the majority of calculations forming the basis of risk beliefs are carried out symbolically.

> The fundamental idea is that the way people perceive risk will be taken to be synonymous with the way they talk about risk. (McGill, 1987, p. 52)

2.2.2 How people talk about risks

If instead of writing this book, our brief was to design tests by which to assess and/or measure people's perceptions of risk as a basis of decision-making, we could not improve upon simply listening to what they said. Naturally, experts may construct sophisticated formalized psychological models to explain what people are doing when they take decisions, but we suggest that this examination of everyday language will give rise to no less a powerful construct because it allows the people to show the diversity of their opinions. There is a materiality to the language that people use to make sense of what they see and experience. In what they say or, more often, do not say, people reveal both what they think about the issues and how they rationalize (and sometimes justify) their own opinions.

However, we must be careful how we ask each person to express their views. For example, if an observer was watching a group of managers as they debated what decision to take where there were major risks, it would not be sensible to ask the apparently simple question, 'Which manager is right?' There are several problems with this question. The first is that it suggests that the observer is able to produce an answer in absolute terms, i.e. an answer capable of objective justification. It also invites the observer to produce a ranking order of other people's perceptions as if one perception is less valid than another, or one person's view is more 'rational' than the others. More importantly, the question makes no reference to the power structures that may be operating within the group. These structures may constrain some of those who contribute to the debate, e.g. they may be required to represent a particular point of view (say, as a trade union representative on the decision-making body), be afraid to voice their true feelings because of a threat to job, feel obliged to agree with the boss as a means of gaining promotion etc.

2.2.3 What people say or do not say can be revealing

As a general rule we would contend that, through the process of social interaction, each person reveals something of how they form their perceptions about risk. This is the only way in which the otherwise private process of thought is made explicit. For these purposes, when people talk about risks, two types of knowledge are being used:

1. descriptive knowledge, i.e. facts about the world; and
2. procedural knowledge, i.e. how the world works.

This knowledge will be acquired during the lifetime of each individual. There are various sources of knowledge:

- personal experience;
- the experience of acquaintances;
- formal education;
- the news media and other mechanisms of communication such as books.

Each person will make judgements about the salience of each new piece of information. Some information will be considered more important because it is a personal as opposed to a reported experience. Others will attribute salience depending upon the authority of the source. The new information will then be fitted into the person's scheme of knowledge. This may take the form of a semantic net which describes the relationships between different elements of knowledge or a script which describes the expected sequence of events, say, when entering a shop to buy food. Understanding how people comprehend risks is a vital part of risk communication (see section 2.6) and in the study of decision-making.

2.2.4 People are worried by many things

The way in which people think about risk may well vary with age, gender, education, employment etc. Thus, an older person may think more about certain risks than a younger person, e.g. health may become a more important issue as one grows older, while longer term threats to the environment may be more important to the young. Further, people worry about a wide range of things. Sometimes the focus of worry will be things that already exist, e.g. whether the unusual noise from the car engine means that it is going to break down. On other occasions people will worry about things that might happen, e.g. whether they will be injured in an accident. The uncertainty of the future often leaves us apprehensive over which of several undesirable consequences may result. If only as an emotional safety device, people therefore restrict their worries to those matters of immediate concern and may not think about risk at large. Indeed, many may not consider any external risk unless their attention is drawn to it by some event.

MacGregor (1991) defines worry as:

> a cognitive process that occurs when we are uncertain about a future event or activity . . . Worry is thinking about uncertainty whereas anxiety includes the gut-level feeling that accompanies uncertainty.
> (p. 315–16)

We tend to worry before an event, often creating worst-case scenarios as a way of preparing for the future. It is a state of mind in which we are preoccupied with a problem and it tends to be negatively related to happiness. Some psychologists treat worry as a way of building up defences against stress. Hence, it is defined as cognitive in that it is closely tied into expectations about future events, usually connected with personal achievement, money and our personal relationships. As worry becomes more pronounced, people will tend to decide to take some form of defensive action.

As a person is moving towards either taking a decision or implementing a decision, an iterative process such as that shown in Figure 2.1 is likely to take place. Thus, subject to the problems of the Hawthorne Effect, the study of decision-making in situations of risk is a study of those people involved in, and affected by, the decision.

2.3 THE PUBLIC'S FORMATION AND AMPLIFICATION OF RISK PERCEPTIONS

Obviously, the extent to which people will feel confident about outcomes when they are in situations of risk will be determined by their familiarity with the particular risk. If the sources of the risk are less familiar or they are seen to have considerable elements of uncertainty connected with

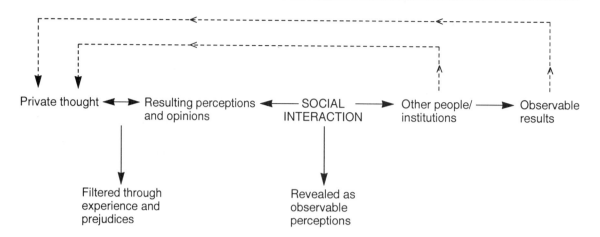

Figure 2.1 Formation of risk perceptions. Iterative process building towards decision as implementation of decision.

them, people will tend to view them with greater apprehension than those more familiar risks where the consequences are known (Slovic, 1987). Thus, we all understand the risks in driving or being carried as a passenger in a car. If circumstances disturb our confidence, e.g. snow falls or ice forms, we can take steps to restore calm by maintaining the car well, driving more carefully and wearing seat belts. In other everyday situations, it may not be quite as easy to identify the action required to relieve anxiety.

We all have to eat but what we choose to eat may have a major impact upon our future health in terms of the risk of heart attacks, strokes, cancer etc. Before scientists and doctors began to identify the various physiological causes and effects, it was easy to buy food. We balanced cost against convenience, knowing our preference for the appearance and taste of the food, and bought what we liked. Now that we have been told that it is difficult to define the links between diet and health, particularly where the source of the problem may lie dormant for many years, do we, for example, buy organic food or 'conventional' food (with or without additives)? The experts may have great difficulty in telling us by how much we have reduced the risks from ingesting residual pesticides, hormone growth stimulants and other chemicals, yet many will now pay the higher prices for organic foods because their perception is that they are safer than the conventional foods. Others will continue to buy the 'same old foods' arguing that if there were real risks the government would have taken action to protect them (Hammit, 1990).

The decisions about which foods to buy could then be further complicated by the introduction of unfamiliar technology. The practice of food irradiation is relatively unknown and only poorly understood. The reactions to this process may be shaped by a variety of quite different attitudes. Some may respond simply on the basis that anything involving radiation is dangerous. Others may be anti-technology when it comes to food production and storage. Some may be concerned on health grounds that irradiated food may be kept longer and become a danger. Others may have read the scientific and economic articles and have reached an opposing view on the merits of the arguments.

2.3.1 Communication, perceptions and amplification

In the routine of life, many people do not think regularly about familiar dangers. They only think about the danger when their attention is drawn to the issue by a factor that breaks the routine. Quite often, this factor takes the form of a communication of information. Indeed, there are somewhat ironic cases when the announcement of plans designed to relieve existing risks has actually increased alarm:

1.   because the original risks were not fully appreciated by the affected people; and
2.   the proposed remedies are not properly understood.

There are many ways in which people's perceptions of risk may be affected and some may cause what is termed the social amplification of risk (Kasperson *et al.*, 1988; Machlis and Rosa, 1990). Here, an adverse event acts as a trigger to the interested group and results in an unexpectedly large increase in the perception of risk. This may be wholly out of proportion to the seriousness of the triggering incident or to the real levels of risk. Thus, instead of a limited direct consequence, a business organization may find secondary adverse effects in the loss of sales, political pressure to increase regulation etc. It is comparable to the ripple effect generated when a stone is dropped into a still pool. Examples of this phenomenon may be seen in the loss of trust in chemical manufacturing plants after the disasters at Sevaso and Bhopal, a fear of nuclear electricity generation plants after the accidents at Three Mile Island and Chernobyl etc. In part, this is encouraged by the extensiveness of the media coverage which helps to put the issue on the national agenda. The exaggerated adverse response is also likely among those who have thought little about the issue and therefore have weak or no real opinions. However, such instant reactions may be unstable and the individual may soon revert to only a weak opinion. But, even if only in the short-term, these triggering incidents also enable special interest groups to promote a stigmatization of the particular industry, and this may cause considerable operational difficulties over a significant period of time.

2.3.2 Imagery and amplification of the perceived risk

By focusing on the individual as an actor, capable of understanding and acting upon imagery, we also reflect the concept of subjectivity and recognize the fact that people have different opinions, perceptions and attitudes. These differences often produce inconsistent risk management strategies where differences in perceptions and priorities lead people to pay attention to quite different sets of risks. So some may choose to eat organic food, engage in regular exercise and go rock climbing, while others avoid living near nuclear power stations, eliminate the use of CFCs in their daily lives and never use products tested on animals.

In making these types of choice, we must accept that the images shown in the news and entertainments media influence perceptions. The impact of negative images may predispose people to form strong risk perceptions and to attach stigma to those considered at fault, e.g. the Exxon Valdez oil spill and the resulting images of damage to the wildlife and their natural habitat. There is no reason why these perceptions of risk and the value judgements leading to stigma cannot influence economic behaviour, e.g. consumer choice to boycott a manufacturer considered at fault. In one sense, the phenomenon of social amplification of risk would be acceptable if the resulting perception was accurate, or as accurate as that formulated by experts. Unfortunately, there is no requirement of rationality in this process, and it can sometimes be impossible to predict how the public will react to any incident.

Indeed, as many researchers and opinion pollsters have found to their cost, it can be very difficult to define reality as an observable objective phenomenon and, even if a working hypothesis can be proposed, what one set of trained observers may find is not something which is necessarily equally accessible to all competent observers. Each person interprets reality in the light of a lifetime of personal experience, modified by that person's interaction in a social environment where what is said and done serves to confirm and verify what they think (cf. Habermas and his concept of the lifeworld – see section 10.1.5). For the observer, the problem is always to exclude personal bias in trying to interpret what is seen. Thus, if the observer has a well-developed political or methodological construct against which to measure what is seen, it is difficult not to treat input data as merely confirming or denying that construct rather than representing data which may form the basis of a new theoretical construct, e.g. if a capitalist came across evidence suggesting working-class oppression, would that be taken as supporting a Marxist point of view?

Little is known about how an image is accepted into the public domain, nor how the dynamics of perception work. All that can be said is that some images appear to have a transitory impact and the general perceptions soon fall back to the status quo. While others become entrenched in the public consciousness and form the basis of a cumulative growth in the perception of risk. For these purposes, the central focus often proves to be an image connected with the total risk of the completed project or that part of the project which has the highest public visibility, e.g. an accidental discharge of toxic chemicals or radiation into the environment. In focusing on one image, other risk components are often marginalized or ignored. Thus, issues such as the costs of cleaning up the environment after the escape, the need to move people from the area for a period of time to avoid contamination, the need to change the legal framework of regulation etc, are not considered even though, in total, they may represent far more significant elements of risk than the one image focused upon.

2.3.3 Distortions in risk evaluation

When an organization is evaluating a project, it may also concentrate on just one or two elements of risk. To some extent, it may be as short-sighted as the public or, perhaps more cynically, it may only treat as important those issues already identified by the public. If management is to commission a more detailed risk assessment, it often takes place towards the middle or end of the project, long after the project design has been agreed. This means that, in effect, the decision to finish the project is almost bound to be made because too many resources will have been committed to the project and too many reputations will be at stake to abandon it.

Thus, for example, as a part of the plant licensing function, the United Kingdom Health and Safety Executive will be evaluating the risks in the new computer operating system for the latest nuclear power station after all the coding has been completed, i.e. after years of work and millions of pounds have been spent. The political pressure to approve the project will be enormous because the delay to commissioning the plant and the cost of redesigning the control system will be significant. It would have been better if a full risk analysis had been carried out in combination with a cost-benefit analysis during the design and development phase of the project because this would have helped to identify weak spots and to suggest cost-effective alternative technical possibilities before entering upon the final phase of the project. In this way, the aim becomes the management of a project to produce an optimal outcome whereas a focus in time upon the end of the project can only produce strategies to reduce the worst effects now recognized in the design (cf. the Norwegian system for offshore gas and petrol installations, see section 1.3).

It is perhaps significant that even though there is little research into the way the public forms its perceptions of risk and it is acknowledged that these perceptions may be unreliable, they have been recognized as an important element when it comes to assessing risk in relation to major public works. Thus, in the Layfield Report (1986) following the inquiry into the Sizewell B Pressurized Water Reactor, the conclusion was reached that,

> the opinions of the public should underlie the evaluation of risk. (Vol. 1, para. 2.101h)

In part, the problem is that reliance on quantitative methodologies and pre-set risk criteria may become mechanical and rigid. While we cannot expect science to remove the uncertainty from risk, what we may hope for is more effective communication of risks to the public so that their views may be better informed and their contribution to decision-making more real (see section 2.6).

2.4   THE FACTORS THAT INFLUENCE THE FORMATION OF RISK PERCEPTIONS

If it is necessary to take a decision about future behaviour and risks are involved, there are a number of factors that will influence the decision made. The following is not an exclusive list of these factors, but it gives a general indication of what each actor might be thinking about as the decision is approached:

- At a selfish level or in organizational terms, is there a material benefit to be derived or disadvantage to be incurred?
- Is this a free decision or are there elements of coercion or economic dependency which limit choice in some real way?
- What have I got at stake – what is the level of personal investment?
- Do I have practical experience which is relevant to this situation?
- As a short-cut to a more time-consuming and objective evaluation of the issues, do I have any prejudices which are not likely to be harmful if relied upon in this situation?
- What does my peer group appear to think of me in general and of this situation in particular, and to what extent should I take account of any pressures from them?
- In terms of accountability should the decision prove wrong, what would be the reaction of my colleagues, the shareholders, the institutional investors, the media and other external commentators on relevant events?

The latter two factors really form a part of a more general set of relationships which represents a circle of interactions that people use as a sounding board when forming their risk perceptions (see Figure 2.2). It is a natural part of decision-making to find out what other people say and to speculate upon what they may do in each scenario, whether they be family, friends, acquaintances, enemies, experts, etc.

2.4.1   How group interactions shape risk perceptions

In working through interactions with different groups, one of the primary concerns is a judgement about which group's views have credibility. The following elements combine to give a basis for that judgement:

- Each person consulted will have varying degrees of knowledge and experience as a base from which to comment; unless a particular person has natural intuition, it may be wise to assume that advice from those with little relevant knowledge is not reliable.
- Each person consulted may have varying degrees of objectivity or self-interest, and this may affect the likelihood of receiving accurate or partial advice; if you ask your spouse for advice, will you hear good advice or what that person thinks you want to hear?
- Differences in the relationships may create a greater or lesser likelihood that full details will be disclosed by the person seeking advice – do

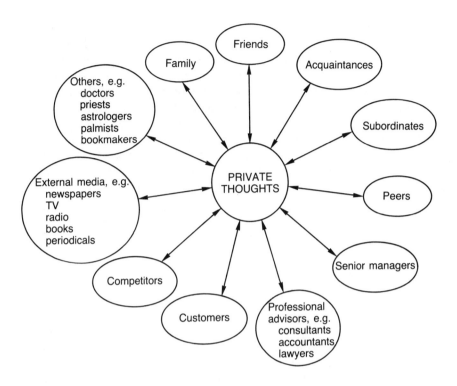

Figure 2.2 Circle of social and business interactions to form perceptions and opinions.

you really want to tell the people you are competing with for future promotion that you are not decisive or will consulting with them make you look more statesmanlike?

- Differences in relationships may create a greater or lesser likelihood that honest answers will be given; in management, will your junior managers be prepared to tell you that you are wrong?

- Differences in the opportunity to interact with some immediately available or others to be sought out, or with some available only for very short periods of time, may lead to significantly different advice being sought or given – if you see someone every day, this may lead you to have a very different view of them as opposed to someone seen only occasionally but thought to be wise; and if you only have a few minutes to ask your questions, what you ask may not be anything like the questions possible in longer meetings.

- Differences in the form of the interactions – some interactions will not be direct but through reading or seeing, e.g. through letters, reports, electronic mail systems, or external media such as newspapers, television programmes etc. remember that people will not say and write the same things – in the spoken form, body language and other intangible forms of communication are possible whereas what is written will be less flexible and more permanent as evidence of what was said.

It would be reasonable to conclude that all attempts to externalize the debate about the forthcoming decision are likely to be helpful so long as the decision-maker draws the right conclusions about the reliability of each contribution. Indeed, even writing private notes may help the lone decision-maker to clarify his or her thoughts prior to taking the decision. When trying to assess the power of any workplace pressures that exist to shape views, you should remember that debating stances and arguments that have been successful tend to be repeated. It can save time and money in not rehearsing the full range of argument in what appears to be a repeat situation. The problem is to ensure that all the main variables in the present situation still match the old arguments. Unthinkingly repeating past decisions is not a sound strategy for the future.

2.4.2 The group and risk evaluation

In the modern organization, the cohesion of the group and team building is considered increasingly important. This can create problems for those who are not high enough in the organization to have been recognized as leaders. If any person whose status is formally subordinate or equivocal within the organization speaks out on major issues but finds that senior managers or the peer group reject his or her views, there is considerable pressure to modify those views so that they conform to the perceived normative views. Of course, the thick-skinned and ambitious may stand out for what they believe is right, but rightness and wrongness are not absolute concepts and, without the support of those who can shape corporate opinion, such 'trouble-makers' may find that continued employment in that organization is not possible.

Indeed, one of the perennial problems for democratic as opposed to autocratic managements is to retain a reasonably coherent corporate understanding on key issues while allowing a constructive debate on strategy to take place. Unfortunately, prejudices can spring up quickly to form the basis of opposing or threatening views. Sometimes, the very existence of opposing views will form a filter to people's openness to the world. This filter may work in different directions, whether to keep things out or to keep things in:

1. Some will take up arms for the preferred point of view, hoping for a quick victory and a restored unanimity. Here, the filter may exclude some aspects of the opposition's stated views because the more committed the fighter, the less receptive he or she may become to the views of others.
2. Others will remain apparently uncommitted, wishing to sit on the fence until the matter is resolved. Their true feelings will remain less obvious to the world, i.e. they filter out clues as to their views when they present themselves to the world.

Only the would-be peacemakers will remain open to the world, hoping to find the key(s) to compromise among the different groups. However, if the organization wishes to maintain morale as it continues in operation, there will always be a tendency towards moderation. The more vociferous the initial stance adopted by the different factions, the more carefully all may begin to act if the feelings of those conducting the argument are not to be permanently damaged. The emergence and the reconciliation of all views arises through interactions within the immediate social groupings. If the maintenance of the group's integrity is important and loss of face is to be avoided, each side's views must be modified until an acceptable compromise is reached, i.e. a consensual form of decision-making.

2.4.3 Interest groups will tend to have their own perceptions

One of the problems in trying to reconcile different views is that many risks are essentially human in origin or effect and they cannot be seen in terms of numbers. Because these decision elements cannot be quantified and processed to produce right and wrong answers, competing views may be equally valid. For example, workers may see a risk to their jobs or to their quality of life if automation proposals are implemented without consultation. The software engineers may have legitimate expectations about the degree of user friendliness to be built into the new systems, but is their view any more valid than the concerns of those who will actually have to make the new systems work? Similarly, managers may see another competing organization in financial difficulties following a fire and offer help during reconstruction. The values and emotions that might form the basis of decision-making in such circumstances should be seen as part of the structure of meaning deriving both from the circumstances and institutions through which people experience the world and, whether directly or indirectly, through other's reports of their experiences.

Indeed, as a general proposition, we would assert that perceptions of risk cannot be understood in a simple numerical or engineering sense. Equal weight in decision-making terms should be given to the way in which people think about, interpret and describe the competence, legitimacy and integrity of the prevailing institutions and influences. It is therefore sensible to investigate how much is known by each group of people. Knowledge is the key to risk definition and assessment. The level of knowledge will be affected by the jobs they have, the information they have access to, their level of interest and other personality factors. Each employee will feel that they run various risks in performing their jobs (people with low self-confidence and high anxiety levels will tend to perceive the risks as being greater). In part, this may affect the type of job selected and the level of job satisfaction they feel.

This more subjective form of study does not deny that some physical phenomena may not be more objectively measured and predicted, e.g. in a market survey, the size of the market in terms of existing sales may be estimated with reasonable accuracy, and projections of growth (or decline) may be extrapolated from past trends. But the social world and its concepts of reality cannot be ignored. Together with the more scientific elements, they constitute what is known as the discourse of risk.

2.5   THE CONCEPT OF DISCOURSE

The concept of the discourse emerges from the work of authors such as Foucault. At a general level, the discourse is everything that is said, written or done within a society. It exists both as a means of communication whereby values are discussed and disseminated throughout society, and as a means of control. Thus, if we can control everything that is written about the world, much as the ironically named Ministry of Truth in Orwell's novel *1984*, who is to say that our version of what has happened is not true? So if we are eminent scientists and we tell you that ozone, something previously only thought of as a therapeutic odour experienced on the seashore, is now in danger of thinning and we may all get skin cancer, how should people act? The public discussion of the issue, hopefully well-informed, should give the people the facts and allow an opinion to emerge. This should then form the basis of action, e.g. the phasing out of harmful chemicals in our refrigerators etc. But if the government of the day found this discussion against the national interest, it could use its power to ridicule the credibility of our scientific report or suppress media commentaries etc. The power of the 'whitewash' has long been recognized.

At a level of particularity, there may be a discourse on individual issues or phenomena. In other words, the overall communication and discussion process within society at large is the meta-discourse, and one may then have an infinite number of sub-discourses as topics come and go in the attention of interest groups or the public. Hence, there is a general discussion as to what constitutes risk and when it is acceptable to take risks. Governments think about such risks as whether to build nuclear power stations and whether it is acceptable to delegate the control of these new stations to safety-critical software control systems. Commercial organizations of size will conduct their own discussions as to how they will take decisions where risks are involved. All these discussions both individually and cumulatively constitute the discourse of risk.

Thus, how the managers decide whether to launch the new product is likely to be more a social than a scientific decision, based upon the feelings of the researchers and the managers about how customers may react to the new advertising campaign, the packaging, the new flavours etc. Indeed, the greater the number of intangible elements in the decision, the greater the guesswork. The way the guesses will be taken, in part, will be governed by the rule system emerging from the discourse in each organization. Thus, people will describe the factors to be considered in a particular way and people will contribute to the discussion according to their status and authority within the organization.

2.5.1   Discourse and language

The way people express their perceptions will reflect the different connotational resources which they have, i.e. at a practical level, people's ability to express themselves is in part a function of the vocabulary they have and the grammatical skill that they can exploit to extract the maximum meaning out of the words available. But, even if many words are available for use, some people will only reveal their wants, fears or concerns – their understanding of the issues may be secondary or, indeed, non-existent. This communication will be achieved not only through what is said, but also through what is unspoken. When people talk to each other, there are many silences, and ideas are sometimes arbitrarily put together in a way which both shortens the form and hides the meaning. Sometimes the words themselves are capable of several possible interpretations and only when you are very familiar with the way in which people speak in that geographical area or in that organization can you say what is meant in this instance. Occasionally, it will not be possible to fill in the gaps of meaning with any certainty. All of these silences, ellipses and lacunae of language constitute the social practices of the discourse used within that social milieu. One of the staff development or training issues for all organizations is therefore to decide how much effort to invest in improving the skills of narrative and argument among its managers.

We believe that where the form and content of the discourse among managers is improved, they will be able to act more effectively, because each will know more clearly what the others mean.

For some within the organization (or other social institutions) language is an instrument of authority, persuasion or deception. Leaders may simply command, whereas in a more equal environment, persuasion may be the desirable approach. There is also the possibility that disinformation has been introduced into the discourse. The style people adopt to communicate and the substance of what they say may be a good indication of their purpose. It should be obvious that there is likely to be a difference in style and purpose between those freely, but passively, making their perceptions known, and those who are invited actively to participate in a more formal or public discourse. Normally, before replying, any person participating in a discussion will consider what the implications of communicating their perceptions may be. For some, they may believe that what they say can have no effect upon the decision-making proposals. This may lead them to make only a nominal contribution – the lack of real opportunity to affect the outcome may be demotivating. Others may see their contribution as a part of a more political activity through which they have an opportunity to promote either themselves or a particular point of view.

Further, the status and self-image of the participants must be considered for it cannot be assumed that all those contributing to the discourse are, or see themselves, as equal. Some may therefore be defensive, others aggressive; some indifferent, others committed, etc. The form of the discourse is also skewed in a different way both practical and linguistic. Because management has been more traditionally a male preserve, the language of the risk discourse is also male-dominated. Through the exclusion of women from the discourse, the language and style of risk-based decision-making has become indelibly macho, and major gender differences in opinion therefore frequently arise. Further, organizations tend to be described in terms of hierarchies which fit a largely male view of the world in which domination and subordination are norms (Ferguson, 1984).

2.5.2 The prevailing culture determines how risk is handled

The basic structure of the risk discourse is a cultural phenomenon. Many of those involved in decision-making try to cloak decisions by using terms which suggest that there are objective justifications for each decision, e.g. managers often use phrases such as the scales or parameters of acceptable risk which suggest some form of measurement and therefore try to suggest that their decisions cannot be challenged. Stated simply in this book, you might think such devices would be transparently obvious and dismissed by those to whom they were addressed. But the artificiality of these devices may never be apparent to the majority because they are embedded in a dense political language and defended by institutional barriers. Whether consciously or unconsciously, all the senior decision-makers establish organizational paradigms for the balancing of uncertainties in decision-making. The discourse of work experience and its related comment and argument then revolves around these paradigms, confirming the consensus of the team or group. If anyone is brave enough to voice different views, they are often dismissed as being irrational or illogical.

It is, of course, possible that this institutional resistance to new views is justified because each new idea has not been properly thought through and it contains more unresolved questions than the established views. This is always likely because it is often difficult for individual nonconformists to gain access to all the information relevant to the policy decision. But the danger is that new ideas are more arbitrarily dismissed because they do not 'fit the facts' as they have been known. If too much creativity and innovation from lower down in the organization is stifled, it may lead to what is known as 'management by quiescence'. This is a form of delayed knowledge acquisition – the majority of those employed in the organization wait quietly to be told what is to be done and they therefore become dependent for information on a complex structure of trust and deferrence. In any event, a lay person outside the 'magic circle' of influence may be alienated by the use of technical language and have no interest in contributing to a debate seen by others as being outside his or her ability to comprehend. This gives positive advantages to the elite group because their views cannot easily be challenged.

In more democractic organizations, formalized decision-making may take more time and involve more people, some of whom may not always be relevant to the immediate decision. But informality may be equally unfortunate in excluding the opportunity for outsiders to subject proposals to critical review. The fact that some of the methods used or proposed have weaknesses should not be concealed because what is required is an open appraisal of the level of confidence that can be placed in the outcomes to each decision-making process. Equally, whatever the nature of the organization, decision-makers should be clear about what are facts and what are values and, perhaps more importantly, what is known and what is not known. In the event that decision-makers become more accountable for their decisions, this openness will also help to deflect criticism or ridicule if the decisions subsequently prove wrong.

2.6 RISK COMMUNICATION

Within the discourse, the process of express communication serves two main functions with respect to the recipients (Figure 2.3):

1. to inform; or
2. to empower.

If the communication is one way, i.e. from an 'expert' to a target audience, the patronizing expectation may be that the audience will simply accept what the expert tells them. If they reject the message, it is more than likely that this will be attributed to a lack of understanding. If the purpose of the communication is to enable the audience to think about the issues so that they may take good decisions about their own safety or make some form of response to the sender, this represents a sharing of power. According to Laird (1989), the public are now more involved in taking decisions because of the decline of deference, i.e. the public is no longer prepared to give respect and trust as of right. Respect must be earned. Whereas government and large industries used to ignore public perceptions, the people have realized that secrecy was often intended simply to conceal incompetence or uncertainty, i.e. so many early decisions have now been proved wrong.

Consequently, today even the most highly qualified experts find their scientific evidence questioned or dismissed as the people take direct action to express their opposition to what may appear to them to be proposals to repeat versions of past mistakes. Indeed, if the commercial or governmental organization does not consult the public early in the

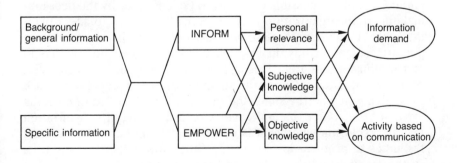

Figure 2.3 Communication. Information communications policy should match the powers of comprehension in the target audience and have the right motivational goals. If knowledge levels are low, some informational input may stimulate high demand for more information.

planning of a project where there may be adverse effects, the public may believe that a cover-up is in operation, that the facts have only been leaked by a concerned employee, that the organization is trampling on local interests etc.

Overall, in a non-elitist sense, there are four main reasons for one group to send out messages to others about risk(s):

1. So that people's general understanding can be improved, i.e. those responsible for sending the message(s) have no particular decision to make – their motive may be merely to enhance the recipients' awareness of the issues, e.g. an employer may send out messages about safety in the factory to help reduce accidents, governments may require warning notices to be displayed on cigarette advertisements and the packs themselves etc. The aim may be to inform people of a previously unknown risk or to alert them to a change in the apparent magnitude of the risk. Equally, the aim may be to report that the risks have diminished.

2. The particular message may have been commissioned by an organization from an expert. The purpose of the report will be to inform decision-makers on the nature and extent of the risk, and on whether there is a need to take action. Because the recipients may not have the technical expertise to understand the detail of the science underlying the report, the expert should take care to set out the evidence impartially and to show how the conclusions have been arrived at. If the report differs from others on the same topic, the reasons for the difference(s) should be explained. If the report has limitations because of the need to simplify the issues, the author should indicate the reliability of the report and tell the reader(s) how to bridge the gap, e.g. by recommending background books, articles or other documents that will help to perfect understanding.

3. The message is sent out to provoke feedback which will help to structure the decision to be taken, i.e. the recipients will identify their main interests and concerns, and so help to define the parameters of the possible solutions to be aimed for by the decision-makers. If an organization is trying to decide where to site a plant that will be the source of some local pollution, it may identify a potential site and study the response made by those who both live in and administer that area. This will help to identify the characteristics of a suitable site and assist in planning the campaign to convince those living in what becomes the real target area not to oppose the arrival of this source of employment. Alternatively, the organization may be exploring whether it is necessary to commit any immediate resources to product development. It therefore needs to consult its customers to establish the level of their satisfaction with the existing products and to discover what other features (if any) might improve the safety of the designs.

4. So that the feedback will provide a direct input into the particular decision to be taken, i.e. following upon two or three above, the

decision-makers have identified the criteria to be applied and the information they will need in making the decision, and they now seek the specified information to fit into their decision template. This may be a positive effort at consultation, or it may be to confirm a decision that has already been taken in principle.

2.6.1 The motives for communicating risks may vary

Those who send out these communications, may have a variety of motives. When governments send out messages about the risk of cancer or AIDS, they are trying to modify human behaviour in giving up smoking, adopting safer sexual practices, etc. Their motives in doing so will be tend to be altruistic, i.e. concern for the health and well-being of their citizens, albeit that other economic and political factors may have been at work. But, for example, when a journalist writes a dramatic scoop story, alerting the public to the very latest apparent threat to their health, a variety of other motives may be at work:

- It may be purely selfish, e.g. to gain credit with the editor with a view to securing a salary increase;
- It may be out of loyalty to the employer, e.g. to boost the sales of the newspaper or to impress the advertisers with the increased sales;
- It may be personal and somewhat malicious, e.g. the journalist fell ill through eating soft cheese and now relishes the opportunity of exposing the risk of listeria;
- The journalist may wish to promote the interests of a group or individual, e.g. the journalist has secretly accepted payment from one manufacturing organization to write 'knocking copy' about a competitor's products, or the journalist may be a member of an organization such as Friends of the Earth and always writes stories which alert the population to threats to the environment.

2.6.2 How to interpret risk messages

When it comes to the interpretation of risk messages, Morgan and Lave (1990) argue that care is needed. Some senders will have an open agenda which makes their motives more clear. The recipients are therefore justified in taking the messages at face value and responding accordingly. Thus, people receiving the messages may decide that taking the newly identified risks is either acceptable or not, and they may or may not worry about the issue. Whatever decision is made, it will hopefully have been a better informed decision. But this assumes that information is always neutral. Sadly, this is not the case. Even the most overt of messages may, in part, be based upon principles that are not known to the recipients. One reason for this is that the average reader may not be able to understand the full explanation or not have the patience to read through pages of background. The simplified message may therefore leave out significant elements which ought to be included if a fully informed decision is to be made.

Sometimes, the explanation of a risk may require a departure from the normal patterns of communication within the culture. Whereas the management of a factory previously have been cautious in discussing risk in the plant to minimize social and legal problems, there may now be a need drastically to change employee attitudes in the face of unavoidable risks. Similarly, if the manufacturer has consistently played down rumours of a safety problem in the design, it may be hard to get the consumer to use the product in the safest way. Against the calm words of yesterday, it may be hard to convince employees or consumers that the risks are real. The moral for employers and for those organizations that depend upon consumer confidence may well be that honesty is always the best policy.

If the sender has selfish motives, the recipient ought to try to disentangle the message. A part of what is said will be of benefit to the sender, but some of the content may be of benefit to the recipient. However, it may be difficult for the recipient to make the distinction even if the need to do so is recognized. The problems become even more acute if the sender has a hidden agenda because the recipient may not know how to begin to interpret the message. If the recipient has no reason to suspect that a bias exists and takes the information at face value, the corruption and/or deception has succeeded. The danger from the sender's point of view is that should the truth subsequently be exposed, all future credibility may be lost. That the sender may have had an altruistic motive in using deceptive tactics will not save his or her reputation. If the recipient suspects the possibility of bias, he or she may try to 'read between the lines', but there is no guarantee that the analysis will succeed.

The way in which people interpret messages will also be influenced by a number of other factors:

- The timing of the message may suggest either that there is significance or no real significance to the content;
- The status of the person sending the message may signal significance or not – in part, this will depend upon the degree to which the person is trusted and respected;
- The style of presentation may have a significant effect – if someone appears excited or passionate, this may catch the emotion of those who hear the statement and have a profound effect; another may have such a dispassionate style, that few can be bothered to work out what is being said;
- If the presentation shows that there may be significant advantages to be derived from the risky enterprise, more may be prepared to run the risks – more negative presentations may produce fewer supporters;
- The extent to which people may take precautions against the risk will also affect perceptions – if little can be done, people may fatalistically keep to their usual activities;
- If the source of the risk is unfamiliar or involves elements which excites the recipient's imagination adversely, e.g. radiation or cancer, the

response is likely to be more alarmed.

2.6.3   Rationality and risk appreciation

In their study of the communication issues affecting difficult social problem areas such as the regulation of residual pesticides in food and radon in homes, Krimsky and Plough (1988) follow the view that the cognitive process of forming perceptions is conditioned by individual cultural and social norms. But when looking at the responses of people to information, they suggest that there is a sharp distinction between two basic types of 'rationality' that may make the process of evaluation and assimilation work:

1. *Technical rationality* – here the individual has sympathy with the scientific method and is prepared to weigh evidence more dispassionately. There may also be a tendency to treat unquantifiable information as unreliable and to exclude it from the decision-making.
2. *Cultural rationality* – this takes as its focus the concerns of the family and the peer group, avoiding the dispassionate approach and trusting personal or reported experience rather than abstract evidence.

They do not suggest that this distinction is fixed for each person. In fact, depending on their status and position in the decision-making environment for each issue, people may change from one form of rationality to the other, depending upon their role in each situation where choices have to be made. Thus, a person may be quite technically rational at work where management decisions are to be taken, but culturally rational when confronted by a planning proposal to put something unpleasant in his or her backyard. Alternatively, lay people can now read up a technical subject and ask some very awkward technical questions of the experts. It must be accepted, however, that not many people are prepared to do this. The solution may therefore be for groups of threatened citizens to hire their own expert to assist in protecting their interests – a somewhat ironic step to 'fight fire with fire'.

2.6.4   The ethics of risk communication

There is little agreement about the ethics of risk communication and the extent to which it may be acceptable to use manipulative tactics to induce recipients to change their behaviour in some way. Obviously, if there is an immediate danger it may be acceptable to use any means to ensure the safety of those likely to be affected. But if the motives are more covert, it is not clear whether codes of practice or laws are required to regulate the senders' behaviour. All that can be said is that all those who are in the business of risk communication should be encouraged to act as ethically as possible. The ultimate aim should be to ensure that society and its component organizations use their resources effectively to tackle the big problems first. This means that all the information supplied to the decision-makers should support rational decision-making. When it comes to dealing with the public, communicators should either be responsibly trying to improve the people's understanding of the issues or working with the public to produce better quality decisions, i.e. risk communication should be seen as a dialogue where all interested parties should have an equal right to be heard. Hopefully, this would make governments and organizations more responsive and make the average member of our society a little less alienated.

Following the Seveso disaster, the Council of the European Communities issued Directive 82/501/EEC which specifies that members of the public liable to be affected by a major accident must be informed of safety measures and how they should behave in an accident. Two later Directives added the requirements that this information should be actively disseminated, repeated and updated at appropriate intervals. The aim is to enable people to cope in the event of a disaster and thereby to reduce risks. If people are training in safety procedures, even at a conceptual level, their vulnerability may be reduced. It is therefore sad that the implementation of these Directives has been slow throughout the Community and that little is done to obey their principles. It seems, therefore, that laws do not work in encouraging high standards of openness on the part of state or commercial organizations. What we should see is more active dialogue between the government and industry to discuss matters of mutual concern, with the public able to observe and contribute where appropriate. If this does not happen, it is likely that the public will increasingly abandon the politics of discussion and move towards protest and litigation to protect their interests.

2.7 CONCLUSIONS

If any organization is to take good-quality decisions when there is an element of risk, decisions must be taken at a senior level within the organization. If managers know what can go wrong, how often it is likely to go wrong and what the consequences might be, they can begin to take more rational decisions about what should be done. This will involve the balancing of different factors of cost and benefit, trading some advantages against other disadvantages as they try to look into the future. But only if this is done with as complete a view of the organization as possible will all the relevant issues be appreciated in taking the decisions.

If managers or the people who may be affected by their decisions are to understand the issues, it is important that all try to speak the same language, i.e. that there is some agreement about the magnitudes of various risks and about the priorities to be accorded those risks. When we talk about risks and safety, about protection and acceptability, we need to have some agreement about scales of measurement and about the legitimate qualitative concerns that will form the basis of risk perceptions. We should also consider the ethical codes and the laws such as the Seveso Directive that should underpin the business of risk communications (section 2.6) and the mechanisms that may result in risk amplification (section 2.3). In part, some of these problems can be solved if we discuss goals and aims more openly, sharing the power of decision-making with those likely to be affected.

Now that we have some understanding of the nature of risk and how people perceive risks, we can move on to a consideration of the decision-making process.

QUESTIONS

1. Think of five words which may be used to describe degrees of likelihood, rank them in order of probability and then consider whether this represents a useful scale of measurement.
2. Think of the different ways in which we use images – as news pictures, advertising materials, corporate logos etc. What processes enable an image to change public perceptions and opinions?
3. Can you think of examples of risk amplification, where the interest group has suddenly become aware of a risk in an exaggerated way?
4. Explain the concept of discourse.
5. When planning communications about risks, what factors should communicators bear in mind?

Notes

1. Her views are quoted in Roskopf and Aiello (1991).

3 Decision-making and risk in the modern organization

INTRODUCTION

In the opening words of their preface, Cooke and Slack (1984) assert that, 'Making decisions and bearing responsibility for them is one of the cornerstones of the manager's job. Quite simply, if managers didn't make decisions they would not be managers!' (p. xv). Thus, just as in the previous chapter we had to consider how people think about risk, we must now investigate what we mean by a decision and how people take decisions. Naturally, people cannot take decisions blindly. We must therefore also begin to consider what information people will need to help them take good quality decisions. Finally, in the last chapter, we saw that language and the relationships that people create are aspects of power. In this chapter, we should identify a distinction of fundamental importance, namely, that managers may have *power over* events and people (i.e. authority) or they may have *power to* implement ideas and decisions. We may properly see these powers as aspects of both organizational and personal capacity or ability. Since organizations depend for their effectiveness on co-operative effort, we should start with the proposition that people tend to be better motivated when they are given power to get things done.

3.1 WHAT IS A DECISION?

The management of all business activities depends upon the process of decision-making. According to Eardley *et al*. (1991), 'A decision is a process or a sequence of activities undertaken by an individual or group(s) with a view to establishing and implementing a solution to an existing or potential problem' (p. 35). Distinctions have been made between two significant types of decision:

- programmable or 'well-structured' decisions; and
- unprogrammable or 'ill-structured' decisions (e.g. Simon, 1973; Richards, 1974; and Soelberg, 1967).

The former decision types usually occur frequently and they have well-defined structures and predictable information inputs. Consequently, they may be solved by using a pre-defined solution process and decision criteria. The more routine the decision, the more likely it is to be solved by the application of what is termed an algorithm, i.e. a formalistic set of rules designed in advance to be applied to every example of a specific situation. A significant proportion of operational decisions may be classified as programmable including credit rating, quality control, equipment maintenance and delivery scheduling.

Generally, unprogrammable decisions are of a more unique nature, having ill-defined structures, unpredictable information inputs and decision criteria that must be formulated to meet the specific situation. It is reasonably common for strategic decisions to be 'ill-structured', although Soelberg (1967) and Simon (1973) recognized that such decisions do exhibit certain common and repeated patterns in their processing, i.e. organizations learn how to take the more difficult decisions. The organization will make these less routine decisions through the application of heuristics, i.e. a system of making choices through the use of non-linear methods. Examples of unprogrammable decisions would be: deciding where to site a new manufacturing facility given that each potential site may have different attributes, which of several projects in research to select for product development, whether to diversify into a new market etc.

The activity of decision-making has received significant attention from a wide, variety of discipline areas, each providing different perspectives on what researchers have found to be a multi-faceted and extremely complex process. This is true at the level both of individual or personal decision-making as well as of organizational decision-making, which tends to involve greater interaction between individuals or groups of decision-makers. It would be clearly impractical and unnecessary to review all of this research in the context of this book. Our intention is therefore only to consider those areas of research that contribute directly to the central concerns of risk and uncertainty. This will include:

- the development of an outline model of the decision-making process;
- a review of the major perspectives of decision-making research; and
- an examination of the research conducted into the role and use of information within this process.

3.1.1 What is the decision process?

The following major elements combine together to form the decision-making process:

1. The personal characteristics of the decision-maker. This includes the following sub-elements:

    - the individual's cognitive characteristics and decision style, e.g. some people absorb information well only if it is presented in a structured fashion, others can accept elements of data in any order and create a framework of reference to support their own understanding of the growing mass of information; some people will worry about their accountability for the decision and move slowly through the process to collect as much information as possible before committing themselves, others will take decisions more arbitrarily, not caring whether the individual decision is right or wrong, so long as more turn out to be right than wrong;

- the individual's capacity and willingness to handle complexity and incongruity, e.g. some people perform inadequately either because they are alarmed when new data does not fit comfortably with existing information or because they do not have the skills to carry out the calculations necessary to resolve the problems; and

- the individual's capacity to handle a sometimes significant quantity of information inputs, e.g. some people panic when too much information comes too quickly and, in their haste, they overlook vital material, while the output of others begins to slow down out of conscientiousness as they try to assimilate all the new information before taking decisions.

2. The decision or task environment. The place where people work is a statement by the people with power about the quality of the environment the others are entitled to expect when they come into work. A pleasant building, well-equipped can be motivating; a poorly maintained old building may signal a lack of concern for the lower ranking employees and lead to a loss of commitment on their part. The way in which people are allowed to work reflects the culture that has emerged for that organization. Both the organizational and the personal environment will have a profound effect on the way in which the decision process operates, e.g. any changes in the political and social framework that represents the culture of the organization and in the personal status of the individuals involved, may produce very different sets of decisions from one period to the next. We have already seen that the discourse within each organization will colour the way in which people will talk about risks and contribute to the decision process (see section 2.5.2). It will also help to shape the way in which people create images and communicate their thoughts (or not) (see sections 2.4. and 2.6).

3. The decision variables. Here we concentrate on the specific dimensions and attributes of the immediate decision, e.g:

- the number of variables that are recognized as being relevant to the decision (remember that other relevant variables may exist but not be identified by the decision-makers either in time or at all);

- it is inevitable that there will be either actual or potential interaction between the variables that have been identified – naturally, the nature and extent of the interaction will vary with each combination or permutation of the variables and it is up to the decision-makers to determine which are the most likely to occur and how significant the foreseen interactions will be should they occur;

- the scale of the resources committed to taking the particular decision (remember that you cannot guarantee better quality decisions just because you make more resources available – all that may happen is that it takes more people longer to make the same poor decision);
- time-scale – this may be under the control of the organization and therefore be an element of resourcing, or the amount of time available may be dictated by the pace of events external to the organization; and
- the number of parties interested in the outcome and their position or status – if only a few people who are relatively unimportant to the organization may be affected, a very different decision may be taken as against a scenario when individuals of critical importance to the decision-makers personally or to the well-being of the organization may be involved.

4.   The decision process. There are a number of methodologies and techniques that may be applied to the different parts of the decision process, i.e. to support and improve the quality of the activities of problem structuring, information specification and collection, data analysis, solution identification and selection etc.

A moment's reflection should show us that although we have separated four elements as constituting a decision, all four will interact with each other in any given decision situation. Thus, for example, when we talk of complexity as a part of decision-making, we are not just referring to the complex nature of each of the four elements themselves, but including the complex nature of the interactions between the elements.

Most of the researchers agree upon the major stages involved in the decision-making process. There is, however, less unanimity on the order in which these take place or, indeed, the constituent elements of each of the stages. Figure 3.1 presents a preliminary outline model of the main stages in the process, indicating what we would take to be the sequence of activities.

Some authors (e.g.MacCrimmon, 1974; and Brunsson, 1982) have tried to highlight the distinction between the 'thinking' or 'decision' perspective and what they termed the 'action' perspective. For example, MacCrimmon suggested that whether or not the trigger operates and action follows the identification of a problem (Stage 1 in Fig. 3.1) would be influenced by:

- the size of the gap between actual performance and the target level of performance set for the individual or group (in turn, the impact of this element depends upon the degree of accuracy attributed to the measurement techniques used and the period of time reviewed – if small gaps are identified by techniques which may have significant margins of error built in and the periods covered are short and not

Problem
Trigger
v
Initial perception/Model
of problem or issue
v
Structuring problem
Components
Alternative solutions
v
Analysis of alternative
solutions and consequences
Preference ranking
Selection criteria
v
Selection/Choice of
alternative solution
v
Decision and commitment
to chosen solution
v
Implementation, communication
monitor and control

Figure 3.1 Outline model of decision-making process.

considered significant, nothing may happen);
- the attention of the decision-maker being drawn to the size of the gap and it being considered significant;
- for a variety of reasons, even if the gap is considered significant, the decision-maker may not be motivated or willing to respond to the signals or to recognize that a problem has been identified; and
- even though the decision-maker may be willing to act, he or she may not have the ability or opportunity to do anything about the problem and so no decision is seen to be taken.

Brunsson identifies a further difficulty that may arise when the decision-maker is motivated to undertake a comprehensive search process. Naturally, the manager will be trying to reduce the existing levels of uncertainty and to identify alternative solutions for the problem(s) in hand (i.e. Stage 3), but if he or she is too successful in collecting new information about the situation(s), the actual result may be to cause even greater uncertainty. Two consequences may follow:

1. the decision-maker may become demoralized in the face of increasing uncertainty and lose the motivation to seek further solutions; and/or
2. the increasing uncertainty may reduce the level of commitment to any particular solution.

Brunsson also has a word of warning for the researchers into the decision process. He suggests that great care should be taken when identifying cause and effect. Thus, although some well-organized decision-makers may lay down the criteria for choosing between alternative solutions at a very early stage in the process, it is just as likely that the process of evaluating the consequences of adopting each of the alternative solutions may result in the definition of the criteria for selection.

Simon (1979) therefore stressed the importance of understanding the heuristic processes involved in unprogrammable decision-making, and argued that a model of the process,

> is an essential component in any positive theory of decision-making. (p. 507)

As we shall see later, there are two approaches to research into decision-making, the descriptive and the normative. On the basis of descriptive research, other researchers in the field (eg. MacCrimmon, 1973 and 1974 and Mintzberg, 1975) have suggested that many of the stages shown in Figure 3.1 may proceed concurrently, or be part of an iterative process, or occur in the reverse order to that shown. For example, Cohen (1972) suggested that,

> [an] organization is a collection of choices looking for problems, issues and feelings looking for decision situations in which they might be aired, solutions looking for issues to which they might be the answer, and decision-makers looking for work. (p. 2)

Researchers of the descriptive processes of decision-making have invariably been critical of the normative models of the process (e.g. Simon 1979). Rose (1974) provided a fairly representative view when he observed that

> one is forced to conclude that present normative models are not immediately applicable to most decision situations even if a decision-making possesses the ability and will to use them. (p. 502)

3.2 A SYNOPSIS OF THE THEMES OF DECISION-MAKING RESEARCH

Beach and Mitchell (1978) reflected the views expressed by many of the more recent researchers on decision-making when they concluded that,

> a substantial amount of research has been devoted to developing techniques (decision aids) for improving decision-making effectiveness. While improved decision effectiveness is an important goal, we also must seek to understand human decision-making as it is, not merely as it might be. (p. 439)

Richards (1974) provided some support for this view by stating that the major thrust in research and development in this field had been in:

- improving the efficiency of the decision-making process for programmable decisions; and

- reducing the information processing costs of programmable decisions.

But, as Brunsson (1982) argues, there is a danger in any research and development activity that focuses on the element of efficiency in decision processes. The difficulty is that outcomes which, for example, suggest ways in which cost savings may be achieved, are often inconsistent with rules that might be developed in the hope of promoting more rational decision-making. This danger will, of course, be increased if cost-cutting measures limit the resources available to support decision-making processes. But we should be careful not to overstate the danger. The fact that we have used the word 'rational' in this context might be taken to require a higher standard of care in decision-making than is actually the case. Indeed, there are a number of myths which are often associated with the concept of 'rationality' in decision-making. For example, we do not expect that when faced by the same set of risky circumstances, everyone will do the same thing, i.e. that there is objectively a 'right' answer to each problem. However, we would expect that the same person should take the same decision when faced by the same circumstances, i.e. consistency is rational so long as the outcome achieved in previous situations was acceptable. To that extent, rationality is no more than one of the criteria against which to measure the degree of utility in the decision outcome achieved.

It follows, therefore, that it is perfectly legitimate for different people to reach different decisions in the same situation. There are many possible reasons for differences to arise, including:

- the methods used and the extent of the search for data undertaken by each person may find different sets of facts upon which to base the decision – these differences may be exaggerated by factors such as:
    - the level of resources made available to support the search activity;
    - the conscientiousness of those performing the searches;
    - the status of the individuals searching for information may limit or enhance their ability to access certain types of data;
    - the amount of luck they have in finding data etc;
- the decision-makers may find the same data but interpret the facts differently (see Section 3.1.1 on the characteristics of individuals); or
- they may consider that the organization's goals and objectives call for different types of decision.

It is often said that the success of an organization lies in its ability to be able to make the most of the opportunities that are detected. But, without a system to reconcile the practice of decision-making within an organization, the organization's response to opportunities can differ widely, depending upon which individuals take the decisions. This may arise, for example, because some individuals may be risk averse while others are risk neutral, i.e. some may be conservative or timid and wish to avoid the risks while the others may be more self-confident or brash and not mind taking the risks.

3.2.1 The descriptive and normative approaches

Following his review of research into rational and other decision-making approaches, Simon (1979) suggested that advances had been made in this area of descriptive research and concluded that

> we have a large mass of descriptive data, from both laboratory and field, that show how human problem solving and decision making actually take place in a wide variety of situations. A number of theories have been constructed to account for these data, and while these theories certainly do not yet constitute a single coherent whole, there is much in common among them. . . . it is now entirely clear that the classical and neoclassical theories have been replaced by a superior alternative that provides us with a much closer approximation to what is actually going on. (p. 510)

When different authors have reviewed the field of decision-making research, they have each sought to classify the major developments in different ways. These approaches depend upon and flow from each author's own particular disciplinary stance. Simon (1979), for example, identified four areas of research including:

- a study of the behaviour shown by individuals when exercising choices related to statistical decision theory predictions;
- psychological research into the microprocesses of individual decision-making;
- empirical (primarily case-study) research of actual decision processes in different types of organization; and
- developments of theory aimed at replacing economic maximization postulates (i.e. factors of utility) with behavioural decision postulates (i.e. cultural, social and political factors).

Driver and Mock (1975) reviewed research into the human information processing dimension of decision-making and its contribution to accounting information systems. They identified cognitive psychology as the seed-bed of the subsequent developments in this field. Figure 3.2 shows the outline classification of these developments.

Having established the primary division between the normative and descriptive approaches, they concentrated their attention on the latter field. They recognized that the descriptive field spanned the spectrum from the research work developing generalist approaches (e.g. Miller, 1956 on human information processing capacity), to the situationalist approaches where the behaviour of each individual differs, albeit marginally (e.g. Newell and Simon, 1972). The centre of this spectrum reflects essentially a contingency approach, as discussed in Chapters 8 and 9, which they refer to as a 'differential' approach. The more recent research has been concentrated in this category, aiming to examine:

- the influence of each decision-maker's valuations ('value') of the different information inputs; and

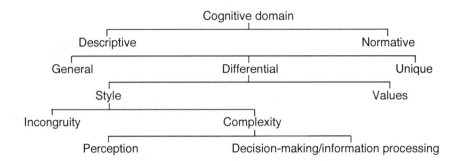

Figure 3.2 Approaches to human information processing. Source: Driver and Mock (1975), p. 493.

- the manner ('style') in which they actually process and use data in making decisions.

Information processing style is seen to be influenced by the nature of the problem situation faced in terms of incongruity (e.g. novelty, ambiguity, uncertainty and risk), and complexity. The latter they further subdivided into two areas of research:

- how complexity influences the perception of the problem; and
- the information received and the manner of processing that information.

Although Driver and Mock specifically related the aspects of perception and human information processing to the complexity dimension (the topic with which their paper was primarily concerned), it is probably safe to assume that they recognized that these aspects could also be related to the ambiguity section/dimension (see section 7.1).

3.2.2 Decision-making perspectives

The research by Astley *et al.* (1982) identified the following four major perspectives on the decision-making activity.

- *The process perspective.* This theme may be identified in the work of Lindblom (1959, 1968 and 1979) who observed a process of 'muddling through'. Cyert and March (1992) studied the impact and role of intra-organizational coalitions on decision processes and behaviour; but the work of Mintzberg (1973, 1979) reveals a highly fragmented and unstructured process of decision-making.
- *The outcome perspective.* This reflects the research of Cohen, March and Olson (1972), suggesting both that outcomes are not necessarily a response to a specific problem and, indeed more alarmingly, that solutions may precede the problem. Thus, if decision-makers discover or develop what they believe to be a sufficiently generic solution methodology, they may actively seek problems to apply it to. The

result may be an unhappy adjustment in the problem elements so that the facts then fit the methodology.

- *The bounded rationality of the decision-makers.* This is to be found in the work of Simon (1977) and of March and Simon (1958). They recognized the inevitable truth that when managers were faced with high degrees of complexity in real world situations, any limitations that they had in terms of cognitive abilities were likely to be exposed. One of the ways in which these limitations might appear was demonstrated by Cyert and March (1963) who showed that the search, analytical and learning processes likely to be employed in the modern organization tended to be inadequate. Similarly, Lindblom (1959, 1968) observed that many organizations relied on a process of incremental changes to their systems by applying historical precedents. The stated aim was to learn from past mistakes and to introduce gradual reform and improvement, but the only result was that managers made 'successive limited comparisons' instead of applying more general yardsticks and measures. These findings suggest that, for a variety of reasons varying from inadequacy in the face of complexity to laziness, decision-makers are likely to seek solutions to their problems that are known to be merely 'satisfactory' or even sub-optimal, rather than aiming for the optimization of an identifiable utility function, e.g. profit maximization. Indeed, many problems are solved by finding solutions that 'work' at a human level, i.e. they reduce the number and the violence of the complaints. Thus, there is a great temptation for organizations to try to simplify their problems and to redefine targets in the light of actual performance. The result is that solutions will be matched to the new and perhaps more modest targets rather than to the best imaginable targets.
- *The institutional rules and procedures for the taking of decisions* which provide both the framework and often the domain of criteria for the decision, as well as conferring power to certain personnel in the organization (e.g. Wilson, 1982). For a more detailed explanation, see section 3.5.

3.2.3 Research approaches

Libby and Lewis (1982) identified four research approaches:

1. To study the interaction between the decision-maker and the information received, examining the influence of the information on decision quality. This first approach was based primarily on the Lens Model (Brunswick, 1952, 1955) and involved the development of quantitative/statistical models of decision behaviour.
2. To study how decision-makers exercise judgement based on probabilistic information by focusing on matching descriptive evidence on decision-making to the normative models of rational behaviour. This approach is derived from the work of people such as Astley *et al.* (1982) into the phenomenon of bounded rationality (section 3.2.2).
3. To study the behaviour of decision-makers leading up to the taking

of the decision. This would include the social and organizational dynamics, activites and processes occurring prior to making a choice (i.e. problem definition, information search, analysis, etc.).

4.   To study the cognitive style of decision-makers. This would seek more directly to relate the personal characteristics of the individual to the quality of decisions and the responses to information load and complexity.

In summary, research has been conducted into all four of the major elements of decision-making outlined at the begining of section 3.1.1. At first, the main research effort was targeted on the development of decision aids and models intended to improve the effectiveness of decision-making – an approach that was to be based on the constructs of the normative model. But as the research continued, there was increasing dissatisfaction with the descriptive power of the normative approach, and this has resulted in an increasing focus towards purely descriptive research approaches. In recent years, most of this descriptive effort has been directed towards the decision-maker and the decision process elements, rather than the decision environment or decision specific variables. This emphasis has been particularly common when dealing with unprogramm-able decisions. There are two probable reasons for this emphasis:

• the expectation is that the research into the elements of the decision-maker and the decision process is more likely to produce generalizable results and theories than research into the elements of the environment and decision specific variables which are likely to be more unique and situation specific;
• from the perspective of the psychologist and behavioural scientist, it is easier to conduct research into the characteristics of the decision-maker and the dynamics of a process in the laboratory situation as opposed to the field.

However, both reasons are less than wholly satisfactory. Thus, for example, McGhee *et al.* (1978) having failed to establish any empirical correlation between decision-maker characteristics and information pro-cessing activity, suggested with support from other psychological researchers that

> future studies of human information processing in the accounting discipline might develop better descriptive models than presently exist if variables, such as task influences on behaviour, are systematically taken into consideration. (p. 695)

3.3 DECISION-MAKING AND INFORMATION RESEARCH

Information and its processing play an essential role in the decision-making process. MacCrimmon (1974), for example, suggested that,

> the entire decision making process can be viewed as the acquisition

and processing of information. (p. 462)

While Earl and Hopwood (1980) regarded information as

> the raw material of decision-making, the *sine qua non* of planning and control and the life blood of organizations. (p. 4)

They further observed that 'the relationship between information and decision has rarely been critically examined' (p. 6). By way of example, they identified a number of presumptions. These presumptions concern the information/decision interface and they are in common use even though they have not been fully substantiated by empirical research. These include the views that:

- the identification of a decision or problem situation will automatically result in the process of information specification and acquisition;
- human beings behave in a rational manner throughout all aspects of their information processing activities;
- the specification of information requirements and the analysis of the resulting information will preceed the choice of alternative solutions;
- the role played by information is invariate across a multitude of different decision situations;
- the availability of good quality information facilitates or eases the decision process rather than actively influencing or frustrating the decision.

A number of studies on decision-making have focused on the role of information in the decision-making process, and the nature of the processing activities undertaken by the individuals involved. The next section reviews the main studies and their conclusions.

3.3.1 The role of the information processing function

When Libby and Lewis (1982) reviewed human information processing research within the context of accounting decisions, they classified the information used according to the stages in the decision process as shown in Figure 3.3. This presentation has been further developed in Figure 3.4 to incorporate the types of information in relation to identifiable activities in the decision process.

This work has produced valuable insights into the manner in which information is handled and subsequently influences the decision-maker. Research by Hoffman (1968) confirmed the somewhat predictable proposition that when people receive inconsistent information cues, this is likely to create feelings of doubt and conflicting choices in the decision-maker's mind. Naturally, the greater the inconsistency in the initial data, the greater the degree of uncertainty generated in the mind of the decision-maker. Similarly, Slovic (1966) found evidence that many decision-makers find it difficult to weigh up positive and negative evidence on different elements critical to a decision. Further, when the situation has real levels of uncertainty affecting critical factors in the decision, there is

Input: Information set / decision cues
          Incorporating variables such as
               • scaling characteristics
               • statistical properties
               • information content
               • method of presentation
               • context of decision

Process: Judgement of decision-makers
          Incorporating variables such as
               • characteristics of decision-makers
               • characteristics of decision rules

Output: Judgement / decision
          Incorporating variables such as
               • qualities of judgements made
               • degree of self-insight

Figure 3.3 Classification of information used in the stages of the decision process.

no single methodology or technique that can be guaranteed to help and decision-makers may adopt any one of a number of possible strategies for making the final choice. But Slovic (1972), and later Tversky and Kahneman (1974), have established that there is a somewhat worrying tendency for decision-makers to anchor their strategy selection and subsequent judgements on the basis of the first information cues received. The evidence suggests that many decision-makers seem unwilling or unable accurately to reappraise future decisions in the light of new information.

Other studies have observed a significant degree of variability in the manner and extent of information search and subsequent processing activity undertaken by different organizations. In trying to establish the factors that influence the degree of variability, Astley *et al.* (1982) stress the two dimensions of:

- complexity – this arises when the nature of the problem is multi-dimensional (i.e. the problem is made up of a significant number of component factors, each one of importance) and there are real degrees of uncertainty as to the nature of the possible consequences to each of the alternative choices; and
- cleavage – there is real disagreement or even conflict between the various interests which become apparent during the process of evalua-tion of the alternative solutions.

These two dimensions interrelate in the decision-making process, having an effect both on the nature of the process itself and the outcome. Indeed, in one sense, the extent of cleavage might be nothing more than one of the factors adding to the level of complexity. Thus, if the decision-makers have divided into armed camps and each group argues from a partisan

Information Inputs	Decision Stage

Situation variables
Performance variances
External or internal signals
Organization policies,
Objectives and plans etc.
	Problem trigger
	Identification/
	   recognition of
	   situation requiring
	   decision

Situation variables Decision, specific information.	Problem definition, structure, formulation

Historical records
Previous experience
Analogous – decisions
Analogous – organizations
	Search and
	   generation of
	   alternative Solutions

Historical data
Data models and analytical
   methods and techniques
Outcome forecasts
Probability estimates
etc.
	Estimation of
	   consequences of
	   alternative solutions

Organizational objectives
   and preferences
Individual objectives
   and preferences
Risk perceptions
	Evaluate alternatives

Decision criteria	Decision / choice

Figure 3.4 Information inputs to the main stages in the decision process.

point of view for a solution that will favour their interests alone, this significantly adds to complexity. In the context of information, they suggest that when either complexity or cleavage is relatively high for a decision, the result will be greater scrutiny of the existing information holdings or increased intensity of information search and processing. We would suggest that the result could just as easily be an arbitrary decision based on little information and no real processing effort. Thus, if managers know that the views of two interest groups are irreconcilable, there is little point in trying to achieve a compromise. Similarly, if it is clear that the level of uncertainty cannot be reduced to manageable proportions unless uneconomic resources are allocated to information search and processing, the decision must either be deferred until uncertainty can be reduced, or the managers must simply guess between the alternatives.

Indeed, Driscoll and Lanzetta (1965) found no significant evidence to support the view that the resources devoted to information search increase as the result of increased uncertainty. In fact, the converse tends to be true. Their findings suggest that more time is spent studying low uncertainty problems than high ones. The reason for this is that effort expended if there is low uncertainty would represent a better investment because there is a better chance of clarifying the issues and a greater likelihood of a better quality decision. They did, however, recognize that increased complexity in the problem situation may change the relationship between uncertainty and information search from a decreasing monotonic function to a decreasing curvilinear function.

3.3.2 The style of the decision-maker

Potentially, many factors may affect the scope and extent of the information processing activity for each decision, but one of the most consistently important will be the personal characteristics of the decision-maker. Driver and Lintott (1973) developed a classification of the style of individual decision-makers. It is based on the two main variables, namely, the way in which they defined the focus of their solution search, and their use of information. The essence of this classification is summarized in Figure 3.5.

The two extremes of style are decisive and integrative. For these purposes, a person would be said to have a 'decisive' style if, typically, he or she focuses on a single solution and processes the minimum amount of information necessary to support a conclusion on this single solution. At the other extreme, the 'integrative' style reflects a decision-maker who is prepared to process large volumes of data without prejudging which is the best among the several solutions under simultaneous consideration. This is distinguished from the 'flexible' style in which different interpretations are applied to the limited data collected when considering alternative decision solutions. A further category developed from the research of Driver (1974) combines the integrative and the 'hierarchical' styles into what he termed the 'complex' style. This is derived from the finding that although the majority of people will tend to be consistent in the style they adopt, some people select the style that best fits the situation. Empirical research based on this model (Driver and Mock, 1975) provided support for the predicted levels of intensity of information search and usage.

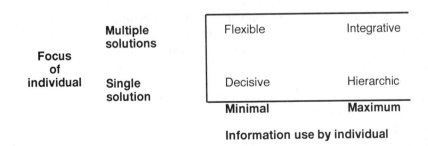

Figure 3.5 Decision-making style.

Indeed, at an intuitive level, we would always suspect a link between personality and the level of resources devoted to information specification and exploitation. But later empirical studies by Savich (1977) and McGhee *et al.* (1978) found no significant relationship between the classification of personality of the decision-maker and the information processing intensity. For the time being, therefore, we leave the matter as inconclusively proved.

3.3.3 Information search and processing strategies

An alternative matrix of potential information search and processing strategies has been developed by Shields (1980). This is based on research into information usage and its relationship to accounting-based performance reports, and it produces classifications depending on the nature of the search pattern and the amount of search. A modified version of this model is shown in Figure 3.6.

The additive (linear) search strategy is discussed by many authors including Slovic and Lichtenstein (1971). Although the linear nature of the strategy implies that the decision-maker will only analyse a limited range of parameters, there is confirmation that the analysis carried out will always be in some depth. The way in which the strategy is applied to different decision scenarios could be either a sign of strength or weakness. A well-prepared, decisive decision-maker could have developed a clearly articulated list of parameters prior to the analysis of the particular decision, and maximizing the use of available resources, concentrates efforts where it is believed the best results may be achieved. A weak decision-maker may have learned that a few parameters have relevance and applies these to the particular decision situation irrespective of the nature of the situation.

The additive difference search strategy (Tversky, 1969) is a more rigorous methodology and it is designed to produce a ranking order of the possible solutions. It depends upon making a number of detailed comparisons between all the identified solutions that are considered viable. Each set of comparisons will be based on a single parameter or dimension, and the differences arising from each comparison are aggregated to achieve a final aggregate difference score between the alternative solutions. Thus, if an organization was taking the decision whether to relocate staff from one

		Primary search pattern	
		Breadth first	**Depth first**
Intensity of search activity per decision	**Low**	Additive difference	Additive linear
	High	Elimination-by-aspects	Conjunctive

Figure 3.6 Model of potential information search strategies.

office site to another, the following represent examples of the separate comparisons between the different possible sites that might be considered.

- The existing information flows will be disrupted by moving the staff, so what new information flows and linkages might be established in each of the new locations?
- If new concentrations of staff are produced, will this lead to a more efficient use of existing office space?
- What are the costs in moving general office and task-specific equipment to each of the new locations?
- Will all the staff move and, if not, what are the training/recruitment implications for each of the new locations?
- What are the costs of relocating the staff in terms of additional mileage allowances, removal expenses etc. for each of the new locations?

Each of these five dimensions would be taken in turn and applied to all the possible sites. At the end of the process, there would be listings of values under each of the five headings which should allow a more objective ranking of the possible sites. Naturally, this process can never be wholly objective both because some of the dimensions may not be quantifiable in strict numerical terms, e.g. the information flows and linkages, and because interested parties may have an incentive to produce biased costings depending upon the result they want to favour. But at least the evidence is set out in a more organized way and should support a better quality decision.

Overall, if either of the additive strategies is used, there is a clear implication that the decision-maker has developed a set of weightings to apply to each of the decision parameters that are considered. These weightings may be either objective or subjective (or have qualities of both). Thus, the decision-makers might decide that parameters having a direct bearing on staff morale might be given a greater weighting than mere cost considerations, and so on.

The conjunctive strategy (Einhorn, 1980) is a filtering process which operates during the preliminary stages of the decision-taking. The aim is to produce a shortlist of candidate solutions. Thus, as a precondition to consideration in the final decision-making, each potential solution must be seen to satisfy some initial threshold level of performance on each of the key parameters. If a solution makes the final shortlist of realistic candidates, further information search and analysis may then be considered worthwhile. As in the additive strategies, the decision-maker must have some prior knowledge of the key parameters and must have determined the threshold levels that must be satisfied.

The elimination-by-aspects strategy (Tversky, 1972) employs an approach in which all the potential solutions are tested against each parameter in turn. If a particular solution fails to satisfy some minimum or threshold level on a particular criterion, it is eliminated from further consideration. The remaining solution alternatives are tested against successive parameters until only a single solution alternative remains which has passed all the parameter tests. This approach also necessitates some prior judgements by the decision-maker to identify the important parameters, their ranking and the acceptable threshold levels.

To a greater or lesser extent, all of these strategies require the decision-makers to spend time identifying the key parameters, their relative weighting and the minimum levels of performance that would be considered acceptable. The amount of information required for this purpose will tend to vary depending upon the criticality of the resulting list. Thus, if the organization has decided to adopt the conjunctive strategy, the managers will know that more information will be specified for search and processing once the shortlist has been drawn up. The initial list of parameters may therefore be relatively crude. But, if the organization has decided to adopt the elimination-by-aspects strategy and the list of parameters is intended to be the sole yardstick by which the selection procedure is to be judged, more care may be required in defining the parameters.

There is, however, a danger in emphasizing the level of care to be devoted to the process of drawing up such a list of parameters. In the case of unprogrammable or unique decisions, it is almost certain that major issues of strategic importance to the organization are involved. When the senior managers recognize the importance of the decision pending, they may begin to act unrealistically, for if they lay down the requirement that managers should draw up what is supposed to be a definitive list of key parameters, they may be expecting too much insight and rationality from the preliminary decision-makers than may be achievable in practice. Lists of parameters should be recognized as guides and measures to the selection process. They do not replace the essential tasks to be undertaken by those responsible for the final evaluation of solution alternatives.

3.3.4 Subjective values in the decision process

At an intuitive level, it should be obvious that people react differently to stress and that one of the sources of stress in the decision process is the amount of information available to support the particular decision. One of the dangers commonly encountered in a democractic environment is having too much 'noise' in the system. Indeed, many studies have described the phenomenon of 'information overload' where too many people are competing for the decision-maker's attention and presenting conflicting versions of reality in what they say (e.g. Driver and Mock, 1975). These studies confirm that the capacity of individuals to absorb and process information is a function of their cognitive characteristics, the decision style they have adopted, and the nature and importance of the decision to be taken.

From the earlier parts of this chapter, we have also seen that the main focus of research into the use of information in decision-making has been primarily on the personal attributes of the decision-maker. The resulting data is usually expressed as a series of consequences, showing how different characteristics affect both the volume and the interpretation of the information that can be accessed by each decision-maker. For example, let us take the question of how well the ordinary person can judge how often events have occurred in the past. Judging the relative frequency of events on a subjective basis is frequently allowed to depend upon the fallible human memory. Unfortunately, the powers of recollection and judgement may be skewed by the degree of contemporary publicity (or lack of it) given to the particular phenomenon both within and outside the organization. Thus, unless something prompts us to remember or research the detail of the past, we tend to misjudge how often things happen or how long ago a particular event occurred.

We should also remember from Chapter 2 that whatever information is collected and offered as a support to the decision process, its content may implicitly and explictly refer to many intangible values. Some of these values will be the values of those collecting the information, others will be the values addressed by those offering the information (for more discussion, section 3.4.1). At many levels, the form in which the information is presented will be a mass of signals. Thus, for example, the order in which information is laid out and so received by the decision-maker may significantly influence both the reader's perception of the parameters identified and stated to be important, and the consequent judgements concerning their weighting. It may therefore be safer for senior managers to adopt a complex style of decision-making. This would require them to vary the strategy selection and the level of commitment to information search and processing in the light of the importance attributable to the particular decision and the level of resource available to support the decision-making.

The chance of information availability is also critical. Who knows what and how it is incorporated into the decision-making process may produce dramatically different decisions in the same basic situation. Subjective preconceptions may also lead decision-makers to accept or reject different elements of data more readily. Hence, data presented in a quantitative form may be considered to be more reliable than apparently subjective opinion or qualitative data. More recent research is now concentrating on issues such as whether decision-makers are sensitive to the size of any sample of data. Thus, for quality-control purposes or for market research, managers are being asked questions on how large a sample they believe would produce significant results and what distribution of results would be expected from varying sample sizes. At present, results suggest that the majority of managers do not know what to expect.

We therefore conclude this section with the proposition that the training of decision-makers becomes significantly more important as they move up the organization's management hierarchy. By the time they reach the strategic levels within the organization, the aim should be to help decision-makers to:

- develop a constructive decision style and to be aware of the main information search strategies;
- start off the search for information from a sensible point;
- eliminate bias from their decisions; and

- to be aware of the more obvious problems in relying on statistical techniques.

3.4 A PRACTICAL VIEW OF INFORMATION IN RELATION TO DECISIONS

The need to take decisions will always be triggered by some event whether it is observed directly in the real world or indirectly through the reception of data, e.g. a deadline has to be met or a customer places an order. Many decisions emerge from a form of stream of consciousness. Each person lives through the day in a somewhat fragmented way, observing events as they occur and responding to the stimuli that catch attention. Many of these events and stimuli will be unexpected and unstructured as people interact with each other. However, one of the things that a manager must do is to build up and sustain relationships with others. One of the main functions of these relationships will be to provide information that may be useful in taking decisions and to allow people to test out and refine ideas before they are presented to a wider audience.

The behaviour that ends in the making of a decision depends upon the ability of the people involved to make reasonable estimates of the costs that may be incurred and the likely returns. These estimates should be based upon the best information available to the organization but this information does not magically present itself for consideration. It is up to the decision-makers to search for that information. For issues with any degree of complexity, it is impossible to scan the environment (both internal and external to the organization) to identify all the alternatives for each decision. So in a 'rational' organization, the economics of decision-making require that the investment of resources is only made to the collection of information so long as the expected marginal return from the information gained exceeds the expected marginal cost in acquiring it.

3.4.1 The communication of information for decision-making

The search for, and the collection of, information is not the only problematic area for the organization. Once it has been found, the information must often be processed in some way and then communicated to the appropriate people. Communication takes time and the system may be affected if those responsible for the processing or dissemination of the information do not have the same goals as those to whom the information is to be sent. Obviously, if the contents of the information are modified, this may have a direct effect upon the nature of the decision ultimately taken. The more evenly balanced the decision to be taken between two alternatives, the greater the risk that subjective bias will influence the outcome. It is therefore important for the organization to be aware of the possible conflicts of interest between the different groups so that allowances can be made for possible distortions in the information communicated. More importantly, the further up the organization the information must travel and the more it is to be summarized or manipulated, the greater the risk that the information may become distorted.

One of the ways in which organizations can attempt to check for distortions is to monitor the feedback data after decisions have been made. If it becomes apparent that the estimates were inaccurate when they arrived at the strategic level, allowances and compensations can be built into the system to reduce the opportunity for similar errors to arise in the future. This will involve the managers in making subjective judgements about the reliability of the sources of the information and of the extent to which the information may have been the subject of interpretative adjustment by those with competing goals. Obviously, the greater the discretion given to groups lower down the organizational hierarchy to filter and manipulate the information in their hands, the greater the risk that the resulting communications may be unreliable in some way. But if their collection or interpretative discretions are significantly restricted, they may become demotivated and lose their initiative in chasing relevant data or in extracting the best results from their data. This may be equally unfortunate for the decision-makers. Thus, if the organization is to survive with a reasonably stable level of performance, the decision-makers must use the feedback data on the results of past decisions as a basis upon which to adapt to the level of falsification or incompleteness in the anticipative data to support future decisions. This may be seen as part of the more general need for the organization to learn adaptive skills to enable survival in the business environment.

However, this adaptation process may not be the best answer. Cyert and March (1992, p. 93) reach the conclusion that 'consistency or completeness [in information] would, at times, create problems in finding feasible solutions'. When an organization is triggered into recognizing the existence of a problem and/or of the need to take a decision, the relevant people may allocate resources to search for possible solutions. In the first instance, very rough criteria may be specified as the basis upon which to filter out the inappropriate solutions, i.e. the cost of a full analysis of every option may be far in excess of the expected return. Once a manageable group of possibilities has been identified, they may be considered in more detail. But there is no guarantee that the organization will be willing or able to devote sufficient resources to the particular decision-making task of gathering complete information to support the final decision. Indeed, the need for some to contribute information may only become apparent after the implications of a specific proposal to implement a decision are recognized. For example, if only one of the possible solutions would affect the sales department, and the staff in that department initially do not consider it likely that that solution will be adopted, they may not contribute to the debate until, in a sense, it is too late.

This should emphasize the point that elements of data are not simply scattered throughout the environment, passively waiting to be discovered in a search activity. More often, the characteristics of the data sought have to be defined in the light of the objectives of the search. The aim will be to identify data that will help to solve the particular problem in hand rather than simply to satisfy a researcher's curiosity. Once the immediate problem is solved, the search for data is likely to be discontinued. Problems will therefore arise if those people who are to make the search:

- do not recognize the need to search for particular data;
- only recognize the need to search for particular data when the decision-makers have more clearly identified which choice between alternatives they are likely to make;
- they innocently misinterpret the nature of the data sought;
- only search for data in a limited way, e.g. limit the search to the area in which the symptoms of the problem are most clearly seen instead of properly analysing the situation to identify the best place in which to search; or
- have their own goals which conflict with those of the decision-makers.

We should also recognize the distinct possibility that the scope of the search for data may be significantly affected by the competences and confidence of those who are to search. Thus, people will always be tempted to give preferences to searches of those areas in which they have the greatest knowledge and confidence. This may save time and give them the best opportunity to appear to do a good job. Unless this issue is specifically adressed in selecting those who are to make the searches, a very limited view of reality may be presented to the organization to support each decision. Managers should therefore plan to improve search performance and to reduce bias by:

- improving the training of existing staff;
- allowing junior and middle managers a diversity of experience so that they will gain a better understanding of the goals and objectives of the organization as a whole;
- always ensuring that the search pattern includes those areas in which the organization is vulnerable; and
- improving their own performance in communicating information needs and in monitoring search performance.

3.4.2 Moving closer to taking the decision

As they approach the taking of a decision, the managers of an organization should have a number of responsibilities in mind when defining the nature of the problem, analysing its component elements and identifying possible resolution tactics, e.g:

- under normal circumstances, the organization will wish to take all reasonable steps to protect its existing asset holdings;
- in the event that some losses appear to be unavoidable from the destruction of, or damage to, organization assets, the management must consider how to finance those losses;
- because if others are injured as a result of the organization's activities, governments now provide for the liability of organizations through

both the provision of a system of courts and remedies, and/or the creation of no-fault insurance schemes, the management must consider how to promote the safety of employees, customers and third parties and, wherever possible, reduce the risks to which employees are exposed and which may cause sickness, injury or death;

- should the state provide for the payment of levies to a compensation fund or if claims against the organization are likely to be successful, the management must plan how to finance all costs and losses arising from injury to these groups;
- if it is foreseeable that other situations of loss are likely to arise from the activities of employees, then appropriate contingency plans must be made.

We should remember that people who take decisions expect that they are going to be implemented. The test to be applied in making the decision is whether it will offer a feasible resolution to the given problem. After all, the main functional justification for the role of manager is that 'things will get done'. This feasibility may be judged by either or both of the following criteria:

- budgetary, i.e. sufficient resources can be made available to support implementation of the decision; and/or
- as against doing nothing, the decision will result in a measurable improvement in performance or outcome.

However, the difficulty for the decision-makers is to be able to make the values of the variables sufficiently explicit so that they may be incorporated into the decision. If we consider the budgetary implications of a proposed decision, it would be expected that there will be costs attached to implementation and it may be hoped that savings will result. If the organization is considering whether to change its production facilities, the costs may be capital in the price to be paid for the new plant and the structural alterations to the workshops, and revenue in the new running costs for each of the proposed production facilities, e.g. if the plant will then run with fewer production workers, savings in wages will accrue. But if a well-balanced and rounded decision is to be made between the different options, how do the managers put values on elements such as:

- the speed and accuracy of the different manufacturing capacities claimed by the sales personnel of the manufacturers or distributors to be achievable through the use of their equipment in each proposal (remember that the sellers will have a positive interest in exaggerating the quality of their wares, thus distorting the data input);
- the quality of the output claimed to be achievable in each proposal;
- the claimed level of safety for the (remaining) employees who will use the plant in each proposal;
- customer responses to the products resulting from the new facilities;
- the corporate image of the organization, e.g. if one process is supposedly greener than the other(s) but more revenue-expensive, which should be chosen?

Even if monetary values could be attributed to uncertain variables such as these, there is no guarantee that the organization would be able to incorporate them into the decision. All that might happen is that the nature of the decision-making would become more complex and that is not necessarily the way in which to achieve a better quality decision. Thus, organizations tend to simplify decisions by excluding from consideration all those variables that are hard to quantify. The result is that many otherwise complex problems are resolved on the basis of subjective expectations and hope.

3.5 HOW ARE DECISIONS TAKEN?

In a relationship of direct power, the wording of the decision outcome will be as an instruction to the subordinates of the decision-maker. The decision may therefore be wholly arbitrary and there may be little accountability if the outcome is unsatisfactory to some of those affected. If the organization is more democratic and participative, the wording will suggest an expectation that appropriate action will follow. Hence, the manager may try to 'sell' the decision as a *fait accompli* to those affected, or may present the ideas that formed the basis of the decision and invite discussion. In a truly democratic organization, decision-making powers may be delegated within defined limits and either the group consulted or identified individuals will take the decision.

In taking decisions, there is an important distinction to be made between substantive and procedural rationality. According to Simon (1978) substantive rationality is a reference to the actual decision outcome which may be judged with some degree of retrospective objectivity as having been competently taken (or not), reflecting all the now obvious variables (or not). Procedural rationality refers to the processes by which the decisions are taken. It concentrates on the data available prior to the decision and accepts all the knowledge and technical limitations that may have operated (section 3.4).

At its simplest level, the decision process will involve some consideration being given to some or all of the following factors:

- a projection of the likely demand for the goods or services under consideration;
- a forecast of the reaction of competitiors to the introduction or continuation of the given goods or services;
- making the organization's goals and objectives more explicit in introducing or continuing the goods or services;
- an estimate of the costs likely to be incurred;
- an evaluation of the alternative strategies for achieving the goals and objectives at an acceptable cost;
- once a short list of possible plans has been selected, all the relevant projections, forecasts and estimates should be reviewed:

  - to ensure that the data is still timely; and

– to try to identify distortions, errors and omissions in the data.

- take the decision that appears most likely to satisfy the organisation's goals and objectives.

For much of the working day, the life of a senior manager may appear unstructured. This will reflect the reality that, like a juggler with many balls in the air, the manager will be considering a range of different problems but will be at different stages in the decision-making process for each of them. Thus, the manager may be trying to define some of the problems, looking for information that may help identify solutions to other problems, consulting with interested parties etc. Each problem may have different elements and different time-scales. If there is a common denominator, it is that the manager will want to retain status and authority and to advance career through being seen to take good decisions and to implement them successfully. The manager may therefore see connections and trade-offs between otherwise wholly unconnected events.

If the process by which decisions are taken is viewed as defective in some way, those to be affected will not be inclined to accept the decision without complaint. The issue of trust is a vital component of the process to be encouraged between decision-makers and those affected. We should recognize that trust does not suddenly come into being just because a 'management' strategy is developed. It is something that develops over time and within a particular cultural context. The decision-makers should therefore consider how others perceive the problem to be resolved and how the various alternative solutions will impact upon them. As a starting point in managing the decision-making process when there are elements of risk and uncertainty, we can best understand the process by answering the following questions.

3.5.1 What is the problem?

The first step will be to identify the risks which threaten the productive assets of the organization. These may be as follows:

- Natural hazards arising through fire, flood or other forms of physical threat.
- People-based hazards arising from theft, sabotage, fraud, negligence etc. Obviously, no matter how the loss of productive assets, whether physical or liquid, may be caused, that loss is likely to interfere with the capacity of the organization to continue its business operations. If the loss is substantial, the organization may not be able to survive without taking major corrective action. To be effective in the reduction of loss, this action must be carefully planned, and the employees well trained in implementing the contingency plans.
- Third party-based matters which may give rise to successful claims against the organization. The uncertainty lies in the number and extent of possible third party claims. Those claims might be for damages to offset losses arising from an alleged breach of contract or from a breach

of the duty of care which may support an action in tort. The latter is particularly difficult to assess because, for example, the cause of the injury to the employees may be long-term and not immediately obvious to them, e.g. claims for silicosis, industrial deafness or other occupation-related diseases which only become apparent over long periods of time. The basis of the claim would be that the possibility of injury ought to have been obvious to the managers who should be reasonably well-informed about the latest scientific and medical research as it affects the processes under their control. If successful, such claims do not have a direct effect on the imediate productive operations of the organization. But, if the insurance provision is inadequate and no contingency funds have been set aside, assets must be sold or the organization's liquid resources used to meet the claims and the costs of the action. The effect is therefore the same as if these assets had been destroyed.

This stage will help to define the possible causes of loss, and so clarify the nature of the problem. There is, however, a danger in attempting to define the causes of the problem. If it is suggested that the process can produce an exact diagnosis, solutions may be presented as a complete cure. This is rarely the case.

One of the ways to ensure the maximum co-operation from the employees is for the organization to engage in a process of consultation. Normally, this will involve meeting with representatives of those employed to discuss matters of mutual concern. For these purposes, we should distinguish between negotiation and bargaining.

3.5.2 How to distinguish between negotiation and bargaining

Negotiation is a form of exploratory meeting in which those involved identify the feasible options open to them in the light of the others' goals. We should emphasize that negotiation is not a way of eliminating conflict, but a way of making conflict more tolerable. It is always possible for this process to become confrontational if those involved decide to test each other's commitment and power. To reduce the risk, those involved in the negotiation should try to create social relationships of mutual respect rather than dominance/subservience. Thus, the goal of the managers may be to reduce losses through theft; the employees representatives may wish to avoid workers' reputations being damaged by unfounded allegations of dishonesty. If the managers adopt a rigid approach based on their claimed right to manage, this may be found highly provocative by the majority of honest employees, and hostility and suspicion may become a barrier to effective communication and agreement. The best answer may be to produce a top–down approach where all those employed by the organization are encouraged to be more honest in their own dealings and to report anything suspicious in the knowledge that the report will be investigated with equal fairness whether the managing director or the office cleaner is involved.

The narrower the range of possible options identified, the more the parties move towards bargaining (Figure 3.7). If people bargain, all those involved are acknowledging that there is a degree of interdependency between them, i.e. one party must want what the other party has and both must believe that an exchange can be agreed at a price. The role of the person chairing the meetings is vital. If the meeting builds on views and opinions that are similar, a solution or price may emerge through consensus. The problem is that each side is negotiating and then bargaining for their own interests which may not be made explicit during the early negotiations. Thus, a fairly consistent but inexplicit aim will be for the managers to retain their authority; the others will have their own needs and objectives which are not necessarily shared.

If the meetings take place at a strategic level through representatives of the management and the employees, the organization will also have an audience outside the immediate forum. Thus, the decisions to be made may have relevance to:

- the public at large which may be informed of events either by rumour and gossip or by the news media;
- national level organizations, e.g. the government, the CBI, TUC etc;
- members of the public indirectly involved in the decision outcomes, e.g. either the family of those employed and the businesses with whom they deal, or the customers of the organization;
- other organizations in the same line of business, e.g. customers, competitors, employer's federations etc;
- to investing organizations such as banks, insurance companies and pension funds; or
- the other employees of the organization.

In all discussions, the quality of the information that is made available to the negotiators and the way in which the final decisions are communicated

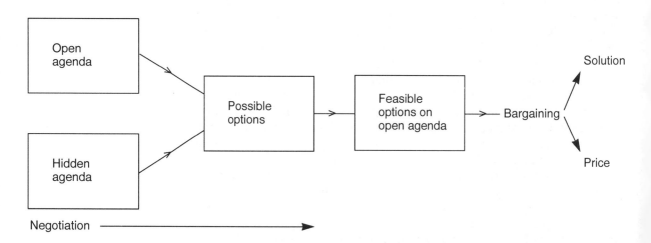

Figure 3.7 Processes leading to bargaining.

are significant. All information has potential value. This value may take different forms:

- being open and free with information may help to establish credibility in the negotiations, i.e. it reduces uncertainty – the more information is kept to the chest, the more devious the provider may appear to be and the less weight may be given to the information when it is disclosed;
- if we have reliable information, it may allow us to take good decisions and to feel confident when implementing those decisions, i.e. it gives us power and motivation;
- sharing information can consolidate group identity and loyalty by making people feel important through their access to this otherwise confidential data;
- it may have value outside the organization, e.g. information on future pricing and marketing strategies would be valuable to competitors or customers;
- at an emotional level, some information will be more or less important depending on the relevance and impact on the recipient, e.g. some information will appear emotionally neutral to an outside consultant, but may appear to threaten loss of jobs to shop-floor workers and therefore be emotionally sensitive to them.

In any negotiating or bargaining situation, there are risks that both those involved and the wider audience may misjudge what is going on. One of the ways to make the communication process less prone to error is to reduce uncertainty in what is said and to clarify why it is being said. Before communication, it is therefore helpful to consider the value of the information to be communicated and its emotional impact.

3.5.3 How big is the problem?

This requires the organization to try to estimate or measure the scale of the risk. Some of the losses foreseen may be remote or routinely small and they may safely be ignored. But if the small losses are going to accumulate into a more real threat, e.g. as petty pilfering by staff becomes an institutionalized perk, or the odds on the looming disaster change, action will be required. The organization must therefore assess the significance of possible losses and produce some form of probability distribution or estimate. This will help the organization to assess the magnitude of the risk and to identify the issues that ought formally to be included in the risk decision-making process. Many issues, both internal and external to the organization have become major strategic business issues because the risks of liability and of intervention by regulators have become significant to the future profitability of the organization. So, for example, organizations are now engaging in product lifecycle analysis to see what risks there might be in the longer term after the product has been sold and used. This has been forced on the European and American manufacturers by the increasingly tough laws on product liability which impose strict liability for injuries suffered many years after purchase.

3.5.4   What does the corporate plan say?

Once management has made its assessments of the foreseen risks, they should be placed within the context of the organization's corporate plan or mission statement. In a sense, there is a single, major task confronting all management teams. It is the need to comprehend and, if possible, to master the complexity of the whole organization. By this we mean that the organization must be able to control itself. The blueprint of this control exercise will be the corporate plan. The best strategy in drawing up an effective plan is to create goals and to define comprehensive models against which to measure performance in trying to realize the goals. At one level, the organization may say that it has the goals of solvency and profit but this is to put the cart before the horse. Actually, the most effective levels of decision-making will aim to define the conditions that must exist in order to achieve solvency and profit, i.e. we rise above the level of simple bookkeeping and move to address the planning of strategy.

Thus, in the continuous routine of planning, one of the tasks undertaken by management will be to evaluate the worth of each machine or production unit as an asset. This will give a basis upon which to decide whether the asset should be replaced, repaired or abandoned if it is damaged. The long-term objective will be to protect the earning capacity and the capital worth of the organization as a whole. So the management team must assess the productivity of each asset and its true worth as a part of the organization's equity rather than simply calculating whether the particular machine or unit is cost-effective in its operation.

This recognizes that the well-being of organizations is not challenged by single problems that arise in a convenient sequence. In relating to their environments, organizations actually face a complex set of interrelated threats and opportunities. For planning a set of responsive tactics, it will therefore often be counter-productive to abstract problems from their systemic contexts. If decision-makers do try to cut up all the problems into neat little boxes, this will suppress information about the relationships between those problems and thereby deprive the decision-maker of access to some of the essential aspects of each problem.

3.5.5   What can and should be done about the problem?

The organization may first wish to seek more information about the problem, and specify what research or other investigation should take place within the time and budget available. This is all part of the process of identifying and evaluating the various risk management strategies that may be relevant to the particular problem. The formulation of risk management strategies works on two levels:

1.   at a strategic level, the best outcome for the organization is an idealization of the future, i.e. the management team will list the most desirable features of the outcome to each problem, and then identify the best way of trying to realize that future;
2.   at a tactical level, it entails:

- making decisions on whether to implement particular loss reduction and/or avoidance projects;
- contingency planning on whether to repair or replace particular
  assets or property should they be damaged or destroyed;
- identifying the detailed sources of finance for the above.

3.5.6   How should any conflicts be resolved?

When confronted by diverse problems, management will do well to
consider a diversity of different strategies. Each of these strategies may
have different champions within the decision-making framework. As the
debate proceeds on which decisions to take, tensions may emerge
between various polarized groups within the organization. If these
tensions cannot be eliminated, conflict may emerge. Charajedaghi (1985)
describes four ways in which to handle conflict:

- solving it by declaring a winner and loser(s);
- resolving it by achieving a compromise that, to some extent, satisfies all
  the protagonists;
- absolving it, i.e. ignoring the problem in the hope that it will go away;
- dissolving it by encouraging the parties to the dispute to work constructively together, thereby transforming the conflict from a threat into an
  opportunity.

The best resolutions to, and dissolutions of, conflict always emerge
through discussions at a metasystems level where partial interests should
be seen in the context of the organization as a whole. This should allow
decisions to be taken in the best interests of the organization.

3.5.7   Should mitigation or compensation elements be included?

One way to encourage the development of trust in the decision-making
process is to build mitigation or compensation policies into the solutions
adopted. If the organization is seen to be acting according to the more
abstract values of equity and fairness, those affected will be far more
likely to accept the decision or fight the decision with less commitment.
The timing of the offer to pay any compensation would be highly relevant
in defusing the opposition. Thus, how the effects of the decision will be
mitigated or how those affected will be compensated sends a vital signal to
the world and may enhance the reputation of those who take the
decisions.

3.6   DECISION-MAKING STRATEGIES

It should now be apparent that organizations treat strategic decision-
making as an exercise in problem-solving. Because of the difficulty in
producing reliable estimates of future reality, the best strategies depend
upon setting general goals and objectives, leaving the detailed decision-

making to relatively short-term matters. The necessary consistency in this more short-term approach should come from the parameters established through the overall pattern of objectives. For our immediate purposes, organizations usually operate upon two principles:

- the KIS rule – keep it simple; and
- wherever possible, avoid uncertainty.

In essence, the organizations that take the simple routes, relying on what they know tend to do better than the speculators who rely on uncertain future events for their success.

To provide stability to the organization and a reasonable degree of consistency over time, managers tend to evolve sets of rules or standard operating procedures. The rules or procedures will represent the learned experience of the organization and should be the first point of reference whenever a problem arises. The greater the degree of decentralization and the higher the degree of delegation to each group, the more likely it is that the overall survival of the organization will depend upon the application of standardized rules and procedures.

If a rule appears to fit the facts and the right outcome appears likely, it may be applied algorithmically. If no specific rules appear directly relevant, more general 'rules of thumb' may guide the heuristic process, e.g. in deciding at what price to enter the market, set a price equal to the cost of the product or service plus the industry norm mark-up. Thus, issues which might appear to be complex can actually be 'resolved' through applying a series of simple rules/procedures. The source of these rules may vary:

- they may be what academics describe as best practice rules and, as such, they are taught to all students and absorbed into the organization through recruitment or they are consciously adopted by the particular organization because they are written up favourably in the management text books and journals;
- they may be industry specific and normative, i.e. the nature of the task may require that certain steps are taken or the manner of competition between organizations may lead to the evolution of certain rules of the game; thus, self-employed and employed accountants and lawyers are bound by sets of professional rules (see Chapter 11 on how this may evidence the existence of autopoiesis within the organization), and those dealing with international commodities will follow the standard operating procedures for forward buying, payment etc;
- they may be evolved by the managers within the organization – cynics may say that when a manager claims as a defence that he or she was following the rules, what this actually means was that no thought was involved in the process.

3.6.1 What are the limits of these rules?

In a sense, there is no limit to the scope of the rules. They may be written in such as way as to apply to all aspects of an organization's activities.

However, at the simplest level, one may group the rules under the following general headings:

- roles and tasks within the organization will have to be defined and the relationships between those roles and tasks made clear;
- information searching and record keeping should be defined, dealing with such matters as the nature of the information to be collected or recorded in different situations, who should be responsible for defining information needs, how often information holdings should be reviewed, the relationship between information gathering and the communication system etc;
- the communication system should be clarified by rules dealing with the nature of the information to be transmitted, how it should be processed (if at all), to whom it should be communicated, when it should be communicated etc;
- procedures for establishing and reviewing the goals and objectives of the organization;
- guidelines establishing the expectations and aspirations of the organization, i.e. establishing the degree of elasticity in the goals and objectives;
- rules for avoiding uncertainty in decision-making;
- rules for making choices between alternatives.

We have tried to reflect the logic of the rule framework in the order in which we have presented this list. Obviously, the organization should start by knowing who should be doing what, have a clear idea what information it needs (in the first instance to set objectives and, second, to take decisions) and know how best to take the simple 'safe' decisions. We acknowledge that this may lead firms to be more conservative than adventurous, but we would prefer organization to make their decision-making sufficiently explicit so that the decision-makers know when they are taking a risky decision and act in a way that appears to give them the best chance of taking a decision where the outcome is more favourable than unfavourable.

3.7 SUMMARY

From the first quote in this chapter, we should draw the conclusion that decisions are intentional behaviour aimed at providing solutions for problems (or in the case of pet problem-solving methodologies, we see problems offered up to the methodology for solution). In reaching the decisions, managers will have to come to terms with uncertainty and the possibility of conflict between different interest groups within the organization. The way in which these conflicts are resolved may lead to sub-optimal results but we assume that each decision will have qualities of appropriateness and acceptability about it given the negotiating and bargaining that may have taken place. To that extent, the whole decision process is political in nature, with the key players manoeuvering for position at every turn and fragile alliances being made for short-term advantage.

The end product of decision-making will tend to reflect limited or bounded rationality. Some of the limitations will come from the conflictual environment, others from the routinization of decision-making through the imposition of standard operating procedures and rules. Although consistency can be a desirable trait in decision-making, it should not be assumed that the same decision is always the right decision. Independently of any rule system, consistency may also be achieved because decision-makers copy each other. Decision-making styles come into and pass out of fashion as cultures shift within organizations and choices are ritualized. So long as these network characteristics retain useful experience in the organization's memory, this will represent a useful adaptive practice for the organization. It will be unfortunate if valuable experience is lost through nothing more than a passing fashion.

We also hope that the decisions are based on the best information that could be found given the level of resource allocated to the search function.

QUESTIONS

1. See if you can propose your own definition of the decision process. (You may find it a useful exercise to draw a flow chart or soft systems diagram to show the linkages between the different component elements.)
2. How do you begin to specify what quantity and quality of information you will need to refer to during the decision-making process?
3. What are the main themes of the research into decision-making?
4. Is it desirable to try to eliminate or reduce the subjective elements in the decision-making process?
5. How should managers measure the scale of the problem and assess which of the possible solutions might be most effective?

At a strategic level, when is it acceptable to take risks?

4

INTRODUCTION

All organizations that claim to work efficiently and effectively have certain objectives and needs in common. At its simplest level, one of the most frequently identified needs is to take the best quality decisions based on the information available. In assessing the quality of decision that can be achieved by each decision-maker, certain assumptions tend to be made. Thus, as people rise within the organization, the natural expectation is that they should be able to get a better view of the position of the organization in its environment and that they may have better access to information about the organization's activities. Hence, as our chapter title implies, the troops about to take up their positions on the battlefield always hope that the general has a good idea of what the opposition is doing. But, sometimes, resource limitations or organizational inefficiencies prevent the key people from forming a complete picture of current reality. Inevitably, this affects the quality of the decisions taken but, despite these difficulties, time and events press on and decisions must be made. Sometimes decisions will be made and those involved will actually have misunderstood the true nature of the decision taken. Sometimes, managers will decide that they must take the decision regardless, i.e. that it is acceptable to take the risk of unforeseen consequences even though they know that their perception of what is happening is inadequate. One way in which to improve the quality of individual decisions is to formulate longer term strategies which will form a broad framework within which to direct and inform each short-term decision.

4.1 WHAT ARE THE LEVELS OF CONTROL IN AN ORGANIZATION?

The activities and functions of an organization occur continuously throughout its structure. If we are to begin the process of making qualitative distinctions between the mass of everyday activities and functions which all those employed by the organization undertake, it is necessary to refer to:

- the volume and frequency of each type of decision that affects those activities and functions;
- the aspect of the business operations to which they relate – the language in which they are described, say, for job specification purposes, may be imprecise and care must be taken in assessing the actual nature of each operation; thus, the activity of pricing may relate to the process of marking up goods on the shelves or to the broad policy-making decision of the pricing strategy to pursue in competition with other organizations;
- the time period which may be short-, medium- or long-term.

Thus, a number of qualitative divisions should be apparent although it is accepted that they are a somewhat crude basis upon which to make a classification. At the lowest level of power and authority within the organization, a significant number of routine programmable decisions will be taken (section 3.1). These decisions will relate directly to specific subsystems and they are taken in line with medium- or long-term policies laid down by the more senior managers. This is the operational level of activity. The tasks of organizing and integrating the day-to-day activities of the organization occur at the intermediate level of authority within the organization. This is termed the management or tactical level. At the highest level, policy and therefore unprogrammable decisions are taken and then passed down for implementation by those at management level (section 3.1). This is metasystem activity and it is called the strategic level. Managers at this level are concerned with the long-term development of the organization as a whole (see Anthony, 1965).

4.1.1 A first attempt at defining strategy

Most authors who discuss strategy do not offer comprehensive definitions, and many of the definitions which have been offered disagree with each other. At its root, the term 'strategy' derives from the Greek word 'strategia' meaning 'the art of war or generalship', and it first appeared in European military literature at the beginning of the eighteenth century as representing the sum total of all the means available to a general for supporting the effort to achieve the desired objectives. It may be contrasted with mere 'tactics' which relate to localized elements in the overall campaign. When translated into the business environment in the middle of this century, 'strategy' broadly was taken to imply the process of commanding the resources of the organization in such a way as to achieve objectives usually stated in terms of monetary profits. Anthony (1965) provided an early and still generally accepted definition of strategic planning as,

> the process of deciding on the objectives of the organization, on changes in these objectives, on the resources used to attain these

objectives, and on the policies that are to govern the acquisition, use, and disposition of these resources. (p. 24)

This was compatible with the view of strategy emerging from the work of the Harvard Business School, initially the leading centre in research and development in this field. Essentially, Harvard considered strategy to be normative in nature (e.g. Learned *et al* 1965; and Andrews 1971). For these purposes, strategy was treated as a situational art – a creative and imaginative series of acts based on the integration of numerous complex but subordinate decisions. In a general review, Bower (1967) described this approach to strategy as adopting a form of problem-solving model in which the decision-maker seeks the means or 'puzzle solutions' to move the organization from its current state to its desired or objective state.

4.1.2 Strategy formation is part of a learning process

For our purposes, we may see the process of forming long-term problem-solving models as the basis of strategies as being a part of a continuous learning activity on the part of the organization. It is interesting to compare the function of a teacher or lecturer with the stimulus of the market place. The aim of a teacher should be to create situations in which the student may learn. (We take it as axiomatic that the activity of learning is gaining the ability to make practical use of the knowledge communicated by the teacher rather than merely demonstrating the rather more mechanical abilities either to regurgitate barely understood facts and concepts in examinations, or to replicate artificial competences out of their contexts.) In the same way as students, what the managers try to do through their interactions with the market place is to increase their ability to use their intellectual and commercial resources effectively in the pursuit of specified objectives. By identifying objectives and attempting to solve the problems of realizing them, the management is engaging in a form of learning activity where the educational feedback is the longer-term commercial performance of the organization. If the managers learn well by effectively monitoring the operations of the organization, modifying strategy when necessary, the organization should become a more effective problem-solver and move to a more desirable state.

4.1.3 Simple definitions often get lost

Through the work of many academics, there has been considerable energy invested in developing the debate as to the nature of strategy. One of the more obvious consequences has been that the concept of strategy in the sense of decision-making aimed at changing the state of an organization, has been subsumed within the boundaries of various newly defined fields of academic endeavour such as strategic management and business policy, but there is little agreement on the definitions for these new classifications. An early work by Chandler (1962) defines strategy as,

the determination of the basic long-term goals and objectives of the enterprise and the adoption of courses of action and the allocation of resources necessary for carrying out these goals. (p. 13)

Steiner (1979) then indicates,

> While there is no consensus in the field, many scholars today have broadened these concepts and view 'Strategic Management' as including the process by which organizational missions, purposes, objectives, strategies, policies, and action programs are formulated, evaluated, implemented, and controlled so that desired organizational ends are achieved. (p. 406)

Snow and Hambrick (1980) provided a more conceptual view when they observed that,

> Increasingly, organization and management theorists are viewing strategy as the mechanism that guides environmental alignment and provides integration for internal operations. (p. 527)

Their thesis is that the more efficiently and effectively the management team manipulates the interface between the organization and its environment so that, for example, resources are made available to match windows of opportunity in the marketplace, the more likely is the organization to prosper. As implied, this view reflects the broad definition accepted by most researchers in this area of management science (e.g. Mintzberg, 1979), though more descriptive and pragmatic definitions are commonly used as exemplified by the previous two quotations.

4.1.4 Major elements and processes in the definition

Duncan (1980) divides the strategy formulation and implementation field into two areas;

- the inputs to the strategy-making process; and
- the elements of the strategy-making process itself.

Included in the inputs to the process are:

- managerial roles;
- organizational design;
- organizational processes (e.g. power, communications (section 2.6 etc.).

He identified the main elements or stages in the process as:

- environmental analysis;
- strategic decision-making;
- strategy formulation;
- strategy implementation.

The major stage excluded from this list is that of determining organizational objectives. Several researchers would argue for the inclusion of this element (e.g. Hofer and Schendel, 1978), arguing that strategy is concerned with both the 'ends' and the 'means', rather than just the means as suggested by Duncan. With this exception, most would agree with the broad stages he identifies and the inputs to the process (e.g. Johnson, 1985).

A typical model of this normative strategic management process is shown in Figure 4.1. The limitations of this type of normative model were recognized by Johnson (1985) as it

> equates management with rationality in decision-making [and] . . . it is limited if the management of the complexity of strategic decisions is to be understood in organizations. (p. 23)

Most authors subdivide the strategic management process into at least two elements, strategy formulation and implementation. The former concerns the processes of developing the strategic plans (stages 2, 3, 4 and 5 in Figure 4.1), while the latter involves the processes of enacting these plans.

The formulation stage is considered by many authors to be the key stage in the process. Thompson and Strickland (1980) refer to strategy formulation as

> largely intellectual and requires the abilities to conceptualize, analyse, and evaluate; it requires shrewd judgement as to what constitutes an entrepreneurially effective strategy and what does not. (p. 154)

Bower (1967) also recognizes the importance of this element, but emphasizes the dimensions of *synthesis* of the analytical results and *discovery* of the ingredients for success and the environmental opportunities which could provide these.

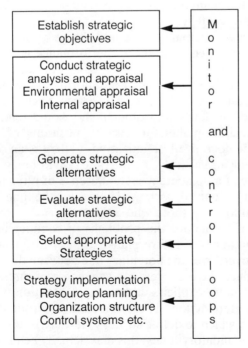

Figure 4.1 Strategic management process.

4.1.5 Major issues in the strategic management debate

So far we have considered three of the significant issues in the strategic management field which continue to be a source of debate and the reason for much of the research, namely the definition of the field, the inclusion of objective determination in the process, and the composition of the stages in the process.

A further issue emerges from the apparent lack of agreement on whether each stage in the process is capable of being clearly differentiated and, if so, in what order the stages should or do occur in the process. A part of the differentiation process will also assist in characterizing the contribution which each one makes to the whole. A major reason for this disagreement is the distinction between the normative and descriptive approaches mentioned above. The former suggests a logical, ordered and progressive development of strategy through each of the main stages (e.g. Newman, 1967), while the latter indicates a more disjointed and recursive process in which many of the stages are conducted simultaneously with minimal distinctions between them (e.g. Mintzberg, Raisinghani and Theoret, 1976).

A significant strand of the descriptive research concerns the degree to which strategies are the product of deliberate or premeditated decision processes, as opposed to emerging unintentionally in response to environmental pressures or internal interdependencies (e.g. Mintzberg, 1979). Snow and Hambrick (1980) explored the difficulties in identifying the 'intended strategies' of the organization, and Quinn (1977 and 1978) established that many managers are reluctant to announce explicit goals or to articulate strategy.

In a perfect world, managers would always be prepared to lay down the criteria against which their future performance is to be judged. It is an obvious part of the process of assessment and accountability both internally through the process of monitoring and control, and externally to the organization's creditors and investors. Such a process, if capable of being carried out fairly and objectively, would tend to allow the most successful decision-makers to rise to positions of responsibility in a thoroughly democratized organization. (There is an organizational paradox in producing a truly democratic environment for the essential characteristic of a democracy is the absence of ultimate authority – there is a circularity of control with the leaders for the time being subject to the collective authority of those who are led.)

But even if we ignore the problems of commercial confidentiality in disclosing the detail of future plans, strategy formulation is not an exact science. It hovers over the boundary line between decision and indecision, trying to reduce the inexpressible vagueness of intuition, aspiration and prediction to more explicit statements of intention which then can form the basis of future action. There is a further question as to the degree of certainty with which to define strategy. If there is too much detail and it is cast in more mandatory tones, this may actually be more of an operational plan and lack the qualities of responsiveness and flexibility essential to encourage initiative and entrepreneurial skills.

Our model so far also assumes that the organization is monolithic. This would mean that it is structured so as to operate with only one guiding intelligence. But many organizations are either inchoate in structure, say because the organization is engaging in a period of dynamic growth and it has yet to devise new structures of decision-making, or polycentric with delegated responsibilities given to functional or geographical divisions. In such cases, the formulation of coherent strategies for the whole becomes less possible. We are also assuming that every organization is capable of predicting exactly what will happen so that proper, measured contingency plans may swing smoothly into action, whereas the decision-making in the real world is, depending upon the prevailing economic circumstances, more likely to be a form of continuous crisis management. Hopefully, the immediate management responses to each difficulty will only be minor tinkerings with the strategic plans so that reasonable continuity of commercial effort may be maintained. But the possibility of major dislocations in the face of adverse conditions can never be discounted.

An associated issue to the degree of deliberation in strategy formulation is the extent or significance of change resulting from this process. Research studies have shown that the formulation process tends to be incremental and adaptive (Lindblom, 1959 and 1979; Mintzberg *et al.*, 1976; Mintzberg, 1978; Miles and Snow, 1978; Quinn, 1978 and 1980; Hedberg and Jonsson, 1977; Schendell and Hofer, 1980; Lyles, 1981; Johnson, 1985). Thus strategy formulation comprises a stream of decisions each having relatively modest impact and causing incremental realignment of the organization with its environment. As Snow and Hambrick (1980) suggested,

> if at all possible, organizations, when faced with external change or pressure, tend to *adjust* rather than *change* their strategies. (p. 529)

Bower (1967) recognized the tendency for decision-makers to apply familiar solutions in the form of rules and procedures to unfamiliar strategic problems. Other research studies outside of the strategic decision field have arrived at similar conclusions in relation to management decision-making, suggesting that organizations prefer to apply familiar solutions to new problems (Cyert and March, 1963; and Cohen, March and Olsen, 1972). Mintzberg (1978) proposed the idea of a 'Metastrategy' for an organization representing an underlying and enduring orientation that the organization has in relation to its environment. In this context, significant change in strategy as opposed to adjustment will only occur if there is significant change in the environment, e.g. technological change or major economic shifts in relevant markets, say, into recession, and the organization feels it expedient to seek a significant re-alignment to its environment.

A further issue raised through the research is whether there is a clear distinction to be made in the terminology between 'corporate-level' strategies and 'business-level' strategies (Hofer and Schendel, 1978). It is suggested that the former is concerned with defining which classes and types of business(es) the organization should remain in or seek to enter, and the latter with how to compete effectively within each chosen area of business activity. In practical terms, this distinction is more blurred as 'business-level' issues will clearly influence the selection of appropriate businesses, and 'corporate-level' issues will influence the decisions on how to compete effectively in each of the markets for the business activities (Figure 4.2).

4.2 A SYNOPSIS OF RESEARCH ACTIVITIES AND APPROACHES

Within the six main stages identified in the strategic management model presented in Figure 4.1, research has concentrated on two dimensions, the content and the processes involved. Research studies into the content element have emphasized:

- the type of issues examined at each stage;

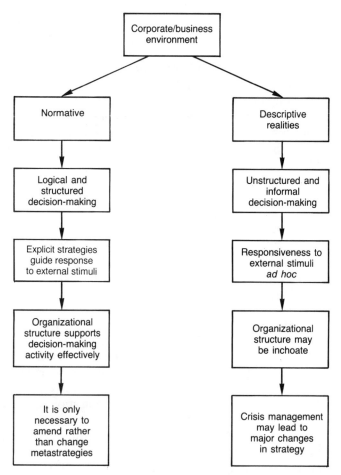

Figure 4.2 The extremes of difference between the normative and descriptive schools.

- the information used; and
- the nature of the output from each stage.

The process studies have emphasized the methods and systems used in the evaluation and analysis of the strategic situation.

It is also possible to divide the developments in this field between the prescriptive/normative and the descriptive models and research. A considerable volume of literature is associated with the normative approaches to strategic management, covering all the stages outlined in the strategic management model. Significant contributions to this approach have been made by Ansoff (1965); Christensen, Andrews and Bower (1973); Hussey (1974) and (1979); Argenti (1968) and (1974).

When Hofer (1975) reviewed the previous research in the strategic management field, he observed that considerably more emphasis had been placed on researching the processes in formulating strategies than on the content of organizations' strategies themselves, and that much of this had been normative in nature. By way of explanation, he suggested that this focus for the research had evolved because the strategy content was assumed to be situational, whereas processes were assumed to be more universal in nature.

To some extent, Hambrick (1980) followed a similar line when he evaluated the research in this field. He also confirmed the perception of processes as being important, but he placed the element of processes into a more broadly defined context of five streams of research comprising:

- strategy – performance relationships;
- strategy – structure relationships;
- strategic decision processes;
- linkages between levels of strategy (i.e. corporate/business level);
- differentiation between intended and realized strategies.

To illustrate both the diversity of the research actually carried out and some of the problems experienced in trying to classify that research, we should also refer to the work of Ginsberg and Venkatraman (1985). They analysed 29 studies in the period 1977 to 1984 and concluded that the main thrust of research in this period related to the impact of environmental variables on the formulation of strategies. They also concluded that the majority of studies concentrated on the individual business-unit strategies rather than on the aggregative corporate-level strategies.

However the themes may be identified and classified, it is clear that considerable research effort has been devoted to a general attempt to evaluate whether there is a link between the application of strategic management processes and practices, and the performance of the organization. An early study of 386 US corporations by Fulmer and Rue (1974) found no positive correlation, though other studies by Thune and House (1970); Herold *et al.* (1972); Schoeffler, Buzzell and Heany (1974); and Schendel (1979), all established some degree of positive association between the application of formal strategic planning approaches and business success.

In reviewing the research in strategic management Steiner (1979) asserted that,

> Research has concentrated more on broad organizational design and environmental variables than on other aspects of strategic management, such as capital allocation, managerial styles, objectives and goals, product expansion, and research and development. Most research has concentrated on the organisation as a whole rather than on major subparts. More research has related to corporate Headquarters than major divisions with particular attention to different control relationships with headquarters and in different environmental settings. More research has been done about contingency theories for business strategies than for strategies at other levels or for other types of organization. Finally, more research has concerned strategic process than strategy content. (p. 413)

He further commented that,

> Not enough research has been done on preferred strategies to acquire environmental knowledge that is most needed in making decisions in different situations. No company can examine thoroughly all environmental conditions which may influence strategic decisions. How does a company determine precisely what environmental forces to examine in making strategic decisions of a particular type? How does a company determine how much effort to devote to what data gathering? (p. 415)

Duncan (1979) produced a similar plea when he concluded that,

> a key problem for organizations is one of defining the organization's domain. In defining domain, organizational decision makers determine the kinds of outputs the organization will produce and the components in the environment it will deal with. The interesting policy question is how do organizations define their domain? What is the process involved? Also how do organizations scan the environments? (p. 428)

4.3   THE CONCEPT OF ACCEPTABILITY

After discussing issues of safety, organizations then move on to consider whether they should take the risks. This involves assessing the acceptability of those risks. The word 'acceptable' in relation to an activity is usually thought of as meaning that the activity or its consequences are pleasing or welcome in some way. For our purposes, that would mean that those who are to run the risks will always willingly consent to the possibility of the foreseen consequences affecting them. To say that a risk which is usually thought of as being unpleasant in some way may be acceptable is therefore to strike a slightly odd note. It might be better to think in terms of the risk being tolerable, i.e. that we bear the risk because we are going to get more good than bad out of what we do. However, because everyday language tends to favour the use of the concept of acceptability, we will adopt that usage.

In scanning the environment around itself and deciding what outputs to produce, each organization will be taking decisions about how acceptable it is to take certain types of risk. At a conceptual level, the organization is making decisions involving both tangible and intangible values. Thus, as examples of the decisions that may have to be taken:

- a certain degree of projected profitability may be a prerequisite to the financial acceptability of a given project;
- the damage to an organization's corporate image if a project goes wrong may affect both commercial and social acceptability;
- it may be morally unacceptable to expose employees to the risk of injury through the failure to replace old and dangerous production facilities.

If the organization is to prosper, it must interact with its customers. It must leave its customers satisfied with the product or service, and collect payment for the work done. In doing so, one strategy would be to ignore all other considerations as if the rest of the world had no relevance to the achievement of that one function. At the other extreme, the strategy might be to cause the least possible disturbance to others in pursuing all its activities. Following its declared strategy, the management team will analyse each proposed decision and try to identify what all the different risks are. These risks will then be measured with whatever degree of accuracy is alleged to be possible. Indeed, a part of the information supporting the decision process should be a realistic guide as to the reliability of each of the methods used to assess the risks. The risks may also be classified and prioritorized and, by judging the social, economic and political acceptability of each of the risks, the managers can decide how safe it is for the organization to take each decision. In making the decision, the managers are judging the level of acceptability. This is a relativistic and judgemental activity and involves the following questions:

- if it is alleged that taking risks of this type is acceptable;
  - what do we actually mean by acceptable?
  - acceptable by whose standards?
  - acceptable for whom to take the risks?

4.3.1 An attempted definition of acceptability

Acceptability is an elusive concept. It may mean that people would be prepared to tolerate the particular outcome, i.e. it would be acceptance in a stoical way. Thus, if the organization makes losses on a particular project, some jobs may have to be lost as the price of failure. The individuals directly involved may regret the necessity but will accept the inevitable with whatever good grace can be mustered. Acceptability may equally be taken as suggestive of some degree of welcomeness in the outcome. Indeed, in some cases where particular projects 'hit the jackpot', the outcome in terms of financial benefits and enhanced status may be actively pleasing to those involved. But no matter whether it causes pleasure or some pain, the practice of acceptance should depend upon the willing consent of those who are to be affected. In seeking a majority vote in favour of taking a particular risk, we should never lose sight of the fact that people may give their consent for a variety of reasons. Hence, for each decision, the management and those in the environment who may have some power to affect the proposed decision should consider the propriety of what is proposed and what the consequences would be in either taking or refusing the decision.

4.3.2 Practical examples of the issue of acceptability

If we take issues such as how quickly to phase out the production and commercial exploitation of CFCs (chlorofluorocarbons), how much action to take to prevent the discharge of untreated pollutants into the environment, whether to use animals to test the safety of products intended for human use, or whether to respond to pressure on issues like the compulsory wearing of seat belts in cars, we are inevitably dealing with a mass of intangible values. It is interesting that ICI, as one of the world's major producers of CFCs, has decided to phase out the production of CFCs more rapidly than the British government had requested. This may be a reaction to the projected decline in the market for the sale of CFCs or it may reflect different values in reducing the supply of a product that may be seriously damaging the atmosphere. It is impossible at this time to do anything other than speculate on the company's reasons for the decision.

We can be more positive about issues such as seat belts in cars or crash helmets on motorcycles. As a preliminary to the decision of whether to legislate on car or motorcycle safety, there was a review of the accident rate in cars and on motorcycles per vehicle mile and an assessment of the degree of injury suffered. The problem with this research is to produce meaningful statistics. The first question is whether the data is differentiated by sex and age. Thus, the risks run by the 18-year-old male may be far in excess of those run by a 40-year-old woman. The time of day the accidents take place can also be significant, as can the presence of alcohol in any driver involved. The size and strength of the cars and other vehicles involved may also affect the nature of the injuries sustained, as can the type of road upon which the accident happened. Hence if there is a minor collision between two cars in an urban environment, there may be only light damage to the cars and their drivers. The result would be rather different if a car runs out of control on a motorway while travelling at 80 mph at a peak time of day. There are always problems when the data is presented solely in the form of averaged values. As to cars, there was empirical research by both governments and the car manufacturers to measure the potential effectiveness of seat belts by crashing cars containing human-shaped dummies. This led to projections of the reduction in injuries that might be expected and the consequential savings in the cost of health provision.

The next question was whether people could be persuaded to overlook the infringement of their personal liberty and to wear either a seat belt or a crash helmet. As part of the process, some car manufacturers responded to the issues by fitting seat belts and further empirical research could then determine whether there was a reduction in the severity of injuries sustained when people were wearing those belts. Similar research into accident statistics sought to distinguish between those riders of motorcycles wearing and not wearing crash helmets. This evidence was used to introduce a discussion in the public domain. On the one hand, did society place any real value on injury reduction? One of the natural consequences would be the reduction in beds taken up in hospitals. This would free money and space to treat non-avoidable injuries. Or were compulsory seat belt and crash helmets so serious an invasion of freedom of individual liberty that they should be opposed no matter what the improvements in general health-care provision? This debate then allowed Parliament to make a better informed decision on whether to use the law to require the wearing of seat belts or crash helmets as a satisfactory resolution of a risk-producing problem.

4.3.3 The standards of acceptability and power

From the debate so far, we should conclude that standards of acceptability are constituted by the discourse (section 2.5) which pervades and defines each cultural domain (section 2.5.2). The judgement of acceptability is an exercise of power which, for these purposes,

> [is] the multiplicity of force relations immanent in the sphere in which they operate and which constitute their own organisation . . . in the interplay of nonegalitarian and mobile relations. (Foucault, 1976, p. 92, p. 94)

Left to themselves, each person would probably choose their own solutions to known risks. Indeed, even in regulated environments, people act without proper regard for their own safety. Hence, although a worker may be aware of the chronic coughs or damaged eyes and ears of those around him/her, a worker may accept those risks rather than endure the daily nuisance of respirators, goggles or ear protectors. But behaviour is modified through the exercise of power at different levels. In his view, Foucault (1975, 1976, 1980) saw the combination of knowledge and power shaping the individual as an object. He identified this shaping action as a continuous process through each person's life. It begins in the discipline of each person's upbringing and the pressures of socialization to conform to the accepted norms. Thus, in schools the teachers make us conform and encourage the young to think about the exercise of power by having monitors and prefects selected from the more senior pupils. All are encouraged to participate in the surveillance and monitoring activities of the peer group which continually reinforces conformity to the perceived normative standards. This practice persists in employment where foremen and supervisors rise from the shop floor to control the workers. Thus, at different times of life and in different roles, we are all persuaded to accept positions which fit into a framework of dominance and subservience.

4.3.4 The reasons for acceptance

Within the hierarchy of formal power relationships, the employer for reasons of cost, paternalism or government regulation, may have a different reason for accepting or rejecting the same risks. Thus, the concept of acceptability may reflect very different things in the diffused power structure:

- that an individual worker has taken a conscious decision after balancing known factors relating to the risk, e.g. the speed and comfort of work when piece work rates are the basis of pay, may lead to sacrificing safety for short-term gain if the taking of safety precautions would lead to lower productivity; this will also encourage employers to turn a blind eye to the abuses of regulation because the resulting higher productivity will enhance potential profitability but, should there be a significant risk of accidents, the profit may be absorbed by the payment of fines imposed for breach of regulations and damages to those injured;
- there may be a historical momentum arising from the discourse to maintaining the status quo – even though the workers and their families know that there are risks, they continue stoically to take them because the same risks have always been taken in that industry; that nothing has been done to reduce or eliminate the risks is taken to mean that running the risks is acceptable! e.g. the generations of miners and pottery workers who have worked in conditions known to cause pneumoconiosis and silicosis, but who achieved a form of value system in which survival became a phenomenon in which to take pride;
- acceptance may continue because no viable alternative can be devised (this may be a technological or an economic matter, e.g. the speed with which pottery kilns can be cooled prior to unloading the fired ware used to require the workers to enter the kilns to remove the ware before it was properly cooled, thereby improving the effective use time of the kilns);
- acceptance may result from ignorance or blind prejudice – for these purposes, the definition of prejudice proposed by Bethlehem (1985) is most useful,

> an opinion or belief held by anyone on any subject which, in the absence of or in contradiction to, adequate test or logically derived conclusions or comparison with objective reality, is maintained as a fact by the person espousing it, and may be acted on as though it were demonstrably true. (p. 2)

Life is too short to find out or test everything so to some extent we all make quick prejudgments to fill in the gaps – in turn, this may lead to intolerance of things which tend to undermine the prejudice, dogmatism in the authoritarian way in which the prejudices are asserted, rigidity in the relative inability to change one's mind, and stereotyping by grouping or reacting towards dissimilar things as if they were similar; the response of the prejudiced individual or group is likely to be to put social distance between themselves and any group not conforming to their view, and it should also be recognized that people's memories are often filtered through the prejudices to ensure that their recollection of history conforms to the prejudices. Remember that a prejudice is distinguishable from a policy decision. Frederick and Wilson (1991) when discussing quantitative carcinogenic risk assessment in the United States of America, define a policy decision as

> a consensus of opinion of a group of scientific experts that has been adopted into regulatory practice to bridge gaps in knowledge to achieve a pragmatic regulatory goal. In the absence of appropriate scientic data, no value judgment is assumed or implied with regard to its accuracy.

Such a consensus would form the basis of reasonably error free decision-making because it would be based upon such evidence as was available, and it would be reviewed in the light of experience:

- There may have been a form of political process and the majority, whether informed or not, may have voted to take the risk – in the light of the previous points, the voting habits of the majority may be shaped by a variety of historical, economic or other imperatives and the vote should not be taken as conclusive of the actual wishes of each individual voter, nor as fair reflection of the needs and wishes of the oppressed minority who may have no choice other than conformity;
- In a more overtly coercive environment, the taking of the risk may have been a unilateral decision by managers or, at a higher level, by government – this may have profound ethical considerations for the society as a whole if, in accounting terms, there is no good return for the many from the risks imposed upon the few. During the Industrial Revolution, the risks were borne by the majority of the working class for the benefit of the few entrepreneurs;
- People may be prepared to accept a known but moderate risk because it is considered preferable to taking other risks which are less well understood even though these risks may actually be smaller;
- People may base their decisions on comparisons with other threats – this is often unscientific, e.g. it may be tempting to assume that because workers in one industry with one set of hazards are generally perceived to be relatively content to accept those risks and seem to be reasonably safe, it must also be proper to accept the working conditions in the immediate industry as safe even though the hazards may be different. The flaw lies in reducing risks to a single dimension, e.g. that of life expectancy, whereas many risks are multi-dimensional. Thus, it would be a nonsense to argue that because you are prepared to run the risk of

injury by driving a car on the road, you must therefore be willing to live next door to a nuclear reprocessing plant because more people die on the road.

All these possibilities should illustrate that standards of acceptability are not necessarily fair, consistent or rational (section 2.6.3). You should also recognize that an individual is primarily worried about the possibility of being injured, whereas society is only interested in the collective risk, i.e. the total amount of damage caused by a particular hazard, balanced against the benefits accruing to society as a whole.

4.4 WHO CONTRIBUTES TO THE DISCOURSE OF ACCEPTABILITY?

All those who have a role sufficient to entitle them to a position of authority and status are likely to wish to contribute to the discourse in a way that will maintain or enhance their status. Thus, whether they be managers, scientists, engineers, doctors, statisticians, trade unionists, environmental protection groups etc, each profession or group will have their own value systems, their own professional standards and their own status to consider when making public statements or seeking to affect the public in some way (sections 2.4.1, 2.5.2 and 2.6 generally). Some groups whose relevance to the particular issues are perceived as being more marginal may be either cautious and precise, or reckless and attention-grabbing, weighing risks rather differently from, say, a commercial management team whose own jobs may depend upon successfully launching a product on to the market. The manner and style of contribution to the debate will therefore be determined by the nature of the cultural domain within which the statements will be made, and by the power relations within the domain.

4.4.1 Acceptability and consultation

In decision-making terms, one of the major problems to consider is the degree to which a process of consultation ought to take place before any decision of importance is taken (sections 3.4.1 and 3.5.2). In some organizations, autocratic management styles lead to unilateral decisions (sections 2.1.1 and 3.3.2). This may have the advantage of efficiency, but it may also lead to a sense of alienation on the part of those whose only role is to obey. The problem for groups whose interests are not overtly considered is to gain access to the discourse which pervades and constitutes the particular domain. More often than not, such groups will have to adopt a directly confrontational approach to force the managers even to notice their claim to be heard. Even if their views are formally admitted to the discourse, there is no guarantee that they will be accorded any weight in the decisions then taken.

At the other end of the spectrum, the effect of consulting with every group (assuming that it is economical to do so) potentially dilutes the impact of each group's contribution. If one group 'has the ear of management', its views may carry great weight. If one group is but one voice among twenty groups of more or less equal status, each voice is small unless there is a degree of consensus. This forces groups either to compete with each other to gain greater status so that managers will consider their views to be more persuasive, or to co-ordinate their views and thereby to submerge their separate identities and interests as the price for gaining influence. Whichever way the situation develops, the interests of each small group are marginalized.

4.5 WHAT ARE THE CRITERIA AGAINST WHICH TO JUDGE ACCEPTABILITY?

The most commonly cited criterion against which to judge the acceptability of any decision is that of reasonableness but such a test, common in the law, tends to be somewhat imprecise. For our purposes, we must make a distinction in the relevant factors to be considered depending on the point of view of each decision-maker and that person's horizon of expectation. For every decision which arises, the decision-maker's point of view may perceive the risk as being specific to some aspect of the organization or it may characterize a third party as the potential victim. In turn, this will change the expectations which each decision-maker will have as to their ability to affect outcome and as to the morality of deciding the extent to which to use that ability.

4.5.1 An example of the test of reasonableness

Let us take as a scenario that the organization is deciding whether to market a product which, while being safe if handled by a person with some expertise, may be dangerous if used by an inexperienced person. The preliminary stages of the decision by the organization will involve market research to find out whether the consumers know of the risk, its frequency and likely severity, and that they are prepared to run those risks in order to achieve the benefits. If the organization finds that the level of knowledge of risk is low, there will be problems in devising marketing strategies that will promote the product while not deterring potential users. Obviously, if the advertising campaign emphasizes the danger in use, the product may simply be thought unsafe and no one will buy it. The issue for decision is how acceptable it is to play down safety considerations, knowing that some people may be injured as a result of buying the product. Naturally, the organization would perceive practical risks. Thus, should too many people be seriously injured, the resulting media attention might be damaging to the organization's reputation and the claims for damages might be damaging in financial terms.

We would suggest that decisions would be unreasonable if the identified risks were not strictly necessary. This might be either because the manufacturing organization could, for a relatively small cost, change the design of the product so as to reduce or eliminate the risk, or because the user could be better educated in the use of the product through some form of advertising-oriented public awareness campaign. However, any proposed changes to the product should always be properly justified. Generally, a manufacturer should not adopt new materials or incorporate replacement components into a design unless they have been shown by appropriate tests to produce significantly safer tolerances than the existing materials or components. The justification for change lies in being able to demonstrate a real benefit from the change through an enhancement to the quality of the product or to its acceptability in the market place.

In turn, from the consumers' point of view, the decision whether to buy will be determined by whether the consumers have a reasonable opportunity to take protective measures, and know how to make those measures effective. In evaluating the degree of reasonableness from the perspective of the consumer, the issues are therefore knowledge and freedom in decision-making. Thus, if there are no other products that will achieve the same quality of results or the safe machines are so much more expensive, the consumer may be constrained in choice and so find running the known risks not unreasonable, i.e. acceptable until a realistic substitute becomes available.

4.5.2 How the extent of knowledge affects reasonableness

Many people live their lives on the basis of custom and practice without having any practical knowledge of the risks that may be involved in using particular products. The underlying assumption is that if the particular product is in everyday use and there have been no obvious problems over a period of time, it must be reasonably safe. This is a form of testing through experience. But there is a general need to acknowledge that this may be no more than an admission of ignorance because the problems have yet to be detected or, more realistically, there has yet to be an informed discussion of the risks in the prevailing discourse.

In defending any civil action for negligence, the law has given manufacturers and distributors access to a number of possible defences such as contributory negligence (where the victims were, in part, responsible for their own injuries and so receive a reduced amount of damages) and the more limited *volenti non fit injuria* (where a person voluntarily running a known risk may be denied a remedy if the foreseen risks become reality – to make the defence work, the defendant must show that the plaintiff agreed, whether expressly or impliedly, to waive any claim arising from the defendant's lack of care). Therefore, the apparatus of the law may deny people a full remedy if they do not take reasonable care of themselves.

If someone buys a bicycle with no defects and through inexperience falls off it and is injured, this is not the fault of the manufacturer. A person of ordinary intelligence ought to appreciate the risks while learning to ride, and take appropriate avoidance measures. The answer would be different if the bicycle was defective in some way. But this last one hundred years has seen a major shift in legal policy from the excesses of *caveat emptor* to the strict liability of producers under the Consumer Protection Act where those injured by defective products may now positively expect to be compensated by those who brought the product to the market. Hence, society no longer finds it acceptable to require the innocent buyer to insure against any possible loss arising from any purchase made.

4.6 WHAT ARE THE RISK FACTORS IN JUDGING ACCEPTABILITY?

We may pose a number of questions which will help to assess the degree to which the particular decision to accept the risk is acceptable. To some extent, the questions are cumulative in their exploration of the issues and, in part, they overlap. We therefore tender these questions as if they were facets cut into the same precious jem stone.

4.6.1 Has the risk been assumed voluntarily?

Here, the issue is the level of freedom in the choice made. If a person decides to smoke cigarettes, this decision is taken against the well-known background of the medical evidence of a link between smoking and cancer. Governments may debate whether to permit advertising and the size of the health warning to be printed on every pack, but still provide free or subsidized health care for those smokers with lung cancer. In part, this is a decision based on morality that one should not penalize a person indefinitely or disproportionately for mistakes made. It may also be argued that the treatment has been paid for through the tobacco duty levied by the state.

If a group of people decide to risk their capital in a new business venture, this may be economic necessity because no local organizations are offering employment. Governments produce laws in an attempt to regulate insolvency but there are always inequities in trying to reconcile the interests of the creditors with those of the indebted. However the balances are struck, the state's conscience can be salved by the platitude that the creditors did not have to deal with that new organization, and the people did not have to risk their capital in the failed business venture.

In trying to assess the acceptability of any risks, people and organizations should act reasonably and responsibly in weighing the costs and benefits implicit in the activities voluntarily undertaken. If we pay a fee to drive a racing car on a private circuit, the risks are acceptable both to the individuals involved because supervision and safety provision will reduce the chances of injury, and to the public at large who are not exposed to the hazards of high-speed driving on ordinary roads. If joy riders drive high-powered cars at excessive speeds on the highway, this is an unacceptable risk. Commercial aspirations always bring organizations to a positive interaction with their environments. The responsible organization should recognize that it is not acceptable if the air we breathe or the environment in which we have to live is polluted. But, for example, should the car manufacturer stop producing petrol/diesel cars because there will always be pollution no matter what technology offers by way of catalytic converters, etc? Or should the car-owning population share cars and use public transport more often thereby reducing the level of emissions? Calculating responsibility factors in such situations of risk to the environment is not a scientific process.

4.6.2   Is it necessary to take the risk?

Some will accept risks in non-essential activities or products which would not be thought so acceptable if the activity or product was essential. Thus, people regularly risk injury through participating in contact sports, but would unhesitatingly think of suing an employer for failing to provide a safe place of work if they fell on a slippy floor and were injured.

4.6.3   Are there viable alternatives to the present practices?

If not, those people taking the decisions either fatalistically tend to accept the risks or act with wilful disregard to the risks. But if there is an element of free choice, the consumers can use their buying power, employees can leave the dangerous factories to find safer places of work and organizations or regulatory bodies can use their power to produce more acceptable outcomes.

4.6.4   Is the risk well-known?

Notoriety has a double-edged quality. If many know of the risks, one possibility is that they will be alert in the relevant situations and, hopefully, be familiar with the more effective ways of reducing the chances of injury and loss. But consider the possibility that exposing people to consistent risks may also make them fatalistic and apathetic. This may increase the incidence of accidents because they are more prone to be careless. If management take the decision to retain this risk in the environment, their rationale may be that it is more acceptable than introducing a new and unfamiliar risk even though the new risk may give rise to lower chances of injury. Once you remove certainty from those at risk, there are prices to be paid while all learn how to cope with the new risks and there is no guarantee that, in the short- to medium-term, there will be any improvement in the loss statistics.

4.6.5   Is it an everyday hazard?

Everyday hazards that affect the majority of people are judged by different standards of acceptability. Thus, we all know that young children are likely to fall when playing and may get bruised or scraped knees, or that it is dangerous when crossing the road. But if safety experts began to tell us about these 'obvious' risks, we would tend to be impatient. On the other hand, some risks are considered unusual and excite the public's interest. Thus, headlines and enhanced news attention will be given to gas explosions and fires which kill families in their homes, to planes that fall from the sky or to industrial accidents that suddenly release poisonous fumes or radiation into the environment. While not undervaluing the nature of the risks themselves, some incidents achieve substantial notoriety. Thus, we get the nine-day wonders of polluted sea water around holiday beaches, salmonella bacteria lurking in eggs and the listeria hysteria. Sometimes, the knee-jerk response of government is wholly out of proportion to the risk to society as a whole and the need to be seen to take action to limit immediate damage, distracts attention from the less well publicized, but no less lethal, risks such as those that affect road users etc.

4.6.6 Should a risk be taken, will the effect be immediate or delayed?

Here the issues are time-scale and the identity of the victim(s). If there is no certainty that the risk will mature and, even if it does, it may take some time to show itself with not everyone exposed likely to suffer adverse consequences, the decision-maker will have different scales of acceptability. The more immediate the risk of retribution for a bad decision, the more cautious the decision-maker is likely to be. But if the risk has a high degree of latency, it is easy for the decision-maker to adopt a gambler's approach or an attitude of 'it never happens to me'. Thus, should the risk affect others and only after a period of time, a non-involved decision-maker may ignore morality and deliberately expose those others to risk for the profit of the organization.

4.6.7 Who is affected by the risk?

Some people in a society may be considered more expendable than others. Whether the exposure of that group to risk will be tolerated will depend upon the prevailing political culture and the alertness of the world to news of any abuses. Thus, if there is a real risk to the average individual, there is likely to be pressure to take action to avert the threat. If the risk is to a limited class of more sensitive individuals, society will have to make value judgements based upon intangible cultural norms.

4.6.8 Are the results of the risk reversible?

If a factory suffers a fire, it may be rebuilt and continue production. However, the fact that reinstatement of the status quo may be possible does not of itself justify limiting safety measures, for the deliberate exposure of both employees and the fire-fighting services to the risk of injury through fire would be unacceptable. Thus, a balance must be struck between the commercial interests of the organization, the degree of accountability for allowing the risk to occur and the extent to which the ability to reverse some or all of the ill effects will mitigate the organization's potential or actual liability.

4.6.9 Is the risk to employees in the workplace?

Historically, there were cultural norms which created apparently acceptable justifications for running greater risks in earning a living than in everyday life. At the simplest level, it may be argued that no one has to work in dangerous conditions and that the level of pay may be higher to compensate those who take the greatest risks. If the trapeze artist in a circus, working without a safety net, falls and breaks a leg, or a boxer suffers brain damage in a championship bout, the risks of such injury were knowingly accepted for the entertainment of the masses. We may regret the particular injury but unless the moral conscience of society is affected by the number and extent of these injuries, parliaments will not legislate to outlaw all dangerous acts and sports as entertainment.

But during the last two hundred years, we can observe a gradual redistribution of social power and rights as to working conditions. Society as a whole has come to care about the working conditions in those industries where injury or disease was common, or about green issues such as the environmental pollution caused by industries. The slowness in achieving a reduction in the number of hazards in the workplace and to the environment, reflects the difficulty in persuading the power-brokers that the economic wealth of the country depends upon reconciling the commercial needs of the entrepreneurs with the practical needs of the workers and the communities in which they live. This has only been achieved recently in the more developed countries, and then only patchily.

Progress has depended upon developing the recognition that the majority of workers have not had complete freedom in being able to select non-hazardous employment. More often than not, if there was a choice, it was whether the worker would risk being maimed in a mine or a factory. This also assumes that the workers had good quality information about the nature and extent of the risks being run. Unlike the trapeze artist who knows there is no safety net and who has trained to reduce the chances of falling, the ordinary worker found that the relevant discourse was often manipulated to exclude access to such information, preaching submissiveness and reinforcing the general acceptability of the prevailing working methods and conditions. If workers became more aggressive, laws were changed to exclude remedies for claiming compensation for personal injuries and disease and, if all else failed, positive policing through the use of troops would deter potential troublemakers.

In the modern context, we have moved beyond the metaphorical view of the worker as a replaceable cog in the machine of the organization, and now see the worker as a vital constituent element in the organization as an organism, team, etc. (section 1.2.2 and Chapter 10). This involves a complete reorientation of view for each worker is now to be encouraged to develop and improve skills within the context of the organization as a caring beneficiary of the work performed.

4.7   EMPIRICAL FACTORS IN THE DECISIONS

Whatever the nature of the general criteria of acceptability underpinning the decisions to be taken, a number of apparently empirical factors are also relevant. The appearance of reliability is encouraged by the attribution of precise values to variables through one or more measuring processes:

1.   Statistical evidence is collected and the evident risks are measured and expressed in terms of probability.
2.   The severity of adverse effects is estimated and appropriate funds are set aside on a contingency basis or sufficient levels of insurance are negotiated.
3.   Through cost benefit analysis and other similar accounting devices, the management will attempt to estimate likely efficacy as a measure of the likely benefits from the proposed scheme.
4.   There will also be estimates of cost as a measure of the price to be paid both in tangible and intangible terms, i.e. both as to assets and resources to be consumed, and as to damage to corporate image etc.
5.   There should also be a formal study of the distribution of any risks as a function of the benefits and costs, i.e. there should be indentification of:

- who will be at risk;
- whether those at risk will be the ones to benefit;
- who will have to pay if the risks arise;
- whether those who pay will be the ones to benefit.

4.8   SOFT VALUES TO BE CONSIDERED

The use of the term 'soft' is intended to refer to matters of personal and social value judgement (cf. section 3.3.4). An empirical methodology assumes that the external social world is made up of 'hard' and relatively unchanging mechanisms which may be measured through a process of observation. This supposedly produces value free data because it is concerned with real and factual phenomena. Soft methodologies adopt a more interpretative model and are concerned with trying to understand and reconcile the multiple and diverse values and problems observable in social systems. The difficulty with such an approach is that without some form of critical framework, the resulting observations and interpretations may be unduly distorted by the values of the observer. Without explaining at this stage how soft systems methodologies may produce a reasonably reliable basis for decision-making, the following three concepts would be relevant to decisions on risk.

4.8.1 The concept of safety

This is the degree to which any risks are deemed to be acceptable both by those who run them and by society at large. The criteria of acceptability will be modified by a number of further factors:

- the freedom of choice in those who agree to run the risks;
- the extent to which proper precautionary measures may be taken to keep the risks within appropriate limits;
- the morality of society taking the benefit of work carried out in circumstances where choice is constrained and precautions are nominal.

4.8.2 The concept of benefit

This is the degree to which the efficacies are judged desirable. Again, this is a judgement both for the workers who run the risks and by the societies that take the benefit of that work. It should perhaps be seen as inequitable for society to take the benefit without also assuming the burden in terms of cost to ensure that the work is carried out as safely as possible.

4.8.3 The concept of equity of distribution

This is a judgement of fairness and social justice. Social justice is a part of the more general standard by which the distributive functions of society are to be assessed. It is a part of any doctrine of political economy. As Rawls (1971) argues, the evolving social system shapes the wants and aspirations that its citizens come to have. It helps to define what its citizens want to be.

> Thus an economic system is not only a device for satisfying existing wants and needs but a way of creating and fashioning wants in the future. How men work together now to satisfy their present desires affects the desires they will have later on, the kind of persons they will be. (p. 259)

In theory, a consideration of politics, economics and morality will be combined in major decisions affecting the distribution of good within a community and mere considerations of efficiency will be a very subordinate issue. But we often fail to make all the relevant issues explicit in centralized decision-making, and leave the working out of distributions to market forces. A system of markets will tend to decentralize the exercise of economic power, and market failures and defects are often serious. States therefore have the problem of deciding to what extent it is acceptable to have a command economy with centrally directed allocation of resources and distribution of public good as opposed to free competition with the risks of abuse of monopoly power, cartels and other restraints on the normal patterns of trade.

Whereas the more preferable system would create social institutions which would promote the idea of justice as fairness within a stable culture, there are problems of isolation and assurance. This reflects the fact that most individuals make their decisions in isolation. As with the prisoner's dilema, even though each person's decision may be entirely rational, all may end up worse off. The assurance problem is to assure all the parties who are to co-operate that the others will carry out their part. It is always difficult to maintain confidence in the overall system when the contribution of each is dependent upon the actions of all the others involved. Thus, if conscientious tax payers are continually told to pay more because an increasing number of people evade their obligations to pay their assessed share, the system will eventually break down.

4.8.4 Combining the concepts

Lowrance (1976) proposes the following combination of ratios:

safety: risk   as   benefit: efficacy.

If we maintain the distinction between hard and soft, the concepts of safety, benefit and equity of distribution are soft and therefore normative, whereas the concepts of risk, efficacy and cost/benefits are considered to be empirical.

If we were to take as an example a decision whether to implement a new industrial process where there is an element of risk to the local community, the managers responsible for the project would always want to measure the successfulness of the process in the longer term in achieving the aims identified in the project specification. This would be considered a natural part of the control and monitoring function of the internal workings of the organization. In the short-term, however, there is a need to allay any fears in the community. Covello *et al.* (1988) have developed a manual for advising plant managers on how to communicate with the public (for more a more general discussion on risk communication, see section 2.6). It analyses the best way in which to make risk comparisons so that the public will find the information useful. They divide risk comparisons into five categories:

1. highly reliable comparisons, say, of the same risk at different times or with an accepted standard;
2. a second choice and less desirable comparison between the risks of doing and not doing something, say, comparing alternative solutions to the problem or making comparisons with the solutions adopted for the same problems elsewhere;
3. a third choice and even less desirable comparison of average with peak risk at a particular time or location;
4. comparisons which would be of marginal acceptability, e.g. comparisons of risk with cost and/or benefit, comparisons of occupational with environmental risks, comparisons with other specific causes of the same disease, illness or injury;
5. largely unacceptable comparisons, e.g. between unrelated risks.

Their advice is that managers should always make the most reliable comparisons if they want to retain credibility. The problem with this classification according to Roth *et al.* (1990) is that sometimes a modest use of comparisons will help lay people to get a feel for the scale of the risk without asking them to make definitive and therefore unacceptable judgements. Thus, it might be useful to say that the likelihood of injury is comparable to the risk of being struck by lightening during a similar time period, or that if exposure to the chemical occurred, the discomfort would be no greater than the pain suffered in having dentistry performed without anaesthetic. Conversely, if the information on first or second order comparisons is framed in highly technical language, such statements will be unacceptable even though completely honest. The need is therefore to balance clarity and honesty against commercial expediency and communication ethics (section 2.6.4). Roth *et al.* conclude that risk comparisons have a legitimate role to play in helping people to understand which factors are worthy of consideration and how they should be weighted in reaching a decision. Their view is that the Covello classification as such cannot be considered rigid, but the spirit of the distinctions is useful. The moral of this analysis may be that all risk comparison messages should be tested for content and context before they are released to the public at large. In this way, messages may be fine tuned to make sure that the right tone is struck. This will be particularly important if the local community is already distrustful or angry about the way in which the plant has been operating (see Chapter 2 generally on how people form their perceptions).

Once the plant has been commissioned, the management will monitor function to include externalities. It should then be possible to identify the benefits that accrue both to the immediate users and to society as a whole, thereby identifying the distribution of the benefits (section 1.3). Thus, if the new process is more cost-effective and produces fewer pollutants to be discharged into the environment, all may then be seen to benefit from the project.

Given data about the process before and after implementation, the risks to workers and to the environment can also be measured in both using and not using the new process. This should create information upon which to give a better answer to the question whether the risks were and are of a type and a magnitude that the public is generally willing to accept. By going through such a process of analysis and evaluation, it should be possible for any organization or government institution to reach a reasonably balanced view on whether to retain or amend an industrial process, regulate or prohibit a process, or take any other action. The point of the exercise is to try to balance the more measurable factors against the unmeasurable values, e.g. of pain and suffering through injury, missed social or commercial opportunities, the beauty or amenity of the environment etc. This analysis should also help to develop suitable risk comparison messages that can be used when communicating new projects to the community.

The aim should always be to make these intangibles more explicit in decision-making and to try to establish better grounds for rational appraisals and comparisons. There is also an argument that the decision-making process as it affects soft values should be more public and democratic so that all those who may have an interest may have some say in the outcome or, if not, at least come to understand the basis of the decisions that have been taken. In recent years, there is a new problem in the speed with which the debate must sometimes be conducted in the glare of the mass media. Newspapers, radio and television often present safety problems as crises. In fact, all that will have happened is that there is a substantial change in the estimate of the risks, in the personal or social acceptance of the risks, or in the plan formulated by those responsible for the management of the policy or industry.

Acceptance is recursive in nature so we will move from a quiet period of stability, through a period of debate and confusion towards resolution and stability again. The particular problem will be identified and reported in the media. The selection of such contributions to the discourse of safety and acceptability is subject to many constraints imposed by the vested interest groups. But if sufficient impact is made on public opinion, the government will be moved to commission reports and a defence of the status quo will be attempted by those responsible in the light of expert comments. Social, political and economic forces then vie with each other to influence the outcome and decisions are taken. In substance little may actually change or the alternatives that hastily emerge may be even worse. But there will be the illusion of progress towards a better world.

4.9 INTENDED CONTRIBUTION OF THIS BOOK

We intend to adopt the descriptive approach to strategic decision-making and will focus on the formulation stages. We recognize that the formulation of strategy involves a number of distinct, though not separately observable, activities by individual decision-makers. Although our work is primarily oriented towards the process elements rather than the content of strategies, the nature of the empirical research that has been undertaken does permit some limited observations on the content element.

The examples we have devised for case-study exploration in Chapter 12 concentrate more on the determination of 'corporate-level' strategy, being concerned with the broad direction of the organization in terms of businesses and markets, rather than 'business-level' strategy. This is reflected in the nature of the strategic situations and alternatives presented.

The focus of the analysis is at the level of the individual decision-maker, and does not incorporate the issue of interactions between individuals or groups in the strategic decision-making process. The contribution that we aim to make within this context is to:

1. identify the degree of commonality in perception of strategic problems and issues;
2. provide an insight into the structuring of the decision-making domain (Duncan, 1979);
3. assess the degree of risk perceived in the situation and the common set of alternative solutions, and more importantly the factors influencing such perceptions;
4. encourage the use of information to support the analytical processes, including the type, content and volume of that information (Steiner, 1979);
5. explore the link between the information processing activities and the perceptions of risk in the situation;
6. determine the extent to which observed behaviour reflects the predicted behaviour of the normative decision models.

We accept that any work which focuses on the individual decision processes without taking detailed account of the usual organizational and environmental situation will limit the potential degree of generalization from the results. For example, no conclusions may be drawn on the influence of the interaction between individual decision-makers in formulating strategies, nor on the political processes involved (Pettigrew, 1973, 1977), nor the effect of organizational culture on the process (Tichy, 1983). However, within the space limitations of a single volume on this subject, it is all we feel able to cover.

4.10 SUMMARY

By way of summary, it is convenient to adopt the characterization of strategy proposed by Ackoff (1990):

1. an organization's strategy will be formulated by the highest level of management and the intention will be that those decisions will affect the organization as a whole – decisions which do not meet these two criteria will be tactical;
2. strategic decisions may be characterized by the setting of relatively long-range objectives, and the formulation of policies (i.e. rules) and the principles (i.e. the values to be preserved) intended to govern the selection of acceptable means by which the stated policies are to be promoted;
3. the focus of strategic planning will be potential and actual changes in the organization's environment which are capable of having a significant effect upon the organization.

The distinction between strategic and tactical is therefore relative in organizational terms, with the tactical or operational decisions concerned with the immediate future and the day-to-day *efficiency* of the organization, whereas the longer-term focus of the strategic decision concentrates on the *growth* of the organization. At the highest level, some decisions will also have a *normative* quality, i.e. they will address ideals rather than practical goals that can be more directly approached. Managers will be interested in the *effectiveness* and *development* of the organization. This will consider the values to be pursued rather than the means of measuring the actual performance (i.e. the efficiency) of management. This does not mean that the managers will not have practicality in mind. Even at the most abstract and conceptual of levels, all organizations must adopt strategies that are to some extent capable of being implemented and monitored. The pursuit of unworldly aspirations is not compatible with normal commercial ambitions.

Haimes (1991) puts in a plea for the creation of and adoption of total risk management (TRM) to match total quality management (TQM). He asserts that if justice is to be done to the processes of evaluation and management of risk, it can only be achieved if the control is aiming to optimize.

> At the heart of good management decisions is the 'optimal' allocation of the organisation's resources among its various hierarchical levels and its various subsystems. The 'optimal' allocation is meant in the Pareto optimal sense, where trade-offs among costs, benefits, and risks are evaluated in terms of hierarchical objectives (and subjectives) and in terms of their temporal impacts on future options. (p. 170)

Such allocations can only be set in motion following a holistic evaluation of the organization, i.e. at a strategic level. The implementation of the policy decisions will then be subjected to the conflicting and competing objectives that drive the detailed decision-making at each lower level within the organization.

This should also lead us to recognize that risk cannot be defined on a single dimension. It is a multi-attribute phenomenon and no single factor can capture all the decision elements that may be relevant to a decision, whether by individual or organization. Each level and subsystem within an organization will have its own beliefs and perceptions, its own aims and goals. The same applies to individuals. Decisions are made by aggregating the multiple attributes into the decision-making process and then resolving the issues of uncertainty (or not) in the time available and with the lowest possible cost. Thus, as in Figure 4.3, some decisions can be characterized as having direct implications that can be stated with sufficient certainty such that decisions can be made with some confidence to produce optimal results. But where confidence is lacking and the availability of time and/or money does not permit a detailed evaluation of the risks, the options selected may be very different and lead to quite different consequences. Obviously, the process described in the figure comprises both factual and value judgments, i.e. both describing the decision attributes and attempting to quantify the risks attached to each decision option, and then reconciling the elements of uncertainty, time, money and confidence within the operational framework of taking the decision.

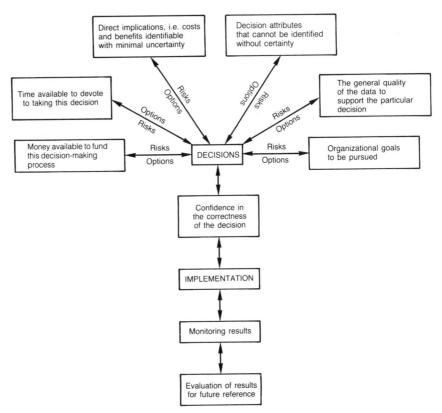

Figure 4.3 Components of strategic decision-making.

QUESTIONS

1. Make a short list of the different major functions and tasks that would take place at each level of control within the modern commercial organization.

2. See if you can write down a list of all the features that would have to be taken into account in producing a comprehensive definition of strategy.

3. To what extent would you agree with the proposition that the strategy formation element is the most important element in the process of managing a large organization?

4. When deciding whether the taking of an identified risk is acceptable, whose views should be taken into account and why?

5. Make two lists of well-known risks. The first list should deal with risks run by commercial organizations that affect the public, the second should be limited to risks that affect only those who work in particular factories. Alongside each risk, then indicate whether you consider the risk acceptable or not. As you do so, consider what factors you are weighing in your mind and reflect upon the values they represent.

Uncertainty and risk in the context of business strategy

5

INTRODUCTION

We now come to the unashamedly theoretical portion of the book in which we shall be examining the detail of the research into the concepts of uncertainty and risk. The intention is to build on the material introduced in the first four chapters, consolidating and extending understanding. This chapter concentrates on the concept of uncertainty but, as you will see when you reach the conclusion section, we have tried to present the information in such a way that it will illuminate our understanding of risk in a business context.

5.1   GENERAL INTRODUCTION

Most would agree that the concepts of risk and uncertainty are integral, if not fundamental, constituent elements of the process of decision-making within organizations. Since books like *Organizations in Action* (Thompson, 1967) the management of uncertainty has been recognized as being of critical importance. This would be particularly the case at the strategic level of decision-making (section 4.1) where the longer term nature of the decisions necessarily involves taking policy-based decisions about future investments or possible market opportunities. When these concepts are discussed in the fields of economics, financial theory or strategic management, the majority of authors make a constructive beginning by recognizing that there is a distinction between the two elements, but then proceed to confuse the issue by using the two terms interchangeably, usually by subsuming uncertainty within the definition of risk. An example of this is to be found in Hull (1980) relating to *The Evaluation of Risk in Business Investment*:

> Risk evaluation provides a quantitative measure of the risk in an investment opportunity. . . . Risk evaluation also has the big advantage that it distinguishes the important uncertainties from the unimportant uncertainties in a particular investment project. . . .

> Generally, risk evaluation quickly focuses managerial attention onto the key uncertainties. (p. 138)

Indeed, in an earlier work which discusses the distinction between the two concepts, Borch and Mossin (1968) suddenly suggest that,

> it no longer serves any useful purpose to distinguish between risk and uncertainty. (p. xiii)

This dismissal of a distinction is justified by the assertion that the introduction of some form of subjective probability assessment of the possible outcomes would be sufficient to overcome the need for any distinction. One of the aims of the next two chapters is to demonstrate that such views provide a narrow and somewhat naive interpretation of risk. Although they are fairly common in the earlier literature, we maintain that it is inadequate to make a primary differentiation of risk and uncertainty on the basis of objective or subjective probability assessment.

The first step, therefore, is to make a clear distinction between the two concepts of uncertainty and risk, and then to discuss the relationship between them in the context of strategic decision-making. The aspect of uncertainty will then be explored in greater depth to consider the factors which influence uncertainty within the context of business decision-making. Finally, the area of risk will be examined to establish:

- the causal factors which influence the nature and degree of risk;
- the link between uncertainty and risk; and
- the influence of risk on decision-making in general.

In the next chapter, reference will be made to the development and use of the risk concept within the fields of economics and financial theory and how this may be applied to the area of strategic decision-making. A model of risk within the strategic decision process will then be developed to indicate and highlight the main causal variables and relationships.

5.1.1   Uncertainty and risk

As we have suggested, uncertainty and risk are integral elements in all decisions whether or not they are explicitly recognized as such or they are merely implicit in the actions of the decision-maker. In broad terms, the state of mind that we term *uncertainty* can be viewed as arising from each person's imperfect state of knowledge concerning future events and, as such, it will influence the degree of confidence that the decision-maker has in the decision to be made. There are two major problem issues both for decision-makers and for those who must supervise decision-making, namely:

1.   to devise a means of calibrating the level of competence that each person has to take the particular decision; and
2.   to estimate the degree of confidence they would feel that their decision was correct.

It is probably a cliché that a decision-maker who is modest and knows his or her own limitations may take better decisions than those who believe themselves to be more competent than they actually are. Confidence and self-esteem are also variable qualities and unless managers take steps to talk with decision-makers with a view to assessing their present state of mind, there may be no basis upon which to judge the reliability of the decision solutions proposed to existing problems. We take this as symptomatic of the general proposition that there is a wide range in the levels of uncertainty. In the particular case, the extent of this range will be determined by a number of factors, including:

- the nature of the situation;
- the volatility of the environment;
- the number of aims and objectives to be balanced;
- the futurity of the decision; and
- the quality of the decision-making unit.

This latter point reflects the fact that uncertainty is not an objectively quantifiable feature which is inherent in a particular decision situation. Rather it is a fluctuating feature whose scale is dictated by the day-to-day composition and competence of the decision-making unit (i.e. individual, group, or organization). This can only be assessed on a relative or comparative basis, and it involves subjective valuations at all levels of the organization. There is also a tendency in the literature to assume that the decision-maker is risk-neutral, which is practically never the case in a real-world situation. However, if any business is to judge the reliability of its decision-making, it should attempt to assess the degree of confidence felt by the decision-makers that they have made the right decision. The greater the potential degree of uncertainty, the more important it is to know how reliable they believe their decision to be. Thus, if they were aware of significant gaps in the information available to support the decision, they might indicate low confidence, and the business can make contingency plans in the event that the decision proves unreliable. It is accepted that adding this element of data to the calculations may predict more risk, but if the organization is aware of the qualitative limitations on the data used or the methodologies and techniques applied, the managers may be better prepared if things do go wrong.

Risk in strategic decision-making may be broadly defined as the general value judgement made by a person of appropriate status within the organization as to which of the possible outcomes to a decision situation are acceptable and which are unacceptable (section 4.3 *et seq.*). Doherty (1985) asserts that the basis of a risk is the lack of predictability as to the nature and degree of each outcome. But he confirms that the concept of risk is essentially neutral. It is vital to understand that the fact that a risk is identified does not of itself imply that any outcome will be either desirable or undesirable. That is a further value judgement made in the light of the goals of the organization. Thus, at a simplistic level, an investment or speculation may produce profits greater than that expected or losses smaller than expected. Such outcomes may be desirable through the boost either would give to investor confidence. They may be undesirable because it may make the organization vulnerable to a hostile take-over.

5.1.2 A list of the different types of risk

At a very general level, it is reasonable to produce a list of the various types of risk that may affect different aspects of an organization's activities, e.g:

- *market risks*   the demand for any organization's products or services will depend on many factors outside the management's control, e.g. the size of the market will be determined, in part by individual spending power and the pressure on the consumer to save rather than spend (a function of consumer confidence in difficult economic conditions), the price of competing products or services, consumer tastes and preferences, changes in government regulations (say, on packaging or safety), etc;

- *financing risks*   the cost of providing and maintaining capital for the organization is subject to government policy as reflected in the movements in the interest and currency exchange rates and in taxation provisions, exchange control regulations and cross-border capital movement restrictions which are, in part, dictated by the prevailing economic conditions – the length of time for which credit facilities must be arranged will also be affected by variables such as the level of bad debt in the market place, whether government or other subsidies and reliefs are available, etc;

- *resource management risks*   the cost and availability of the raw materials required for manufacture may be affected by strikes, bankruptcies or technological change, there may be an insufficiency of trained labour available etc;

- *environmental risks*   anti-pollution and safety regulations may constrain the way in which the organization is able to operate and the costs that it incurs.

5.1.3 Uncertainty, risk and government regulation

With particular reference to environmental risks, Lowrance (1976) points to the fact that, with the growth in scale and centralization in society, we have relied increasingly upon government regulations to control safety and environmental problems. The choice of what to regulate is driven by the power of the discourse, i.e. the contemporary concerns most vociferously reflected in public opinion (see section 2.5). Hence, pressure from trade unions and the public may lead the legislature to regulate to promote greater safety in the workplace. Similarly, pressure from doctors and other experts may lead to the regulation of the standards for the testing of new drugs or the conditions under which food may be stored prior to sale.

We should also recognize that governments may act positively as well as negatively. A number of important risks including natural disasters, economic dislocation, sickness and injury, may sometimes give rise to government relief. Relief is distinguishable from insurance in that recipients are not charged a premium, e.g. relief from taxation under a regional development scheme or compensation for modification of regulations. Kaplow (1991) warns that government relief for risk distorts incentives because individuals no longer bear the full cost of their actions. If people know that the relief to be made available will act like a cushion against potential losses, decision-making will be distorted because it will lead managers to make non-optimal decisions. This will arise because individuals may form an incorrect perception as to the real extent of the probability of their loss, i.e. build in the expectation as to the availability of government money.

5.1.4 Using the law as a means of regulation can create problems

One of the problems for the private sector is that governments tend to work on an *ad hoc* basis to appease public opinion and to win votes. Because of this lack of any real systematic long-term plan for legislation, effective planning is difficult for those organizations that may become the subject of regulation with, as yet, unquantified costs attached. In a perfect world, legislation would not be necessary because:

1. industry and commerce would control itself – hence, once the true costs of past and future mismanagement become apparent, the organization ought to select the best way of controlling longer term costs rather than trying to dispose of the problem via the route of least short-term cost; or because,
2. failing that control activity, the consumer would give buying preference to the organizations with the best track record of control.

As it is, the profit motive which underpins the activities of commerce in the Western world tends to resent environmental expenditure which shows no immediate return. Of necessity, therefore, there is a policy that legislation should regulate the things that the people themselves cannot control. This may be because the average person does not have the expertise or because there is no 'green' substitute, e.g. drug testing and safety, environmental protection arising from fuel extraction and energy production etc.

There is, however, an inherent problem in using laws to control risks. If laws are to have the right quality to be enforceable, they must be certain and precise in their use of language to define what those affected are to do. If there are doubts and ambiguities, there are constitutional barriers to prevent courts from rewriting the statutes. This would, in effect, be the act of legislating and only a parliament may do this. If risks are the subject matter of these laws, their nature is, by definition, uncertain. Thus, a state may have a policy to control emission levels, but where the levels are set for each industry, these levels may be wholly arbitrary because there is insufficient information on the exact nature of the risks to health and to the environment. The setting of the trigger levels for state intervention on any issue therefore becomes a task of major importance to all involved. In turn, this raises the question, 'what level of proof as to the nature of the danger is required before the state will intervene?' Since the nature of the risk itself and the probability of harm flowing from it may be hard to assess, it is difficult to decide what the acceptable levels of exposure are without relying on subjective values. The moment one admits that the decision whether to intervene is not objective, the fair-minded state must always discuss proposed regulations with the affected industries before taking action.

One way of setting a medium- to long-term agenda for government (and, therefore, the relevant industries and service providers) to follow would be to identify situations where the ordinary market forces have failed to operate to improve standards. However, there is the difficulty that if the consumer is not apparently prepared to pay the price to introduce safety features, upon what basis should the government make those safety features mandatory? It may be necessary for government to create a system of incentives so that a commercial organization can share in the 'profit' of a cleaner and safer environment. This system might contain elements such as tax allowances, rebates and investment credits. There could also be a public register of new and available technology that may help to reduce the threat to safety. This would be a system of carrots, but if sticks were also used it raises the question of whether modern society is over-regulated. Although many governments do work on the basis of compulsory benevolence, mouthing such high moral justifications as 'prevention is better than cure', it will be the consumer or tax payer who is forced to pay in the end. But if criminal and civil court actions are too expensive and slow and the government regulations cumbersome, what other possibilities exist?

1. voluntary self-regulation by the profession, trade or industry, often after consultation with government and as an alternative to formal government regulation;
2. certification by the British Standards Institute and other certifying and licensing bodies;
3. direct consumer action, often invoked by the Consumers Association or various radio and television programmes.

These examples serve to indicate the diversity of risk confronting the modern organization. The interaction between all the risks will hopefully provide a means whereby the organization can earn a profit, although it must be acknowledged that the aggregation of risk is a complex matter. Should the state produce regulations, the costs to the industries affected may be substantial. If the regulations are not realistic in terms of what today's technology can achieve, that line of business may have to be discontinued until the technical problems can be solved at an economic cost. Further, if the state is to retain the trust of the electorate, it may feel obliged to monitor the scientific data, and to continuously upgrade the scope and effect of the regulations in line with available technology. This may place heavy costs on the industries who may have to write off the plant installed to meet the last regulations. Such risks give commercial organizations strong incentives to lobby governments in an attempt to prevent over-regulation and to set the lowest standards. The result may be compromise regulations that target the most feared risks, and leave out those risks where the uncertainties are high.

A better strategy for governments would be a two-stage regulation. In the first part, government would, after consultation, set minimum standards for the protection of those at risk. This minimum standard should be positively policed to encourage compliance. This minimum standard would also represent a benchmark from which to set future targets. However, since there is always the possibility either of error in setting the standard or of an improvement in the available technology, the second stage should be a discretionary power in nominated government departments to reassess the standards and to change compliance levels in particular situations where the regulations have been shown to be inadequate. But those negotiating the standards and drafting the regulations should take care that nothing that appears in the regulations should discourage any organization from voluntarily achieving higher standards.

5.1.5 Probability risk analysis

Linnerooth-Bayer and Wahlstrom (1991) report that in the United States and, to a more limited extent, in Europe, probabilistic risk analysis (PRA) has emerged as a major methodology to aid regulatory policy-making. They consider it important to separate risk assessment from risk management, i.e. separating the scientific findings and policy judgements from the political, economic and technical considerations that influence the choice of government policy. The problem is that

> Large uncertainties, and even ignorance, dominate many areas of risk to the extent that the very lack of knowledge is unsuspected. (p. 239)

PRA is used as an aid to political policy processes, e.g. to provide overall estimates of a technology for policy-making purposes, public inquiries and environmental impact statements, and to aid regulatory decisions and licensing procedures. It depends upon the creation of a tree, but the growth of the branches may be in either of two directions:

1. possible chains of events called event trees are constructed which lead to unwanted consequences: or
2. working backwards, chains of faults called fault trees are constructed in the search for accident precursors.

The risks are quantified by estimating the probability of each event or fault and combining this with an estimate of the damage likely to be caused. The main weakness of PRA lies in this quantification process because the data cannot be guaranteed adequate and no analysis of that data can be guaranteed accurate and complete. This is increasingly a problem as the level of complexity and interdependence of technological systems grows. Consequently, the results will depend on subjective assumptions and judgements in creating and analysing the model. It is therefore important that the results are expressed not as single numbers, but as probability distributions reflecting the certainty of the numbers. Indeed, the expression of uncertainty is one of the basic ideas underlying PRA. However, as Linnerooth-Bayer and Wahlstrom (1991) observe,

> There is a natural tendency to define a problem in such a way that the analytical results are valid and credible. This tendency has been apparent in the nuclear field. As an official at the UK Atomic Energy Agency observed, hazards which can be evaluated with confidence have been given comparatively more attention than other hazards. (p. 243)

Nevertheless, PRA has informed public debate on the social acceptability of nuclear power generation, where to site potentially hazardous installations such as liquid natural gas terminals etc. (section 1.3.4). The problem is that, unlike decisions, policies need to reflect a consensus of view to be viable. This involves each party participating in the pluralist process in an attempt to convince all the other parties of the correctness of their argument. Unfortunately, each party in the debate tries to use scientific evidence to make their own arguments appear more credible. Because the outcome of PRA is influenced by the subjective judgements as to what to put into the model, the issue of uncertainty tends to be devalued or overlooked when the arguments are presented. Indeed, the very expertise that uses PRA and comparable methodologies and which ought to be scientific and detached, is being politicized.

As we have seen in the preceding chapters, there is a phenomenon of plural rationality, i.e. different people view the world differently. They have different ways of defining issues, different criteria of reasonableness and different concepts of rationality. These perceptions tend to be rooted in social contexts and the acceptability of risk is coloured, if not actually determined by these cultural factors. This makes it very difficult to arrive at a consensus as to government policy through a purely technical definition of risk and uncertainty.

5.1.6 Risk and uncertainty separated

The aspect of risk is often treated in isolation from uncertainty in conceptual models. In some cases according to Moore (1983), this is a distinction between repeatable and non-repeatable events. Games of chance are said to be repeatable events (e.g. each spin of the roulette wheel, throw of the dice or turn of the card) and to the actuary, deaths in the community are repeatable events as each person in a large community may either die or not in each year. But what the rate of inflation will be or the base interest rate at a given time are non-repeatable events because they rely upon a unique combination of circumstances not under the control of any one person or group of persons.

The problem is to decide whether this distinction is useful. A person organizing a large outdoor event can insure against disruption through rain (the so-called pluvius cover) and individual items of value may be insured when employing a furniture remover to carry goods from the old house to the new home. To the proposer, the event is non-repeatable because this particular event will not recur in the same form, but many people organize outdoor events or move valuable items from one part of the country to another so the insurance company will be exposed to risk from a number of comparable transactions. In deciding whether to accept the insurance proposal, the underwriter must balance experience derived from previous comparable policies (which will give rise to relative frequencies), against the particular circumstances outlined by the proposer(s), making adjustments to the crude statistical measure by the application of more subjective considerations. The distinction is therefore not very useful because its only function is to indicate that when each person or organization forms a perception of risk, that perception will be a function of their individual perspectives, values and needs.

Similarly, at a conceptual level, some researchers tend to consider such unrealistic questions as, 'given certainty of outcomes to a given decision situation, what would be the preferable decision?' While a number of conceptual and normative models have sought to identify key variables likely to influence the risk perception, these have generally been considered to be too narrow in their treatment. Libby and Fishburn (1977) observed that,

> While the applicability of this (the mean-variance model) and other normative models to aggregate market behaviour has been studied extensively, the degree to which these models describe individual managers' actual risk preferences has received little attention in the business literature, even though the individual level of analysis is relevant to many decisions made within the firm. (p. 272)

In reviewing the empirical work in the field of risk, Libby and Fishburn (1977) concluded that

> In contrast to the abundance of studies involving small monetary amounts, there are relatively few efforts to explore systematically choice behaviour and perceived risk in realistic business situations. Most of the investment literature is normative in nature and uses a model similar to the Markowitz (1959) mean-variance model. (p. 279)

Bourgeois (1985) in linking risk and uncertainty to strategic decision-making, commented that

> Administrative theorists can take a cue from financial theory, where the central paradigm for the last decade has centred around the concept of risk aversion, that parallels our uncertainty avoidance. Unlike administration, finance has long recognized that risk, measured by volatility, is acceptable at any of various levels, so long as the

expectation of or demand for a higher rate of return accompanies the acceptance of risk. (p. 570)

There may be a high degree of interaction between the elements of uncertainty and risk in any particular decision situation. For example, decisions involving a high degree of uncertainty such as product developments designed to exploit new technology are also likely to be perceived as high risk situations. Hence, high levels of uncertainty may influence risk perceptions, though the degree of correlation between these two elements and the range over which uncertainty influences risk remains unclear. It is also likely that decision-makers may perceive risk in decision situations where there is a high degree of certainty about the possible outcomes and their consequences. Indeed, many of the normative models developed in the field of decision theory assume this.

A further question related to an integrated model of uncertainty and risk is whether or not perceived risk influences the degree of perceived uncertainty. This inter-relatedness of the two concepts provides some explanation of why many studies on decision-making adopt a composite definition embracing both uncertainty and risk. The following sections will seek to develop and analyse the two elements separately initially, and then seek to synthesize the findings on the two elements.

5.2 UNCERTAINTY

5.2.1 Definition of uncertainty

We think it useful to start with a statement of the blindingly obvious, viz. uncertainty is the opposite of certainty. Certainty exists when a particular consequence can be unambiguously predicted to follow a given event. Uncertainty is said to exist in decision situations where the decision-maker lacks complete knowledge, information or understanding concerning the proposed decision and its possible consequences. There are two basic types of uncertainty:

1. uncertainty arising from a situation of pure chance, e.g. the throw of a dice or the turn of a playing card – this is known as aleatory uncertainty; and
2. uncertainty arising from a problem situation where the resolution will depend upon the exercise of judgement – this is known as espistemic uncertainty.

Unless otherwise stated, you may assume that when we refer to uncertainty in a business context, we intend to refer to espistemic uncertainty. Rowe (1977) stated that

Uncertainty exists in the absence of information about past, present, or future events, values or conditions. Although there are various degrees of uncertainty, the basis of the concept of uncertainty is the absence of information about parts of a system under consideration. (p. 17)

The key element in this definition is that the uncertainty only relates to a part of the system under consideration. According to Shackle (1969), the concept of uncertainty has to have boundaries. If decision-makers in the real world were faced with complete uncertainty, they would in effect be powerless. In many respects uncertainty is a measure of the decision-maker's level of confidence or assurance in relation to the situation he or she faces. A high degree of uncertainty would reflect a significant lack of understanding and knowledge of the situation resulting in a low level of confidence and assurance. In statistical terms this level of confidence is measured on the probability scale as follows:

Probability = 0.0   equates to a complete lack of knowledge and understanding about a prospective situation and, hence, a low level of confidence.

Probability = 1.0   equates to perfect knowledge and understanding about a prospective situation and, hence, a high level of confidence.

These probability estimates may be based on directly observable and quantifiable data, i.e. 'objective probabilities', in situations where there is complete knowledge of the possible outcomes and the underlying mechanisms influencing their occurence (e.g. throwing an unbiased dice). If we ignore the very simple dice-throwing models and concentrate on the more complex real world, uncertainty is said to be objective when the decision-maker has perfect knowledge of all the outcomes that can be associated with a particular event and the probability of occurrence can either be calculated on an *a priori* basis or by applying statistical techniques to past experience. This data may be manipulated in mathematical models but, as McKone (1991) comments,

At best, mathematical models only approximate real systems, and therefore their predictions are inherently uncertain. In evaluating the reliability of risk assessment models two questions must be asked: (1) How large is the uncertainty in the model predictions? and (2) How much confidence can be placed in the results? To address these questions, exposure and risk should be presented as probability distributions so that uncertainty in risk and exposure can be characterized by expectation (mean) and spread (variance). (p. 9)

When the magnitude of the uncertainty is significant, decision-makers must identify strategies for reducing uncertainty. Indeed, Galbraith (1973) was positive in stating that as uncertainty increased, so too did the information processing requirements of the competent organization. In situations where the level of knowledge of outcomes or their influencing mechanisms are incomplete, the estimates of reality may be based on the personal assessment of the individual(s) involved, i.e. 'subjective probabilities'. Uncertainty is said to be subjective in the sense that decisions are going to be based on people's opinions. Opinions and judgements are based on:

- the available information;
- people's previous experience; and
- each person's cognitive functions which synthesise both into a hopefully realistic future scenario.

Cohen and Christensen (1970) defined subjective uncertainty as

> a state of mind, often associated with incomplete knowledge, which may characterize the way we interpret what we see, hear or read, and the situations we find ourselves in, and even our feelings, emotions, decisions and actions. (p. 5)

At a strategic level in the larger organizations, a significant proportion of the decisions will be unprogrammable, i.e. unique and non-repeatable events (section 3.1). The decision-making will also be taking place in a complex social and economic environment in which it will be difficult if not impossible to specify all the possible outcomes. In one sense, therefore, all decisions will be based on subjective judgements. This may be said to arise because all decisions are taken in the present, and so the predicted outcomes can only exist in the imaginations of the decision-makers, i.e. exist subjectively.

To help communicate our thoughts and to exercise choice, we tend to talk about the issues by using the language of chance, e.g. to say that there is a 30% chance of an event occurring is to say that in every hundred situations the desirable outcome will arise thirty times. An alternative way of measuring subjective probability is to infer the degree of belief from preference by using the expected utility theory. This theory was pioneered by Ramsey (1931) and it is based on the preferences we may have between different bets. Thus, the subjective probability in an uncertain event E is said to be p if the decision-maker is indifferent as to whether a gain is made or not. However, the work of Ellsberg (1961) suggests a more realistic hypothesis that people prefer to bet on defined rather than vague events when the gains may be moderate or high. Should the prospective gains be small, people may prefer vagueness to clarity. This is now known as the effect of ambiguity and its scope has been the subject of lively debate (e.g. Fishburn, 1988). Thus, in a game in which A bets moderate or large sums on whether a red or a green ball is to be picked from a box containing one hundred balls, it is suggested that people prefer to know how many of the balls are red and how many are green, i.e. people's choices do not simply depend upon the degree of uncertainty, but also upon the precision with which it can be assessed.

5.2.2 Factors influencing the degree of uncertainty

The phenomenon of espistemic uncertainty can be brought about by a number of factors, the more important of which are outlined below:

1. *Inadequate information*   Here the quantity or quality of the avail-

able information will not be sufficient to help the decision-maker to recognize the existence of a problem or a situation requiring resolution. As we saw in Chapter 3, a number of studies on decision-making have recognized that the first stage in the decision-making process is some form of 'trigger' – a set of facts or circumstances warning the manager to initiate the process. In extreme cases, the decision-maker may be totally unaware of any problems likely to affect the organization's performance and so will propose no action. In all probability, all concerned will be feeling confident even though, in reality, this may turn out to be false confidence.

Alternatively, the decision-maker may be aware of adverse trends in the organization's performance but may not know what to do. The uncertainty may arise from an inability to identify the specific source of these problems or from a lack of understanding as to whether the possible solution tactics are within his or her control. Such uncertainty would probably reflect either an inadequacy in the organization's information system or a failure of perception on the part of the decision-maker. Writers have suggested various more specific causes of uncertainty relating to the information system. Cohen and Christensen (1970) recognized the possibility that the intrinsic uncertainty might arise from the form or content of the data used by the decision-maker. While Rose (1974) related the degree of uncertainty in a decision to the amount of information possessed by the decision unit, and Spender (1980) linked uncertainty to the incompleteness of information. These causes might suggest a database design defect in failing to collect, or allow the production of, data to match the problem, or it might be an operational failure on the part of the decision-maker in failing to structure query sets effectively.

2. *Lack of clarity in structuring the problem* If the decision-maker experiences any significant difficulty in decomposing the problem situation into components that can be more easily understood, this may also cause a lack of confidence in the decision situation. For example, it is sometimes difficult to identify the key relationships both between the constituent elements of the problem and between the problem and other factors both internal and external to the organization. The main causal variables may also be unclear. A problem may also arise if too many variables are included in the analysis. If the decomposition produces too many stages in the process problem to be analysed and uncertainty is increased with no improvement in accuracy, only the most important components should be considered in the analysis. Thus, if an organization finds that its production schedules are disrupted because necessary raw materials are not in stock, a number of factors may be relevant. A sample of possible reasons would be:

● the production department may not have communicated their needs to the warehouse in time;

- the stock control system may not have shown the likely shortfall in time;
- the purchasing department may not have placed the orders for replacement stock early enough;
- the finance department may have been slow paying for the last orders, causing the suppliers to demand payment in advance for the immediate orders etc.

Before the organization can begin the process of remedying the problem, it must first identify the causes of the immediate difficulty and determine whether these causes are likely to be repeated. As should be obvious, there are a number of possible causes and any one of them may be the sole cause of delay, or the delay may arise from an interaction between some or all of them. Further, dealing with only one part of the system could be damaging to the rest unless all the relationships are examined in the problem solution strategy.

A failure to produce a clear structure for the problem may result either from the lack of experience, skill or expertise on the part of the decision-maker, or, just as often, from the novel nature of the problem encountered. Moreover, this failure may arise even though the decision-maker has access to good quality information. Unfortunately, access to information does not, of itself, enable the decision-maker to use the information available effectively to formulate the problem. As Cohen and Christensen (1970) emphasize, knowledge of the effect of a problem does not necessarily imply knowledge or understanding of its causes.

3. A further issue related to problem structuring which may compound the degree of uncertainty is the *inability to identify alternative solutions* to the situation. If the decision-maker has found it difficult to identify all the component elements of the problem and to specify the manner of their possible interaction, this will have significant repercussions in the capacity to identify alternative solutions. In the extreme, though possibly not the exceptional case, the decision-maker may develop sound solutions to the wrong problem.

Even if the decision-maker does manage to produce a satisfactory problem structure, there is no guarantee that the decision-maker will be able to identify or analyse the full range of potential solutions. This may be due to the personal inadequacies mentioned in point 2 above, or due to a host of other constraints which may include:

- the amount of time available;
- the amount and quality of information available; and
- the capacity of the individual to analyse or synthesize only a limited range of alternatives.

Constraints such as time and the quality of information may be imposed by external pressures, such as those produced by the activities of trade competitiors, or by internal budgetary considerations. Managers should always remember that spending more money on getting more information and waiting for that information to arrive will not of itself produce better quality decisions. It is a balancing act. On the one hand, the awareness that not all of the potential solutions have been fully explored or analysed is likely to create a degree of uncertainty in the decision-maker's mind. This may cause stress and lead to health problems or an increased turnover in staff. Spending money to analyse more possibilities may reduce profitability but produce greater peace of mind. It is for each organization to decide how much of its budget to devote to feeling better about decisions. This does assume, however, that the extended analysis does not simply produce greater uncertainty if, at the end of the exploration, no more clear solution emerges.

4. The *futuristic nature of decision-making* is probably the most frequently referred to source of uncertainty within the literature (e.g. MacCrimmon, 1974; Kogan and Wallach, 1967). To some extent, all decisions are an exercise in crystal ball gazing. Since all decisions are essentially a commitment of resources now with the consequences not evident until some time in the future, the decision-maker would clearly like to be able to see into the future. The futurity of time involved may vary considerably from the sometimes almost instantaneous fractions of a second when pressing a key to initiate a computerized task to several years in the case of developing new products or technologies.

Some suggest that there is a direct proportionality between the degree of uncertainty and the length of time until the consequences of the decision will result. This implies that the decision-maker would be more confident or certain about decisions that are fully effective within a short period of time rather than over a longer time horizon. While such a broad statement may be valid within a constrained time-scale, it is unlikely that the degree of uncertainty perceived by a decision-maker is directly proportional to the total time period throughout the full range of potential time periods. It is not wholly sensible to reduce the emotions and feelings of a decision-maker to a simple proportion sum. It is more likely that, once a certain time horizon has been reached, a form of emotional safety valve or cut-off mechanism will operate. So if a high level of uncertainty has already been reached and time is to be extended, there will only be a marginal and not a proportional increase in the amount of uncertainty perceived.

For example, let us assume that the management is trying to arrive at a composite assessment of the total uncertainty facing the organization (even though this is not necessarily a useful piece of information to determine). It finds that the organization is already operating at high levels of uncertainty in taking decisions about product development. Information inputs then suggest even higher levels of future uncertainty in the development of the organization's markets. Such news will receive a lower weighting in the cumulative calculations. If we assume that the organization is going to continue in operation rather than devolve into a paralysis induced by fear of the unknown, all that happens is that yet another unknown factor is simply added to the list to be considered in due course.

One of the reasons why organizations may view increasing uncertainty with some equanimity is that decisions which address a long horizon, such as strategic decisions, are likely to be compound decisions. Thus, rather than being a single global decision covering the complete period, in practice, each strategic decision will be made up of a stream of co-ordinated decisions with shorter time horizons (e.g. Mintzberg *et al.*, 1976). In other words, there may be a stream of sequential decisions within which various specific decisions are made or to be made. Hull (1980) indicated that even an apparently single decision situation may encompass a stream of subordinate decision points at which changes or amendments to the plan proposed by the metadecision may be made, when he concluded that

> the possibility of abandoning the project exists at various points during its life.

Cohen (1972) has also suggested that there might be differential perceptions of uncertainty between individuals using the same time horizon. Time has both subjective and objective qualities allowing some the luxury of perceived time to think, while others consider themselves under time pressure from the outset and rush the decision-making.

5. A significant factor influencing the uncertainty or lack of confidence about the future outcomes of specific decisions is the *availability of information*. MacCrimmon (1974) suggests that

> to say uncertainty exists is analogous to saying that there is a lack of appropriate information. (p. 56)

Rose (1974) defined the degree of uncertainty as,

> the extent to which a decision unit possesses all the economic information necessary to use a given decision model. (p. 501)

Although everyone would like perfect information upon which to base their decisions, it is not conceivable in a practical situation that a decision-maker would expect objective or perfect information about the future. But it is likely that the decision-maker will base his or her subjective perceptions and predictions of the future on the information currently made available by the management information system (MIS) and its databases. The decision-maker will try to analyse the available data to establish historical and topical trends and use this information to create a subjective prediction of the future environment within which the decision will be implemented. The quality of the data available to the decision-maker and the capacities of the processing and analysis packages will therefore substantially influence the quality of the manager's resulting subjective judgements and predictions. The qualitative features of the design of the MIS implemented by the organization which are likely to be of particular influence are the range, type, detail, accuracy and timeliness of the data available. If there are inadequacies in one or more of these features and these inadequacies are known to the decision-makers, there is likely to be increased uncertainty or lack of confidence in their predictions.

6. A further factor that influences uncertainty relates to the *objectives to be satisfied* within decision-making. This may arise because the objectives have not been defined with any real clarity or because there is a conflict between the requirements of the objectives that the decision-maker is trying to reconcile within the context of the decision. Substantial evidence exists (e.g. Thompson and Tuden, 1959; Richards, 1974) to support the view that, in the majority of business decisions, there are a number of objectives which influence or constrain each decision. Some of these objectives may, to a greater or lesser extent, be capable of specific quantification, e.g. profit, sales revenue, or cost-saving objectives. Others may be more qualitative by nature and prove more difficult to quantify, e.g. the organization's image and goodwill, or its social responsibility on issues affecting the environment.

    Irrespective of how easy or difficult it may be to quantify any objective, there remains the issue of inherent conflict between objectives. For example, if a decision is proposed which would maximize sales revenue or market share, this might only be achievable at the expense of the objective on minimum profitability in the short-term at least, and possibly at the expense of social responsibility in the longer term. The extent to which each objective is given weight in the decision will produce alternative solutions to the problem of what to do. What may make decision-making even more difficult is that the parameters used by the decision-makers in judging the merits of the alternative solutions to a situation are often themselves ill-defined, likely to alter over time as the organization's situation changes, and to conflict with each other. Faced with such 'woolly', changeable, and often inconsistent parameters to guide his or her decision-making, the decision-maker is likely to experience less confidence or greater uncertainty about the decision situation faced and about which of the solutions to select.

7. The level of confidence concerning the *post-decision stage of implementation* may also influence the decision-maker's perception of uncertainty. In making a decision or selecting the most appropriate option to solve a problem, an inherent consideration is the capacity of the organization to implement the proposed solution effectively and efficiently. A football coach may develop spectacular set-piece plays on paper, but may never dare to use them in the championship

game because the players have not developed the necessary consistency of practical skills to make success assured. Similarly, the business decision-maker must consider feasibilty either in general terms or, more specifically, in terms of the organization's capacity to implement the decision given its financial and manpower resources, structures and systems. The processes involved in implementation are not entirely predictable as the experience of most organizations will testify, and this unpredictability will generate further uncertainty in the decision-maker's mind while formulating solutions to the problem in hand.

8.   An underlying causal variable of uncertainty reflected in the previous seven sources of uncertainty, is the *personal qualities of the decision-maker* (e.g. Nees, 1978, 1983; Cohen and Christensen, 1970). Qualities such as the experience, skills, training and cognitive abilities, for example, will influence the degree of confidence or assurance assessed by individuals in a given decision situation. We can recognize that these qualitative attributes will influence the degree of uncertainty perception from individual to individual, and training and staff development strategies can address perceived deficiencies in these qualities. But no matter how successful these strategies may be, they cannot result in the complete elimination of uncertainty in a decision situation.

According to Heath and Tversky (1991), this may be proposed as a competence hypothesis, i.e. people prefer to take decisions in a context in which they consider themselves to be knowledgeable or competent rather than in a context in which they feel ignorant and uninformed. For these purposes, the word competence includes skills as well as knowledge and understanding. Competence will be enhanced by knowledge, familiarity and experience, and diminished by a lack of relevant information (especially if it is available to others). The reasoning behind this hypothesis is that in addition to any monetary pay-off, there will be credit or blame attaching to the outcome. These psychological pay-offs of satisfaction or embarrassment may be purely based upon a self-evaluation, or they may be derived from the evaluation of others. If the outcome was purely depending upon chance, success or failure would be a matter of luck and people would not be judged harshly if the wrong outcome arose. Competence helps people to take the credit when they succeed, and it may help people to defend themselves if they make the wrong choice, i.e. just one error in an otherwise unblemished track record. If people are ignorant and they merely guess, they also do not know how to claim the credit for their decisions and they may be exposed to blame when they are wrong. But the greater the declared expertise, the more risk there is to reputation if the wrong judgement is made. Heath and Tversky's experiments confirm a preference for skill over chance when predicting future events, and that a feeling of competence or confidence in knowledge outweighs the effects of vagueness. This leads them to the conclusion that

> If willingness to bet on an uncertain event depends on more than the perceived likelihood of that event and the confidence in that estimate, it is exceedingly difficult – if not impossible – to derive beliefs from preferences between bets. (p. 26)

5.2.3 Range of uncertainty

The degree of uncertainty in specific decision situations will be dictated by these primary factors and, more specifically, by the perceptions of both decision-makers and those responsible for supervising them. It is possible, therefore, to conceive of a range of levels of uncertainty in decision-making ranging from perfect certainty at one extreme to complete uncertainty at the other.

Decisions which might be said to involve complete certainty are likely to have the following features:

- a clear and unambiguous identification of the problem, its constituent elements and its causes;
- perfect information about all the relevant variables in terms of both quantity and quality;
- a well-developed model of the problem which incorporates all the variables likely to influence the decision outcome and a perfect understanding of the manner and scale of their interaction;
- an exhaustive list of all the possible solutions;
- an unambiguous statement of the organization's objectives which is specific, quantifiable and internally consistent;
- perfect knowledge of the future consequences of each possible solution and their implications for the organization in the short- and long-term;
- the availability of all the resources and sufficiency of reliability in all the structures and systems necessary for the successful implementation of the chosen solution;
- the presence of perfectly rational and experienced decision-makers with unlimited analytical and cognitive abilities.

In the context of business decisions, it is difficult to conceive of any practical situations which would satisfy all or, indeed, any of the above conditions fully. In fact, the only circumstances in which we might be able to visualize some degree of complete certainty would be in analysing simplified hypothetical decision situations such as one might encounter through the use of normative models in the area of economic or financial theory.

At the other extreme of the range, decisions involving complete uncertainty are more difficult to characterize, but the following factors would be involved:

- no decision-maker is aware that a problem exists;
- the MIS only provides poor quality or irrelevant information;
- even if management is aware that the organization is performing

poorly, it is unable to identify the problem;
- the decision-maker is unable to decompose the problem into its constituent variables and so cannot determine the manner and scale of their interaction;
- the organization has never clearly defined its objectives nor the constraints within which it must operate, leaving decision-makers to struggle with an unclear and inconsistent set of objectives;
- the decision-makers do not have sufficient information from which to formulate a complete range of alternative solutions;
- there is a lack of adequate information as to the likely consequences of each decision solution in both the short- and long-term horizons.
- the organization lacks adequate resources, structures and systems and is unable to implement any significant decision solution effectively;
- the organization is managed by irrational decision-makers with limited experience, skills or cognitive abilities.

In practice, the state of complete uncertainty, if it did exist, would essentially represent a situation in which no decision of significance could be made with confidence. This would arise when there was no basis on which to identify or structure a problem, let alone to undertake analysis or selection of solution. Happily, the typical situations encountered in the real world fall within the middle of the range of uncertainty, with increasingly fewer situations as one approaches the extremes of the range. There is, however, a wide diversity of degrees of uncertainty within each typical business situation, depending upon the nature of the decision to be taken and the nature of the decision-maker.

Anthony (1968), for example, classified business decisions into three groups *operational*, *management/tactical* and *strategic* (see section 3.1). Decisions in each of these groups are distinctive in terms of their basic characteristics, the level in the organization at which they typically occur, and the levels of uncertainty usually associated with them. Like other writers in the field, Anthony identified increasing levels of uncertainty as one progresses through the operational–management–strategic levels of decision-making in the organization. However, the distinctiveness between the uncertainty levels in these groups is not as sharp as this model might imply. It is possible, for example, to conceive of operational decisions with greater uncertainty than corresponding management decisions. Thus, decisions taken by actual sales representatives in the field as to whether to confirm a big order on credit to an existing customer rumoured to be trading while insolvent, may be more uncertain than the management decision on the stratification of credit limits by reference to the size of customers and/or the turnover on their accounts during the last twelve months.

Some research findings (e.g. Kunreuther, 1989; Hogarth and Kunreuther, 1989) demonstrate that insurance actuaries and underwriters charge higher premiums when the uncertainty about the values of probabilities and values is high. For example, both risk averse and risk neutral actuaries will demand a higher premium when the probability of loss is estimated to be either 0.1 or 0.3 with equal probability, than when it is known with certainty that probability is 0.2. It is natural that insurers should wish to add a premium element to reflect their inability to assess the probabilities and the extent of possible losses accurately. Indeed, the greater the complexity and the novelty of the proposal, the more likely it is that the premium will be increased to reflect uncertainty. As Abraham (1991) puts it,

> Insurers can deal effectively with risk, i.e. a specifiable probability of loss; but they are likely to deal much less effectively with uncertainty, i.e. an unspecifiable probability of loss. (p. 363)

It would be consistent with the expected utility theory (for a discussion of maximum expected utility, Section 5.1) that this additional premium element would produce a state of indifference in the mind of the insurer between providing coverage and not providing coverage. The problem for insurers is that in a competitive market, if the terms of the policies are reasonably comparable and the competing organizations have similar costs and profit targets, the company charging the lowest premiums is most likely to get the business. This is known as the winner's curse, i.e. you win the auction at the price you did not want to pay (for a detailed explanation, see Bazerman and Samuelson, 1983; and Thaler 1988). The pressure on insurers is therefore to offer coverage at a price lower than that needed to produce the indifference. Insurers react in the following ways:

- the premiums are only slightly increased, but the terms of the policy are redrafted to limit the scale of the potential liability;
- work is done to produce more sophisticated mathematical techniques to reduce the uncertainty in the risk assessment process;
- the risk is spread between many insurers through the reinsurance market – this institutionalized pooling of risk also helps to build up a common database as to the estimates made by experts as to probability and magnitude of risk and as to the real-world outcomes; this more reliable information can then be factored back into the premium setting process but the frequency and severity of liability is subject to covariance and insurers cannot easily diversify a pool of risks that covaries – this reduction in the capacity to diversify risk has been one of the causes of the high losses in the insurance markets in areas such as environmental liability;
- the insurers find ways to reduce competition – this enables them to increase the premiums to the levels required to produce indifference; it also attracts the attention of those governments with restrictive practices and anti-competitive policies and laws.

This research demonstrates the entirely natural tendency for all decision-makers to want to build a buffer into the price against uncertainty. Sometimes, the amount of this buffer will be set intuitively. Others pretending greater sophistication may adopt a technique such as the expected utility theory.

5.2.4 Types of uncertainty

Rowe (1977) distinguished between two classes of uncertainty that are said to exist in the decision-making process, namely descriptive uncertainty and measurement uncertainty:

- *Descriptive uncertainty* represents an absence of information and this prevents the full identification of the variables that explicitly define a system. As a result, the decision-maker is unable to describe fully the 'degrees of freedom' of a system. In terms of the general model of uncertainty that we outlined above, this would relate to the features of problem identification and structuring, solution identification, and the degree of clarity in the specification of objectives and constraints.
- *Measurement uncertainty* also represents an absence of information, but this relates to the specification of the values to be assigned to each variable in a system. As a result, the decision-maker is unable to measure or assign specific values to the variables comprising a system. In terms of the general model of uncertainty outlined above, this would relate to the factors of information quality, the futurity of decisions, and the likely effectiveness of implementation.

While no specific reference is made to the role of the decision-maker's experience and skills within this classification of uncertainty, it can be deduced that the quality of the experience and skills available will influence the level of both descriptive and measurement uncertainty.

Rowe (1977) then identified three general sources of uncertainty which he classified as:

1. *Behavioural uncertainty* This is a reference to the difficulties likely to be associated with predicting the actions or reactions of individuals or groups of individuals both within the organization and external to the organization, in response to specific actions or decisions. In the context of business organizations, examples of this type of uncertainty would be the prediction of:

    - consumer attitudes to an organization's new range of products;
    - the reaction of competitors to those new product developments; and
    - the responses of individuals and groups within the organization to decisions affecting their work.

2. *Natural deterministic uncertainty* This will arise exclusively from natural sources and, as such, the causes of this uncertainty will be outside the control of human beings. However, there is usually some degree of regularity or pattern associated with their occurrence which can provide some basis for prediction. Thus, one of the natural threats to the physical structure of buildings and some aspects of day-to-day operation would be the weather. With the aid of satellites and high-powered computers, weather can be forecast to some degree of accuracy by comparative analysis of previous weather patterns and their associated meteorological measurements.

3. *Natural random uncertainty*   This also arises from natural phenomena but, unlike natural deterministic uncertainty, this uncertainty has no perceivable regularity or patterns associated with it. The result is an almost total inability to predict their occurrence, and so it represents an extreme level of uncertainty. Typical examples would be natural disasters such as earthquakes and volcanic eruptions. It is interesting to note that, with the advance of human knowledge and the improvement in the technology of measurement and analytical systems, man is increasingly able to establish patterns for such apparently random natural phenomena. In due course, this may result in the reclassification of some causes into the natural deterministic class of uncertainty. But, overall, the elimination of this source of uncertainty is unlikely as new phenomena are continually being uncovered, many of which may ultimately result from technological developments themselves.

While this classification may be useful at a purely conceptual level, the practical business decision-maker would find it extremely difficult to categorize uncertainties in this way. It is clear that there is considerable overlap between the three categories and, despite academic debate, no general agreement on how to distinguish between natural deterministic and natural random uncertainties. Some commentators have also argued that a number of perceived behavioural uncertainties may themselves originate from natural deterministic or random sources. For example, it is a matter of speculation as to what extent, if at all, human behaviour is determined or influenced by weather conditions or the possibility of natural disasters.

Rowe used this general classification of uncertainty to establish the potential scope for the reduction of descriptive and measurement uncertainties, as shown in Table 5.1.

A number of conclusions emerge from this analysis. As a statement of the obvious, the phenomenon of uncertainty is a product of the environment. It may originate from the internal environment which constitutes the organization, or from the external environment within which the organization operates. It may arise in either a regulated manner (natural deterministic) or in a random manner (natural random). The decision-

Table 5.1   Classification of uncertainty and scope for uncertainty reduction

Process	Scope for uncertainty reduction	
	Descriptive	*Measurement*
Behavioural	Limited by ability to define all variables of human behaviour	Limited by degree of rational behaviour
Natural deterministic	Theoretically unlimited but limited by practicalities	Limited by precision of measuring system to some absolute limit
Natural random	Theoretically unlimited but limited by practicalities	Cannot be reduced by any present known method

maker's capacity to reduce the descriptive uncertainty in these two cases is limited both by the availability of information about the internal and external environments and, more importantly, by the quality of the cognitive abilities that can be brought to bear upon the available information.

Naturally, all organizations will want to reduce uncertainty and will therefore attempt to collect measurement data for processing. However, in the case of natural deterministic uncertainty, the successfulness of the measurement exercise will be constrained by the quality of the management information system and the availability of financial and manpower resources. In the case of natural random uncertainty, the quality of the MIS and the availability of resources will have only a minimal effect on reducing the level of uncertainty.

Factors based upon human behaviour as a source of uncertainty may be more difficult to measure than, say, rainfall or seismic activity. The capacity to reduce descriptive uncertainty is constrained by the ability to identify and define the full range of human behaviour variables and their interrelationships. Behaviour for these purposes will emanate from both inside and outside the organization. It may be easier to observe and measure behaviour within the organization because managers are dealing with a limited class of people, present within identifiable buildings at predictable times and for hopefully convergent purposes. The moment we look outside the organization, we have problems in defining the significance in size of any particular sample, quite apart from the problems of actually observing the behaviour of the sample and measuring its responses. Measurement uncertainty in this context may be reduced if, and only if, the behaviour patterns in a particular decision can be assumed to be rational – a frequently unwise assumption even if one can determine what the rational decision ought to have been in each case.

This model suggests that even though the decision-maker will never be able to remove uncertainty from a given decision situation, a number of steps may be taken to reduce the levels of uncertainty, i.e:

1. The organization should plan to improve the scope and quality of the information system, both internally and externally (this refers to both the collection and the processing of the data);
2. Both through formal training and structured self-development programmes, the organization should aim to enhance the skills of all the key decision-makers in information handling, analysis and synthesis;
3. Both formally and informally, the organization should encourage the development of relevant knowledge and experience in the key decision-makers so that they better understand the mechanisms of the decision process itself and the variables that are significant in the decision environment;
4. If decision-makers develop an increased awareness and understanding of the rational and irrational human behaviour patterns within and outside the organization, they may be better equipped to make

more informed measurements and to take less irrational decisions based on those measurements.

However, whether these or other steps are taken, there can be no guarantee that the decision-makers will make better decisions. Even the most conscientious of people with access to good quality data, may not be able to make good decisions in situations where elements of uncertainty remain.

5.3 DECISION CLASSES AND UNCERTAINTY REDUCTION

If we combine the views of Rowe (1977) on the types of uncertainty and the scope for reducing such uncertainty with the classification of decision types proposed by Anthony (1968), we may be able to provide the basis for a more useful model for analysing uncertainty in practical decision situations. For these purposes, let us establish the following predictions concerning the scope for uncertainty reduction in relation to the different types of decisions in organizations.

5.3.1 Operational decisions

(a) Descriptive uncertainty

Because decisions of this type are more routine and potentially programmable, they are likely to involve a limited range of behavioural uncertainty variables. They may also be easier to observe because many of the variables are internal to the organization. The fact that these decisions will probably recur frequently should enable the more senior decision-makers to develop relatively complete models of the problems to be resolved. These models will include the following elements:

- the structural elements;
- the resource implications;
- analysis and decision-making methodologies;
- alternative solutions;
- constraints; and
- clear objectives to be applied for selecting appropriate solutions.

The natural deterministic and natural random types of uncertainty will always have the capacity to impact on this type of decision. But this is likely to be sufficiently infrequent that they may be excluded from the general models of decisions at the operational level. Their relevance will lie as a series of defined contingencies within each model. In the event that any such trigger is tripped, more senior managers will assume responsibility for the affected decisions. The essence of descriptive uncertainty reduction in this area is through the development of effective vertical information systems to enable the organization to monitor performance effectively. This upward flow of information should also facilitate the continuous development of managerial knowledge and skills.

Any new problems in this field can, in the first instance, be handled by applying 'standard models', i.e. solution strategies that have been successfully applied to similar problems in the past.

(b) Measurement uncertainty

The majority of operational decisions will only have an effect within the organization and relatively few individuals are likely to be affected by each decision. Because these decisions have such limited influence, it may be safe for the decision-makers to assume that all those involved will act and react on the basis of economic rationality. If there is a generally competent information system operating within the organization and the time between the decision and its outcomes is limited, it should be possible for the decision-maker to assign values to individual variables with a reasonably high degree of accuracy. If a non-standard response is subsequently detected through the control and monitoring process, appropriate action may be taken.

However, we must frankly admit that, even in the simplest operational decisions, the descriptive validity of these decision dimensions within the models may be highly debatable. Given the inability of computers to comprehend natural language, attributing 'values' to behavioural variables is at best an exercise in approximation. This is not to deny that many of the recent developments in computer technology within business have been directed towards improving the information database and analytical tools in relation to operational decisions. Indeed, some of these developments have undoubtedly enhanced the decision-maker's knowledge and understanding when making decisions. But their claimed capacity to achieve a real reduction in uncertainty must be viewed with some scepticism.

5.3.2 Management decisions

(a) Descriptive uncertainty

Because of the scope of decisions at this level within the management hierarchy, each decision is likely to involve a wider range of behavioural variables. It is also likely that decision types will recur with a lower frequency than at an operational level. The combination of these facts produces a lower degree predictability of behaviour and, in comparison with operational decisions, an increased level of uncertainty. The range of natural deterministic and natural random variables that may influence decisions in this category will be significantly increased. Further, the more outward looking management/tactical perspective will draw these variables from sources both internal and external to the organization. Thus, in planning a review of the discount structure for cash and credit customers in the Midlands, the decision-makers will be influenced by factors such as:

• the current in-house costs and overheads for that area of operation and the projected costs of implementing any change, e.g. changing the values and software verification controls in the sales and relevant finance packages, printing new price lists, advertising the change, staff training etc;

- the attitudes of employees to changing software controls and to relearning responses to customers' oral queries;
- the discount structure operated by competitiors and their likely reactions to any change in the pattern of competition;
- the likely reaction of existing and prospective customers etc.

Whether the decision-maker will be able to reduce the level of descriptive uncertainty in this class of decision will be a reflection of that person's skills, knowledge and experience. As in the case of operational decisions, a number of computerized tools and techniques have been developed to aid decision-makers in the analysis of these decisions. One of their purposes is to support the identification and measurement of uncertainty. For example, Hull (1980), Brown *et al.* (1974) and many other authors in the fields of decision analysis, operations research, finance etc. have proposed the use of sensitivity analysis and problem simulation techniques as methods of resolving or reducing uncertainty in capital investment decisions.

(b) Measurement uncertainty

Models that are based on assumptions of rational behaviour may assist decision-makcrs in the analysis of situations and, in some cases, they may be a sufficiently close approximation to the actual behaviour to permit direct simulation of the decision. In most cases, however, either a directly applicable model will not be available 'off the shelf' or inadequate time and resources will be available to construct a model from scratch. It will therefore be left to the decision-maker to adapt one of the standard models of analysis to the specific situation. The difficulty is that this modification process to make the model a better match to the real world situation will limit the usefulness of the model. As a result, the constraints of the model will normally require considerable simplification of the data or a disaggregation of the variables. This will prevent a detailed study of the variables and their interrelationship in the practical situation faced. A further price to be paid is that it may also be necessary to modify the organization's MIS to make it capable of providing partial data on the decisions faced in the form required by the model. This will apply particularly to the natural deterministic sources of uncertainty both internally and externally. The complexity of the operations to extract data on the natural random type of uncertainty from the MIS will be considerably increased, as will the capacity for resulting errors in output.

5.3.3 Strategic decisions

(a) Descriptive uncertainty

The nature of strategic decisions implies a higher level of exposure to uncertainty from both internal and external sources, as the consequences of these decisions will have a wider and more significant impact on individuals and groups both internal and external to the organization and over longer periods of time. The natural deterministic sources of uncertainty will therefore be more intensive, and the incidence of significant natural random uncertainties will be greater than at either the operational or management/tactical levels. As well as the increased exposure to uncertainty, senior managers will find the scope for reducing uncertainty more constrained. The main reason for this is that a high percentage of the decisions are non-recurrent, and the constant novelty in the nature and content of decisions limits the potential build-up of knowledge, experience and skill that would be directly useful in reducing such uncertainty.

(b) Measurement uncertainty

There is an almost infinite range in the patterns of behaviour and in the objectives that may be relevant to this type of decision. In general, it is a sad fact that the management information systems installed in most organizations are ill-equipped to support this type of decision-making and to aid in the reduction of uncertainty. This is not due to a general lack of technological competence or efficiency. Although it must be admitted that some designs have such fundamental flaws that one would have to doubt the competence of the designers. The primary difficulty lies in having to predetermine the type, quantity and quality of the information needed to support each type of strategic decision. It will also be necessary to prejudge who should have this information and at what time in the decision-making process. All these design decisions must be made in the knowledge that each future decision may have qualities of novelty and uniqueness. It is not therefore possible to produce comprehensive and verifiable decision support systems at a strategic level. The best that can be done is to devise a useful toolkit for the use of strategic decision-makers.

5.4 WHAT ARE THE UNCERTAINTY REDUCTION STRATEGIES?

We might start with the truism that uncertainty is such a feature of everyday life, that organizations should simply learn to live with it. Thus, many theorists have simply suggested that organizations apply game theory to their decision-making. Alternatively, it is suggested that organizations manufacture certainty through the calculation (creatively or otherwise) of certainty equivalents. These equivalents are usually termed utilities or expected values.

Cyert and March (1992, p. 167) take a more realistic line in advising organizations to concentrate on taking a sequence of short-term decisions. By breaking future scenarios down into a series of smaller steps, decision-makers can reduce the number of longer term decisions where there may be greater uncertainty. This is a form of incremental management, where each problem is solved as it arises. Although this may, if not properly controlled, devolve into crisis management, managers would hope to stay on course by having:

1. timely feedback data on performance levels arising from the most recent decisions; and
2. a clearly defined set of goals as a constant framework of reference.

Further, organizations can impose standard operating procedures and rules on to their environment, hoping that by controlling at least a part of their environment, they can reduce the uncertainty. Thus, for example, many lawyers are trained to think backwards, i.e. they are trained to take a situation after it has arisen, analyse how it arose, and attribute fault and liability to pay compensation for loss suffered. How much better it would be if the lawyer looked forward at all the things that might go wrong and advised on the implementation of liability exposure reduction strategies, say, in precontractual negotiations and the resulting contract terms, or in the way in which potentially dangerous products are checked for quality before being released for sale etc.

There will also be a temptation to try to reduce uncertainty in ways that may be unlawful. The law on restrictive trade practices and monopoly abuses seeks to outlaw agreements and concerted practices between organizations that should be competing with each other. But there is a very narrow dividing line between the unlawful and the quite proper monitoring of the activities of competitors. It is natural for competitors to shadow each other's prices and to match each other on factors such as terms of supply and after-sales service. It is natural for industries to agree accounting standards and other self-regulatory codes of conduct. It is natural for industries to sell lists of customers and to share other data, say, on credit worthiness, on new manufacturing techniques, on the impact of new laws on their operations etc. That this produces predictability instead of uncertainty is a welcome by-product for the organization. That it may reduce profitability is not necessarily unwelcome if there is reasonable stability in the market place. The problem arises if patterns of trade are distorted to the prejudice of the customer. In such cases, the law will enforce uncertainty in the market environment by attempting to restrict the collusive exchange of information between organizations.

5.5 SUMMARY

The next chapter will explore the various definitions of risk as developed within the fields of economics, financial theory, decision theory, behavioural research, and strategic management. Throughout the discussion of these approaches to risk, an attempt will be made to synthesize these views and to develop a composite definition of risk appropriate to strategic decision-making, and to identify the major components of a model of risk within this context. For the time being, we therefore propose the following propositions as a working definition of risk:

1. At a strategic level, each organization will want to generate a general protection system which parallels the ordinary commercial systems.
2. The intention of this protection system will be to reduce or eliminate the risk of loss.
3. The identification of systemic vulnerabilities and their associated threats and hazards will enable the management to form a view as to the acceptability of each foreseen risk of loss.
4. This assessment of acceptability will in part be based on two measurements,

   (a) of the probability that the loss might be sustained, and
   (b) of how great the loss might be.

5. In general, the significance of the loss will be determined by the extent to which the organization depends upon that system, and the values, both tangible and intangible, that may be prejudiced should the system fail to operate as it should.
6. But until the organization comes to terms with the reality of uncertainty, it is unlikely to make reliable decisions.

QUESTIONS

1. Make a short summary of the points you would make to distinguish uncertainty from risk.
2. Can laws be a useful device for regulating risks and, if so, what form of methodology should underpin government policy making?
3. Explain which are the most important of the factors which affect the degree of uncertainty.
4. Briefly explain the range and types of uncertainty.
5. Outline the main uncertainty reduction strategies for each of the main decision classes.

Models of risk and decision behaviour 6

INTRODUCTION

Continuing the more theoretical approach from Chapter 5, we now come
to two chapters which concentrate on the concept of risk itself. The aim in
this first chapter is to explore definitions of risk and then to examine how
one may model risk. Finally, we shall look at techniques such as portfolio
theory and CAPM, and try to establish the key factors in any realistic
model of risk.

6.1 A POSITIVE DEFINITION OF RISK

In his introduction to *An Anatomy of Risk*, Rowe (1977) expresses
succinctly both the problem of definition and the state of current research
aimed at producing a definition.

> Certainly the analysis of a seemingly simple concept with which man
> has always dealt pragmatically, has not resulted in significant solu-
> tions. The subject of risk is in reality very complex. (p. 2)

Over the generations, the term 'risk' has been variously defined. In the
broader context of life and the manner of its living, risk is seen as a part of
the basic exercise of survival. In the different fields of study and research
that humanity has from time to time explored, the range of definitions
moves through a cycle. It begins with the scientific and rational appraisal
of the pay-offs that can be identified with some degree of certainty. It then
moves through the various techniques of prediction that can be applied to
assess and compensate for the variability of the returns foreseen on a
given investment, and it finishes with the merely practical avoidance of
unwelcome consequences.

The definition of risk in a classical sense was provided by Knight (1921)
as the situation in which the decision-maker has three advantages:

- knowledge of the problem structure;
- an understanding of the complete range of possible outcomes; and
- the ability objectively to assess the likelihood of each outcome occurring.

At its simplest level, therefore, Knight saw risk as a form of measurable as
opposed to unmeasurable uncertainty. He was writing at the start of the

1920s. This period, just following the First World War, was a time of optimistic scientific rationalism. In a form of romantic euphoria, people wanted to believe that anything was possible through the appliance of science. Hence, the definition of risk as a measurable form of uncertainty matches the prevailing upbeat feeling of human success and boldly asserts that it is possible for the decision-maker to achieve perfect knowledge about the foreseen outcomes and the likelihood of their occurrence. If such levels of performance were achievable and the decision-maker was only aiming to maximize a single variable objective function, say, for example profit or some utility measure, then it would probably be possible to construct a rational mechanism for the analysis and selection of the most appropriate solution strategy. Otherwise, it is an unrealistic expectation. But despite the naive and mechanical nature of this definition, it has been uncritically accepted as underpinning much of the theoretical work on risk in the areas of game theory, economic theory and financial theory.

Indeed, we cannot dismiss the significant contribution of these theoretical explorations to an understanding of risk. But they remain essentially normative and, as such, they are not wholly comfortable when applied to the analysis of risk in the practical business environment. Hence, Mac-Crimmon (1974) argued that Knight's distinction between measurable and unmeasurable uncertainty was untenable on both logical and empirical grounds, and concluded from his empirical study that,

> few executives made this risk–uncertainty distinction at any time, none made the distinction in all the situations presented, and on reflection very few thought that such a distinction was reasonable. (p. 458)

6.1.1 A more negative view of risk

Rowe (1977) sounded a more negative note in moving towards a definition of the nature of risk when he argued that

> if risk implies something unwanted or to be avoided, risk is then associated with consequences that involve losses to the risk-taker. (p. 23)

Finally, he defined risk as

> the potential for realization of unwanted negative consequences of an event. (p. 24)

and risk aversion as the 'action taken to control risk' (p. 24). This latter comment clearly indicates that he views risk as an endogenous variable within the decision-making process.

Willett (1901) not only identifies the link with uncertainty, but also the negative consequences of the decision when he defined risk as

> the objectified uncertainty regarding the occurrence of an undesirable event.

Denenbury et al. (1974) further stress this negative aspect by defining risk as the 'uncertainty of loss'. Bettis (1983) highlights the diversity in risk definitions by recognizing two variations,

> the term 'risk' is taken in modern financial theory to be a precise technical term defining the probabilistic distribution of market returns. In the strategic management literature, however, it is often taken (among other things) as a manager's subjective judgement of the personal and organizational consequences that may result from a specific decision or action. (p. 413)

This is a more rounded and sensible view of the phenomenon, and it builds upon the views of Cohen and Christensen (1970) who related the definition of risk to what is at stake in the decision and the potential pay-off(s). They recognized that these outcomes may be expressed in values that adopt the terminology of money, safety, health, reputation or, indeed, the quality of life itself. To that extent, all risks reflect both tangible and intangible values and the practice of decision-making must always be subjective and judgemental to some extent.

Research into the nature of risk within strategic decision-making has been considerably less exhaustive than in many of the other related fields. Although we would accept that the development of normative models and the associated research in many of these complementary fields have provided useful insights into the concept of risk in general, it is our view that they fail to provide a realistic descriptive base for the concept of risk in assessing strategic issues. We think that the issue of risk measurement is of particular importance to strategic decision-makers for two main purposes:

- risks should be measured as a part of the general process of identifying potential hazards or situations posing a threat to the survival of the organization; and
- if it appears that the organization may be vulnerable, those situations posing a threat to the continued development and achievement of the organization's objectives should be monitored and such action as is reasonable should be taken to reduce the likelihood of loss.

Within the modern organization, this need to reduce the likelihood of loss may be seen in the routine for risk managers to liaise with their organization's legal department. There is a case for arguing that all proposed corporate decisions should be appraised in the light of the legal environment. Thus, precontractual representations about future performance need to be vetted, draft contracts need to be interpreted, advertising copy and product labelling need to be verified, quality control procedures and the resulting product safety need to be assessed, tax and business organization laws need to be monitored etc. Risk management in many senses is preventive law, i.e. you try to deal with the cases before they arise, aiming at reducing the number of opportunities to become embroiled in expensive and stressful cases before the courts where bad publicity may be damaging to corporate image and awards of damages or of fines may damage the corporate pocket (whether directly or through increased insurance premiums).

6.1.2 Hazards and threats

Although he tended to characterize the hazard for the firm as being predominantly financial in nature (a limitation that we would deny) Bettis (1982) expressed similar concerns at the strategic level when he defined risk as follows:

> Risk is usually taken to indicate some degree of hazard. For a firm the hazard is financial in nature. While bankruptcy and insolvency are extreme examples, lesser hazards such as a modest earnings decline are more common. (p. 22)

It is also useful to refer to Cohen and Christensen (1970) who distinguished between the term 'hazard' which they defined as the actual or potential outcomes, and the term 'risk', which is the subjective consideration of these outcomes. The essence of their distinction is that the hazard is independent of the risk, and will occur irrespective of the risk perceived. However, risk perception is clearly a function of the potential hazards, i.e. the organization will always wish to decide whether the particular risk is acceptable (section 4.3).

We would agree that the distinction is sound but would disagree as to the limited meaning given to hazard. Any strategic management team will try to identify the vulnerabilities of the organization to loss or damage. It is a sad fact of life that once people have been positively involved in running the interactive systems which together comprise the organization, weaknesses will be exposed that may cause the organization significant loss or damage. Those weak or vulnerable points can only be identified by examining future scenarios to classify elements as either threats or hazards. Each of the systems which comprise the critical functions of the organization must therefore be examined. If the points of weakness might be exploited, whether by accident or design, and:

- the purpose of those systems might be frustrated; or
- there might be damage and loss to the organization or its personnel;

the managers will have identified a threat or hazard. In each case, the outcome, will be either frustration of a function or purpose of the organization, or loss or damage to the organization or its personnel. But, the nature of the hazard or threat will be as infinitely variable as the nature of the systemic vulnerability affected.

If we move into the commercial market place, we can see that the trend towards more consolidations, mergers and acquisitions has resulted in the creation of fewer, larger manufacturing, processing or other facilities. Although this may be justified through the achievement of economies of scale, it also has the effect of increasing the risk of business interruption if the key facility is disabled through accident. New technology increases the threat of obsolescence and new ideas bring their own risks, e.g. the Just In

Time stock system may reduce the amount of capital tied up in stock at any one time, but may equally paralyse a manufacturing process if deliveries are unexpectedly disrupted, say, by a lorry drivers' strike in France. Indeed, such is the general increase in the pace of change that unpredictability is now a fact of life. To add to the problem, far more money may now be at stake in the business deals of the multinational organizations or through major accidents such as the Exxon Valdez.

In an attempt to provide a framework of reference, Bettis (1982) identified several sources of risk which would present a potential hazard to an organization, examples of which include:

- short-term sales fluctuations;
- changes in consumer tastes;
- changes in technology;
- changes in government policy;
- changes in competitor's strategy;
- changes in organization's framework;
- changes in organizational membership, etc.

Each of these, he argues, would present a potential hazard to the organization, but he recognizes that the financial consequences of some of these occurrences may be evident more rapidly than others. For example, fluctuations in sales may have an immediate effect on earnings and liquidity, while changes in technology may only be evident in the longer term. We would agree that each of these might represent a hazard at a macro level, i.e. to the organization as a metasystem. But what it fails to do is to reflect the equal possibility of microhazard, i.e. a hazard which represents a threat only to a subsystem of the organization. Thus, if there is inadequate documentation of one of the operational computer systems, the sickness of key operators could paralyse the particular function of the organization until other staff work out how to use the computer system. This could damage the organization's image for reliability in being able to perform this function, disturbing consumer confidence and reducing short-term profitability.

6.2 RISK MANAGEMENT STRATEGIES

Once all the major hazards have been identified, the organization must devise risk management strategies. At its simplest level, this will involve assessing the trade-offs between:

- the benefits to be derived from a given reduction in the risk; and
- the costs incurred in achieving this reduction.

If the decision-makers make the levels of uncertainty explicit when forming their strategies, their real concerns and values may be made more apparent. Thus, if it was proposed to take precautionary measures for social or political purposes, e.g. to reduce the risk of polluting the local river and harming fish stocks through the accidental discharge of hazardous waste chemicals, a decision could be taken which reflected non-utilitarian factors. In our pollution scenario, the components of the decision might be:

- the level of toxicity associated with the chemicals that might escape;
- the amount of the toxic chemicals that might escape and therefore expose animals or humans to risk;
- what technologies exist either to reduce the risk of escape or to minimize the risk of injury following escape;
- what are the benefits and costs of each potential strategy in reducing the risks of injury.

There are considerable uncertainties connected with each point. Thus, even though the management may be able to assess the level of toxicity in each chemical that might escape, it is extremely difficult to assess the dose that might be ingested by each animal (whether directly or indirectly) and what the effects of that exposure might be. It may be difficult to estimate the severity of the potential threat to the environment. The escape might be limited or major. It might flow directly into the water or seep through the soil into the water table. It might be upstream or down stream of various local social sites of recreation on the river etc. Questions of technology should be somewhat more clear-cut because engineers should be able to inform managers of the latest safety systems and clean-up procedures. But, if new plant is to be installed to contain waste better or to reduce its toxicity, will the capital cost and, perhaps, the increased production costs be borne willingly by the customers through the price mechanism, or should the organization absorb the costs out of existing profits?

Balancing all the factors of this type is an exercise in handling significant levels of uncertainty, but if managers knew that they were deciding to increase prices specifically to fund environmental protection measures, appropriate public relations steps could be taken to justify the price increases to customers and to enhance the reputation of the organization as a 'green' and caring concern. In short, more rational decisions would be made (see section 3.11).

6.3 MODELLING RISK

As Ramani and Finlay (1991) are able to state (with some degree of relief), 'National hazards are a rare occurrence.' (p. 405) So using the Poisson probability distribution, the frequency of both natural and man-made disasters may be measured quite easily, but their severity is more difficult to assess. Hence, we tend to express severity in terms of the number of deaths and injuries, and in the monetary value of property destroyed and damaged. They advocate using a Gumbel Type II extreme-value distribution approach for estimating hazard severity. Once a hazard has been assessed, the cost of corrective action can be estimated and the investment justified using the following formula:

$$\text{justification} = \frac{\text{consequences} \times \text{exposure} \times \text{probability}}{\text{cost factor} \times \text{degree of correction}}$$

The formula depends upon appraising the entire situation resulting from a disaster and rating the consequences on a scale from 1 to 100 depending on their severity where:

> 1 = minor cuts and bruises and minor damage to property; and

> 100 = a catastrophe which causes numerous fatalities, major disruption to services and extensive damage to property.

When all the elements have been rated, they are substituted into the formula and one decides that, say, for any result rating in excess of 10, the cost is justified.

This is but one example of the many normative or conceptual models in a wide range of discipline areas including economics, financial economics, operations research, decision analysis and psychology in which the influence of risk on the individual decision-making process has been represented. The remainder of this chapter reviews the general nature of these models, their main parameters and conclusions, and assesses the validity of these models in attempts to describe decision behaviour at a strategic level when confronted by risk. A more detailed evaluation of the models developed in the field of economic theory and their application in financial theory will be undertaken in section 6.4 and Chapter 7.

Levy and Sarnat (1984) outlined the main stages in the development of theoretical models in the area of economics and financial theory to explain decision behaviour in relation to investment decisions. These models are set out in the following paragraphs.

6.3.1 Maximum return criterion

This criterion of decision-making is based on the assumption that the decision-makers are only concerned with the process of forecasting the maximum possible returns when selecting alternative strategies. If this was the only declared basis for making decisions between competing investments at a policy level within the organization, it suggests that the decision-makers are taking a very limited view. This would arise because the decision-makers would not only fail to incorporate considerations of the likelihood or probability of these returns being achieved, but would also ignore the ethical considerations of particular types of investment and other intangible issues. The potential scope of this model would therefore only be representative of practical decision-making in a situation of near or perfect certainty and of limited accountability. Given that perfect certainty is little more than a philosophical abstraction, this approach is of little practical value.

6.3.2 Maximum expected return criterion

The basis of this model is that investment decisions should be based on selecting only those investments which are likely to achieve the maximum expected return. We therefore go beyond the less realistic maximum return criterion by taking account of probabilities. For these purposes, the expression 'expected return' is defined as

the mean of the random distribution of possible returns weighted by their respective probabilities of occurrence.

If managers make their selections on the basis of this criterion, they may hope to achieve the maximum 'weighted average' return from a given situation, but there are three problems in the uncritical use of this criterion, as follows:

1.   Its essential weakness is that it ignores the actual distribution of returns within the expected or weighted average value.
2.   It assumes that decision-makers will be indifferent to the spread of the distribution. By way of example, let us take two alternative possibilities based on the need to price a new product prior to its launch on to the market.

    (a)   Some decision-makers might prefer to plan for a lower expected return which has a higher degree of certainty. The managers might therefore prefer to pitch the price of the new product lower than the average market price in the hope that this will gain market share. Although this would produce a lower gross profit margin per sale, it might guarantee a greater likelihood of sales. In statistical terms, there would be either a smaller distribution of possible returns around the lower mean value, or there would be a closer orientation of probability estimates around the expected value.

    (b)   Other decision-makers might prefer an option which offers a higher expected value, but which has a wider distribution of possible outcomes around the expected value. The managers might start by asking its customers to pay a high price, but allow a discretion to local agents on discounts for quantity. The selling organization therefore gives itself the chance of some sales at high unit value and other more likely sales at a lower value. Thus, there would be a wider set of probability estimates associated with each outcome, making the achievement of the expected value less certain.

3.   It fails to reflect the preferences of the decision-makers towards the potential scale of absolute losses. These preferences would have been evident when the assessment of the original outcome distribution was undertaken, but they would then be weight-adjusted into the final expected return value. For example, when the decision-maker is reviewing all the possible outcomes from pursuing each of the strategies, there may be a high level of risk attaching to one situation because of the magnitude of the potential consequences. If the decision-maker decides to go ahead regardless, this can only be based on the judgement that the probability of the particular outcome occurring is relatively small. The maximum expected return

criterion implies that the decision-maker will take a balanced or weighted view of such potential hazards or consequences in arriving at a total risk appreciation of the situation. It will be apparent that the decision to go ahead means that the probability of gain appears to outweigh the chances of the very high loss and so makes the venture seem worthwhile.

6.3.3 Maximum expected utility

The expected utility approach was originally developed by Ramsey (1931) and Von Neumann and Morgenstern (1944). They showed that the concept of utility can be introduced into decision problems in such a way that an individual who acts solely on the basis of expected utility is also acting in accordance with his or her true tastes. The model is developed on the basis of a number of axioms, as follows:

1. Any two alternative outcomes are comparable, in the sense that the individual either prefers one to the other, or he or she is indifferent between them.
2. Both the indifference and preference relations are transitive, i.e. if the individual prefers option A to option B and B to C, then he or she also prefers A to C.
3. Where a risky option has as one of its outcomes another risky option, the first risky option can be decomposed into its more basic alternatives.
4. If an individual is indifferent between two risky options, they are interchangeable in any compound option.
5. If two risky options involve the same two alternatives, then the option in which the more preferred outcome has a higher probability of occurring is itself preferred.
6. If option A is preferred to option B and option C then a lottery can be defined involving A and C which is indifferent to B.

Although Tversky (1967) questioned the descriptive validity of the utility approach to risk in decision-making if empirical evidence was available to support the decision, he nevertheless recognized that there was value in the approach. This value lay not only in the accuracy of the predictions it might make, but also in its capacity to represent a framework for the study of the behaviour of individuals in making choices.

More recently, Levy and Sarnat (1984) have been evaluating the modern theory of utility and they recognize that the axioms listed above logically precede the relevant utilities. In fact, the appropriate place for the statement of utilities is to be attached to the various options themselves. This helps to reflect the underlying preferences of the decision-makers. Hence, the order of events in the decision procedure first requires that the decision-maker subjectively assesses the individual utilities of the alternative outcomes to each option and then assesses the subjective probability of the occurrence of each outcome. This assessment will produce an expected utility for each alternative option, and the decision-maker will then select the option(s) most likely to maximize the expected utility. Although the absolute magnitude of the expected utilities from each option will vary according to the utility function used, the relative ranking of the options on the basis of maximum expected utility will remain the same irrespective of the utility function used.

This model provides a useful theoretical approach to resolving the problem of the relative ranking of alternative decisions in the cases of risk, but it leaves unresolved the issues of how to determine the subjective probabilities and the utility functions to be applied. Further, if the axioms outlined above had to be met literally, they would prove severely restrictive in real-world situations. The problem is that to describe a utility function in mathematical terms, we have to do three things:

- identify the variables;
- make assumptions about their probability distributions; and
- determine constraints.

Leaving aside the problems of identifying all the relevant variables and constraints, it is generally true that the more we have to make assumptions, the less valid the likely output from the model.

6.3.4 Individual utility profiles

Utility theory has also developed ideas for the assessment of individual utility profiles, i.e. to help characterize the preferences of individuals in decision-making situations. In general, individuals can be classified into three groups according to their utility towards risk, namely as:

- risk lovers;
- risk averters; and
- risk neutral individuals.

In conceptual terms, this classification provides a useful contribution to understanding decision-makers' behaviour when risks are involved and, to some extent, explains the apparently irrational behaviour of some risk-seeking decision-makers. But there are a number of difficulties in considering the application of such risk-utility profiles to the practical situation of strategic management. The first difficulty is that the main thrust of the profiles is limited to individual utilities and, in turn, this will be dependent upon each person's psychology. Although this will be useful when evaluating organizations where individuals have considerable management discretion (i.e. in the more autocratic and hierarchical organizations), it may be more difficult to conceive of group or organizational risk profiles, given that group or team decision-making is more prevalent in the strategic decision area. The basic problem lies in establishing the basis upon which to construct a profile of the group's utilities towards risk (section 7.4.1 for comments of the phenomenon of risky shift). Although it may be comparatively easy to assess the risk characteristics of the individual members of a group, it may not be so easy to identify the appropriate variables and their interactions upon which to assess the group's risk profile.

A further difficulty in the application of this concept is that even if these group profiles could be constructed, their use as a predictor of actual decision behaviour is likely to be severely constrained. The reason is that the risk attitudes of groups or individuals will vary according to:

- the detail of the decision situation faced;
- the current environment in which the decision is to be taken;
- the membership of the decision-making group; and
- the extent to which the individuals feel in control of the situation, i.e. if they have been successful in the past and this success is directly attributable to their special skills, they may feel more confident in risk-taking.

In the case of strategic management, where the decision situations are usually novel, and the managers are reacting to a more dynamic environment, it would be impossible to construct the necessary range of decision situations in advance to determine fully the utility profiles. In essence, the 'risk-utility' profile is not only a function of individual preferences at a given point in time, but is clearly influenced to a substantial degree by the parameters of the current decision situation, i.e. the situational factors tend to be more important than the individual's preferences.

The situation faced by the organization might threaten its survival. Managers might be stimulated to take great risks to save it or, caught like the proverbial rabbit in the lights of the on-rushing car, they may be paralysed into total inaction. Equally, if the organization has surplus assets, it may develop a more consciously risk-taking strategy. The feeling may be encouraged that they can afford to lose on one or two deals. This will be particularly likely if:

1. the managers do not think of themselves as gambling with their own resources, but speculating with the organization's assets; and
2. the resources used are new to the organization – a more conservative approach may be taken over traditional assets.

Alternatively, like GEC, the UK-based electrical engineering company it may sit with its cash mountain until the right opportunity materializes. Obviously, if resources were scarce, tight controls might lead to very conservative strategies.

In a discussion of the slightly more unusual phenomenon of worker co-operatives, Doucouliagos (1992) suggests that workers tend not to be entrepreneurial, i.e. there is an implication that they are risk averse. He explains this on the basis that, particularly when alternative employment opportunities are limited, workers tend to have more to lose than capital owners. For, should their own business fail, they will not only lose their jobs, but their own money (and often money they may have borrowed from friends). But this view may be overly simplistic. The running of conventional businesses is not risk-neutral. Markets may be volatile and it may be the failure of the conventional organization that spurs the otherwise redundant workers into action. Indeed, if workers set up a limited liability company, there is no real reason why they cannot be as entrepreneurial as the rest of the business world. Thus, just as limited liability encouraged the ordinary shareholder to be less risk averse in making investments, the ordinary worker, with some training and education, has exactly the same potential to make optimal business decisions as the 'ordinary director of any other company'. In fact, it would be highly patronizing to assert any other view and, with their own money at risk, they may be motivated to take greater care of the business than a director who feels that there is nothing more than reputation at stake.

6.3.5 State preference theory

This approach to investment decisions is based on the assumption that the assessment of alternative investment options will be influenced by the consumption opportunities in alternative states of the world or the economic environment, i.e. prosperity and growth in the market will offer rather different investment opportunities from recession and depression. Hence, the utility of return in one state of the economy may generate greater utility than the same return in another possible state. For example, the utility value of £1 in a forecast state of depression may yield a higher utility than £1 in a state of forecast growth and prosperity.

6.3.6 Mean variance criterion

This model of the treatment of risk in decision-making highlights the prospective variability of the potential returns from an investment alternative. The degree of risk involved in an alternative is directly related to the degree of variability of the alternative outcomes to a given situation in relation to the mean return for that situation. Hence, high variability of returns equates to high risk, and low variability equates to low risk. The development and evaluation of this criterion in the area of financial decisions is undertaken in the following section.

6.3.7 Classifying the models

This listing of the various normative models should illustrate the extensiveness of the search for models to describe and explain the way in which decision-makers handle risk in the real world. Although, the descriptive quality of each of these models may be insufficient to aid decision-makers in practical strategic decisions, they cumulatively highlight a number of the key issues in the risk analysis situation in practice. The parameters that most influence the perception and assessment of risk include:

- the absolute size of the potential returns or losses achievable in each decision situation;
- the need to strike a balance between the possible returns or losses and the likelihood of their occurrence;

- the inherent utility in the identified alternative options;
- a desire to seek a relative ranking of the potential alternatives;
- the decision-makers' desire to seek the maximum possible benefit (utility) within the risk constraints;
- the attitude of each decision-maker towards risk may vary;
- the value of prospective returns from an investment will be influenced by changes in the forecast environment;
- the wider the projected variations in alternative returns from a given investment the greater will be the risk perceived by the decision-maker.

Libby and Fishburn (1977) developed a classification scheme for such models based on two dichotomies:

1. parametric versus expected utility models; and
2. partial order (or dominance) models versus weak-order models.

6.3.8 Parametric and utility models

These are based on the returns distribution and the associated moments, e.g. variance and skewness. *Utility models* are based on a comparison of the expected utility between alternative distributions of returns. Libby and Fishburn (1977) recognized that there may be certain parametric models which are equivalent to expected utility models, and that the two groups are not, therefore, mutually exclusive. We would not deny that the expected utility models may be a good descriptive basis upon which to evaluate certain individual decisions in investment contexts, but we would suggest that these may be equally appraised in simpler models which are based on just a few key parameters. As Libby and Fishburn (1977) stated:

> Despite the fact that the expected utility model may be a good descriptive model for some individuals' decisions in investment contexts, many investigators have hypothesised that it may be possible to describe such decisions more simply in terms of a few parameters of the distributions, rather than in terms of a general utility function. A number of parametric models that attempt to capture the salient features of risky decision making have been developed. These models provide relatively simple descriptions of behaviour that are computationally efficient, readily measurable, and can be easily communicated to others. For these reasons, the parametric models have been the target of much of the behavioural research . . . (p. 275)

They also questioned the potential application of those models of a utility type to practical situations. The major problem lies in each decision-maker's need to define and measure utility in a practical environment. The manner of definition and measurement would have to meet the constraints imposed on these models and it is likely that they would become unrealistically limited.

6.3.9 Partial and weak order models

Libby and Fishburn further classified the range of models into the two groupings of partial order models and weak order models. *Partial order* or dominance models are based on the proposition that the user can:

- identify one alternative solution as 'better than' others for achieving a given objective or meeting an express criterion; and
- provide a ranking of preferences across the available alternatives.

However, difficulties may be encountered where there are a number of unresolved or residual alternatives which are not clearly dominated by one solution. This might arise in those cases:

- where the decision-makers perceive the value(s) arising from each alternative either to be equal or not to be sufficiently different so that they are indifferent as to which outcome actually occurs; or
- where the value(s) arising from each alternative are counter-balanced by other factors in the objective function, i.e. there may be a counter-balance between the size of possible returns and the variance of the returns to which the decision-maker is indifferent.

Decision-makers using the *weak order* models divide the distribution into indifference classes where all the achievable outcomes are ordered from best to worse according to the criteria identified as relevant to the particular decision to be taken. These criteria will be set by reference to the decision-maker's preferences or utility. A comparative example of the application of partial order and weak order models is given in Table 6.1.

In the case of both the partial order models and the weak order models, the following preferences would hold:

$$A \text{ preferred to } B \text{ as} \quad \text{mean}_A > \text{mean}_B$$
$$\text{and} \quad \text{variance}_A < \text{variance}_B$$

$$A \text{ preferred to } C \text{ as} \quad \text{mean}_A > \text{mean}_C$$
$$\text{and} \quad \text{variance}_A < \text{variance}_C$$

Hence, both models would determine that investment A dominates both investments B and C. However, the balancing of factors to produce a preference between investments B and C is less clear. So it may be seen that although the mean return on B is greater than that on C, the variance of potential returns on C is lower than that on B. Unfortunately, the partial order model approach is unable to resolve a problem of this type, i.e. where the parameters are in conflict and do not suggest a clear preference. The weak order model approach would attempt to resolve the problem by direct reference to the decision-maker's own utilities and preferences. The aim would be to compensate between the objective parameters in the model so that subjectively higher preferences in one

Table 6.1 Weak order model

Decision parameters	Alternative investments		
	A	B	C
Returns (mean: £million)	2.0	1.5	1.0
Variance (standard dev.)	1.0	1.6	1.2

Table 6.2 Parametric weak order model

	Models not accounting for individual differences	Models accounting for individual differences
Single parameter	Max. expected return Min. loss probability	Max. probability of target return
Multiple parameter Compensatory	—	Trade-offs related to: mean-variance mean-semivariance mean loss probability mean-confidence limit mean-target semi-variance mean-probability of below target return
Non-compensatory	Ruin probability – Mean lexicographic other lexicographic	Constrained expected return maximization

parameter may offset small inverted preferences in the other. This is achieved by a two stage process, i.e. through:

1. the construction of individual utility preferences for pairs of parameters; and
2. determining the trade-off curves between pairs of parameters with the same utility values.

If we apply this to the above example, it might be found that the decision-maker's utility for return and variance on investment *B* were the same as the utility for the return and variance on investment *C*. In such an event, the decision-maker would be indifferent between the two investments. But if the utility from the pair of parameters on *B* appeared to exceed that derived from *C*, then the decision-maker would prefer investment *B*.

Libby and Fishburn (1977) have produced a classification of the existing parametric weak order models of risk by evaluating whether or not they allow for individual differences, and the extent to which they are compensatory as shown in Table 6.2.

Although the single parameter models may be the simplest to use in the choice situation, they are considered to be inadequate in terms of their descriptive power, i.e. they fail to reflect the multiple concerns that may face the decision-maker in a practical decision-making situation. The multiple parameter models have, therefore, received most attention and more researchers have attempted their development. A review of the parameters used to assess risk in the models identified in Table 6.2, would result in their classification into three distinct groups as follows:

(a) Variability of returns

A number of models utilize the variability of potential returns from an investment as the basic parameter of risk. The specific measures used to measure variability include:

- variance of returns;
- standard deviation of returns;
- mean semi-variance of returns; and
- mean confidence limit.

(b) Variability of incurring losses

By reflecting a concern with the possibility of a negative outcome to an investment, this measurement of the possibility of incurring losses reflects a different and, perhaps, more realistic angle to the measurement of risk. The measures used in this context include variability measures and the concept of probabilities:

- mean semi-variance of returns;
- mean probability of loss;
- probability of ruinous loss; and
- minimum loss probability.

(c) Achievement of target returns

This third group of measures is concerned with the measurement of the probability or chances of achieving predetermined returns as the main basis of the risk parameter and includes:

- maximum probability of target returns;
- mean-target semi-variance of returns; and
- mean probability of below target returns.

The essence of the conclusion that emerges when risk measures are related to variability of return is that the wider the distribution of potential returns then the greater the risk faced. This was the basic assumption underlying much of the early work in this area (e.g. by Keynes, 1937), although other authors suggested that the third moment of the returns distribution (i.e. assymetry or skewness) may also have an impact on the level of risk (e.g. Hicks, 1946). The second group, which reflects the emphasis on losses, would support the view that risk perception is more concerned with the lower end of the returns distribution and the chances of incurring losses rather than with the broader assessment of the whole distribution. The third group switches the emphasis towards an assessment of the chances of achieving target returns as the basic measure of risk, although the target may be determined as a minimum or maximum target level of achievement. The minimum level of achievement in this context could be taken as the zero profit level and would, therefore, reflect the avoidance of loss group referred to above.

In judging the descriptive power of these models in relation to practical decision-making, it has to be recognized that the use of dual parameter variables could produce models which are both computationally efficient, and capable of quantification and measurement. Their identification of risk in terms of the spread of the distribution of returns, the assymetry of this distribution, and the chances of achieving below target returns or losses, together with the acceptance of a mechanism for decision-makers to trade-off returns against risks from a potential investment, provide a partial description of the risk analysis process in practice. The deficiencies of such models lie in:

- their narrow definition of the factors influencing risk;
- the assumption that decision-makers are necessarily rational; and
- the assumption that all decisions are influenced by the desire to minimize risk.

The range of factors influencing risk perceptions in strategic decisions are developed later in section 7.1. The clear indication that emerges is that there are a number of variables which may be considered to have a power of influence, and that many of them could not be measured in terms of the variability of returns. Indeed, the factors affecting the selection of alternative strategies may be highly subjective and are therefore unlikely to be rational in a purely economic/financial sense of the word. We should draw the conclusion that the potential returns and risks involved in an investment are only two of a number of potential influencing factors. While we cannot deny that risk will always be an important consideration in strategy selection, it is conceivable that many strategies implemented will not be those that would minimize risk even assuming that the decision-maker had assessed the risks in advance.

Generally, Cohen and Christensen (1970) have been critical of these pure risk models for their failure to incorporate individual attributes such as skill, judgement and the degree of interest in the decision situation and outcomes. They further questioned the value of such models, suggesting that

> if the idea of 'rationality' is to have any place at all it must be limited to a series of repeatable decisions, so that the reward is maximized in the long run. A decision based on average results in the long run must be distinguished from a decision which has to be made once only, a distinction which points to a weakness of the Expected Value models. . . . Many businessmen and even economists now recognize that 'one shot' decisions in practical life cannot reasonably be made on the same basis as decisions which relate to a series of repeatable occasions. The expected average pay-off is not a 'rational' guide for a 'one-shot' decision. (p. 85)

Given the nature of strategic decisions as essentially 'one-shot' and 'non-rational', the models as developed would appear to provide no significant contribution to either understanding or aiding such decisions.

6.4 RISK IN ECONOMIC AND FINANCIAL THEORY

In the context of financial theory, we find that the concept of 'risk' has been defined in broad terms as the variability of returns generated by an investment. For example, Levy and Sarnat (1984) use the term 'risk' to describe an option whose return is not known with absolute certainty, but for which an array of alternative returns and their probabilities are known; in other words, for which the distribution of returns is known. The distribution may have been estimated on the basis of objective (either a priori or a posteriori) probabilities, or on the basis of purely subjective probabilities.

Given our distinction between uncertainty and risk in section 5.1.2, it strikes an odd note to return to the proposition that uncertainty should be seen as an extreme case of risk in which

the possible range of returns is known but the probabilities of occurrence for each alternative is not.

Further, in the final sentence of the first passage quoted above, they assert the existence of a process whereby uncertainties can be converted into risks by introducing subjective probabilities. Following their logic leads to the conclusion that since probability beliefs in the area of financial investment are almost invariably subjective, the concepts of risk and uncertainty may be treated as interchangeable.

When Salter and Weinhold (1979) were developing a risk/return model that could be related to the phenomenon of business diversification, they defined risk as

the variability of returns or – in more precise, statistical terms – as the dispersion of negative and positive deviations from an expected return. This dispersion of returns can most usefully be thought of as a probability distribution . . . (p. 85)

In addition to a definition of risk that stresses the variability of returns, financial theory also recognizes a strong correlation between the level of risk or degree of variability, and the rate of return. As Salter and Weinhold (1979) indicated in their model:

The returns of a particular security is the compensation to investors of bearing its risk; the greater the risk, the greater the required return. (p. 84)

Following this proposition would lead us to anticipate a strong correlation between the level of risk and the rate of return on a security. By way of example, let us compare the low risk investment in a government bond with a high risk investment in the ordinary shares issued by a newly quoted company on the Stock Exchange. We should expect that, in the former, the potential variability of return is likely to be low, whereas ordinary shares will usually be securities with a potentially high degree of variability of returns. The essential feature of this perception of risk is that it deals directly with the variability of future returns from an investment.

6.4.1 The problem in linking risk to investments

There is a fundamental problem with any definition of risk which is related to the variability of returns from an investment. Because of the nature and structure of formal investments, there is a further implied element to be reconciled with the definition of risk which either:

- incorporates a test to determine the actual level of uncertainty as to the value of the potential returns (if any) to be derived from the investment, e.g. from ordinary shares in companies affected by a recession; or
- assumes the absence of uncertainty through a system of fixed dividends or returns within predefined limits, e.g. in government bonds, building society or similar investment accounts, preference shares etc.

Within the framework of financial theory and its associated models it is quite usual to assume perfect certainty as to the future returns achievable from an investment, in the sense that it is a given parameter in the model. For example, portfolio theory develops from the assumption that the future returns from a range of alternative investments are known or given parameters, and seeks to develop normative proposals as to how the risks associated with these alternatives may be combined to satisfy the individual risk/return or utility functions of potential investors. Thus, if an investor was seeking to minimize total risk, he or she would seek a portfolio of securities with a low degree of variability in aggregate returns. But an investor willing to accept a high level of risk would select a portfolio of securities providing a potentially high degree of variability in aggregate returns. As compensation for accepting this increased risk or higher level of variability, the investor would also anticipate a higher aggregate return.

6.4.2 The capital asset pricing model

The capital asset pricing model (CAPM), developed from portfolio theory, distinguishes two types of risk within the total risk inherent in a business's securities, namely:

- *Systematic risk* This is the degree of variability of returns in a particular security relative to the average degree of variability of returns in all securities in the market. This element of total risk, which is normally termed the Beta value, measures the variability of returns due to the common denominator factors which influence all securities on the market, e.g. interest rates or inflation rates.

- *Unsystematic risk* This is the degree of variability of returns in a particular security which cannot be explained by the 'normal' factors which influence all the securities in the market. As such, this reflects factors which are peculiar to a particular company and therefore affect only the degree of variability of its returns, e.g. that there may be an industrial dispute in a particular company or that a hostile takeover battle may have resulted in the acquisition of a company with a poison pill.

Total Risk = Systematic Risk + Unsystematic Risk

or

Total Variance = Market Related + Company Specific
of Returns   Variance   Variance

The hypothesis upon which CAPM is based is that it is the level of systematic risk which is of importance to the potential investor. The investor will therefore attempt to match this risk or the market-related variability in potential returns with the expected return from the security. So if the new security appears to offer the potential investor either a lower level of systematic risk for the same expected return that he or she is currently receiving from the portfolio or, alternatively, offers a higher expected return for the same level of systematic risk, then the investor would increase his or her utility by investing in that security. If, however, the proposed security offers either higher systematic risk without the compensatory increase in returns, or lower expected returns without the compensatory reduction in systematic risk, then it will prove unattractive to potential investors.

The CAPM usually expresses the expected return from a security as follows:

$$E(R_i) = E(R_f) + B_i (E(R_m) - E(R_f))$$

where:

$E(R_i)$ = expected return from security
$E(R_f)$ = expected return from risk-free securities
$E(R_m)$ = expected return from a portfolio comprising all securities in the market
B_i = securities systematic risk

The Beta value (B_i) expresses the level of systematic risk for a company's security relative to the level of risk for all other securities in the market. Although we have chosen to show a single period model, there is no reason in principle why this could not be extended to a multi-period model in which the Beta value would measure the future degree of variability of returns relative to market returns over a number of years. In this respect, the Beta value would be a measurement not only of risk *per se*, but also of the uncertainty surrounding future returns for the company security and for the securities in the market as a whole.

6.4.3 The problems in calculating reliable Beta values

In theory, the problems associated with multi-dimensional forecasting are usually eliminated, in part, by the proposal that the Beta values for a security may be 'appropriately' based on historical data. The justification for this proposal is that systematic risk or the relative variability of a company's returns varies only slowly over time. However, the empirical evidence on the stability of the Beta values for a security over time suggest that they are relatively unstable. Levy and Sarnat (1984), for example, state that

most betas change over time, which makes the calculation with past data almost useless for future investment decision making.

Blume (1975) also found instability but detected a tendency for Beta values to regress towards unity or the market average. The suggested reasoning for this tendency is that organizations with above average risk (Betas > 1) will seek to reduce the riskiness of their operations and hence reduce their Beta value towards 1. Conversely, we are to presume that organizations with below average risk (Betas < 1) would seek to increase the riskiness of their operations and hence increase their Beta value towards 1. While there may be intuitive grounds for supporting the proposition that any organization may aim to reduce the riskiness associated with their operations, there would appear to be less intuitive support for the converse view that commercial organizations that have operated successfully in the past will wish to increase the riskiness of their operations in the future. However, if it is clearly recognized that,

1. risk in this context is essentially an expression of the variability of the accounting returns; and
2. that high risk is equivalent to above-average variability in the firm's returns across a number of periods, and
3. that low risk equates to below-average variability,

then it is possible to understand the intuitive logic for a regression of Beta values towards unity.

In the context of the CAPM, it should therefore be evident that the concept of risk is directly related to the earnings stability of the company and its securities. A company which produces a relatively stable earnings flow (including dividends and capital gains), though not necessarily above average in terms of size, will achieve a low Beta value, whereas relatively unstable earnings flows will be accorded a high Beta value. Salter and Weinhold (1979) emphasize this effect and its contradiction with strategic logic as

> given a business opportunity producing a cash flow, the risk/return model emphasizes that market value will be affected by managing systematic risk rather than unsystematic, or company specific risks. Ironically, managers spend most of their efforts on these very real company specific risks. Managers do this because company specific risks (such as competitive retaliation, labor relations, or even bankruptcy) are both obvious and immediate, as well as being potentially disastrous to personal and organizational welfare. The risk/return model argues, however, that management strategies that lead to either stabilized cash flows relative to the level of the economy, growth in free cash flow, or improved investor confidence about future cash flows will tend to lead to reduced systematic risk and increased market value for the firm. (p. 106)

Kudla (1981) was unable to establish any link between the strategic planning activities of organizations and their level of systematic risk. Naturally, the ability of any organization to affect systematic risks will be a function of their dominance within the market. Most commercial organizations are relatively small in their operations and so are unable to have any real effect on their environment. If a particular organization has achieved real power, it may be able to affect the pattern of trade within the market place as a whole. The problem for such large organizations is that the obvious use of what amounts to monopoly power may be unlawful. But Kudla did identify a reduction in the levels of unsystematic risk as a result of strategic planning. It is therefore reasonable to conclude that organizations will be able to have an impact on factors specific to their own activities. In more general terms, he also questioned the effectiveness of the communication channels between each business and their investors, both large and small, and challenged assumptions that a single organization can influence the responsiveness of the market to changes in systematic risk. Thus, if changes in interest rates might lead an organization to desire a restructuring of its level of debt, it might not be able to go to the market to ask for further funds without undermining investor confidence in the short-term. Discussing restructuring proposals with only one or two sources of finance might place a strain on relationships where the level of exposure is already high, i.e. if management go only to the banks who have lent the most money, this may provoke those banks into less desirable responses.

In reviewing the operation of the CAPM, it is interesting to note that the scale of the absolute profits or losses of a business is omitted from the model. The model is structured so that it measures risk on the basis of profits and losses relative to the market average (i.e. systematic risk), and any further variability in returns which cannot be related to market trends are treated as unsystematic risk associated with the particular business. This emphasis on 'relative' risk contains an implicit assumption that high profits and losses in absolute terms must engender high risks for the business and its investors. While there may be an intuitive link between high absolute losses and high risks, there would appear to be less intuitive or practical logic for assuming that high absolute profits must involve high risks. We think it likely that if a decision-maker begins to forecast increasingly high absolute, as opposed to relative, losses he or she will perceive higher risks. Conversely, if increasingly high absolute, as opposed to relative, profits are forecast, the decision-maker should tend to perceive lower risks, unless the manner of business operation gives specific cause for concern.

The justification offered by the proponents of CAPM for this stress on the importance of systematic risk as opposed to unsystematic risk is that the latter can be avoided by the investor through the process of diversification, i.e. the investor moves the pattern of investment away from securities which are affected by unsystematic risk and towards those securities which will provide the same return but contain only systematic risk. Naturally, the investor is unable to diversify his or her portfolio to avoid systematic risk because those risks are the risks faced by all the securities in the market. This behaviour in excluding securities affected by unsystematic risk from a portfolio is usually offered as an example of rationality in decision-making and of self-interest in retaining employment. As Brealey (1983) pointed out in his review of portfolio theory,

> the (portfolio) manager should not expect to be compensated for the risk that can be diversified away. The only risk that he gets paid for taking is the kind that stems from broad market movements. (p. 165)

Salter and Weinhold (1979) have suggested that there are a number of possible strategies open to management if they wish to influence the level of systematic risk. These include the following:

1. Undertaking strategies aimed at producing related diversification. This attempts to reduce the variability of the organization's cash flows as a result of increasing the size of the operating margins relative to fixed costs of the business. In the language of the product market portfolio model, this is likely to occurs in two situations, i.e.

   (a) when a company becomes a low cost producer; and/or
   (b) the dominant competitor within a market as a result of the combined effects of the experience curve and increased sales growth and market share.

2. More effective asset selection and management by a diversified organization, which will generate either a faster growing or a more stable free cash flow than available in a comparable portfolio of independent businesses.

3. Increased diversification enabling management to include some individual businesses in the portfolio which have high unsystematic risks attached to them but which have, or lead to, low systematic risk. Less diversified companies may be unwilling to employ such strategies because of the potential high organizational and financial costs accompanying them.

If we move away from proposals which seek to improve the organization's exposure to systematic risks through the process of diversification, there are some clear steps that managers in the non-diversified organization can take to control or reduce systematic risk. The aim must be to take decisions that result in increased stability of profits or cash flows relative to the market average, thereby achieving a reduction in systematic risk. For example, the following would all assist in reducing systematic risk in the short- to medium-term:

- concentrating on existing product/market niches;
- improving or maintaining market share in existing markets;
- improving efficiency and concentrating on cost reduction activities; and
- avoiding excessive diversification (particularly into unrelated business activities).

The basic threat to the effectiveness of these non-diversification strategies in reducing systematic risk lies in the longer term. If the organization focuses tightly on a limited product or market area, it becomes more vulnerable if that area is subject to prejudicially fundamental changes.

Thus, niches in markets are sometimes eradicated by changes in technology or business practices, competitors may be stimulated into price wars if market share increases are perceived as threatening etc.

A further weakness in the CAPM is its failure to address the interactive nature of the relationship between systematic and unsystematic risk. Although the CAPM emphasizes the importance of systematic risk and, by implication, directs the strategies of the organization towards reducing those risks at least in line with the general market trends, no explicit recognition is given for the role that the reduction of unsystematic risk can play in reducing systematic risk. If unsystematic risk is defined as those risks which are specific to a particular organization and not reflected in the risks facing the industry or market as a whole, then examples of this type of risk would include:

- changes in the demand for a specific organization's products or services;
- the impact of competitors' practices on a specific aspect of business operations;
- operational problems or dislocations such as labour disputes specific to an organization; and
- difficulties encountered with organizational structures, processes, systems, or key personnel.

Strategies which address issues such as these and which would, if effective, reduce the company-specific or unsystematic risk, are also likely to influence the stability of the cash flows/profits relative to the market, i.e. reduce the level of systematic risk. The clear distinction between systematic and unsystematic risk which is made in the normative model of the CAPM breaks down in the practical world of strategic decision-making. Strategies which may appear to be directed towards reducing systematic risk are also likely to alter the level of unsystematic risk, and vice versa. Consequently, the day-to-day reality of decision-making is concerned with both types of risk but, for most practical purposes, decision-makers do not differentiate between the two types whether in analysing business situations or in developing and formulating appropriate strategies.

6.5 KEY VARIABLES INFLUENCING RISK

The earlier sections in this chapter have begun the process of examining the models developed within the field of economics and financial theory. We have established that these models may provide a computationally efficient approach because the dual variables commonly used are capable of measurement. But the effect is unsatisfactory and artificial because the use of the distribution of returns as a proxy for the concept of risk provides a somewhat constrained definition of the risks faced in strategic decisions. This section reviews further models of risk which seek to broaden the definition of risks actually faced by decision-makers. These models seek to establish the key variables that influence risk.

Bettis (1982) developed a model which links an organization's performance to strategic decisions, industry structure characteristics and risk.

$$performance = f(IC, S, R)$$

where IC = industry characteristics
S = strategy
R = risk

He further postulated that risk is essentially an endogenous variable because strategic managers tend to assume, both explicitly and implicitly, that risk is a variable that can be managed. For example, typical risk-reducing strategies might include diversification, participating in joint ventures, and entering into insurance or other similar loss avoiding agreements. His model indicates that the nature of risk is itself primarily dependent on the industry characteristics and the strategy pursued.

Bettis and Hall (1982) and Bowman (1980) also support this view of risk as an essentially endogenous variable and argue that a well-devised strategy could simultaneously reduce risks and increase returns. Overall, the theme of the argument on risk reduction is mainly related to the ability of the organization to reduce the variability of the returns generated. The simplified model of risk presented by Bettis (1982) is:

$$RISK = f(IC, S)$$

where IC = industry characteristics
S = strategy developed

This model was further elaborated in terms of both risk itself and the influence of risk on the performance of an organization, as follows:

1. *Performance*

$$ROA = b_{10} + b_{11}(ADV) + b_{12}(RISK) + b_{13}(LACAP) + b_{14}(RD)(RL) + b_{15}(RD)(RC)$$

where:

ROA	= return on assets (net income after tax/total assets)
ADV	= advertising expenditure (advertising expenditure/sales)
$RISK$	= risk (see following equation)
$LACAP$	= plant investment (net plant/employees)
RD	= R & D expenditure/sales
RL	= diversification strategy – into related/linked product/markets
RC	= diversification strategy – into related/constrained product/markets.

2.   *Risk*

$$RISK = b_{21} + b_{22}(LACAP) + b_{23}(RL) + b_{24}(RC)$$

where *LACAP*, *RL* and *RC* are as defined above.

The model specified in the above equations identifies performance as a function of the industry characteristics, strategy and risk, while risk itself is a function of the industry characteristics and strategy.

Examples of industry characteristics at large would include factors such as the level of concentration in the market and the size of barriers to entry. Within the organization, Bettis selected the relative scale of advertising (to sales), research and development (to sales) and capital investment (per employee) as the primary measures of the characteristics of an industry. The various types of strategy were differentiated on the extent to which any new product or market area was related to the organization's existing products or market areas. This classification of strategy was based on the typology developed by Rumelt (1974) in his study of the strategy, structure and economic performance of large American industrial corporations. Rumelt classified the diversification strategies adopted by organizations into four groups:

- *single business* –   organizations committed to a single business;

- *dominant business* –   organizations relying primarily on revenues from a single business;

- *related business* –   diversified organizations in which the diversification undertaken is related to existing activities;

- *unrelated business* –   diversified organizations in which the diversification undertaken is not related to new businesses or existing activities.

Within the *related* classification, Rumelt further identified two subgroups, *related-constrained* (*RC*) and *related-linked* (*RL*). The related-constrained organization is typified by a diversification strategy which primarily relates all new activities to a specific central skill or resource already possessed by the organization. For example, an organization with skills in precision engineering would seek to develop other products and/or markets around this particular skill. The related-linked organization is typified by those organizations whose diversification is linked to some specific strength or skill already possessed, but not always constrained or limited to the same skill or strength. For example, an organization whose primary activity lies in the manufacture of consumer durables, may diversify into retailing on the basis of marketing and sales skills, or offer computer software services on the basis of its existing organizational expertise in this field. Related-linked and unrelated diversification are distinguished on the basis that the latter gives rise to an entirely novel activity which does not develop from any existing skill or strength of the organization. Rumelt's research established that only a small percentage of organizations fitted the unrelated or conglomerate category of diversification. Perhaps because of this finding, Bettis's models exclude reference to the unrelated diversification strategy option, even though this is likely to present the highest risk alternative in most strategic decision situations.

The nature of the strategic thrust adopted by the organization is viewed by Bettis as a determinant of organizational performance and will affect the level of risk. As to risk itself, Bettis (1982) sees it as a function of the relative scale of capital investment undertaken representing the industry characteristic together with the type of diversification strategy pursued into either related-linked or related-constrained product/market areas.

In a further use of Rumelt's diversification strategy classification, Bettis (1981) employs regression analysis methods to analyse the performance differences between related and unrelated diversified organizations. His results indicate a significant positive association between risk, measured as the standard deviation on the return on total assets, and return for large diversified organizations. However, he recognizes that these results when compared with the results of similar studies on risk/return relationships lead to an ambiguous situation in which,

> no clear pattern has evolved for explaining the relationship between risk and return at the level of accounting data. (p. 391)

Bowman (1980), like Bettis, recognized that corporate strategy is a means of altering both risk and return. Bettis (1981) recognized that risk and performance are both a function of industry structure and conduct, and proposed a simultaneous equation approach to jointly modelling risk and return. The model developed for this approach has been outlined above and using the sample of 58 large diversified firms from his 1981 study Bettis (1982) found that:

1. using ordinary least squares regression methods on the single equation model for return on assets produces a marked positive relationship between risk and return with a relatively low standard error;
2. using two-stage least squares regression methods on the simultaneous equation model for return on assets produces a small negative relationship between risk and return, though the standard error in this case was large.

Rumelt (1974) suggested that the major risks perceived by organizations were less concerned with short- to medium-term variability of returns, and more concerned with fundamental changes in the product life-cycle, industry trade cycles and economic cycles. He commented that

> the risks associated with product life-cycles, rather than with variability per se, provide the primary motive for diversification, and are those from which diversification can provide the most important relief. (p. 158)

Thus, we may conclude that secular shifts in demand due to product obsolescence, changes in technology and industry-wide patterns of demand/supply are the major sources of risk that organizations seek to address and resolve through corporate strategy. These primary risk parameters which relate to the industry characteristics are essentially exogenous. But while the risks associated with the strategic responses made by each organization and the scale of investments are influenced by such exogenous factors, they may actually be considered as primarily endogenous. By this we mean that even though the aim may be to have some effect upon matters outside the organization, managers actually take decisions over matters within their control and the risks related to these decisions will always be specific to the organization taking them.

QUESTIONS

1. Try and write down a simple, yet satisfactory, definition of the concept of risk.
2. Write down a list of five of the major hazards and threats that would face the modern commercial organization and then see whether you can identify risk management or reduction strategies that would be reasonably cost-effective.
3. To what extent do you feel that the various models of risk presented in this chapter add to our understanding of the concept of risk itself?
4. Can you think of any circumstances in which the returns generated from an ordinary business decision can be estimated with the same degree of accuracy as from the investment of funds in a fixed or variable interest account?
5. Formulate a simple pair of definitions and some examples of systematic and unsystematic risks.

A more detailed view of risk | 7

INTRODUCTION

We now return to two issues of fundamental importance to the long-term commercial well-being of all organizations, namely,

- what steps or processes should an organization go through to enable it to form a reasonably realistic view of the risks that it faces; and
- what information will enable it to gain an understanding of the nature of the problems and the possible means of their resolution.

As we have seen, strategies must not only be devised; the most likely to succeed must then be implemented. The process of strategy formulation depends upon the ability of the decision-makers to measure and/or estimate the scale of the danger, while strategy selection depends upon the willingness of individuals to accept different levels of risk. Although we would always hope that managers would be prepared to take responsibility for their decisions, no matter what the risks, many managers are reluctant to take risks. This risk aversion may be maintained even though the objective evidence in their hands may favour the taking of that more risky decision. This sad fact of life will then lead us on to a more detailed assessment of the actual framework within which an organization will take strategic decisions.

7.1 RISK PERCEPTION WITHIN THE ORGANIZATION

In analysing the nature of the risks inherent in all decision-making situations, Cohen (1972) suggested that the following elements would be present:

- *Intrinsic risk* This is the sum product of all the *de facto* dangers,

  - which are inherent in each decision situation, and
  - which will make a real contribution to the decision consequences; and

- *Extrinsic risk* This represents the decision-maker's own view of the intrinsic risk, i.e. it arises from the processes of identifying and interpreting the available evidence.

The scope and effect of the intrinsic risk will always be a matter of objective reality. For these purposes, there are a number of irrelevancies, i.e. it does not matter:

- how the facts may be ascertained and perceived; nor
- who may be involved in the observation process; nor
- what the time-scale of the observation may be (in fact, the full extent of the risk may only become apparent a long time after the events);

ultimately the intrinsic risk is capable of being described empirically. On the other hand, a number of extrinsic risks may arise, i.e. a different version of reality may emerge from each individual's subjective perceptions of reality. It is a paradox that people may watch the world but not see the world as it really is. Because of their different backgrounds and motivations, and whether consciously or not, each person may give a different emphasis to what they identify as important in the mass of available data. Thus, when two different decision-makers independently consider the same situation, various outcomes are possible:

- they may both identify all the risk factors that are relevant to the immediate decision, i.e. they may both fully comprehend the intrinsic risks (a possible, but unlikely, outcome); or
- because of differences in their interpretation of the data, they may both fail to identify the complete set of risk factors in the situation and therefore:
  - they may each identify completely different sets of risk factors; or
  - they may both identify the same risk factors; or
  - some of the factors identified will be the same and the others will be different.

Both of the decision-makers will have characteristics that will affect their ability to identify the risk factors and contribute to the production of this differentiation (section 3.1.1). These factors include:

- the availability of information to each person given their status and position within the organization – sometimes it may be a feature of the communication system that different decision-makers are presented with completely different views of the data collected by the organization, or it may be more subjective, e.g. one decision-maker is less approachable socially whereas the other regularly meets fellow employees in social contexts and picks up a lot of information not available to the other;
- the way in which the information is framed or communicated may create ambiguity and/or a sense of imprecision about the elements of the situation in which the decision is required – there are a variety of possible reasons for this type of distortion (sections 2.3.3, 2.6.2 and 3.2), including:
  - the incompetence of those searching for the data or communicating the results of their searches;
  - the oversimplification of the complexity of the situation; and

- a conflict of interests between those defining information needs and those actually searching for the data;

- the extent or lack of each person's accumulated knowledge and experience may cause significant differences in each decision-maker's perceptions of the scale or importance of each element of information; hence, one decision-maker may be new to this type of situation and have a very different view to that held by another who has had favourable outcomes in similar decision situations.

Following upon this last point, Cohen and Christensen (1970) have also proposed that in addition to the differences in risk perception that may occur between different individuals, it is likely that the individual's perception of risk and willingness to take risks may vary between situations (sections 2.4 and 6.3.4). They begin by distinguishing between the characteristics of *stability* and *constancy* that managers may demonstrate when deciding whether to take risks:

1. The use of the word stability suggests that, even though the environment may change, the individual's risk perception and risk acceptance would remain the same for similar decision situations. Thus, if a sales manager changes employment from an organization distributing clothing to an organization selling electrical goods, that manager is likely to use the same basic selling strategies even though the nature of the product may change.
2. Constancy refers to similar risk perception and risk acceptance in different kinds of decision situation. Thus, a production manager may take decisions on whether to implement a new process where there may be cost economies but some elements of risk to the employees and, in later years as a director, apply the same approach to deciding whether to diversify the product range.

However, if people change the nature of their roles or if there are changes in the external environment that they must relate to, they may react by changing their perceptions of risks or their willingness to take risks. Hence, as in (2.) above, when managers are promoted to posts of increasing seniority in an organization, they may gain access to much information previously kept confidential. Their new view of available information may lead to a complete re-evaluation of their prior perceptions of the risks run by the organization. Indeed, this reappraisal may be forced upon them by new responsibilities. Similarly, although qualities of predictability may be useful in some decision-making situations, more dynamic qualities may be required to take advantage of sometimes fluid market opportunities. At an operational level, managers may be valued because of their ability to implement the decisions of others. To make the transition to higher levels within the organization, the same dependable managers must begin to show initiative and, perhaps, flair if the organization is to develop the requisite qualities of responsiveness and creativity in fast moving market conditions where the risks are greater.

7.1.1 Risk perceptions and acceptability

One of the key factors in setting the level of risk considered acceptable (see Chapter 4) was identified by Choffray and Johnsonn (1979) who developed a model of individual decision-maker's risk perceptions. This model is based on two elements:

1. The likelihood of undesirable consequences occurring – this was considered to be a function of two broad variables:

   - product economic factors which relate to the cost-effectiveness and/or the profitability of the product or service; and
   - product performance factors which relate to the reliability and dependability of the product or service (factors that, today, we would consider part of a test of quality).

2. The intensity with which these undesirable consequences are likely to be felt both at the individual and the organizational level. As with the definition of extrinsic risk given in section 7.1, this was considered to be a function of each individual's perceptions of the consequences of the decision both at the organizational and the individual level. Naturally, these consequences were themselves considered to be dependent on the product economic and product performance factors outlined above.

This research aimed to analyse the risk perceptions of both individuals and groups who were responsible for making industrial buying decisions. In each case, the decision was which of three types of industrial air-conditioning systems to buy. The conclusions are derived from questionnaire reponses from 120 managers and engineers. Their findings confirmed their two initial propositions, namely:

1. that there would be significant differences of risk perception between the individuals participating in the study; and
2. that each of the factual elements comprising the risk would have a different potential for impact depending on whether the individuals were acting on their own or in groups.

Thus, it was evident that the product performance factors had a greater impact on individuals who were placed lower in the organization's management hierarchy, and that product economic factors became increasingly important as the individual's level in the hierarchy rose. These findings tend to support our more general view that differences in each individual's risk perceptions will arise from differences in:

- their educational and functional background;
- their present position in the decision-making hierarchy;
- the level of success in the performance of the organization;
- the availability of reasonably accurate and timely information;
- their previous experience; and
- a range of psychological factors depending upon whether their previous experience was favourable.

Similar findings emerged from the research of Sheth (1973) who found that risk perceptions tend to differ among decision participants as a result of differences in educational background, sources of information and reference groups. The model developed by Sheth was also an integrated model of industrial buyer behaviour. He established that the major factors influencing the expectations of decision-makers about potential suppliers and their products were:

- the background of the individuals involved;
- the information sources available to individuals;
- the level of active search undertaken by these individuals;
- perceptual distortion of the available information;
- degree of satisfaction with past purchases.

7.1.2 The effect of distortions in the risk perception

In the list of risk perception factors identified by Sheth (1973) above, it is significant that he highlights the effect of the process of perception itself, for this may lead individuals to distort the available information (for another explanation of how distortion may arise, see section 3.3.1 on the communication system). In dealing with this phenomenon, Sheth states that:

> Each individual strives to make the objective information consistent with his own prior knowledge and expectations by systematically distorting it. For example, since there are substantial differences in the goals and values of purchasing agents, engineers, and production personnel, one should expect different interpretations of the same information among them. Although no specific research has been done on this tendency to perceptually distort information in the area of industrial buyer behaviour, a large body of research does exist on cognitive consistency to explain its presence as a natural human tendency. (p. 53)

He then deals with the consequence that, intuitively, we ought to expect in the real world, namely, that where there are disagreements between expectations and the apparent evidence, a further search for information and a more careful consideration of the available information may be undertaken to resolve or minimize the conflict. However, whether this additional effort is actually made will depend upon two interacting factors, namely:

- whether the cost of the further time and work can be justified economically; and
- the extent to which prejudices will prevail over the apparent weight of the evidence (for a fuller explanation, see section 4.3 on prejudice as a factor in the acceptability of risk).

7.1.3 Risk perceptions at a strategic level

If we limit our enquiry to strategic management for a moment, then we might anticipate that there will always be differences between expectations and the results of research into the risks involved in the alternative strategies under consideration. These differences will arise from factors such as the background of the individuals involved, their information sources and the search activities engaged in, the degree of perceptual distortion operating both within their organization's information system and in their own minds, and the level of satisfaction with past strategies. All these elements may contribute to the development of differential expectations or assessments of the risks involved in the alternative strategies. In the area of industrial buying behaviour, Sheth (1973) suggests that the best way to resolve such a conflict of views is to apply the processes of problem-solving and persuasion. The problem-solving process is applied where there are disagreements on individual expectations and involves:

- a fuller analysis of the existing information to identify shortcomings and omissions;
- the search for additional data to improve the information holdings;
- a reconsideration of the problem in the light of both the existing and the new information with the intention of producing;
- a solution to the problem on the merits.

The alternative process of persuasion might be used where, for example, there is a disagreement on some specific criteria to be used in evaluating a particular supplier or, in the strategic situation, where it is necessary to choose between strategies proposed by different senior managers. The aim would be for the decision-makers to arrive at a satisfactory solution through discussion, negotiation and bargaining (for a fuller discussion on the nature of negotiation and bargaining in relation to problem-solving, see section 3.4.1). While he claims that the processes of problem-solving and persuasion are both useful and rational methods of conflict resolution, he does conclude that

> there is ample empirical evidence in the literature to suggest that at least some of the industrial buying decisions are determined by ad hoc situational factors and not by systematic decision making processes. In other words, similar to consumer behaviour, the industrial buyers often decide on factors other than rational or realistic criteria. (p. 55)

Indeed, when examining the more general human information processing and decision behaviour, Driver and Mock (1975) suggested that

> many studies reveal that ambiguity, novelty, incongruity, and uncertainty produce very different responses in men. Some people seek uncertainty and manipulate ambiguity or risk with ease. Others shy away from uncertainty and even distort data to avoid risk or ambiguity. (p. 495)

This highlights the psychological element in decision-making where uncertainty and risks are involved. Kogan and Wallach (1967) examined the psychological dimensions of risk-taking behaviour, concluding that the reliability of risk perception and the willingness to take risks were a function of the particular decision situation, the individuals and the group involved. Perhaps significantly, their research produced no evidence of universal rules to apply in the generality of risk-taking behaviour across different situations.

Most recently, Loomes (1991) concludes,

> It may be that any attempt to find a single unified model of individual decision making under risk and uncertainty will fail simply because no such model actually exists. Given that there are a number of alternative decision models that can claim to represent rational behaviour, at the very least we should not rule out the possibility that different individuals have learned to handle risk and uncertainty in different ways, so that no single model can accommodate them all. (p. 105)

This is a view that carries great weight and should lead us to treat all allegedly comprehensive models with a healthy scepticism.

7.2 RISK MEASUREMENT AND ESTIMATION

Developing the analysis of risk from the previous conclusion that risk perceptions will vary among the individuals involved in the decision process, we will now consider the aspects of the identification, estimation and evaluation of risk in terms of conceptual models. These models seek to develop a framework for exploring:

- the sources of risk;
- the exposure of an organization to risk;
- the relationship of risk to the consequences of a decision; and
- the approaches to measuring risk.

Thus, it would be a highly rational strategy for all organizations to aim to identify their weaknesses and vulnerabilities. But the problem is how to keep a proper sense of proportion in the estimation and measurement of risks so that managers can decide what level of resource to devote to risk avoidance and then concentrate all the resources made available in those areas most at risk.

7.2.1 The measurement of risk

Otway (1975) who was considering societal risks, identified two aspects to the process of measuring risk:

1. *Risk estimation*   This can be considered as the identification of the consequences of a decision and the subsequent estimation of the magnitude of associated risks.

2. *Risk evaluation*   This can be considered as the complex process of anticipating society's (or for our purposes, the organization's) responses to risk, or alternatively defined as evaluating the 'accept-

ability of risk' – for a full discussion of the concept of acceptability, see section 4.3.

Kates (1976) further developed this view by defining three stages in risk measurement:

1. *Risk identification* – this involves the reduction of descriptive uncertainty (section 5.2.4).

2. *Risk estimation* – this involves the reduction of measurement uncertainty (section 5.2.4).

3. *Risk evaluation* – this may involve either action to avoid the incidence of undesirable consequences or to reduce their effects if unavoidable, or risk acceptance.

7.2.2 Risk estimation and evaluation

From the above, it should be apparent that the processes of estimation and evaluation are a part of the measurement process, i.e. estimation is an initial stage and results in preliminary values which may subsequently be refined by more formal measuring/evaluation processes. Rowe (1977) developed a five-stage process for risk estimation, as follows:

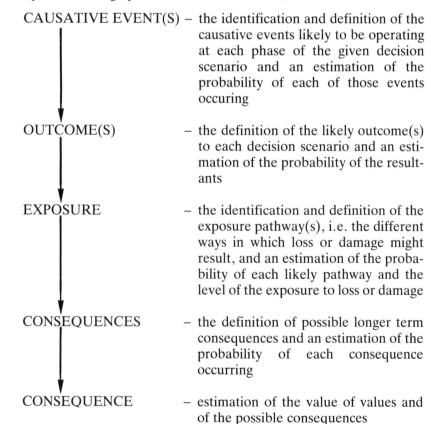

CAUSATIVE EVENT(S) – the identification and definition of the causative events likely to be operating at each phase of the given decision scenario and an estimation of the probability of each of those events occuring

OUTCOME(S) – the definition of the likely outcome(s) to each decision scenario and an estimation of the probability of the resultants

EXPOSURE – the identification and definition of the exposure pathway(s), i.e. the different ways in which loss or damage might result, and an estimation of the probability of each likely pathway and the level of the exposure to loss or damage

CONSEQUENCES – the definition of possible longer term consequences and an estimation of the probability of each consequence occurring

CONSEQUENCE – estimation of the value of values and of the possible consequences

At its simplest level, the estimation of risk falls into two major parts, namely probability determination and consequence value determination:

1. *Probability determination* comprises the first four elements in the above model and involves the estimation of the probabilities of occurrence of causative events, outcomes, pathways and exposures, and consequences.

2. *Consequence value determination* reflects the consequences to the risk-taker and involves the identification and estimation of the values of these consequences. Thus,

$$\text{RISK} = f\,(P_c + C(_v))$$

where:
P_c = estimated probability of consequence occurring
$C(v)$ = estimated consequence values

The model presented by Rowe suggests an additive functional relationship between probability and consequence values. It is likely, however, that the two factors may have an interactive effect and, through their interaction, have a direct influence on the estimation of risk by the decision-maker. For example, if an individual foresees that there may be extremely hazardous consequences to him or herself if a particular strategy is adopted, this will influence the individual's assessment of the probability of occurrence. Thus, a desire to promote personal survival may lead the decision-maker to place a higher probability value on occurrence and so lead to the selection of a more conservative and safer strategy. Conversely, if the individual makes a low probability of occurrence estimate, it would allow the individual, for any reason of personal convenience, to exaggerate the possible consequences.

Rowe (1977) identifies a number of variables or factors involved in each of the five stages in the risk estimation process:

1. Causative event(s): these events objectively represent the primary sources of risk facing an organization, and they can be classified according to:

   - the type of source from which the risk may flow; and
   - the nature of each event depending upon whether it is continuous or a 'one-off', discrete occurrence.

2. In their own right, events may be classified according to the following factors:

   (a) whether they are initiated by people, in which case they may be:

   - purposeful;
   - accidental; or
   - incidental.

   (b) or whether they arise through the forces of Nature, in which case they may arise in two ways, i.e:

- through a process (random or natural law);
- in a mode (whether direct or indirect).

3. When they arise, events may be subject to one or more temporal factors, i.e:

    (a) they may have qualities of continuity – this may produce constant or varying levels of activity and, if the latter, the cycles may be either periodic or aperiodic; or

    (b) they may be discrete – this may give each event a singular or unique quality, or the events may be multiple, i.e. be sequential, repetitive or combinational.

4. Normally, events will have outcome(s) – this element of the classification represents the potential effect of each event whether on the organization at large or on individuals within the organization, and outcomes may be considered in terms of:

    (a) their aspect which may be:

    - desirable;
    - undesirable; or
    - give rise to a response of indifference.

    (b) the temporal factors which may be:

    - continuous in nature, whether producing a constant or varying level (periodic or aperiodic); or
    - discrete, whether singular or multiple (sequential, repetitive or combinational).

5. The extent of the exposure to risk. While the classification so far aims to identify the source of the risk and the broad outcomes should the events occur, this element identifies the factors that are likely to determine the impact of an event and its outcome both on the organization at large, and on the other areas of the environment. To that extent, this part of the process may be considered the evaluation element. The factors involved are:

    (a) controllability: research work by the managers may show that:

    - the likely events are potentially controllable, whether by direct or indirect action; or
    - that to some extent, the events are likely to be uncontrollable and so represent a greater danger to the organization and/or to individuals.

    (b) Recipients: different individuals and groups may be at risk in different ways and to different degrees depending upon the controllability of the risks:

    - some individuals may be affected directly by the outcomes to a particular event, and their physical or emotional health, their financial or social status may be prejudiced in some real way;

- some individuals may be affected indirectly but in an equally real way;
- identifiable groups of people or the general population may be affected directly by some or all of the outcomes to a particular decision;
- identifiable groups of people or the general population may be affected indirectly;
- environmental and social institutions may be affected in a way that would require a real response from a government agency.

(c) Pathways: whenever an organization identifies possible alternative strategies, this might involve the organization in adopting different routes towards the resolution of the problems. The differentiation between these routes will depend upon:

- the degree of avoidability in each of the risks considered and the extent to which each strategy will maximize or minimize the level of exposure to danger;
- the degree to which the choice of strategy to be made is free or constrained in some way; and
- the nature of pathway which may, for example, be to negotiate a solution, to identify a cultural change that will indirectly assist a reduction in risk, to make financial resources available to mitigate losses etc.

6. Consequences: this element of risk estimation involves the assessment of the possible consequences of a particular event based on the prior assessment of the nature of the event, the possible outcomes and the exposure of the organization to these outcomes in terms of risk. The aim of the assessment is to determine the nature of the possible effects, their likely impact on the organization and when the consequences are likely to be sustained. This is a two-stage process and will involve:

(a) a summation of pathways, i.e. the managers will assess the total and partial effects for each of the pathways under consideration; and

(b) an evaluation of the exposure–consequence relationship, i.e. the managers will attempt a measurement of both the temporal factors in terms of whether the effects are likely to be immediate or delayed, and of the recipients depending on whether they are actually identifiable or merely at risk on a statistical basis.

7. Consequence values: this final element of the risk estimation process involves an evaluation of the possible consequences on different

groups including individuals, groups, organizations or society as a whole at local, national or an international level. This involves an identification of the individual risk agents and the value groups in society both at a national and at an international level. The organization must also be aware of the identity of external risk evaluators who may have the role of regulators, enforcers or ombudsmen.

It is important to recognize that the elements incorporating causative events, outcomes, exposure and potential consequences combine together to determine the probability or likelihood of each particular consequences occurring. The final element represents the basis on which there may be an evaluation of the possible consequences for the decision-making unit.

7.2.3 A practical example of risk estimation and evaluation

To help our understanding of the key stages in the risk estimation process suggested by Rowe (1977), it is useful to consider a practical example of a strategic decision to be taken by Whatco Ltd. Let us assume that a research group based in a university science park patents a new development in technology which is related to Whatco Ltd's primary products. It would be sensible for Whatco Ltd to consider whether to approach the patent holders for a licence and, if so, upon what terms. The estimation of the risks involved for Whatco Ltd and its alternative strategies to accommodate this new development could be assessed as follows:

- *Causative events*: the development in technology may be regarded as being initiated by people. In such a case, there are several possibilities, namely:

  - it may be that the patent holders decide to exploit their own patent and therefore become a competitor – this would be an exploitation of their invention in a purposeful manner to achieve a competitive advantage in their entry to the market;
  - the patent holders may license some or all of Whatco Ltd's existing competitors and give them a competitive advantage;
  - the patent holders may agree to license only Whatco Ltd and give it a competitive advantage; or
  - the patent holder may license all those currently producing which will tend to maintain the status quo in terms of competitive advantage.

All research developments, whether they are planned or accidental, or an incidental byproduct of research in another field, would clearly influence the risk estimation for Whatco Ltd. In this particular example, because of its importance, the event may be considered as discrete and singular, even though research work is likely to produce a continuous stream of developments to the technology relevant to that industry. In the light of all the information available, Whatco Ltd would then attempt to establish the likelihood or probability of this event having a real impact on its own performance.

- *Outcomes*:   in the first instance, the assessment of the possible outcomes from this particular technological development will tend to be based on whether it is seen as a threat to, or an opportunity for, Whatco Ltd. This would also incorporate an assessment of whether it is likely to have a short-term or 'one-off' impact on Whatco Ltd or whether it will have a more continuous or sustained impact. If research activity is high and new patents of immediate utility are appearing regularly on the market, the effect of any one patent may be short-term as the pace of development refines and improves performance. Missing one patent, albeit important, may therefore not have a major impact in the medium-term if we assume that new developments in the pipeline may allow Whatco Ltd to leapfrog back into a genuinely competitive position. Indeed, if an organization was routinely to adopt every new development, this might not be cost-effective as the pay-back period for the capital investment in each new development might be very short before each invention is superseded. But if research activity has been low and developments few, failing to exploit this patent may be critical to the long-term viability of Whatco Ltd.

- *Exposure*:   given the assessment of the event and its range of possible outcomes, Whatco Ltd would seek to identify the level of exposure that its products and markets face from each likely outcome, whether in a direct or an indirect sense. Indirect exposure could result from events which impact on other associated products and markets, or on the environment as a whole. Thus, for example, if the effect of the patent will be significantly to reduce manufacturing cost for the mid-range product, this may have profound implications for the whole pricing structure for the product range and might necessitate the redesign or abandonment of products either above or below in terms of price and quality. It would be conceivable that Whatco Ltd could identify several different pathways in which the technological development might be exploited and therefore have an impact, some of which might be direct and others indirect. The evaluation of the potential of Whatco Ltd to control or avoid exposure from alternative pathways of direct or indirect impact would clearly be an important element in estimating the risk involved.

- *Consequences*:   the consolidation of the previous elements on the effect of this development in technology would be reflected in the estimation of the consequences. The consequences may, for example, include the loss of market share for Whatco Ltd's existing products, loss of technological or market leadership or the development of distinctly new product/market areas which the organization could profitably exploit. In addition to identifying such outcomes, managers would also have to consider the likely time-scale attaching to each consequence. It may be possible to conceive of a particular event having both short-term and longer term consequences for an organization as indicated in outcomes above.

- *Consequence values*: this final stage in the process would seek to evaluate the values or costs of the identified consequences on Whatco Ltd. For example, an assessment of the loss of market share, sales value or profits may be typical measures. However, other measures may include the costs of developing the new technology and incorporating it into the organization's products, or the costs of creating alternative competitive advantages to offset the estimated consequences to the organization. If the new patented processes may not be as safe as the existing processes, this may give rise to issues of acceptability in exposing employees or those living near the manufacturing plants to greater risk, and cause problems with regulatory bodies.

7.2.4 Risk measurement and probabilities

Rowe (1977) classifies three forms of risk measurement on the basis of the nature of the probability and consequence measurements. This classification includes *objective risk*, *subjective risk*, and an intermediate classification termed *modelled risk*.

Probability measurement can be as follows:

- Objective, i.e. where the measurement is achieved by a process of repeated trials under identical conditions.
- Synthesized, i.e. where the results are modelled from similar probabilistic systems, but not measured objectively. An example of this approach to measurement based on operational decisions is the analysis of queuing situations. Here data collected from observations over a given period of operation are used to determine probabilities, and these are then used to simulate the queuing situation to establish the probabilities of failure to achieve the desired levels of service.
- Subjective, i.e. where the results are based on estimates from a few trials or derived from mere conjecture.

The approach to the measurement of consequences can be distinguished on the following bases:

- Objective consequences are derived from the description of events that are both observable and measurable.
- Observable consequences emerge from the measured behavioural responses of groups to objective or subjective consequences, i.e. the researcher will provide a series of possible consequences, say by designing a questionnaire or a test marketing exercise. The responses of the sample to the questions or the new products will then be assessed, and the results used as a basis for predicting the responses of the total population concerned (e.g. in market research surveys and forecasts).
- Subjective consequences represent the value of a consequence to a particular risk agent.

Objective risk occurs only when the probabilities and consequences can both be assessed objectively. This relates to the classical definition of risk in which a degree of certainty is achievable, i.e. it is possible to identify the range of possible outcomes, together with their values and the probability of their occurrence (see section 6.1). Shackle (1961) termed this 'distributional' risk, as all of the possible outcomes in the decision set are known and the total probability of unity is distributed across the members of the set, though not necessarily evenly. Simple examples of this type of risk are tossing a coin or throwing a dice (i.e. situations of aleatory uncertainty – see section 5.2.1).

Subjective risk occurs when either the probabilities and/or the consequences can only be measured subjectively. Shackle referred to this as 'non-distributional' risk, where incomplete knowledge of the members of the outcome set prevents the complete allocation of objective-based probabilities to the known members of the set.

Modelled risk can result in three situations:

1. when the consequences are objectively measurable and the probabilities have to be measured synthetically;
2. when there are observable consequences which support the calculation of synthesized probabilities;
3. when there are observable consequences which support the calculation of objectively measurable probabilities.

Relating these ideas on the three categories of risk to practical decision-making and to strategic decisions in particular, it should be clear that objective risk is rarely encountered in practice as few decision situations would permit the objective assessment of both the probabilities of occurrence and their consequences. Subjective risk is likely to be more common because decision-makers can build models of a decision by using subjective estimates of both probabilities of occurrence and consequences as a substitute for objective estimates. The major problem in this approach, of course, is that subjective estimates and measurements may prove to be very unreliable. Modelled risk therefore provides an interesting alternative approach, and it has been used extensively in the work undertaken to develop an understanding of risk in strategic decisions. For these purposes, objectively measurable consequences may be derived from empirical studies, market research or other sampling approaches designed to assess the likely consequences on customers, shareholders, employees etc; and synthesized probabilities may be derived from past knowledge or experiences, and through the identification of patterns of behaviour in previous decisions of a similar type.

7.3   RISK-TAKING BEHAVIOUR

A further dimension of risk in decision-making is the extent of the willingness shown by decision-makers to pursue decision alternatives where the risks are seen to be greater. Given that it will be for the decision-maker to attempt to measure or to form a perception of the level of risk, we must examine what factors then influence the likelihood of taking those risks (see also section 6.3.4).

Kogan and Wallach (1967) suggest that an individual's behaviour leading up to the decision whether to take a known risk is influenced by the following factors:

- *Situational influences*   These are elements which are particular to each person at the time immediately before the decision is to be taken, including:

  - that person's individual skills and competences;
  - the degree of consistency in the availability of good quality information and the cost of further information collection;
  - the level of expectancy attaching to the possibility of gain or censure from the foreseen outcomes;
  - the value of the gains or the severity of the censure following the likely outcomes;
  - the perception as to the role (if any) to be played by elements of chance; and
  - any real or imaginary incentives that will affect the choice to be made.

- *Personal characteristics*   These are the factors in the decision situation which describe and define the interests of relevant people other than the decision-maker, including:

  - demographic factors of sex, race, age and social class;
  - personality and motivational factors; and
  - the interaction between these characteristics and the situational qualities as they affect the decision-maker which gives an estimate of degree of control or influence that all involved may, or ought to have, over the decision situation.

- *Cognitive and judgemental*   These aspects reflect the qualitative abilities of the individuals directly involved in the decision situation. Each person's cognitive and judgemental capabilities help to set the degree of confidence felt by the individual in that situation and will predispose him or her to have a view of whether to take the risks or not. Some may act with a cool head and take risks following a detailed calculation of all the variables. Others may act with a recklessness borne of enthusiasm or desperation, not caring to engage in too detailed an evaluation of the apparent odds of success. All may succeed but, for future reference, one might wish to distinguish between the skilful and the merely lucky.

Following a review of the psychological research into these dimensions of individual risk-taking, Kogan and Wallach (1967) concluded that

> while we have learned from the work on individual differences that some degree of trans-situational consistency in risk-taking is to be found, perhaps the degree is small enough in terms of the over-all

picture so that we can afford to overlook it and concentrate rather upon task and situational determinants when we seek to understand individual risk-taking. (p. 208)

Further support for this view that risk-taking behaviour may be less a factor of the individual personality traits and more a factor of the decision situation was provided by the research of Slovic (1972) and Bassler *et al.* (1978). Their work suggests that the risk-taking behaviour of individuals cannot be assessed in one situation and then be extrapolated to the generality of situations encountered. Rather, it suggests that risk-taking behaviour is situation specific and determined by the interaction between the personality factors and the situational factors.

7.4 RISK IN STRATEGIC DECISIONS – OUTLINE MODEL

When a decision-making unit is charged with the task of strategy formulation, the assessment of the level of risk will be dictated by a number of situational variables and the degree of uncertainty perceived to be associated with each of them. Our first step is to outline a general model of strategic risk with a view to providing a structure to the analysis of risk. This is followed by a review and assessment of the conceptual and empirical research work in the strategic management and related fields to develop a more comprehensive view of the model.

The assessment of the level of risk will be influenced by three groups of situational variables, namely framework variables, problem/solution specific variables and decision-maker variables. This analysis is a modified version of the work of Baird and Thomas (1985). We should recognize that these variables will interact mutually both within groups and between groups. At a strategic level, the combination of variables and the pattern of their interaction is likely to have qualities unique to each decision situation. The result of the interactions will be that a risk perception is formed in the decision-maker's mind:

- *Framework variables* These comprise a range of elements which together prescribe the overall situation within which the organization is operating and within which it must formulate its strategic decisions. The framework variables can be subdivided into three types, i.e:

  (a) environmental – incorporating the economic, social, legal, political and general technological aspects of the external environment; support for the existence and relevance of this variable was provided by Rumelt (1974);

  (b) industrial – incorporating the products, markets, industry structure, specific technological developments and the competitive structure and strategies within the industry; support for this element was provided in the models of Rumelt (1974) Bowman (1980) and Bettis and Hall (1982).

  (c) organizational – incorporating the organization's structure, systems, decision-processes and objectives;

- *Problem/solution specific* These variables encompass a number of features related to the organization's abilities to formulate and resolve a specific strategic problem or issue. They include the following:

  (a) identification of the problem and its likely consequential effects;
  (b) structure of the problem and an understanding of the key variables and the interrelationships involved;
  (c) alternative solutions to the problem and their respective implications;
  (d) objectives and constraints influencing the resolution of the problem;
  (e) complexity of the decision task in its various dimensions (Cohen and Christensen, 1970);

The work of Bettis (1982), Bowman (1980) and Bettis and Hall (1982) all recognized that to some extent risk is endogenous and, therefore, the organization will always have some degree of influence and control over risk through its process of strategy selection.

- *Decision-maker variables* These may relate either to an individual decision-maker (section 3.1.1) or, more commonly, to the decision-making unit in an organization which will be made up by those individuals who are involved in taking the strategic decisions (for further material on group decision-making, see sections 2.4, 6.3.4 and 7.4.11). Consequently, the following factors may be viewed either at the individual level or at the group or unit level. If we are considering a group or unit, the performance of the group will not be the aggregation of the individual's characteristics. Each person's behaviour will tend to be modified as a result of interaction within the group. The factors are as follows;

  (a) knowledge of the framework and problem/issue specific factors outlined above;
  (b) information seeking, i.e. a desire or ability to improve one or more group member's understanding of the problem (Kogan and Wallach, 1964, 1967);
  (c) experience of previous strategic problems and their solutions, whether within the particular organization or in comparable organizations (Nees, 1978, 1983);
  (d) skills in the formulation, solution and implementation of strategies within the particular organization (Kogan and Wallach, 1964, 1967);
  (e) biases shown by the decision-makers because of their specialization, knowledge or allegiances in terms of particular functional or product/market areas. At its simplest level, this may mean that people will represent the interests of the department or section in which they work. It is a fact of corporate politics

that these departmental interests need not be wholly compatible with the interests of the organization as a whole and one of the continuing problems for management is to reduce the level of dissonance between the different interest groups. At a more sophisticated level, people may be predisposed to hold particular views because of their knowledge or professional training (sections 2.4.1/2/3 and 3.4.1);

(f) incentives involved in the decision in terms of potential gains and costs. Sometimes these gains and costs will be direct (section 1.3.1). Otherwise they may be indirect but affect how alliances are made between interest groups within the decision-making unit. (Kogan and Wallach, 1964, 1967);

(g) the beliefs held by the decision-makers concerning the many facets of the strategic situation outlined above.

The work of Sheth (1973) and Choffray and Johnston (1979) outlined previously in section 7.1 supports the view that risk perception is a function of the individuals involved in the decision-making process and their backgrounds.

7.4.1 Group risk perception at a strategic level

Cooke and Slack (1984) refer to the phenomenon of risky shift (p. 96), i.e. a shift towards accepting a more risky solution when people take a group decision (section 2.4 *et seq*. and section 6.3.4). Various explanations are offered to explain this, i.e:

1. if people are going to share responsibility for the decision, those who would otherwise be deterred by the idea of accountability at an individual level should things go wrong, may feel less inhibited and take riskier decisions;
2. it is often the case that those people who are prepared to take risks also show the best leadership qualities and have a strong influence on the decision-making process;
3. the more people who contribute their expertise to the group decision, the greater the potential to take a decision based on a fuller exploration of the issues; this better quality discussion may cause otherwise more conservative individuals to reappraise their concerns about the risks involved;
4. in the sometimes macho world of management decision-making, making high-risk statements in a male peer group situation is seen as more socially acceptable than offering a more cautious line.

Whatever the reason may be for the existence of risky shift, it is a factor that organizations ought to consider if the management style moves away from the autocractic towards the participative and democratic. Indeed, it may be an advantage for the organization because it helps to improve its creativity and its risk-taking ability. If the group is working well, it will tend to canvass more potential solutions and bring more expertise to bear on selecting the best strategy. With more people involved, the commitment of individual members will be improved and communication following the decision is easier. However, if the group does not work well, poorly co-ordinated, high-risk strategies may result from a discussion between individuals determined to avoid responsibility for taking the decision.

This outline model of risk determination within strategic decision-making may be summarized as follows:

$$RISK = E_r + I_r + O_r + P_r + DM_r$$

where:

E = environmental variables
I = industry variables
O = organizational variables
P = problem specific variables
DM = decision-maker related variables

The model presented above implies an additive relationship between the five variable groups in determining the level of risk perceived in a given decision situation. It is likely that in practice the variables would be interactive with each other in influencing the risk perceived. For example, certain decision-maker characteristics may be more sensitive to organizational variables, and changes in industry variables are likely to influence the organizational variables.

In considering the implications of this model it must be recognized that the term 'risk' is essentially a reflection of the decision-maker's perception of risk based on the variables presented on the right-hand side of the equation. The most significant and influential factors in the formation of this risk perception will be the degree of uncertainty related to these factors, and the aggregation of perceptions on the consequential losses associated with the decision. In conceptual terms, the composite risk perception which emerges in each specific situation will result from a set of differential weightings applied to the main groups of variables and the constituent variables within each group. This outcome would be consistent with contingency theory, in that the risk perceived will be dependent on the decision variables and individuals involved in a particular decision. The weightings applied in a specific situation are likely to be unique to that situation. Hence, the issue facing researchers in this area is not to identify the value of weightings used in specific decisions, but to:

1. identify the variables that are the most important in influencing risk perception or those that invariably have a high weighting attached to them;
2. understand the processes by which decision-makers convert this information into their perception of risk; and
3. understand how risk perceptions influence the decision choice.

In this sub-section, we have tried to build on the material covered in earlier chapters to develop an outline model for strategic decision-making. The next stage is to introduce the contingency management theory and then to develop a limited domain model of strategy formulation and of information processing to provide a more integrative model of the impact of information on risk assessment and the consequences for strategy formulation.

7.5 SUMMARY

In the last three chapters, we have explored the twin issues of uncertainty and risk. These were defined respectively from the decision-maker's point of view as a lack of confidence about future events and a desire to avoid unacceptable consequences from a decision. Although the main thrust of the discussion has been based on a separate analysis of these two elements, we should not lose sight of the reality that they are inextricably entwined in the practical decision environment.

Uncertainty can be viewed as an important element in the assessment of the risk perceived in a particular decision. By way of example, we will take two simple situations. In the first, a decision-maker has the luxury of certainty about the future and so can identify all potential outcomes to the decision to be taken. If such were the case, the decision-maker's major concern in reaching the decision would be to balance the major risk parameters against the performance objectives (e.g. returns, growth, market share etc.). But as our second example, let us take the more realistic situation in which the decision-maker is uncertain or lacks confidence about both future events and decision consequences. Here, uncertainty will act as a form of 'smoke-screen' to the decision-maker, preventing the clear analysis of the future. If something could be done to reduce the level of uncertainty, it might help the decision-maker to clarify some of the issues in the pending decision. But it is unlikely that there would be a sufficient reduction in overall uncertainty to clarify all the aspects or issues in a decision. Indeed, it is also possible to conceive of the process of uncertainty reduction actually increasing the level of risk perception. This would happen if, during a search for more information, issues surfaced into conscious consideration which previously had been obscured or ignored.

$$\text{risk}_{\text{perceived}} = \text{uncertainty} + \text{risk}_{\text{extant}}$$

The risk perceived in a decision situation is considered to be a function of both the level of uncertainty and the level of risk that is extant in the decision. This latter level of risk will itself be influenced by uncertainty in terms of the clarity with which the decision-maker can perceive it.

We should now see information'as a key determinant in relation to the level of uncertainty. The relationship between information and uncertainty depends upon:

1. whether good quality and timely information is available to the right people in the management structure; and

2. whether the individual and the organization have the capacity to search for, collate, process and evaluate that information.

If the information system works well, it can lead to a reduction of future uncertainty. But even though improvements in information processing and evaluation can reduce uncertainty and increase the decision-maker's confidence, it is not likely that uncertainty can be completely removed. This is not to diminish the importance of a reduction in uncertainty. Any significant reduction in uncertainty will have two major advantages, i.e:

- it will assist in the clarification and crystallization of issues in the decision situation; and, consequently,
- it will have a beneficial influence on the decision-maker's general level of understanding and help him or her to form a more realistic perception of the risks.

In our analysis of risk, we have adopted a number of different viewpoints, but in the books and articles that have gone before, the approach to risk analysis which has received the greatest attention is that based on a measurement of risk in terms of the variability of the returns distribution from a decision. A range of models utilizing this approach and emphasizing different moments of the returns distribution together with different criteria for trading off risk and return have been developed. We acknowledge that these essentially normative models of decision behaviour have the advantage of simplicity and the ability to quantify risk, but we follow the line adopted by some commentators that such models are inadequate in their failure fully to describe the practical processes of risk assessment in decision-making. Their primary concern is with the consequence values (as defined by Rowe, 1977) as a given parameter (Section 6.4 *et seq.*). This leads to the use of subjective probabilities as a proxy for objective probabilities and the creation of rules for the selection of strategies based on utility or other criteria involving trade-offs between values and probabilities. We feel that their lack of attention to the processes of establishing the consequences, the likelihood of their occurrence and the aspect of risk perception are significant deficiencies in the descriptive quality of such approaches.

The major factors that we identified as combining together to influence the degree of risk perceived in a particular strategic decision were:

- environmental characteristics;
- industry characteristics;
- organization characteristics and structure;
- types of strategy;
- problem specific variables;
- decision-maker variables; and
- organization's information processing systems.

The assessment of risk made by managers in any particular situation is likely to be contingent on the above variables, and Baird and Thomas (1985) suggest that the most effective advance in research into risk in strategic decision-making would be made by:

1. identifying which of the variables listed above have a universally high weighting in risk estimation;
2. establishing how the information systems and processes at the organizational and individual level contribute to estimating risk in these key parameters; and
3. evaluating the process of risk perception arising from these variables and the availability and processing of information.

The new lines of research being developed seek to identify the key variables and the information processes used to identify and to clarify the risks perceived in formulating strategic decisions. Using Rowe's model of risk estimation, we believe that it is possible to divide the process of risk perception into two stages:

(a) determination of probabilities of occurrence through:

*   evaluation of causative events;
*   identification of outcomes;
*   determination of exposures;
*   assessment of consequences;

(b) determination of consequence values, i.e. the quantification of the values of each consequence.

QUESTIONS

1. Take a standard business situation and identify what risks might actually represent a danger to the organization. Then, take each of those risks in turn and explain why different individuals within the organization either might not be aware of it or misunderstand its true nature.
2. Explain why there may be differences in the risk perceptions.
3. At its simplest level, what are the components to a measuring process, i.e. is there any point in distinguishing separate processes of estimation and evaluation?
4. Distinguish between objective, subjective and modelled risk.
5. Produce a critique of the outline model proposed for risk determination at a strategic level within the organization.

8 Contingency theory applied to research in strategic management

INTRODUCTION

It is remarkable how often people and organizations are overtaken by outside events. Sometimes, there will be express warnings but the people at risk choose not to heed them. Sometimes, the warning signs will be less clear and their implications will not be appreciated. On other occasions, people will understand the warnings but will have no real choices. All that they can do, with whatever degree of detached interest that can be maintained, is to watch their own downfall. We now come to contingency theory and, at its simplest level, what we must decide is whether it is possible to identify general rules for organizations to follow in responding to different types of events in their environments.

8.1 DEVELOPMENTS IN MANAGEMENT THEORY

We will start this chapter with a synopsis of the main strands in the development of management theory which have provided the foundations for the development of research and theory in strategic management. This will involve us in tracing the development of contingency theory within the general field of organization theory, indicating its contribution and limitations. Finally, we will examine the application of contingency theory within the field of strategic management.

The development of theory and the practice of research into the management of organizations, have been characterized by the diversity of academic perspectives that have been at work. Not surprisingly, the result is a fragmented body of knowledge and theory. That this is an unsatisfactory state of affairs was highlighted by Koontz (1961) who, in his original review of this field, concluded that

> The variety of approaches to management theory has led to a kind of confused and destructive warfare. (p. 175)

He identified six distinct schools or approaches to the development of management theory:

- *Management process* This is based on empiricism and relies on the distillation of general principles from practical experience. Primarily, it is linked to the traditional or universalist approaches typified, for example, by the work of Fayol (1949).

- *Empirical* The main thrust of this approach which was pioneered by the Harvard Business School, is linked to the development of case studies. Thus, it depends on the process of accurately documenting particular situations and experiences, and then using these studies to develop a knowledge base for future managers.

- *Human relations* This is centred on the study of interpersonal relationships within the organization.

- *Social systems* This recognizes the process of management as a part of the social systems comprising the organization and its environment, and it also seeks to analyse the system of cultural inter-relationships.

- *Decision theory* This originates from the discipline area of economics and it seeks to develop rational approaches to, and criteria for, decision-making.

- *Mathematical* This depends on the development of mathematical models and solution techniques to guide managers, particularly at the operational level of decision-making.

In a later review of the developments in management theory, Koontz (1980) revised his earlier classification, increasing the number of approaches from six to eleven, i.e:

- *Empirical or case study* This remained as described in his original study.

- *Interpersonal behaviour* This centred on a study of interpersonal relationships.

- *Group behaviour* This focused on the behaviour of groups rather than individuals.

- *Co-operative social systems* This recognized organizations as social systems involving the co-operative interaction of ideas, forces, desires and thinking groups of people.

- *Sociotechnical systems* This concentrated on the human–technology interfaces within organizations.

- *Decision theory* This remained as decribed in his original study.

- *Systems* This recognizes that each organization is a metasystem. Thus, each organization itself comprises a series of interacting sub-systems, and it interacts with other systems in the external environment both at a metasystem and at a subsystem level.

- *Mathematical or management science* The title being expanded but the definition remaining the same as in the original study.

- *Contingency or situational* This emphasizes the importance of the particular situation or variables facing the manager in determining the appropriate actions.

- *Managerial roles* This is identified with Mintzberg's approach of empirically researching what managers actually do, and then deriving conclusions from this data about their roles and operating procedures.

- *Operational theory* This seeks to develop a core of knowledge, concepts, principles, theory and techniques related to the actual practice of management.

For our purposes, it is possible to re-classify these approaches into five broad categories:

- *Behavioural* This incorporates the inter-personal behaviour, group behaviour and co-operative social systems approaches.

- *Systems* This incorporates the systems and sociotechnical systems approaches.

- *Quantitative* This incorporates the decision theory and management science approaches.

- *Empirical* This incorporates the empirical or case, managerial roles and operational theory approaches.

- *Contingency* This represents more of an orientation than a specific body of knowledge as we shall see from the discussion below.

Each of these more broadly stated approaches provides an invaluable perspective on the functioning of management and a contribution towards the development of management theory. Indeed, because of the reclassification, some common ground is more apparent within each of the classifications, and some degree of interaction in the development of ideas would be expected. But the interaction between the proponents of each of these categories has been limited and, until a greater degree of integration between each camp is achieved, there is little prospect of formulating a unified theory of management.

While recognizing some movement towards disentangling ('the jungle', Koontz, like other modern researchers, accepts that there is still no unified theory of management. He believes that the potential solution to this problem lies with the operational theory approach. His reason is that this draws on the pertinent knowledge from the other fields outlined in his eleven schools above to enhance and enrich the existing body of practical knowledge in management. It is interesting to note that Koontz (1980) does not believe that the contingency approach can make a major contribution to the research. Indeed, even though he does recognize that there may be differences between them, he classifies the contingency together with the situational approach.

It is now clear that the contingency view is merely a way of distinguishing between science and art – knowledge and practice. (p. 368)

In essence he is arguing that contingency theory reflects a truism that the practical application of any theory or body of knowledge will always be dictated by the situation.

Luthans (1973) criticized Koontz's adherence to the process theory or empirical approach to management, as he considered that traditional management process theory had failed to unify management theory. He identified three new paths of development in management theory, the quantitative, behavioural and systems approaches, and recognized that both the quantitative and behavioural approaches were orienting back towards the systems approach. He argued that the contingency view as opposed to the situationalist view had greater potential as

the open, as opposed to closed, systems view is able to cope better with the increased complexity and environmental influence facing today's managers. (p. 69)

8.2 AN INTRODUCTION TO CONTINGENCY THEORY

There is an alternative means of categorising the approaches to developing management theory and research. Whereas Koontz adopts a discipline-based classification, we would advocate a classification based on three factors:

- the nature of the concept, methodology or philosophy applied in the research;
- the nature of the models used; and
- the resulting theory and prescriptions.

This could produce three categories:

1. The *universalist* category or approach to management theory is developed on an inductive premiss, i.e. that by analysing all the particular instances, it is possible to derive a series of general underlying principles and practices that operate within organizations. It is hoped that the application of the best of these principles to all management situations will then achieve improvements in the general effectiveness and efficiency of organizations. The main source both of this body of factual knowledge and of the resulting theories is real world observation which falls under two headings:

   - a general view is taken of the actual practice of management; and
   - a more particular view is taken of the methods used to resolve specific problems and issues as they arise.

   The main examples of this approach are the research efforts of the so-called traditional management theorists including Fayol, Follet,

Taylor and Weber. They have been responsible for the development of what is now known as a closed-systems perspective of the organization, i.e. the researchers concentrate on the internal structures and processes, both administrative and managerial, which are intended to achieve effectiveness. It is a closed perspective because they do not give signficant consideration to the external environment within which the organization operates. The resulting rules and prescriptions for organizational health have been sufficiently simple and pragmatic that traditionalists have been able to argue that they could be applied to any organization irrespective of the nature of the external environment facing it.

2. The *situationalist* category or approach is based on the premiss that all organizations are unique. Although many organizations will have similar features, the proposition is that every organization will have qualities of uniqueness which stem from the differences in each organization's:

- external environment;
- internal structure and culture (which will be given individuality by the personalities of the people involved);
- processes; and
- goals and objectives.

In many cases, the degree of uniqueness identified between the given organizations might be marginal. Despite this, the supporters of this approach argue that it would be unsafe to derive and propose any universal principles which might be proclaimed as a panacea for the improvement of efficiency and effectiveness in all organizations. Instead, the proposed prescriptions or solutions would be those most appropriate either to the specific situation or to the variables that are of significance to the individual organization at that time. Consequently, the emphasis for the manager in practice would be on a two-stage process, i.e:

(a) a comprehensive analysis of the situation as the manager perceives it; and then

(b) an application of experience and established methodologies to develop an appropriate resolution for the particular problems in the immediate situation.

This approach is more likely to result in the development of a toolkit of analytical techniques to aid the individual in the role of managing a unique organization rather than helping to develop a coherent and cogent body of theory.

3. The *contingency* category or approach represents a compromise position between the two extremes of the universalist and situationalist approaches. As Kast and Rosenzweig (1973) indicated in their discussion of contingency theory within the context of organizational research, contingency theory represents,

a middle ground between: (1) the view that there are universal principles of organisation and management, and (2) the view that each organisation is unique and that each situation must be analyzed separately. (p. ix)

8.2.1 A definition of contingency theory

At its simplest level, the aim of the contingency theory is two-fold:

(a) it seeks to determine whether there are relationships between particular elements in organizations' environments; and
(b) by observing the responses of different organizations to these elements, to provide guidelines to other organizations facing similar, though not necessarily identical, environmental influences.

There have been a number of research studies of a contingency nature in the fields of organizational behaviour and management theory. Thus, Lawrence and Lorsch (1967) took a global view of the organization in its context. They evaluated the general effect of the external environment on an organization's effectiveness and derived a number of contingency propositions. If effectiveness is to be increased, they suggested the appropriate form of organization structure and the management styles that should be adopted for given types of external environment. Similarly, Burns and Stalker (1961) developed a contingency model that links the achievement of organizational effectiveness to the design of appropriate structures and managerial styles to suit the external environment facing the organization. Thompson (1967) proposed that his notion of coalignment was the key to effective management. This is a reference to the process whereby the organization continuously adapts (or aligns) itself to the external environment.

Instead of starting with the environment as a summation of different components, Woodward (1965) emphasizes a particular environmental element, namely technological change, and develops a contingency framework which links the structure and operations of the organization to the rate of technological change in the external environment. Perrow (1970) also indicates that organization structures should be adapted to meet the needs of the technology facing the organization. Chandler (1962), on the other hand, takes the converse approach and starts from an evaluation of the effect of different strategies adopted by an organization on its structure, and produces a contingency model linking strategy and structure to the nature of the external environment. Reference should also be made to the work of Channon (1973) which developed a similar contingency model as a result of research into UK industry. Korman (1972) provided a valuable means of distinguishing between the contingency and universalist approaches based on the following algorithm:

(a) *Contingency theory*

$$Y = f_i (X) \text{ at } Z_i$$

where: Y is the criterion variable

X is the organizational variable
Z is the contingency variable

Thus, different values of Z represented by situations $i = 1, 2, 3 \ldots$ will result in different functional relationships f_i as i changes. The way in which the organizational variable influences the criterion variable will change as the situation changes.

(b) Universalist position

$$Y = f(X) \text{ for all } Z$$

Irrespective of the value of Z or the situation, the functional relationship between the organizational variable and the criterion variable will remain the same.

Contingency theory has provided a valuable avenue for the development of research in the management and organizational theory fields. While the universalist approach initially proved capable of providing concise operational guidelines, subsequent research failed to validate their appropriateness to the wide variety of environmental conditions faced by different organizations or, indeed, the changing nature of the environment for the same organization. The problems of applying many of the universalist prescriptions have been further exacerbated by increasing complexity and the new dynamism of both the external environment and the internal operations of most organizations. As Kast and Rosenzweig (1972) concluded, contingency theory,

> recognizes the complexity involved in managing modern organizations but uses patterns of relationships and/or configurations of subsystems in order to facilitate improved practice. (p. 463)

The situationalist approach has proved a more effective vehicle. Researchers have been better able to accommodate the diverse research results that strive to incorporate both the large number of environmental variables and their complex interrelationships. However, it has proved very difficult to transcribe the research findings and hypotheses back into an operational context, and few generalized rules or guidelines have been derived to assist decision-makers in practice. This leaves the contingency approach which is proving more useful:

- by identifying key variables in the external environment; and
- by using these variables to classify the nature of the organization's environment; and
- subsequently developing prescriptions to aid operational decisions,

the contingency theory has provided a partial solution to the problems encountered by both the universalist and situationalist approaches. Steiner (1979) recognized that,

> What is new with contingency theory is that it takes a new approach in seeking to describe for given situations, structures, and actions that

best meet the needs of the organization. This is a new unifying approach to organizational design which is now being applied to different areas of management theory, including strategic management. The contingency approach is richer than the universal principles approach to theory-building. Inherent in it is more rigor, a deeper appreciation of inter-relationships in situations, and an effort to identify causal relationships. (p. 406)

Schoonhoven (1981) in reviewing contingency theory developments concluded that

> contingency theory is not a theory at all, in the conventional sense of theory as a well-developed set of interrelated propositions. It is more an orienting strategy or metatheory, suggesting ways in which a phenomenon ought to be conceptualised or an approach to the phenomenon ought to be explained. (p. 350)

The conclusion from her review of the research studies in the organization field suggests that contingency theory is concerned with the objective of improving organizational effectiveness in response to uncertainty in the operating environment. The main variables or structural dimensions used to achieve this include:

- rules and operating procedures;
- decentralization of decision-making; and
- the professionalization or training of staff.

Schoonhoven identified four problems inherent in the development of contingency models in this field:

1. There is a certain lack of clarity in the terminology used to explain the relationships in the model. Most studies prescribe the need to achieve 'fit', 'congruence', 'conformity' or 'consistency' between the structural elements of the organization and its environment. This terminology can be ambiguous when it comes to applying the research results to specific organizational situations.
2. The nature of the interaction between the variables involved is often not clearly developed or explicitly recognized. For example, in a contingency model linking organizational effectiveness with professionalization, incorporating training, skill development, specialization etc., one would expect the following:

environmental uncertainty (independent variable)
↓
professionalization training/training (intermediate/interacting
variable)
↓
organization effectiveness (dependent variable)

The explicit relationships would appear to suggest that, given a degree of environmental uncertainty, the level of professionalization or training of staff could be adapted to ensure organizational effectiveness. Thus, by recruiting staff with more sophisticated skills or by identifying and targeting skill shortage areas, the management staff may be better able to define information search requirements and to identify the relevant data in the environment. This might make the organization more effective in the face of uncertainty. The implicit relationship, often ignored, is that changes in the training or skill development may alter the actual or perceived degree of uncertainty, i.e. an interaction between the intermediate variable and the independent variable. As the training enhances the skills of management, their new knowledge may clarify that which was previously uncertain and, in future, reduce the number of situations in which they will perceive the existence of uncertainty. It is also possible to conceive of interactions between the dependent variable and both the intermediate variable and the independent variable. For example, increased organizational effectiveness may facilitate increased training/staff development. This may be through the creation of additional revenue to support the training exercise, or the new effectiveness may liberate time during which the training may take place. Further, the increased confidence that may flow from increased effectiveness may itself reduce the perception of vulnerability to, or uncertainty in, the environment.

3.   Few studies elaborate the form of the specific interaction involved. Thus, it is not clear whether the relationship between the variables is additive or multiplicative, i.e.

whether $Y = X_1 + X_2$ or
$$Y = X_1 X_2$$

The following questions are also left unanswered:

- Is the interaction within the model designed to achieve some maximum or optimum level?
- Are there more than one maximum/optimum solutions possible?
- Are there any threshold effects which would deter further changes in the action variable?

4.   Operational and computational procedures impose further assumptions on the contingency framework. These assumptions include linearity, symmetry and monotonicity in the relationships. Thus, we would be obliged to predict that both low uncertainty combined with a low structural variable, and high uncertainty combined with a high structural variable, may achieve effectiveness, and the relationship will change in a linear pattern in between. An example would be low environmental uncertainty linked to a low level of organizational centralization resulting in effectiveness, e.g. a matrix form of organization with a well-developed team culture may do very well if relatively straightforward tasks and decisions are required to do well in the given market. On the other hand, if high uncertainty is linked to a high degree of centralization, the potential autocratic manage-

ment style may enable the organization to respond very quickly and effectively to opportunities in a rapidly changing market. The implied assumption is that a low level of uncertainty combined with a high structural variable will result in diminished effectiveness, or vice-versa. In our view, Schoonhoven overstates this problem and, in particular, the latter implication, by assuming that contingency models which explore the extreme ranges of a variable are necessarily implying the nature of the relationship in the intervening range.

Schoonhoven's empirical research involved a study of seventeen acute-care hospitals. She attempted to take these four problems into account and her conclusion established a multiplicative interaction between the state of technology in the environment and the organization structure in achieving effectiveness. The assumption was that the relationship was also symmetrical and non-monotonic.

Another issue to be considered in relation to the contingency theory approach is the extent to which it would be legitimate to operationalize the results of the research. There are always problems when trying to tread the path between two approaches as different as the universalist and the situationalist. With some justification, it can be argued that contingency theory may help to improve the quality of models achievable by using the universalist approach, but the end-product may lack its generality of application. Equally, the contingency theory may provide greater scope for generalized prescriptions than the situationalist approach, but lack its descriptive powers.

8.2.2 Contingency theory and limited domain models

In recognizing the potential limitations of contingency theory, we should perhaps consider many of the contingency models to be little more than limited domain models. By doing so, we would clearly be recognizing that the range of external and internal environmental issues encompassed within the model are severely restricted in relation to the range and complexity of variables that may face organizations in practice. This would not be to devalue the power of the approach. Thus, even though a set of findings following upon a contingency research project may not be capable of representing a generalized model appropriate to all organizations, they could be highly relevant to those organizations upon which the particular variables described impinge significantly.

An illustration of this is provided in Figure 8.1. Organization A would be strongly influenced in its operations by environmental variables 3, 5 and 6; to a lesser extent by variables 1, 4 and 8; and almost negligibly by variables 2 and 7. Organization B, on the other hand, would be more strongly influenced by variables 2 and 7; to a lesser extent by variables 1, 3 and 6; and almost negligibly by variables 4, 5, and 8. Clearly, a wide variety of different organizations could be plotted on to this environmental space so that their resulting positions reflected their particular environmental pressures. If we then concentrated our research efforts on the subset area for Organization A indicated in the diagram, which we may properly call a limited domain, we could begin to establish the nature of the environmental variables that might face all organizations falling in whole or in part within this area. The greater the degree of commonality between the variables, the better our ability to develop theories and prescriptions that might help the management of such organizations. Further, it would be seen to be realistic to accept that these theories or prescriptions would be of more limited value to organizations such as B, which faces the same variables, but ranked differently in order of importance.

A typical research design created within the spirit of the contingency theory would:

1. aim to study the interaction of one or two variables within a limited area of the total space occupied by the organization to be studied; and then
2. seek to provide propositions related to the total organizational space.

The main distinction between this generalization process and that adopted in the universalist approach lies in the fact that the contingency approach:

1. is constrained to a limited number of variables; and
2. the resulting propositions and prescriptions are qualified in terms of those variables.

A typical research design which formally adopts the limited domain approach would aim to study a larger number of variables but within a

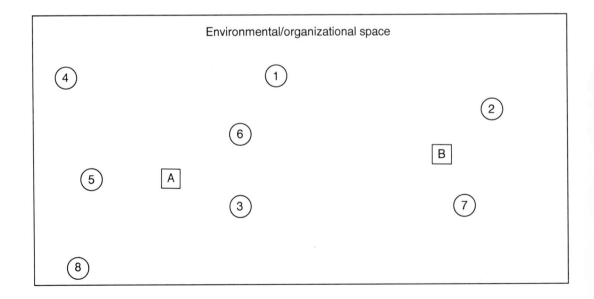

Figure 8.1 Contingency theory – limited domain subset.

smaller or more limited domain. Further, the research would not seek to generalize the results for the entire organizational space, but would restrict propositions to the original domain and the domains immediately surrounding it. The potential of such an approach is to achieve much greater descriptive validity and application, but it will lack the potential to develop into more generalizable propositions.

A not unexpected consequence of the extensive development of essentially limited domain contingency theories has been the attempt to integrate these theories into a general contingency theory. Carlisle (1973); Hellriegel and Slocum (1973); Kast and Rosenzweig (1973); Luthans (1973); Mockler (1971); and Tosi and Hamner (1974) have all sought to collect and integrate the findings of individual contingency research studies into a general contingency model. Moberg and Koch (1975), in reviewing this trend, identified several problems in attempting this integration including the problems of:

- identifying where the overall boundaries fall between the contingency theory and the individual limited domain theories;
- reconciling the differences in the various definitions offered for contingency variables;
- identifying the nature and extent of the interactions between domains; and
- resolving the resulting ambiguities and loss of precision when trying to piece together what they regarded as a patchwork of research findings.

They concluded that

> [the] present aggregative treatments of contingency views strive to move the contingency appreciation too far and too fast. In overgeneralizing from the crude beginnings of situational research, they serve only to suppress the very questions theorists are beginning to ask; for clearly the findings of contingency research have limits too. Despite caveats which offer a word of caution or apologize for the tentativeness of these schemes, present aggregative models both overstate the convergence among existing findings and understate the problems of applying them. (p. 122)

8.3 CONTINGENCY THEORY APPLIED TO STRATEGIC MANAGEMENT

The development of theory and empirical research in the strategic management field has parallelled the development and application of contingency theory in other fields of management research. It is perhaps not surprising, therefore, that the contingency approach has featured significantly in research work in strategic management. Focusing on the strategic level of decision-making also tends to sharpen the appreciation of the uniqueness of each organization's situation. While it is true that this may be a justification for a situationalist rather than a contingency approach, researchers have recognized that the latter provides greater potential for developing more generalized propositions and models than the former.

Harvey (1982) provided a succinct statement of aims for the contingency orientation within strategic management as

> the contingency approach to strategy suggests that, for a certain set of organizational and environmental conditions, an optimal strategy exists. (p. 81)

Hofer (1975) concluded his review of research developments in the strategic management field by supporting the contingency approach as the only sensible approach to the development of research and theory in the field. Similarly, Ginsberg and Venkatraman (1985) argued that

> [it] is perhaps a truism that any theory of corporate or business strategy must be, by definition, contingency-based. (p. 421)

They justified this statement on the following three grounds which, at the present time, would seem to have great force, namely that:

1. no matter what the modern gurus of the art of management may say to the contrary, there is no best way to organize;
2. despite the best efforts of all the researchers, it has not proved possible to develop a universal set of strategic choices that can be applied routinely in all major decisions; and
3. their review of all the literature suggested that the main paradigm used by researchers is based on the proposition that managers match the strategy to the environment.

In reviewing developments in the contingency approach within strategic management, Steiner (1979) noted that there were numerous contingency theories covering different parts of the field, but no integrated theory to link these various contingency theories,

> It is, however, far from becoming a discipline where underlying comprehensive theories tie together major parts of the phenomenon involved . . . However, we shall not see soon, in my judgement a well-rounded comprehensive theory of strategic management. The best we can hope for is more penetrating limited domain contingency theories and more work on integrating such limited domain theories. (p. 416)

Steiner identified four major research thrusts in the development of contingency theories within the strategic management field, deriving from the case tradition, organization theory, empirical research and experience, and conceptualization theories:

1. Examples of the case tradition included Hofer (1975), who developed normative hypotheses linking the product life-cycle position to appropriate strategies. These were based on a number of contingency variables including:

- market and consumer behaviour;
- industrial structure;
- competitors;
- suppliers;
- broad environmental pressures; and
- the organization's characteristics and resources.

Clifford (1973) also examined strategies contingent on the environmental variables, while Ackerman (1975) developed a contingency theory based on the social effects of decisions.

2. The organization theory field has proved to be a rich source of contingency approaches that are applicable to the strategic management field. The effect of the environment on the structure and strategies of organizations has been researched by Chandler (1962); Wrigley (1970); Channon (1973); Scott (1973) and Rumelt (1974). Each of these studies were developed within a broad contingency framework and produced models linking strategy and structure to environmental conditions. Richman (1964); Farmer and Richman (1965) and Newman (1971) examined the influence of a range of environmental conditions on the actual internal management structures, processes and practices of organizations. Anderson and Paine (1975) took a more limited perspective and developed a contingency approach towards strategy content based on the twin environmental variables of perceived environmental uncertainty, and the perceived need for strategic change. Cook (1975) developed four hypotheses which were related to the type of strategy to pursue contingent on the perceived environmental pressure, and the degree of organizational responsiveness.

3. Empirical of experiential approaches have tended to develop contingency frameworks from the analysis either of databases or of accumulated individual practical experiences. The former approach is typified by the PIMS (profit impact of marketing strategies) studies. These have identified some 37 variables that are seen to have a powerful and predictable effect on profits, the most important of which are market share, long-run industry growth, short-run market growth, corporate size etc. The Boston Consulting Group developed similar conclusions as to the influence of market share on profitability, and incorporated the effects of the experience curve as an explanatory and intervening variable. Several other studies have developed contingency proposals that are linked to appropriate processes for strategy formulation and planning systems.

4. The conceptualization approach has generated a number of contingency frameworks, the most notable and earliest of which was that of Ansoff (1965), who produced a comprehensive conceptual model of corporate strategy. Glueck (1972) also produced a comprehensive contingency model for the strategic management area, comprising 71 separate hypotheses.

Steiner (1979) concluded that contingency theories,

> serve more to illuminate and educate the scholarly observer of organisation strategy than to provide solid guidance to operational managers. (p. 414)

He also considered that contingency theories developed in the strategic management fields were,

> with a few major exceptions, a limited domain theory which focuses on several important theoretical areas while ignoring broad interconnections with other models and systems. (p. 414)

Like the fields of organizational theory and management theory, many researchers in strategic management have sought to unite the limited domain theories into an integrated or general contingency theory. Ginsberg and Venkatraman (1985) proposed a systems framework for the integration and evaluation of the limited domain contingency findings in strategic management. As shown in Figure 8.2 this incorporated four groups of contingency variables, environmental (input variables), performance (output variables), organizational (process variables), and strategy (viewed as a linking variable).

Using this model they sought to classify some 29 limited domain research studies according to their primary focus on the formulation stages I, II, or III, or on implementation. Their findings suggested that the primary focus of these studies were on the formulation I stage, and they suggested that

> future strategy researchers should accord a more prominent role for organizational and performance variables as contingency influences on strategy formulation . . . that emphasizes the influence of the

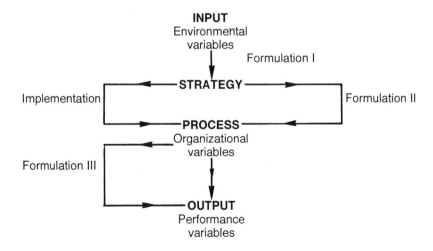

Figure 8.2 Systems framework for stategic contingency theory.

values and perceptions of top managers on organization strategy and effectiveness. (p. 430)

Paine (1979) provided another approach to an integrated contingency theory of strategic management. This was based on the construction of a matrix of appropriate strategies and capability profiles. Although the matrix he constructed was limited to nine cells, there is no theoretical reason why this could not be expanded. By assessing the contingency profile of environmental uncertainty facing an organization together with an assessment of the gap between the current position of the firm and its goals, an appropriate strategy could be selected from the matrix. The difficulty in applying this approach is that even with the fairly considerable research that has been undertaken, it is not really possible to make satisfactory entries in the nine cells in this exemplary matrix, let alone support an extension of the matrix.

8.4 SUMMARY

Research into the strategic management field has developed from a number of different discipline-based sources. The general result has been a fragmented body of research findings and theory constructions. There have been several attempts to draw the various research findings together into a unified theory of strategic management. This has followed on from the establishment of the field of strategic management as an identifiable field of social science. In this effort, the contingency theory orientation as opposed to the universalistic or situationalist approaches appears to offer researchers a more appropriate vehicle for developing and integrating research findings. There are, however, two main problems in the application of contingency theory, i.e:

1. it can be difficult to produce generalisations that will be of real assistance to decision-makers in practice; and
2. the descriptive powers of the approach are limited.

There is no doubt that the contribution from both the universalist and situationalist approaches to strategic management theory and research has been significant and is likely to continue. But even though the contingency theory may be somewhat deficient in terms of its descriptive powers and its ability to provide generalized theories when compared to the other two approaches, it nevertheless does provide an invaluable bridge between these two extremes. In writing this book, we have tried to build on the substantial body of universalist-oriented research on risk in decision-making, and to link this to the more descriptive or situationalist-oriented empirical research on decision-making. The framework which emerges from linking these provides the basis for developing a contingency model of the risk element in strategic decision-making.

QUESTIONS

1. To what extent do you think it a useful exercise to try to identify and then classify different schools of thought on strategic management (i.e. instead of looking for differences, would it not be better to concentrate on identifying similarities)?

2. Produce a simple definition of contingency theory and show how it differs from the universalist and situationalist approaches.

3. Do you think there are reasonable solutions to the four problems identified by Schoonhoven?

4. Explain what a limited domain model is and show how its use may assist a contingency approach.

5. Make a list of ten contingency variables that will always have a real effect on the performance of the commercial organization.

A contingency model of risk in strategic decisions

9

INTRODUCTION

The aim in this chapter is to produce a consolidation of the various analyses made in the previous chapters into a general contingency model of strategic decision-making, highlighting the major groups of variables involved. A limited domain model is then developed from this, and it focuses on the risk and information variables and their interaction in the process of making strategic decisions.

9.1 CONTINGENCY MODEL: STRATEGIC DECISIONS

As we have tried to show, strategic decision-making is influenced by a wide range of variables which have complex and often ambiguous interrelationships. Our task is to develop a generalized contingency model of the strategic decision process. To help us achieve this, we have classified the contingency variables into four broad categories by reference to their common characteristics, namely:

1. *Task environment characteristics* These are the variables which represent the nature of the overall framework within which the strategic decisions take place.

2. *Decision-specific characteristics* These are the variables which reflect the nature and attributes of the specific strategic decision to be taken.

3. *Decision-making unit characteristics* These are the variables which relate to the characteristics of the individual or groups involved in the decision process.

4. *Information characteristics* These are the variables which concern both the quantitative and qualitative dimensions of the information available and of the information systems that are designed to support the strategic decision-making process.

9.1.1 Task environment characteristics

The process for taking any decision (and a strategic decision in particular) cannot take place in a vacuum. The process necessarily takes place in an environment which will be made up of a number of elements, the most important of which are as follows:

- *External environment* There are a number of demands and pressures which flow from the environment in which the organization operates. Included in the list of pressures and demands are the economic, social, technological, marketing, legal and financial issues relevant to the organization's market(s), i.e. the customers, suppliers, competitors, employees, central and local government, and other interest groups or agencies within the community all play their part in limiting or encouraging the organization's activities.

- *Organizational environment* Within the organization, there must be a framework within which the decision-making process will function. This framework will be constructed from formal and informal organizational structures; it will be supported by an appropriate level of resource which includes making sure that people with the right skills are present at the right place and at the right time; performance levels will be monitored; processes and procedures will be continuously modified to match the organization's needs; and internal power relationships will be shaped to provide a supportive environment within which to work and to provide efficient and effective management.

- *Organizational objectives and culture* This will be made up of the missions, purposes, objectives, policies, plans and the standards of conduct and performance expected of the organization and its members. Some of these will be formalized within the organization's own mission statement or other statements of objectives and policies, while others will be observed informally within the culture of the organization and its operating environment.

9.1.2 Decision-specific characteristics

Each strategic decision faced by an organization will, by its nature, tend to be unique. This uniqueness may be characterized broadly into two areas:

1. The nature of the strategic problem. This involves two component elements:

    - the scale of the problem in relation to the normal strategic issues faced by the organization; this will usually be measured in terms of the financial or resource implications for the organization, but it may also affect the amount of time available to the managers to consider each element of the problem before having to make their decision; and
    - the degree of complexity, ambiguity, unfamiliarity and instability associated with the specific strategic problem or issue. Our use of the word 'instability' in this context is a reference to the dynamic nature of many of the strategic issues and problems faced by modern organizations. It also reflects the increasingly fluid nature of some of the environmental characteristics which may change with such rapidity and to such a degree as to alter the nature of the

issue or problem faced by the organization from week to week (or in some cases, from day to day). This is very likely if the nature of the business activity is speculative or interactive, i.e. the state of the market is determined by the actions of competitors, e.g. currency exchange rates in a non-regulated market or commodity prices.

2. Decision conditioning factors. Within each strategic decision to be taken, there will be a range of factors which may either support or constrain the approach to its solution. Examples of the more important factors include:

   - the significance of the decision to the organization;
   - the degree of irreversibility in the decision once it has been taken;
   - the extent to which members of the decision-making unit are to be accountable, whether individually or collectively; and
   - the time and resource constraints which apply to the process of identifying a solution to this particular problem.

9.1.3 Decision-making unit characteristics

There are several characteristics that relate to the decision-making unit. These factors will influence the decision-making at several different levels, i.e. input, process and output:

- the skills and expertise of those who make up the unit will dictate the initial choice of decision-making style and the information content immediately available to support the decision, and will affect the extent to which further information needs are specified;
- the skills of the individuals and the extent to which they are supported by the resources of the organization will affect the processes and methodologies employed in the decision-making; and
- the track record of the unit in terms of previous success and failure will have an effect on the extent to which the solution to the immediate problem is likely to be effective.

The two major groupings of such factors include:

1. *Group or individual* Strategic decisions are more likely to be the product of group effort than individual effort, though the influence of particular individuals may be significant in certain organizations. In some cases, the main decision processing and strategy formulation may be conducted by an individual and then ratified by a group before implementation.

2. *Individual characteristics* This includes the knowledge, skills, experience, abilities, motivation and personality of those primarily concerned with strategic decision-making, all of which may be important influencing variables. In many respects, these features may be found within a group situation, though the interaction of individuals within the group may result in the group aggregate of

each characteristic representing less than the summation of the individual members' characteristics.

9.1.4 Information characteristics

Information provides the vital interface between the task environment and the decision-making unit. Factors which will influence the effectiveness of this interface include:

- the types and quantity of information available;
- the quality of this information; and
- the incremental costs of improving both the quantity and the quality of the information.

The information of concern in such decisions relates to both external and internal issues. Inherent in these factors is the overall quality or effectiveness of the organization's information systems. By this, we mean both the processes of data collection, analysis and synthesis, and the communication mechanisms which will use both manual and electronic means.

9.1.5 The interaction of the characteristics

The four elements outlined above constitute the framework within which strategic decisions are made, and their interaction will dictate the effectiveness of each decision made. We must emphasize that these major elements are clearly not independent, and the degree and nature of their interaction results in increasing complexity. It is the unpredictable manner of these interactions and the resulting complexity that have frustrated systematic research and have impeded the development of universal propositions and a theory for strategic decision-making. A schematic diagram of the four elements is provided in Figure 9.1, showing the broad nature of the interactions.

Thus, when undertaking strategic decisions, the decision-making unit acts within the overall framework dictated by the characteristics of the task environment and those of the decision itself (decision-specific). The variables within each of these broad elements may interact on an individual basis between the elements. For example, significant changes in either product or process technology (task environment) will potentially influence several variables within the decision-specific element such as scale, unfamiliarity, significance and, possibly, the time constraints on making a decision. Also, the variables of complexity, scale, significance and irreversibility (decision-specific) contained within a strategic decision faced may impose changes on the organizational environment and organizational objectives variables in the task environment.

Information provides the link between these elements in the decision-making framework and the decision-making unit. The information systems provide the inputs to the decision-making unit to assess the current state and future trends in the strategic environment, and to evaluate the specific nature of the decision faced. It follows that the effectiveness of the

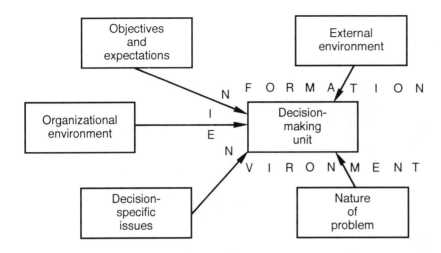

Figure 9.1 General contingency model of stategic decisions.

decision is influenced by all four factors, and is contingent on the appropriate matching of the individual variables in terms of both the content of the strategic decision and the processes used in formulating it.

A final important point related to the model is the bi-directional interaction between the decision-making unit and the task environment. This reflects the view that the decision-maker can both influence the decision environment and be influenced by it. Obviously, the extent of the impact that the decision unit may have on the task environment will vary with the nature of the decision but, even where the decision is likely to have a major effect upon the organization's strategy, the impact on the task environment may often be considerably limited. The reason for this is that, within the organization itself, we would expect the task environment to provide a reasonably stable framework within which decision-making is to take place. The institutional committee structures and boards tend to change only slowly, reflecting a tendency in most cultures to a conservative view of the need to change existing power relationships.

As to the external environment, the impact is likely to be limited unless the organization holds a dominant position in the market. We should remember that if the impact would constitute an abuse of a monopoly or dominant power, it might be unlawful and so should be avoided. An important implication is that the information environment and systems provide the means for the decision-making unit to achieve influence and control. The more effectively the decision unit collects information and exploits it, the better the quality of the decision is likely to be. If it is a decision intended to have an impact upon the either the internal or the external task environment, the way in which the decision is communicated could be the primary determinant of success, e.g. in convincing those affected of the need to change.

9.1.6 Risk-relationships within the model

The introduction of risk into this general contingency model provides a further dimension which enhances the model's descriptive capacity in relation to strategic decision-making. The overall stages in the decision process and the impact of risk on the perceptions of the decision-making unit are illustrated in Figure 9.2.

Inherent in the task environment facing the organization and the decision-making unit are both uncertainty and risk. In broad terms, environmental uncertainty results from the unpredictability of future changes in the environment, while the risk emanates from the potential failure of the organization to respond or position itself appropriately to meet these changes. For example, future changes in consumer tastes may be difficult to predict and are hence uncertain, but a failure to respond to such possible changes may pose significant risks to the market share, profitability and, possibly, the survival of the organization.

The decision-specific characteristics such as complexity, scale and irreversibility will also influence the level of risk extant within the decision. The nature and magnitude of the risk prevailing in the decision environment are potentially to be transmitted to the decision-making unit via the information system within the organization. The information inputs actually received by the decision-making unit, together with the characteristics of that unit, will shape the perceptions of risk in each particular strategic decision situation. We should be clear that the overall quality of the information system and the decision-maker characteristics are crucial factors in transforming the risks prevailing or extant in the decision situation into risk perceptions. The quality of the resulting decisions and the effectiveness of the decision process will largely be determined by the effectiveness of this risk transformation process. The three broad outcomes to the process of transforming prevailing risks into perceived risks are:

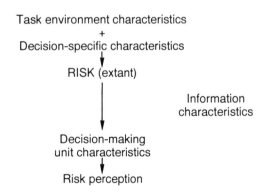

Figure 9.2 Stategic decision process contingency model: incorporating risk dimension.

risk perceived = actual risk (extant)
risk perceived > actual risk (extant)
risk perceived < actual risk (extant)

Unfortunately, the decision-making unit has no means of establishing, other than perhaps in the *ex post facto* analysis of the situation, the degree to which the risks perceived match the actual risks prevailing in the decision. A further complication is the transient nature of both risks and risk perceptions. Thus, as situations develop, it is likely that different values will be attributed to the scale and importance of parameters in *ex post facto* risk than in *ex ante* risk. In some senses, however, the problem is hypothetical as there are no effective means of measuring the actual risks perceived in the highly complex environments faced by business organizations, other than by some form of subjective scaling. But whether subjectively or not, the key issue for all organizations from the decision-making point of view is to try to optimize the match between perceived risk and actual risk at the time of choosing between alternatives.

An important feature to recognize in the formulation of risk perceptions is the influence of the interaction between the decision-maker characteristics and the information system. For example, lack of knowledge, training or experience in the case of the decision-maker (whether as individual or group) may result in the failure to make a full evaluation of the risks transmitted by an effective information system. Equally, an ineffective information system may provide misleading information on the risks facing the decision-maker, irrespective of the quality of the decision-making unit.

9.2 LIMITED DOMAIN MODEL: STRATEGIC DECISIONS

We introduced the role of limited domain models within the contingency approach to strategic management in Chapter 8. The focus of this section is on a limited domain of the overall contingency model outlined above, namely the information environment and its impact on risk perception. A systems model of this limited domain is provided in Figure 9.3. The risk input is recognized as being a function of both the task environment and the decision-specific characteristics. We now intend to concentrate on the process of the relationship or interaction between the information envi-

Figure 9.3 Systems model: risk perception formulation.

ronment and the decision-maker, examining the way in which the information system may transmit or influence risk perceptions, and the decision-maker's interactions with the information system in response to differing perceptions of risk.

9.3 RISK RESOLUTION AND INFORMATION SEARCH: OUTLINE MODEL

An outline model of the information search and processing stages in relation to risk resolution is presented in Figure 9.4. This model describes the stages of information search, followed by the processing and analysis of information, and then the evaluation, extraction and synthesis of the information to be made available to support the decision process. In a hierarchical organization, the search for, and immediate processing of, information is likely to be carried out below the strategic level. The processes designed to summarize and present a view of the data actually collected may introduce distortions into the information output to the strategic level (for more detail, see section 3.3.1). We therefore posit that the stages of information processing and evaluation carried out at a strategic level must result in a subjective judgment by the decision-maker as to the extent to which the information available is reliable and can resolve the elements of risk in the decision situation.

We have used the terms 'risk aversion' and 'risk avoidance' in previous chapters as opposed to 'risk resolution' to distinguish those actions taken by the decision-maker to reduce or eliminate any undesirable conse-

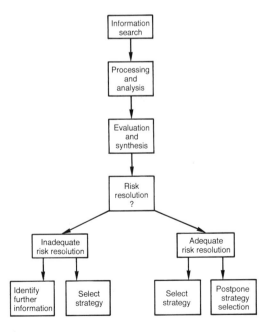

Figure 9.4 Information processing and risk resolution model.

quences and to minimize the likelihood of their occurrence. By using the term 'risk resolution', we do not intend to imply that the risks are either eliminated or reduced in any way. It is used in the sense that the decision-maker has a sufficient level of confidence concerning the decision faced as a result of considering the information collected and its analysis (for a further examination of this issue, see section 5.1.1). This level of confidence will be reflected in the decision-maker's subjective view that he or she has sufficient:

- knowledge of possible outcomes;
- understanding of the potential consequences and scale of such outcomes;
- appreciation of the probabilities of each likely outcome occurring; and
- understanding of the underlying mechanisms that determine the scale and probability of the outcomes.

The degree of sufficiency concerning these factors will be a function of the decision-maker's level of confidence in the decision situation, and will vary between no knowledge and perfect knowledge depending on the characteristics of the decision-making unit. We should emphasize that the level of knowledge is most likely to fall somewhere between the two extremes and not at the extremes themselves, i.e. a complete lack of knowledge or perfect certainty will be most unusual in the real world. At its simplest level, the decision-maker's task is to formulate a subjective assessment of:

1. the risks inherent in the decision task environment and the decision specific variables; and
2. the risk involved in basing the decision on what appears to be the currently available information and, hence, knowledge of the decision situation.

The outcome to the risk resolution stage is presented in the model as two alternatives:

1. The decision-maker considers that the risks associated with the set of alternative strategies under consideration has been adequately identified and resolved, and consequently has sufficient confidence to undertake the choice of strategy.
2. The decision-maker considers that further identification and resolution of the risks involved is both possible and necessary in order to generate sufficient confidence to undertake the choice.

The model proposes four actions on behalf of the decision-maker as a result of the assessment of the extent to which the risks are resolved or are acceptable on the basis of the information collected, analysed and synthesized (see Figure 9.4).

9.3.1 Inadequate risk resolution

If the subjective judgement of the decision-maker is that the risks perceived to be inherent in the decision situation faced have not been adequately resolved, and so he or she feels a low level of confidence concerning the situation, one of two actions is likely to result:

1. *Information identification and search*   The decision-maker will identify what additional information appears necessary to resolve the risks involved, and specify how the subsequent search, analysis and evaluation of the additional information should be undertaken. In order to build up confidence, we would suggest that this should be an iterative process that would continue until the decision-maker feels that the risks as then perceived are either acceptable or sufficiently resolved. There are other factors that will have a positive influence on what interim decisions are taken at this stage, the two most important of which are:

   - the extent to which further information is available or may be made available for inclusion in the decision process; and
   - the cost of collection and analysis which may outweigh the benefits to be gained in improved risk resolution.

   As mentioned previously in sections 3.1.1 and 9.1.3, it is recognized that the criteria used to judge the adequacy of the information available and the potential for further information to improve the understanding of the risks involved are essentially subjective and related to the decision-maker's experience, personality and other characteristics. Corbin (1980) reviewed a number of research studies undertaken to assess the use of information to reduce uncertainty, and concluded that

   > although subjects did not search until complete knowledge was gained, they waited for a particular level of uncertainty to be reached, a level independent of initial uncertainty or speed with which uncertainty could be reduced. (p. 60)

   Reference to related research on 'risk tolerance' indicates that risk cut-offs exist as a function of personality variables (e.g. Brim and Hoff, 1957; Cox, 1957) and situational variables (Lamm, 1967).

   A further feature to recognize is that the search for further information effectively postpones the decision. The motives for such postponement may be the genuine desire to gather further information, or it may be an intentional or subconscious decision to delay making the decision itself. The motives for such postponement are discussed further in section 9.3.2.

2. *Strategy selection*   This particular outcome may reflect one of three possible situations:

   - *The influence of time or cost constraints (or similar decision-specific variables)*   This first situation is likely to be a fairly typical description of many practical decisions where either the time or other resources available to permit further information search and analysis are limited before a final decision or strategy selection is required. The decision-maker may often be compelled to make a decision even though fully aware of the inadequate assessment of the high risks involved;

- *The decision-maker's self-confidence* This second situation represents the cases in which the decision-maker, while recognizing the inadequacy of the information available, feels sufficiently confident to select the strategy by evaluating and resolving the risks involved on the basis of his or her past experience or intuition; or

- *The decision-maker's ignorance* This final situation covers those decision-makers who are ignorant or unaware of the true inadequacy of their resolution of the risks involved and, hence, proceed to make decisions on the basis of the information currently available.

In the first two cases, the decision-maker is taking an essentially pragmatic decision to select a strategy. Thus, because the decision will be taken in the full knowledge that the information currently available is inadequate to produce a satisfactory resolution of the risks inherent in the decision, there will be both an intellectual and an emotional preparedness to cope with the consequences if they prove to be undesirable. In the third case, the undesirable consequences may appear to come without warning and therefore be all the more unfortunate in their effect.

9.3.2 Adequate risk resolution

Once the decision-maker has reached the subjective conclusion that the risks inherent in the decision situation faced have been sufficiently resolved, and he or she feels the desired level of confidence concerning the situation, one of two actions is likely to result:

1. *Strategy selection* In most respects this outcome reflects the normative model of decision behaviour under risk. The decision-maker continues the search, analysis and evaluation loop for further information related to the strategic situation until he or she is completely satisfied that the risks involved have been adequately resolved. It is somewhat difficult to conceive of a practical situation in which the decision-maker would fully resolve the risks involved in a range of alternative strategies so that purely rational decision criteria could be applied in the selection of the most appropriate strategy to fulfil the organization's objectives. A more realistic view of this outcome would be that the decision-maker is sufficiently satisfied that the major risks which have a real effect on the strategies involved have been identified and resolved. The result is that there is a reasonable basis on which to judge the risks involved in alternative strategies when selecting between them. This again implies a subjective judgement on the part of the decision-maker concerning the adequacy and sufficiency of risk resolution, and it is a

reflection of his or her confidence in the given decision situation.

2. *Postponement of strategy selection*   This final outcome to the information search/risk resolution process recognizes the situation in which the strategy selection may be delayed or postponed even though the decision-maker considers that the risks involved have been adequately identified and resolved. Earlier, we referred to the possibility of this outcome when the risks have not been sufficiently resolved. The consequences would then often be the continued activity of information processing which would delay the choice stage. The postponement contemplated here may be of a temporary nature or may be an indefinite postponement. Possible reasons for such postponements may be that:

- there have been changes in the external or internal environments which have occurred after the start of the decision-making process, making it inappropriate to reach a final decision at this time;
- there is a body of considered opinion that although the strategy may prove effective in the future (say, if there were to be changes in the environment) the timing of the strategy may be inappropriate at present;
- it may be expedient for tactical reasons to delay so that there can be an assessment of the strength of likely opposition from, or of the strategies of, competitors;
- the often necessary process of assessing the degree of support or opposition to the potential alternatives within the organization can take place; or
- the individual can try to avoid the responsibilities associated with making such a decision through the procrastination.

Corbin (1980) provided support for this view of the non-decision outcome to decision situations, by recognizing two groups of reasons for failure to decide, i.e:

- what he termed the non-perception of an occasion to make a decision; and
- the refusal to make a decision.

Corbin suggests that the latter reason of refusal or delay in making a decision may arise from four sources, i.e. that the decision-maker is:

- inspecting further alternatives;
- tapping alternative sources of information;
- going through a process of deliberation; and
- waiting for a goal object to become available.

Barnard (1938) in his study *The Functions of the Executive*, identified this outcome as an element of sound management skill when he wrote,

> The fine art of executive decisions consists in not deciding questions that are not now pertinent, in not deciding prema-

turely, in not making decisions that cannot be made effective, and in not making decisions that others should make. (p. 194)

Implied in this statement is the view that high risk perceptions either of an organizational or individual nature are valid reasons for the postponement of a decision. Brunsson (1982) also provided support for what he termed 'the wait-and-see' situation of no action on a decision. While Astley *et al.* (1982) recognized discontinuities in the decision process due to the desire of decision-makers to:

- seek more information;
- gain time to aid comprehension;
- gain commitment; and
- clarify the situation.

MacCrimmon (1974), Thompson (1967) and Child (1974, 1975) are examples of other authors who identified similar risk avoidance and decision deferment behaviour.

9.4 SUMMARY

What we have now shown is that the perception of risk is an important interacting variable between the main groups of contingency variables in the strategic decision-making model. This aids the interpretation of the interaction between the decision-maker's information processing activities and the information environment. We then established that the process of risk resolution is the key influencing variable in this interaction. In a sense, this is the final refinement of the explanations we began in Chapter 2 when we discussed issues such as how people think about risks and form their perceptions of what may happen. At each stage in the argument which followed as to the nature of decisions at a strategic level when there are elements of uncertainty and risk, we have tried to build up increasing levels of sophistication finally to reach this point. We think that the model, as developed, has significant explanatory scope in relation to both the normative and the descriptive views of the decision process; for example, decisions undertaken within time or other resource constraints and situations where there is evidence of procrastination or postponement of the decision.

The next steps require us to refine our understanding as to the nature of an organization and its relationship with its environment, and then to begin to take a more practical view of business decision-making.

QUESTIONS

1. Create a list of specific examples under each of the four classification headings identified in section 9.1 (e.g. under which heading would you put an informal telephoned warning from a sympathetic individ-

ual employed by a trade competitor that his/her organization is about to cut prices across the product range?)

2. Draw you own diagram to describe the nature and extent of interaction between each of the four variables.

3. Produce a simple explanation of how the element of risk affects the interactions you have shown in your diagram.

4. To what extent would you agree with the following statement?

> The risk resolution element is not a process, it is the subjective feeling of confidence experienced by the decision-maker just before the decision is taken.

5. Discuss the proposition that the adequacy of the risk resolution process (?) and the quality of the strategy selected (if any) are always likely to be determined by the quality of the information available to the decision-maker.

Further thoughts on the nature of an organization 10

INTRODUCTION

We now begin the move towards the more practical case-study elements of this book. But before we abandon the wholly theoretical view of the relevant elements in the calculations and assessments affecting risk and uncertainty, we must come back for another look at the nature of the organization. There are many new views and ideas as to what an organization is and how it relates to its environment so, as a bridge between the contingency theory and the practicality of decision-making at a strategic level, let us delve a little more deeply into the modern organization.

10.1 THE COMMON DENOMINATOR ELEMENTS OF AN ORGANIZATION

We are obliged to begin this chapter with the general proposition that there is no single theory as to the nature of an organization, but we may start this more detailed evaluation with a number of 'truths':

1. The business organization is a problem-solving and decision-making body.
2. Uncertainty in the environment is a positive constraint on the capacity of the organization to survive.
3. The modern organization must relate to its market, but the relationship is not clear cut. The large organization will have some degree of control over its market and will be able to exercise some elements of discretion within the market. However, it does not perceive the market objectively – it sees the market through a series of organizational filters. Further, information about the market is not absorbed automatically, it has to be searched for. Often this research does not take place unless there is an indication of current or future failure and so the nature of the inquiry may produce a highly focused view of one aspect of the market place (section 3.1.2).
4. In its relationship to the market, the organization will, in competition with other organizations, aim to make a profit. For these purposes, we may assume that a profit is the difference between revenues and the sum of fixed and variable costs.

5. In addition to the profit motive, organizations may have other goals and objectives, e.g. growth, survival, producing a pleasing environment in which employees may work, providing employment opportunities for the disabled and the disadvantaged etc. These objectives will emerge from the interaction of forces both internal and external to the organization and how the organization decides what objectives to adopt is a result of compromising between the desire to maximize profit and the need to be seen to meet other obligations, e.g. to employees, shareholders, banks, customers, governments etc. We should also recognize that the process of compromise tends to be continuous and that this may lead to different goals and objectives being given priority as the balance of forces shifts within the organization. In turn, this may cause the organization to make different decisions at different times even though in similar situations.

6. The essential nature of an organization is as a mechanism for allowing people to offer their individual labour in a way that allows the many to benefit from each individual's competences and skills.

7. Producing purposive social activities requires the creation of management structures and the implementation of effective information and communication systems.

8. Given that not all decision-making is driven by the needs of the market, the discretions exercised by the organization will be subject to decision strategies or rules so that decisions may be more consistent.

9. As organizations develop, they create standard operating procedures that are intended to apply to the routine tasks. These procedures are the learned responses to standard stimuli and represent the memory of the organization.

10. According to Cyert and March (1992), 'Once organizational objectives and decision strategies are determined, the organization can be viewed as an information-processing and decision-rendering system.' (p. 21)

10.2 THE ORGANIZATION, HISTORY AND THE SCIENTIFIC METHOD

Traditionally, organizations have been described by structure charts which, in visual form, aim to capture the essence of the roles that people have, and the systems that operate such as those dealing with information and communication. The problem has always been that it is difficult to capture the subtleties of informal human relationships in a diagram. Although the law offers us the fiction that a corporation is a person with capacities very similar to those of a human being, the real world denies the existence of a corporate mind. This creates a major theoretical problem because although people may form opinions and adopt goals, organizations cannot think for themselves nor formulate goals. They are no more than pale reflections of the groups of people who have agreed to work together. The first question is therefore whether the so-called scientific method can help us to understand the nature of an organization.

History is a process which records a changing state of affairs. In making and analysing this record, it is possible to assume some degree of continuity so that we can look for patterns of cause and effect. The aim would be to help us to predict likely outcomes in the future should similar circumstances arise. It is suggested that the more often we can detect particular effects, the greater the degree of certainty in being able to project what may happen in the future. This represents the so-called scientific method whereby a hypothesis is offered for evaluation should apparent regularity in causation be detected. If other observers are able to replicate the predicted outcomes in suitable experiments, the hypothesis then becomes a theory. If no one can disprove the theory, it becomes the accepted view of the world.

The difficulty in applying this approach to history is that each historical event is unique. The same people can never meet in exactly the same circumstances. Further, in designing experiments or models, disinterested observers cannot replicate an event in the abstract, expressing all the latent possibilities for different outcomes and reflecting all the influences that could have led to the selection of one outcome rather than any other. Thus, when we come to look at social systems as opposed to natural world phenomena, we must be more cautious in adopting a scientific approach. After all, only if all the right conditions are met, will the random seed that falls to earth blossom forth into the beautiful flower.

The historical record shows that the development of, and interactions in, social systems are not linear and always tend towards the anomalous. Indeed, the very process of the scientific method is itself a social process whereby customs emerge among the members of the relevant group of scientists. How any particular hypothesis becomes the received wisdom for the next generation of scientists is a complex process. It is based upon the status and reputation of those who propose and seek to verify the hypothesis. As Galileo and others have discovered, challenging the establishment theories and the reputations of those who support them, is sometimes a dangerous political act of intellectual terrorism, stimulating a repressive response.

If scientific methodologies are suspect in dealing with social systems such as the commercial organization, we must now consider what other approaches may assist us.

10.3 AUTOPOIESIS AS A MODEL FOR SOCIAL ORGANIZATIONS

At a social level, the organization may be seen as a form of partnership or coalition. It may begin with an agreement between people with money (whether they be privately wealthy individuals or organized into groups such as banks) and entrepreneurs that a particular business opportunity is to be financed over a period of time. This opportunity will exist because the entrepreneurs and their prospective customers agree that the product or services to be provided are desirable. People with the relevant skills will then be recruited to produce the product or services and to achieve delivery which satisfies demand at a price that is economically satisfactory to all involved. Thus, when the organization is taking decisions, it must consider whose interests are likely to be affected and reflect those interests (or not) in the final decisions taken. Frequently, this will involve reconciling the different goals and motives of the individuals and groups whose interests were involved. The most successful organizations are those who take decisions with the least conflict between the different goals because then the most individuals are committed to making the particular project succeed.

Among the modern theories, one of the most interesting attempts to address the dichotomy between the individual and the organization is that of autopoiesis. The concept of the autopoietic system emerges from the study of cybernetics which, for our purposes, is the study of the structure, behaviour and control of the processes of systems. The term 'autopoietic' was first used by Maturana and Varela (1980) to describe living as opposed to non-living systems, e.g. a horse pulling a cart rather than an internal combustion engine powering a lorry. They identify the key characteristic of living entities as their autonomy. This does not deny that living entities interact with their environment. It simply recognizes that there is a defined boundary between the entity and its environment.

They then assert that living systems are by their nature mechanistic, i.e. their behaviour and capacity for development are a product of the properties of, and the interaction between, their component elements and any neighbouring elements. Thus, autopoiesis is a system that maintains its own organizational unity and, despite exchanging, replacing and restructuring some of its component elements, the system maintains its identity, i.e. it is homeostatic.

To understand the idea better, following Mingers (1989), let us compare a single cell taken from the human body and a chemical factory operated by ICI. Both are dynamic and contain complex component elements. They are both capable of producing chemicals by engaging in sophisticated processes. To a greater or lesser extent, both are capable of effecting internal changes but the nature of those changes are structurally determined, i.e. they are contingent responses triggered by events (whether internal or external to the organization) but the nature of each response is limited by the physical capacities of the organization. Thus, if the organization does not have eyes to see impending danger, it cannot take evasive action.

When the cell produces chemicals, some will be retained within the cell to support future processes and others will be exported from the cell (sometimes as mere waste). Each production process may call upon stocks of 'raw materials' already held, or supplies may be imported from outside the cell. To that extent, the cell is self-sustaining. It continually produces itself by manufacturing the very component elements necessary for sustaining continued existence. Another way of describing this would be that a cell is organizationally closed. Thus, although a cell may transform input into output, it does so only to maintain the integrity of its own existence. A factory, on the other hand, is produced and maintained by other systems. Although it mimics the cell by producing some chemicals which may be either retained or expelled, it does not sustain itself.

10.3.1 The role of the observer

Naturally, the way in which any observer perceives the entity and distinguishes it from its environment will depend upon the purpose of the observation. Each observer may have quite different reasons for identifying any particular group of potential components as constituting a unity. It is important to recognize two critically important rules:

1. autopoietic unities may become coupled together; if the resulting organization is relatively loose, this will be a mere colony; but if the identities of the coupled unities become merged into a greater whole, the newly emergent system will be autopoietic in its own right – that the metasystem may then decompose over a period of time or replace any of its component unities does not disturb this classification;

2. a distinction must always be made between an organization and its structure – an organization is the general relationship between the components which enables us to recognize the unity as belonging to a particular type of class (just as we might recognize that paper, printing and the process of binding constitute a book), whereas structure is concerned with the actual components which constitute this particular example of the more general class (so by reading the title and the contents of the book, we know which book it is).

Many different structures may produce unities of the same organizational class. So books may come in different sizes, with hard boards or paper backs, in different colours, written in different languages, with or without pictures or illustrations etc. Even if we were to change the structure, say by rebinding a paperback with boards for longer shelf-life, this would not change its organizational class. A pulping operation on an unsold book returned to a publisher would, however, destroy the identity of the book even though, to a greater or lesser extent, the chemical composition and physical mass of the residual pulp might remain reasonably similar to the ealier book.

By analogy, it is interesting to observe the attitude of the law to this issue. In *Asfar & Co Ltd v. Blundell*, a cargo of dates was contaminated by sea water when the hatch shifted in heavy seas. The insurers tried to argue that the dates were not lost. The judge commented,

> The ingenuity of the argument might commend itself to a body of chemists, but not to business men. We are dealing with dates as a subject matter of commerce, and it is contended that, although the

dates were under water for two days, and when brought up were simply a mass of pulpy matter impregnated with sewage and in a state of fermentation, there had been no change in their nature, and they were still dates. There is a perfectly well known test . . . whether, as a matter of business, the nature of the thing has been altered.

That the judge admits the possibility of the argument appealing to chemists points to the problem of the interest of the observer in making the classification. Thus, when approaching the task of observation, the observer should seek evidence by interacting both with the particular organization and its environment, making all the judgemental choices and reasons explicit in the resulting classification so that other observers may have a basis upon which to assess the reliability of that classification for their own purposes.

10.3.2 Commercial organizations as autopoietic systems

Many authors such as Beer (1980) have suggested that because human-based organizations achieve autonomy and maintain their identity despite changes of structure and the turnover in personnel, they may be viewed as autopoietic or that autopoiesis is a useful metaphor in thinking about how organizations work. Zeleny and Pierre (1975) express the potentially attractive view that

A unique autopoietic organisation, a network of values, norms and precepts, is self-created, self-maintained and self-grown.

However, such a view may be overly optimistic. Many human organizations are not well integrated, creating unequal power structures where quite different sets of values may emerge and motivate factional behaviour, e.g. to compete for resources or to achieve degrees of influence or dominance. This line of thought suggests that an organization would have an institutionalized metasystem which links the subsystems in a shifting pattern of relationships. It may therefore be reasonable to argue that, so long as the co-ordination of effort by the metasystem is aimed at preserving the existence of the whole entity, the organization is still autopoietic.

If this view is right, it would also suggest that there are hierarchies of values and norms within every organization and that the most successful managers are those who produce the most effective reconciliation of all the divergences. Left to themselves, each subsystem might be too wrapped up in trying to ensure their own survival to contribute to the well-being of the whole. Hence, the dynamic to the formation and maintenance of an autopoietic system is metasystem intervention to break down the colony grouping into a single entity. But some combinations of groups may prove unmanageable because the difficulties in resolving the problems of the relationships cannot be overcome. There are various situations in which this might arise:

- increasing specialization of function and interest within the different

components may lead to unbridgeable gaps of purpose;
- the manner of the metasystem intervention is resented and does not result in constructive dialogue;
- there may be difficulties in communication between the different components;
- each component may be subjected to different triggering stimuli from the external environment and respond in divergent ways; etc.

There is a further, more philosophical difficulty. It may be argued that human beings cannot be a part of an autopoietic system because humans are not physically produced by the system. We would suggest, following Robb (1989a, 1989b, 1991), that this misunderstands the nature of human social and commercial organizations. Although human beings may physically co-operate and pool their labour, their physical presence is not significant in social organizational terms. The vital components are the human properties of each contributor. The skills and attitudes of those for the time being involved will constitute the culture of the organization, setting its tone and defining its boundaries. The common values and norms will emerge as a part of the mind-set of those involved. Robb (1989b) says,

> Some modern organisations do appear to me to be much more than a temporary coalition of individuals who act on their own behalf. Such are the structures that many, if not all, of the individuals in such organisations so converge in their actions, and their thoughts, that their individuality becomes blurred, if not lost entirely. Insofar as the members of the organisation play out their roles as components of the organisation without regard to the personal consequences, so they are less whole as human entities. Inasmuch as they depend on the organisation for their survival, they are properly seen as components of it, and as components their freedom to choose to act against the preservation of its unity is curtailed. (p. 347)

For Robb, the primary issue is that there is a pooling of meaning and understanding through all the mechanisms of conversation and communication. If the social or commercial organization is sustained by this continuous production of shared understandings then it may genuinely be considered autopoietic. That the individual humans who work in the organization may come and go is irrelevant to the nature of the organization so long as the organization:

1. maintains control over the interactive processes to arrive at these shared meanings and values; and
2. is able to police the boundaries of itself to ensure that the environment distinguishes its separate existence as a unique entity. (For an application of this approach to the accounting profession, see Robb, 1991.)

The end-product would be an adaptively rational system (following Cyert and March, 1992, pp. 117–18), i.e:

- as an entity, the organization is capable of existing in a number of different states;
- at any one point in time, the organization may prefer one state to the other possible states;
- outside the organization, the environment contains factors that may stimulate the organization to react – these factors are outside the control of the organization;
- the organization has the capacity to respond to the external stimuli by taking decisions that may effect a change in the state of the organization in relation to its environment;
- given its past experiences, the organization may take decisions aimed at producing prefered states, i.e. the autopoietic organization may learn from its experiences and adapt itself to a changing environment.

10.4 THE ORGANIZATION, COMMUNICATION AND THE PROCESS OF CHANGE

As we have tried to show, if an organization is to survive and develop, it must encourage effective communication, i.e. those whose efforts are to be co-ordinated must all come to understand what is to be done. According to Habermas (1984, 1987), effective communicative action depends upon reference to three worlds:

- an objective world, about which statements can be true or false;
- a social world in which, by custom or agreement, things can be right or wrong;
- the subjective world of each speaker which the speaker may accurately describe or not.

Any society's culture and language will evolve with the capacity for coding and overcoding, i.e. the words and signals used may have a literal meaning (coding) but acquire additional layers of meaning because of the context in which they are used (overcoding). Using any manner of communication relies upon a vast array of shared meanings and assumptions about meanings common to the group. All group members build up a stock of ways in which to interpret what they see and hear. Habermas says that this constitutes an individual's 'lifeworld' and it is a reservoir of rules of thumb used to communicate and interpret data about each of the three worlds.

One of the problems within the modern bureaucratic organization is that much of the communication is standardized into written forms. Frequently, the normal spoken language is abandoned in favour of an institutionalized form of writing and this artificiality may create a barrier to the communication of meaning to the readers. When planning change, it should be recognized that both oral and written forms of conversation are important. If there is a possible loss of meaning in translation from written to spoken form or vice versa, or if there is a diffusion of meaning within the text, these problems should be addressed to ensure that accurate shared understanding is achieved. In many ways, the spoken language is a more free and subtle method of communication because of the addition of facial expressions and body language. It is closer to the social context than writing which, by its nature, will normally take place at a separate time and place from the act of communication.

Indeed, the theatre semiotician Patrice Pavis (1982) has suggested that a drama acquires meaning only as the audience decodes the visual iconography (set, costume, lighting etc.) and the textual content; and that this decoding is based upon the semiotically produced expectations which make myth, metaphor and puns work – such that one word may stand for many, one image evoke a mass of meanings and emotions. There is also the power to communicate meaning by inference or silence. Similarly, the literary historian Hans Robert Jauss (1982) suggests that in drama, an audience's response to a particular performance will be founded upon its collective experiences of previous performances. These previous performances establish the audience's 'horizon of expectations' but, should the performance move beyond the horizon, the audience's response will become unpredictable.

For our purposes, the issue should always be whether the method and manner of communication has transmitted meaning which genuinely has been absorbed by the collective consciousness of the group addressed. The more the method moves towards the conceptual and the abstract, particularly in the written form, the greater the need to verify that its content has not been lost. Only if there is a formalized feedback system can the consistency of lifeworlds be monitored and appropriate corrective action taken should differences be detected.

10.4.1 The functional contribution of the lifeworld

The more a lifeworld is shared between individuals, it will stabilize group membership and produce a high degree of social integration. Any disturbances to this reinforcement of understanding will tend to result either in non-cooperation or in conflict. This does not mean that there cannot be change. But it suggests that if any proposed change is to be successfully implemented, it must be compatible with the present state of the values known to be common to the shared lifeworlds of those to be changed. These common values are called 'themes', i.e. at some time, they will have been explicitly discussed by the group and a common view established. Thereafter, the fact of the agreement will allow the issue to remain inexplicit in everyday conversations until it is necessary to address some proposed modification to the common view. This subsequent discussion is part of the process of 'rationalization'.

Habermas suggests that this need to rationalize will become more common as the group's activities become more sophisticated. Indeed, he refers to decision theory and the rationalization process as being a part of 'strategic action' where common understandings are moulded in particular ways. Often, this strategic action will rely upon the use of power or deceptions to break down barriers to success. But, if this moulding process is really to be effective in motivating managers and workers to change, what is proposed must involve each actor's lifeworld to some extent. Should the rationalization process fail to strike sympathetic chords in the lifeworlds, alienation or lack of trust will enter the lifeworlds and the proposed changes will tend to fail.

Successful organizations represent co-ordinated fields of purposeful activities. The co-ordination arises from core concerns and functions which are agreed by the group and are accepted into their lifeworlds. In turn, this sets the agenda for creating the goals of the individual power centres within the organization. Where the organization is coercive in nature, i.e. uses power to legitimize and validate the use of authority to direct outcomes to debate, conflict and doubt will inhibit progress towards shared values. Thus, if any organization is to plan for change, it must:

- try to establish a framework within which a real conversation can take place between individuals who are objectively members of a group, regardless as to their declared place within the hierarchy of the organization;
- encourage group members to contribute freely to the conversation;
- treat all contributions as equally valuable whether they point to convergences or divergences of view;
- establish explicit sets of criteria by which to test the legitimacy of any decisions that the group may wish to make.

It is accepted that one or more of the social subsystems within the organization is likely to achieve a degree of dominance of emphasis within the conversations. The existence of dominance may be tested by the ability of any one group to shape the structure of the organization as a whole. In Marxist terms, this would be the achievement of hegemony which, for our purposes, would be the ability to organize the masses. However, it should be recognized that, in the modern organization, this may not be the owners (assuming that they can be identified in a pluralist shareholding environment) and it may not be the declared managing directors. It will be the group whose views consciously shape the future evolution of the organization. If any organization is going to make good progress, it must therefore encourage the emergence of a hegemonic subsystem with access to all the main lines of conversation within the organization and allow that subsystem to promote conversations as to the future evolution of the organization.

10.4.2 The lifeworld and organizational culture

Habermas's lifeworld respresents a unifying concept to the theory of organization cultures as described by Handy (1978, 1981). For these purposes, a culture should be seen as a conglomerate of ideas, value systems and norms which can be observed both in external relationships with other entities in the environment, and in internal structures, rules and dominating strategies where management decision-making styles, planning and authority delegation set the tone of the work place environment. Handy suggested four main types of culture as follows:

1. *The function or role culture*   In these organizations, there is central-ized decision-making and everyone's function or role is carefully defined. Bureaucracy prevails but with a logical and cost-effective remit so that large organizations are managed well in stable trading conditions. However, problems will arise through a lack of respon-siveness in more turbulent conditions. Here, conversations are for the purpose of control.

2. *The task or goal culture*   This is a more creative environment which is based on a net or matrix format. There is great freedom to change with decision-making based more on expertise than formalized position within a management hierarchy. The tone of the organiza-tion is to 'get the job done' so task or goal orientation prevails. Here, conversations are intended to inform rather than to control.

3. *Power or club culture*   This is a centralized organization where political games involving some risks to status or job tenure are played. Everyone is unified in support of the organization but the character of the environment may be either paternalistic or autocrac-tic. Here, knowledge is power so conversations are frequently strategic in nature.

4. *Person culture*   Here the organization is only a service to the individual and the primary management function is the co-ordination of facilities for those working within the environment. This form of culture is common in multi- or uni-disciplinary groups of experts whether in partnership or large departments. Here, conversations are intended to communicate with the others in the group but with a view to maintaining each individual's interests.

If the organization is decentralized, control is maintained by operational rules and the process of socialization, rather than through the excessive use of hierarchy. Rules and standards are the explicit route by which decision-making can be delegated down through the organization. Social-ization can permit delegation and achieve consistency more unobtru-sively, i.e. to the extent that decision-makers come to accept the same lifeworld, we may expect them to take similar decisions in similar circumstances. Perrow (1972, 1979) calls this the paradox of decentraliza-tion, that control can possibly be greater in a decentralized organization. The problem is that achieving this level of socialization may be very expensive in terms of the time and expertise required to achieve it. But in high risk enterprises, the improvement in control and co-ordination can be invaluable.

10.5   CHANGE AND RISK

In any situation where there is a choice to be made and one or more possible outcomes involve loss or damage to those involved, the everyday usage signifies that there is a risk involved. Naturally, we will always try to organize things so that uncertainty is reduced, but if no guarantee of outcome can be given and the outcome may have a negative value, i.e. it is something not desired by the organization, it is up to the managers to adopt risk reduction or avoidance strategies. The aim will be to:

- reduce the likelihood that the undesirable outcome will occur;
- reduce the magnitude of the potential loss;
- reduce both the likelihood and the magnitude of loss.

If we adopt Handy's theory for a moment, because any decision that is to be taken by any person within the organization may involve some element of risk, management's aim must be to produce a culture in which the best decisions can be taken. This means that rationalization conversations on key themes will have to take place to produce a greater degree of sharing in the lifeworlds of those employed, i.e. the managers will have to talk to each other.

The process that we are describing is not simple consultation before management dispenses wisdom, i.e. a coercive approach tempered by the pretence of democracy; it is the adoption of a different form of organization. If we now think of culture in metaphorical terms as being an emphasis on shared norms and values, we might prefer to see the organization evolve into a 'team', i.e. some form of unitary political system, or a 'coalition', i.e. a pluralist political system. Such metaphors may better capture the spirit that is required if effective decision-making is to be achieved by involved and committed employees.

How an organization plans to restructure itself and then tries to manage the implementation of those changes is likely to be a major challenge to the existing culture and will be an inevitable source of conflict. Some of the outcomes of this conflict may not have been desired by those that set the process in motion but, if the ultimate end-product is a better organization, it will have been worth the effort.

In trying to plan to make better decisions, one of the factors that will have to be addressed in the various conversations between subsystems is the way in which the organization will handle uncertainty and risk. To that extent, we see the issues of risk and uncertainty as merely additional factors to be weighed in answering the more general question of 'How should the organization move towards taking optimal decisions?' The hegemonic group should be looking to guide the conversations to consider how to achieve greater reliability of decision, i.e:

- final decisions in retrospect should be seen to have been correct;
- if alternative solutions were canvassed, they should have been viable albeit less cost-effective or unsatisfactory in some other way;
- the appropriate techniques and methodologies should have been used for the evaluation of the options (assuming that there was adequate time) and the reasons for the decision must have been made clear to those involved.

'But individual choices do not always appear immediately rational without the total context that explains the strategy followed – that is, individuals' choices may be both intelligible and acceptable to themselves but difficult to justify to a third party without reference to some wider context' (Cairns and Marshall, 1991, p. 87). Thus, the strategy may be to suffer several smaller losses to avoid one large loss. It cannot be assumed that the utility of any given loss is a linear function of the size of the loss. Any system of post mortems must therefore place each decision in its proper context so that there is a greater chance of a fair judgement on the behaviour of those involved.

Managers have a particularly important role to play as communicators. Many researchers have confirmed that managers spend a significant amount of their time communicating orally (e.g. Mintzberg, 1973; Keegan, 1974). As the level of uncertainty increases, so too does the requirement to process information and the managerial positions become essential clearing houses to link different groups together. The more judgemental the decision-making, the greater the need to have socially similar people employed in the key roles so that this communication process runs with the fewest possible number of errors.

10.6 HOW ARE ORGANIZATIONAL GOALS SET?

If an organization is to maintain its autopoietic status, it must achieve an understanding of its shared meanings and values. The practical manifestation of these meanings and values will be in the form of goals. According to Cyert and March (1992, p. 35), the key element in the bargaining process to arrive at organizational goals are the 'side payments', i.e. money, personal treatment, enhancement to status or reputation, acceptance of authority etc. These will frequently be addressed through policy commitments. Although the marginal cost of making each policy commitment is usually quite small to the other members of the potential coalition, the commitments will often relate to the allocation of scarce resources and the extent of the side payment therefore becomes a constraint.

A further problem is in persuading all the interested parties to make their needs and aims explicit. How far each party's position is investigated will depend upon the amount of time available and the skills of those managing the process. Further, the extent to which the new policies are tested for consistency with the existing policies may be a function of non-rational elements, e.g. the aggressiveness of the groups involved.

Even though it may be acknowledged that the immediate outcomes are not wholly satisfactory, the interested parties may agree to adopt the goals and their concommitant side payments on an interim basis. This may be reviewed and revised in the light of experience, e.g. budgets may be reallocated as needs become more clearly defined and tasks may be redefined as the people involved come to understand what is involved. Often this will involve an allocation on the basis of the new status quo. Thus, if one manager begins to exercise greater discretion as the particular role grows, this new 'authority' may be formally recognized and confirmed through a new contract (and, perhaps, a higher salary).

The problem is that because of time constraints, the past tends to become the blueprint for the future. Thus, it saves time to assume that last year's budget will serve as a model for this year, with the only change being to increment the whole in line with inflation. The organization therefore has to wait until either:

1. the aspiration levels of the interested parties force a challenge to the existing institutionalized expectations; or
2. the organization suffers from the consequence of not reviewing and changing an earlier rule, e.g. a major accident occurs and those injured make significant claims for damages.

A failure to make changes need not be harmful. Hence, it may lead to the creation of 'slack', i.e. a surplus of resources after making all necessary payments. This slack may be paid to members of the coalition even though it is not strictly necessary, e.g. salaries may be paid at a higher level even though there is no lack of loyalty and, even if the employees left, highly competent replacements could be appointed on a lower salary. In the boom years, this slack may be paid out as bonuses to shareholders and/or as a reward to the enterprising staff. In the lean years, it can be a cushion against disaster, allowing cuts to be made without damaging performance so long as a sense of equity is preserved in the distribution of the cuts. Thus, the organization can manipulate the slack to adapt itself to changes in the economic environment.

10.7   THE ORGANIZATION AND THE POLITICAL ENVIRONMENT

When the term 'political risk' is applied to the commercial organization, the usual meaning is that unwanted consequences may result from political activity. Within the organization, the political activity will take place within the constraints imposed by the prevailing culture. Thus, different members of the coalition may press for different goals at different times. In part, this will depend upon the demands being made by other parties in the bargaining system and people will modify their aspirations in line with their predictions as to likely outcomes.

Outside the organization, national governments may interfere with the way in which the organization is allowed to function, i.e. the commercial or business organization is a system within an environment and political events occur in that environment. At one extreme, there may be wars or civil unrest, or the actions of the state may involve the expropriation or nationalization of assets, i.e. the interference is direct and causes a discontinuity in the normal operation of the organization. At an intermediate stage, there may be discriminatory taxes or unfair competition from publicly subsidized competitors, i.e. the interference is less direct and still allows the organization some opportunity to make a profit. At a micro level, there may be some interference with parts of the organization's operations, e.g. local planning authorities may prove unwilling to allow buildings to be erected unless relatively expensive changes are made to reduce environmental impact, but this does not represent a major event for the strategic planners.

For the commercial organization, the impact of political events may appear to be indistinguishable from economic events. Thus, the nature of some legislation may be entirely economic in effect, e.g. currency devaluation, exchange control regulations, transfer pricing rules etc. Hence, the effect upon the organization may be to create significant uncertainty in the following areas:

- new constraints may affect the way in which money is moved from one part of the organization to another and affect investment decisions – this may take the form of new rules about the transfer of capital or profits, or the way in which the accounting system must show how profits or losses are calculated;
- if the political environment is unstable, people may wish to avoid working in that area or the government may restrict the movement of people – remember that instability is a property of the environment and it may either be a risk to the organization's profitability or an opportunity to earn greater profits depending upon the nature of events;
- at an international level, there may be problems about technology transfer, e.g. before the end of the Cold War, computer and other 'high-tech' equipment could not be sold to the Eastern Block countries, or the states involved may not police copyright, patents and other intellectual property rights, preferring to see their economies expand through piracy and unlicensed copying;
- there may be uncertainties affecting ownership and control of the organization – in the more unstable parts of the world, direct political interference may affect ownership or require that local people are positively involved in the running of the operations within their country; alternatively, states may interfere where the way in which the organization is run appears to be against public policy and self-regulation is ineffective;
- there may be uncertainties affecting the operational activities of the organization where local policy-making may be more volatile and arbitrary.

However, as the above list should indicate, economics and politics are distinguishable. Politics as a term refers to the legitimacy accorded to the use of power within a society, whether at a national or at a local level. Economics is concerned with the production and distribution of wealth within a society. Not unnaturally, there will be interaction between those who have wealth and those who have the power. Hence, those who have the power may seek to influence the way in which wealth is generated, i.e. politics will help to define the framework within which economic activity takes place. While those with wealth may seek power to protect the current distribution of wealth. Sometimes, the risks will be highly industry-specific. If the organization is involved in the production of economically and strategically significant products, their position may be very different from that of an organization which produces luxury, non-essential goods. Thus, if an organization has achieved a position of dominance in the production of necessary commodities it may either enjoy a protected position or become a target. A producer of non-essential goods may be ignored (the long-term fate of the organization being left to market forces), or it too may become a target for action. To think in clichés and stereotypes for a moment – an oil industry may fear nationalization in some parts of the world, while those who build and equip luxurious palaces may find work in places as unexpected as a socialist Romania. You should recognize that there is no certainty that any political event will have an effect upon business operations.

From the organization's point of view, there are two distinctions of a political nature that will have to be weighed in the decision-making process:

- a distinction must be made between types of political activity which are a part of a process of continuous change and those which represent discontinuous change (i.e. quantitative as opposed to qualitative change) – it is easier to forecast future trends where the process of change is more continuous than discontinuous, e.g. when a government has been in power for some years, it is easier to predict their actions but if, following a general election, a new government is voted into power, there may be significant uncertainty on how their sometimes vague election promises are to be converted into working legislation;
- a distinction must be made between gradual and rapid change – the more slowly change occurs, the easier it is to follow the trends and to approximate certainty; if the situation is dynamic and volatile, and no one trend is dominant, all the predictable outcomes may appear equally likely and uncertainty will prevail.

The uncertainty lies in the inability to predict what will happen to the investment represented by the organization and the revenue accruing to it when the various possible political events impact upon the day-to-day business operations. Most decision-maker's responses will be highly subjective. In dealing with the possibility of expropriation, Shapiro (1978) suggests sophisticated techniques for adjusting cash flow projections using the assumptions in the capital asset pricing model. He also suggests that these assumptions are varied depending upon whether the risks are systematic or not. The idea is to produce better quality assumptions on the expected value of cash flows and their distribution, but no matter how objective the managers try to be in collecting information and analysing the political situation, there will always be distortions in the estimates arising from subjective factors.

10.8 THE LAW AND THE REALITY OF POLITICAL AND ECONOMIC UNCERTAINTY

When people and organizations plan their future strategies, they will take the political and economic environment into account. Sharpston (1990) suggests that there are three levels of expectation that may result, namely:

1. expectation – a subjective belief that has not been formed through a careful appraisal of the available evidence;
2. reasonable expectation – this is an economic prediction based on a logical analysis of the available information; and
3. legitimate expectation – here, the individual or organization believes that it is legitimate to expect a particular form of treatment by the government or state institution.

We have already established that business decisions are usually taken on the basis of imperfect knowledge, i.e. that even if it was achievable, most organizations cannot afford the time and other costs of acquiring perfect information. Thus, risks cannot be eliminated and it is always reasonable for business decision-makers to expect a discrepancy between risks perceived and risks extant. The law will therefore not give a remedy if an expectation or reasonable expectation is not fulfilled – that is the essential nature of the business activity. Equally, states must be able to retain flexibility to deal with changing circumstances as and when they arise. If this involves changing policies or the laws at short notice, this is unfortunate but not necessarily something that the prudent manager could not have foreseen. After all, economic crisis is rarely an overnight phenomenon. It more usually emerges over a significant period of time and the seeds of each crisis can be observed by the economically alert manager as they germinate.

But, if there is a major qualitative change in policy that could not have been foreseen by the prudent manager, and that manager had actually been led to believe that there would be no change, the courts may give a remedy for breach of legitimate expectations. It must be shown that there were discussions between the organization and the state and that the organization then acted on the expectations created. Naturally, it must be possible to prove the nature of the discussions and to show that the beliefs about future government action were plausible. Further, managers are expected to read the papers and to keep up to date with changes. To gain access to the remedy, there must be no serious hint of change before it arrives. All these parts to the rule should indicate that it is very difficult to invoke the remedy, but the European Court of Justice first stated what has become its consistent policy in 1978,

> any trader in regard to whom an institution has given rise to justified hopes may rely on the principle of the protection of legitimate expectations. On the other hand, if a prudent and discriminating trader could have foreseen the adoption of a Community measure

likely to affect his interests, he cannot plead that principle if the measure is adopted.[1]

To that extent, therefore, the European business managers may have some protection, particularly if they deal in the more highly regulated areas of commercial activity.

10.9 THE BOUNDARY BETWEEN THE ORGANIZATION AND ITS ENVIRONMENT

Cooper (1992) reminds us of the distinction between distal and proximal thinking, i.e:

• distal thinking deals with effects and outcomes; and
• proximal thinking relates to processes and events.

The idea of trying to identify a boundary between an organization and its environment is essentially a distal project because it views the organization and its component systems as being in a fixed or finished state with strong boundaries to establish and maintain its separate existence (i.e. as autopoietic – see section 10.3). But, as we have seen in section 10.8, whether or not an organization can claim a legitimate expectation depends on the contact between individuals employed by the organization and individuals employed by the relevant government institution. This would run contrary to the idea of an organization as a 'thing' that can be measured in some way. It would be better to apply proximal thinking to see organizations as mediating networks, i.e. as being made up of groups whose composition may change from time to time and which relate together either continuously or not, depending on their functions. Thus, instead of talking about a boundary between groups or between the organization and the outside world, it might be better to think of an organization as an effect generated by the social contacts between the people involved in pooling their efforts for their common purpose(s).

Naturally, endless fluidity in group membership is a recipe for chaos so, if only to create some certainty in the mechanisms for the management of the organization, people have to be assigned functions and they are allocated to particular groups. However, as information technology empowers more people who work within the organization, the idea of group boundaries may become less meaningful. This leads us to make a number of propositions (based on Star, 1992) about how problem-solving and decision-making takes place, as follows:

1. Actions and intellectual events are always situated in the place where the people involved perform the relevant tasks.
2. The intellectual resources of the organization (i.e. its cognitive capacities) are distributed and collective. Thus, many individuals make up the organization (i.e. they are distributed throughout the various places in which organization activities take place). Each individual has his or her own abilities. At any moment, depending

on the status of the individual, that person may be the mind of the organization as it relates to an 'outsider', or that person's contribution may be collective through the co-ordinated activities of one or more groups.

3. Thus, the boundaries of knowledge in large organizations are highly fluid and complex. As between people, what the organization knows at any moment in time will depend on which individuals or groups are pooling their knowledge. The effectiveness of this sharing will always depend on social interactions and the problems of self-interest and motivations referred to earlier (see sections 2.2.3/4, 2.3.3 etc). In information systems terms, it will depend upon which people have been able to access the best quality data at the relevant time. This might be thought of as a design or training problem, i.e. it is simply a case of building a good system and ensuring that the people are trained to use it properly. Unfortunately, to produce an effective design requires a good understanding of two elements:

    - how the organization actually works; and
    - how the people might be persuaded to work if an automation project is undertaken.

    For all the reasons canvassed throughout this book, neither question can be answered with any degree of certainty.

4. The ability of the organization to solve problems and to take good quality decision depends upon being able to assign the task to the right place within the organization to take advantage of the knowledge and skills located there or to be collected there.

5. Information technology can potentially go anywhere and make data available everywhere. To that extent, it breaks down the old social boundaries and requires the development of new ways of dividing up the work. One likely outcome as more people may become involved in problem-solving and decision-making is that the form and structure of the organization is continually modified through the process of negotiation, i.e. as people become aware of each new problem, they offer their knowledge and skills for exploitation. Thus, the cognitive resource is relocated where the most knowledgeable and skilful are identified on that issue.

Nothing said in this section should be taken as devaluing the concept of autopoiesis. That a boundary cannot be mapped with any degree of certainty does not mean that there is no boundary. All that it means is that the boundary line is being continually redrawn to match the cognitive and functional capacities of the organization. The organization remains aware of what is 'inside' it as opposed to 'outside' it. It will achieve this awareness through the principle of self-referentiality discussed by Gastelaars (1992). He builds on the idea of discourse analysis to show that all groups identify distinctive processes of inclusion and exclusion, i.e. to produce a set of differences between the internal and the external, by reference to which the internal may be defined. To that extent, even though internal barriers and boundaries between the groups constituting the organization may be disappearing, and greater fluidity in the interactive processes performed by the organization in relation to the world may arise, an organization may still be autopoietic.

10.10 SUMMARY

In the popular imagination, the running of successful organizations is in the hands of entrepreneurs. Flood (1992) defines an entrepreneur as,

> a person (or group) who initiates and manages enterprising new commercial ventures which have risk of profit and loss. (p. 15)

The process of initiation depends upon the ability to make the best choices at the outset, whereas management is the continuation of the activity once it has begun. As strategies mature, situations change and further input may be required to revitalize the efforts which continue to be made.

The best practice of initiation and management allows managers to receive optimal support when they are planning and making decisions, and complements their efforts to maintain or improve performance. The success of each venture inevitably depends on the social systems which constitute the organization. We have tried to show that organizations are like self-sustaining living things but that they may be present wherever the work of the organization is being carried out, be it in a formal office environment or a hotel bar where prospective clients are being entertained. If the survival pattern and growth of the organization is to have the desirable qualities of predictability and stability, those responsible for management must have access to good quality information. This information will be derived from the control and monitoring functions of the organization and it will allow the managers to make more confident decisions about future opportunities and the constraints that may affect performance. The more long-term the planning, the more likely it is that the managers are thinking strategically.

The problem is that, to a greater or lesser extent, all human beings are subjective, i.e. they have their own hopes, dreams and opinions, none of which needs have any objective validity. Yet the need of the organization is to co-ordinate the activities of all these different people so that their participation in the organization will result in viable decisions being taken. The greater the degree of uncertainty or risk attaching to each decision, the greater the need to ensure that the debate which leads to the decision being taken is constructive.

QUESTIONS

1. In a few sentences, write down a definition of autopoiesis as it applies to organizations.

2. Robb extends the application of autopoiesis to include the professions. Because groups like the Law Society and the British Medical Association lay down rules and police standards, do you think it legitimate to consider them autopoietic? Would you give the same answer to groups like the CBI or TUC which represent the interests of member organizations?
3. Within your own course or work environment, write down a few of the elements that are a part of your lifeworld.
4. How would you describe the culture in your course or work place?
5. What rules should apply to regulate the relationship between an organization and its environment?

Notes

1. *Asfar & Co Ltd* v. *Blundell* (1896) 1 QB 123 at p. 127, per Esher, MR.
2. *Luhrs* v. *HZA Hamburg-Jonas* (1978) ECR 169.

11 Risk and uncertainty revisited

INTRODUCTION

Somehow, the abstractions of theory can have a safe and detached emotional quality. But as you approach the reality of a decision where risks are involved, the hairs can prickle on the back of the neck if things are not apparently going to plan. We must now carry the theories forward into the world of an organization made more real. Let us consider what managers ought to do and how they ought to do it if they are to have the best chance of optimizing the outcomes to their eventual decisions.

All organizations usually have a system of checks and balances to try to ensure that decisions are in line with declared policy. In the case of a commercial organization, these policies will be stated in terms of target rates of return, maxima and minima figures of authority etc. This approach is not without its problems. The trend at a strategic level has been to define aims and objectives with increasing clarity instead of leaving the policies with enough fuzziness to encourage flexibility of response. Some organizations have therefore fallen into the trap of accepting or rejecting market opportunities on arbitrarily set criteria, decisions which can damage long-term profitability or performance. It would be more desirable for strategic managers to give their delegates an understanding of the level of risk the organization is prepared to take in pursuing its corporate mission. This will leave the employees some flexibility and creativity to follow up the activities of the entrepreneurs, i.e. to act as intrapreneurs. This may be defined as

> an innovative employee(s) of an organisation who (re)vitalizes management to sustain and strengthen enterprising new, establishing or established ventures. (Flood, 1992, p. 15)

11.1 PRACTICAL RISK MANAGEMENT

In business today, many of the risks have become more complex and harder to identify, quantify and control. Yet, on a day-to-day basis, senior managers are required to take commercial decisions with differing levels of risk attaching to them. These decisions may be characterized as investments, gambles or speculations. The following distinctions are useful:

- Investment will normally involve the placing of funds in the hope of receiving a favourable return. The most usual criterion against which to judge the acceptability of the investment opportunity is:

  - the higher the expected risk, the greater the expected return (see section 6.3.1/2).

- Investment differs from gambling because the expectation of gain is more positive.
- Speculations are transactions where the outcome is variable but there is a useful economic function, e.g. commodity futures and traded options.

An organization will not usually gamble because it cannot then control the risks, but it may speculate, say, by launching a new product, because there are better methods for predicting outcomes. The difference between speculation and investment therefore lies in the levels of risk involved.

11.1.1 Risk management defined

One of the strategic decisions taken by some organizations has been to build up the function of risk management. According to Doherty (1985) risk management may be defined as those investment decisions taken by an organization in anticipation of, or as a consequence to, foreseen losses and the selection of appropriate financing strategies. In one sense, therefore, risk management may be seen as a part of the organization's general financial planning and control activity. However, there are also technological overtones to the activity in that losses may flow from the processes undertaken by the organization. This requires a level of technical expertise to be able to identify the possible loss-producing situations and to measure the possible costs and benefits of a risk reduction project. But, whatever the detailed methodologies applied, in the final analysis, the acceptability of all projects must be measured against the organization's objectives.

11.1.2 The organization and the Stock Exchange

If we adopt a conventional business model of the organization, among the objectives for the commercial company quoted on the Stock Exchange will be value maximization. To some extent, it has become axiomatic that the welfare of the owners of any business is best assured by maximizing the share value. So it will be a natural tendency for managerial concerns to focus on the interests of the existing, as opposed to future, shareholders. One explanation for this would be that the managers may be seen as the agents of the shareholders for the running of the company. This view may be justified because, in extreme circumstances, the directors can be removed from office under the articles of association in a general meeting if a majority of the shareholders are dissatisfied and support a vote of no confidence. In more general terms, the value of the shares on the Stock Exchange provides a measure of performance, representing the market's assessment of the expected future earnings of the company based on the presently available information. This market assessment implies that managers will aim to maximize the future earnings capability of the shares. Since share values respond to reported and observed performance, capital markets impose a form of financial discipline on decision-making.

Under normal circumstances, we may assume that a commercial organization will wish to maximize its profits, i.e. the return to those supplying capital to the company, plus the residual surplus after deducting costs from revenue which is available to the equity holders. There is a problem in that the paid managers take the decisions not the shareholders, and their interests may not coincide. If the shareholders have a diversified portfolio of shareholdings (section 6.4.1), e.g. such as the large institutionalized investment organizations, a poor performance from one company may not be significant. But managers cannot afford to be complacent about their own jobs so they may adopt a more risk averse set of strategies, i.e. they may 'satisfize' not maximize in an attempt to ensure their own survival. However, even satisfizing may not be sufficient to avoid insolvency in severe recessions. To some extent, this conflict between shareholders and management can be reduced by requiring managers to have shares in the company and by giving performance-related pay and bonuses (section 1.3.1), but there will always be tensions because managers have loyalties to the organization and the people who work for it (section 1.2.2 on the shift from ownership to the organization as a biological entity in its own right).

An additional problem in these more difficult economic times is that companies which do not have a positive approach to management may become targets for hostile takeover with consequent loss of jobs. Further, if managers wish to retain their appeal to prospective employers, they must appear to have promoted the financial viability of their present (or last) employer. Both these factors may have a significant effect on the level of risk considered acceptable by the managers.

11.1.3 The organization and the cost of labour

We have now established that the level of trading in the stock exchange is a direct reflection of the perceived financial worth of a company. For employees the concerns are more immediate than the likely yield on money invested, the worth of the company being judged by the level of wages and salaries, and the practicality of the terms and conditions of employment offered. Both assessments of value are subject to the same laws of supply and demand. The demand for capital depends upon the degree of success in the performance of the company, i.e. the demand for the company's product or services. A relevant factor in this latter demand will be the competitiveness of the price for the product or services. In part, this will be a product of the cost of the labour required to produce or supply it.

Not unnaturally, if prospective employees think that there is a risk that the job may not be secure, they will usually ask for a higher salary. Whether this request is likely to be successful will, in part, depend upon the strength of the economy. If there is a shortage of jobs, the company can afford to offer low wages and salaries on a 'take it or leave it' basis. If there is competition between companies for skilled labour, an offer of higher wages and salaries will be necessary to recruit and retain staff of the right quality. From the employers' point of view, a further consideration is whether the law favours the employers so that a company is able to dismiss staff easily. If so, only more altruistic concerns will inhibit the commercial decision to reduce overheads by shedding staff if the market falls. Quite apart from its role at a mechanistic level in a negotiating and bargaining session, where threats and brinkmanship may play a vital part in achieving the desired result, we must therefore see risk as a key factor in the substance of wage and salary negotiations.

11.1.4 The interested parties weigh the risks

A number of factors will combine together to determine the price adjustment of share values and of products and/or services. The main factors are:

- the extent of risk aversion in investors and customers;
- the degree of risk involved in the different projects; and
- the relative bargaining strengths of the parties.

If the risks are known, the external parties will tend to require that a risk premium is payable, e.g.

- venture capitalists and bankers lending to a company in financial difficulties may add a surcharge to the interest payable on loans above a certain limit;
- employees may demand higher wages as the price of continued loyalty; or
- customers demand to pay less for the product if quality and after-sales service may be poor.

Thus, if the company is to continue in being, there is a market resolution of the conflicting claims of the various interest groups that constitute the organization and its environment. If the risk levels are seen to increase, the natural commercial pressures will make it more difficult to negotiate with risk averse customers. If the risks are wholly or partly offset by the implementation of improved management strategies, the organization's more defensive negotiating position may be relieved and, when market confidence is restored, the additional costs of the new security measures passed on to the customers. The resulting market prices will reflect the costs and benefits to both parties to each deal at the time it is made.

Finally, there is an issue about the extent to which costs should be internalized or externalized. Often social responsibility issues such as environmental pollution controls will, if the costs are passed on to the customers, damage trading positions in a highly competitive market. The costs of such controls may be absorbed comfortably, in the extreme case, by a monopolistic firm with excess profits, or by an efficient organization with a financial surplus, or by all competing organizations which respond equally to government regulation. Otherwise, social goals do not sit happily in a list of the commercial organization's objectives.

11.2 THE ROLE OF THE RISK MANAGER

In examining the roles of the modern managers, Friedel (1991) makes an interesting set of comparisons and contrasts between the conventional business manager and the risk manager:

- it is the task of senior managers to lead the organization, but the task of the risk manager is to protect the organization;
- one of the main goals of a senior manager will be to look forward into the future to identify opportunities for growth, but the task of the risk manager is to look forward for danger and to move cautiously to reduce risks;
- much of the practical world of decision-making is dominated by the short-term interests of the organization, whereas risk managers are dominated by the long-term;
- the job of the risk manager is to be the bearer of bad news about the future and no one really wants to hear that in the confident, up-beat world of management.

Thus, the whole philosophy of building up awareness of risks may be at odds both with the entrepreneurial instincts that may help to make good leaders, and with the corporate goals and objectives as well. So while the risk managers may want to plan increased risk or loss retention levels to help insulate their organizations from market swings (Section 11.5), the leaders may want to use the capital of the organization to fund their next attack upon the market. Yet, as Smith and Williams (1991) rightly point out,

> the objective of a risk manager is the same as that of other managers: to increase the value of the firm. (p. 58)

11.2.1 The risk manager and crisis management

We might adopt the cynical view that managers do not want to be bothered about the future unless a crisis is looming. Taback (1991) takes the practical view that,

> Before a crisis occurs, there is usually a warning period during which an astute management team can recognize the signals and events that increase the likelihood of disaster. During this period, the company can accomplish the most at the least cost. Even if it cannot prevent the disaster, knowing it is coming makes the company better prepared. (p. 66)

In other words, crises do not simply happen. They arise out of the context of the business (see the issue of legitimate expectation in Section 10.8). Some form of defensive planning at a strategic level is therefore sensible to allow the organization to make a reasonably well co-ordinated effort to respond to the emergency at a time of maximum turmoil. The best plans involve the following stages:

- risk identification;
- flexible response planning – it is impossible to predict every crisis so each plan should only establish a framework for responses, leaving the detail of decision-making to the disaster team;
- responding to the emergency by limiting damage and interruption to operations, protecting the most critical operations and implementing disaster recovery plans;
- returning to normal operations – not necessarily simply recreating the pre-emergency nature and level of activity, but learning from the experience and benefitting from the opportunity perhaps presented by the destruction of buildings to rebuild to meet different market challenges.

As to risk identification, let us start with a list of headings:

- *Operating risks*   i.e. the way in which the organization undertakes its major area of business activity causes harm to employees, customers, those living near the factories etc. Thus, operating departments should be positively involved in identification, evaluation, control, incident reporting and internal investigation.

- *Infrastructure risks*   i.e. that there will be disruption to the major services of water, electricity, gas, transport, communications etc. So every function within the organization should contribute to the identification of exposures, and indicate the strengths and weaknesses of each department to react (both individually and collectively) in the event that any of the events occur.

- *Financial risks*   i.e. that the operations of the organization will not produce sufficient earnings to cover costs. So the finance department should oversee budgeting, review asset holdings and valuations, monitor performance, examine the alternative strategies for risk financing etc.

- *Legal risks*   e.g. that new laws will affect the way in which the organization carries out its operations or that liabilities will be incurred through the negligence of employees. So the in-house or external lawyers should review contracts, advise on exposure to liability, defend and pursue claims etc.

- *Insurable risks*   i.e. a potential loss that can be covered by a policy of insurance. So the finance and administration departments should analyse exposure to loss, deal with the issue of cost of loss allocation to the responsible departments and assess the cost-effectiveness of the alternative loss control and avoidance strategies, remembering that the payment of insurance premiums reduces immediate profitability.

One way of evaluating risk management policies is to look at the cost of risk under each heading. Thus, albeit crudely, if an organization were to try to identify all the main financial effects of their activities, including the price paid for insurance policies, a measure of performance might be achieved. This measure would assess cost-effectiveness against the organization's market value and its cash flows, i.e. it would measure positive values as well as negative costs. However, although the loss of funds may be directly observed when disasters happen, it is more difficult to monitor positive performance because it is not clear how to attribute cause and effect when share values rise and fall. All that can be assumed is that investors will be more likely to invest in organizations that achieve stability and long-term growth. Thus, economizing by discontinuing a portfolio of insurance policies might improve short-term profitability but not impress the investors with the management's wisdom. But introducing effective quality control systems, e.g. by implementing BS5750 or IS09000, might enhance market value because investors may believe that there will be fewer claims arising from defective products and that therefore longer term profitability will be improved.

11.2.2 The power of the investor

One of the problems for the manager concerned with formulating a risk management strategy is that it may be necessary to ask how a well-informed outside investor might view the organization. When using information prepared in this way and communicating it to other managers, it is important to make it clear where the manager's allegiance lies. This would be particularly important if the manager in question held shares under the now common incentive schemes. It would also be relevant in the field of management ethics if one group were particularly advantaged by management's decisions.

One of the reasons for considering the views of investors is that a commercial organization planning to meet risks can either withhold a proportion from profits in each year, or can issue shares through a rights issue, i.e. issue a prospectus to existing shareholders indicating in general terms the purpose of the loan. If a new company is to be floated, a more detailed statement of aims and strategies will be required to go to the market. In a sense, the company will always be trying to convince investors that the expected rate of return will be better than that receivable from the risk-free investment in, say, government securities or a building society. The key element in the potential investors' decision whether to invest will be determined by the degree of perceived risk in the proposed project(s).

As we have seen, internal risks come from items such as research and development, quality of work, costs involved etc. Externally, the risks revolve around the nature of the market opportunity and the state of the economy. Growth in the economy, changing consumer preferences, the state of labour relations and the rate of technological change are exogenous and outside the direct ability of the organization to control. This adds considerable uncertainty to the risk appraisal process. But, as Moore (1983) puts it,

> For a business to succeed, entrepreneurs require the ability to seize opportunities identified and avert the threats presented by the outside world. (p. 82)

Many commercial organizations prefer to finance risky projects out of retained resources because it avoids the need to convince outsiders of the project's viability. It also avoids problems of commercial confidentiality in alerting competitors to future plans, and issues of ethics in how accurately to describe the degree of risk to investors, both current and prospective.

11.2.3 Ethical issues

Gibson (1991) emphasizes that the question of ethics is also relevant in the process of cost of loss allocation. If the policy of the organization is that losses should be borne by the cost centre responsible, it may be a simple matter to determine which department is responsible. However, even in this simple situation, departmental managers are likely to dispute liability and to defend claims in much the same way as the whole organization may try to fend off potential liability to third party claimants. Naturally, one of the best forms of defence is attack, and managers may end up accusing each other of fault. It may be possible to achieve amicable settlements where the losses are shared or the most senior managers may have to make formal judgements as if in court. The difficulty in this type of situation is that self-interest often prevails and the resulting settlements or judgements may actually be inequitable, i.e. the objective reality of fault is obscured by the manipulations of those at risk.

If the organization's policy is more complex, e.g. there is a pooling scheme between departments or the organization practices a loss retentions policy, the ethical problems may become more acute. If there is a pooling arrangement between departments, the very existence of the scheme may encourage managers to dispute liability and to aim to redistribute the loss in their favour. If the scale of the retention is varied depending upon a classification of risks, there is tremendous scope for argument about whether an actual risk matches the classification or not. Alternatively, if a loss has to be financed out of the sale of existing asset holdings, debenture holders may be concerned if managers propose to sell assets that might otherwise be caught within the floating charge. This concern would be all the more pointed if the managers' incentive scheme depended upon only ordinary or preference shares. The converse would be to fund borrowing to meet the liability out of existing revenues. This would reduce the likelihood of being able to declare a dividend and deny the ordinary shareholder but not the preference shareholder. Allocating the loss between the different groups may therefore be a difficult ethical problem if the managers have a direct interest in the outcome.

11.3 RISK MANAGEMENT AUDITS

In theory, large organizations will have either recruited staff with the expertise to mitigate risks, or will have trained staff to recognize risks and, where time permits, to seek expert advice before committing the organization to action. As a rule of thumb, let us propose that large organizations will not be interested in high-risk, low-return projects because the returns will not be worth the effort invested. If the profits are likely to be low, the rational organization will be less willing to put capital into risky projects, and will try to spread the risks through joint ventures where expertise and costs can be pooled.

This does not mean that big organizations do not take big risks. A big organization can often afford to take big risks where there are considerable levels of uncertainty provided that failure could not threaten the overall well-being of the organization. Smaller organizations cannot afford to take risks that would run the real risk of bankruptcy even if success could boost profits substantially. If an organization has ten substantial projects and they are all dependent upon truly independent risks, the successful can pay for the unsuccessful. But if the ten projects are all dependent on the same risk, then the big organization is in the same position as the small organization with its future dependent upon a single project. It is therefore essential for all organizations to monitor the effectiveness of their risk management functions and the best approach is that of the risk management audit.

11.3.1 The duties of the directors

The directors of a modern company have a series of duties to protect the company, its assets and the shareholders from harm. These duties are based upon a duty to use reasonable care in defending the organization's primary income-producing base, both tangible and intangible, i.e:

- land, buildings, plant and equipment;
- the technology employed and associated intellectual property rights;
- the employees;
- its financial resources;
- corporate image and reputation;
- customers and suppliers.

According to Duncan (1991), the obligation to produce income can be balanced against other organizational or social objectives. These may include providing a safe place and a safe system of work, and selling environmentally friendly products. In the sense of direct cause and effect, this may be a conflict between economic and non-economic goals but, indirectly, an organization will benefit from improved production if employees suffer fewer industrial injuries and sales may be enhanced by building a reputation for caring about 'green' issues. Thus, the decision may be partly ethical and partly promoting the organization's economic interests.

11.3.2 The role of insurance

When discussing potential losses, most managers tend to think in terms of the adequacy of the existing insurance cover, but insurance will only rarely cover the total loss, i.e. in a product recall situation to rectify a design defect, even if the contingency was insured, the claim will not cover items such as:

- loss of reputation;
- lost productivity when retooling to meet the new production requirements;
- retraining;
- the cost of management resources diverted from other tasks; and
- loss of market share.

We should also recognize that the existence of an insurance policy cannot prevent the accident from happening nor the loss from being sustained. Even if we assume that the actual loss falls within the terms of a valid policy, it simply provides a part of the loss finance and, insofar as money can be a compensation to injured victims, it helps to relieve pain and suffering. It is therefore sensible for managers to work towards ensuring that all major risks are clearly identified and adequately controlled through properly planned risk management measures. Insurance should be seen as no more than a final line of defence against loss exposures that cannot otherwise be defended against.

11.3.3 Who should be involved in the risk audit

The risk management audit process must be under senior management's control,

> because it directly affects the people who are employed within the physical structures occupied by the organisation, the political framework within the organisation and the special interests entrenched within the existing hierarchy . . . Only the most senior of managers can assess the impact of disasters at a macro-organisational level and, without proper macro guidelines, the micro-assessment achievable by individual departments is likely to be unco-ordinated and ineffective. (Eardley, 1991, pp. 290–1)

In addition to the internal audit and security departments whose function will be to achieve proper levels of accountability within the organization, Eardley (1991) identifies eight groups that should contribute to the audit process:

- the finance department which will be responsible for producing detailed costing, appraisals and projections;

- the legal department which may advise on the existing laws and the possible extent of third party liabilities;
- the public relations department which will advise on how to protect the corporate image and reputation of the organization;
- the industrial relations/personnel department must be involved on all aspects of a risk management exercise since the implementation and operation of any controls and disaster recovery plans will always depend upon the co-operation of staff and their unions;
- engineering, production and buildings departments can give positive guidance as to the factors of criticality in their areas of responsibility;
- the computer services department which can advise on risks to the information system;
- the management services department (if any);
- outside consultants who can bring a breadth of experience to bear and can enable the organization to avoid the most obvious mistakes.

The aim should be to put together a team with the best possible range of skills and experience to undertake an audit process that falls into the following parts:

1. to identify and analyse the major material risks facing the organization which will involve a review of the organization's resources, the vulnerabilities to harm and an assessment of the magnitude and criticality of the most probable losses;
2. to assess the organization's efforts to control those risks through security measures, disaster plans, safety and other training programmes, and the risk finance methods;
3. to compare the probable risks with the existing planned responses to determine adequacy of protection;
4. to recommend improvements in the identification, control and financing of the most critical risks.

11.3.4 The audit methods

The audit process will rely upon a variety of different techniques including interviewing key members of staff, making inspections of facilities and buildings, reviewing existing documentation affecting security systems and disaster planning etc. Those involved may also elect to use scenario-based methodologies such as:

- perpetrator analysis and job sensitivity analysis which define the characteristics of those who may represent a threat to the organization. Some targets will be more attractive to different attackers. This will in part be determined by the opportunity that each class of perpetrator has to attack the organization and the levels of knowledge, expertise and authority (if any) that would be required to exploit those opportunities. Job sensitivity analysis reviews the operation of the organization from the point of view of the potential attacker and identifies the assets most at risk in order of probability of loss or damage. This form of evaluation is based on a number of general propositions, namely that:

- the more senior the employee, the greater the opportunity to work outside normal controls;
- it is easier for a subordinate to avoid supervision when managers are under pressure;
- many subordinates now have more sophisticated skills than their managers.

- threat scenario analysis. Once the targets and the potential perpetrators have been identified, the planners should ask which of the vulnerabilities would be most likely to allow the attack to succeed, and what the relative impact of attack by each class of perpetrator would be. This should help to identify the most cost-effective risk control strategies;
- penetration studies represent a direct examination of the existing security systems to see whether they represent a reasonable response given the criticality of the protected object.

The overall problem with risk audits is that there are no generally accepted risk management principles or standards similar to those operating within accountancy against which to measure the adequacy of the risk management efforts made. In part, this is because the needs of each organization will tend to be unique,

> comparisons with other organisations can be misleading because each organisation will have developed in a different environment and as a response to its own internal and external pressures. The security solutions adopted by other organisations may therefore not be appropriate if simply transplanted into the immediate organisation. (Eardley, 1991, p. 293)

As Duncan (1991) therefore concludes,

> the quality of the audit is only as good as the experience, expertise and methodology of the individual performing it. (p. 54)

11.4 LOSS CONTROL METHODS

If a person buys an item using a credit card and then discovers that the same debit appears twice on the monthly account, he or she is likely to react immediately. Once the cause of the duplication is established, i.e. it proves to be a mistake or fraud, steps can be taken to prevent it reoccurring. While the difficulty is being investigated, the person may quite legitimately refuse to pay both sums claimed. In the commercial world, many organizations seem to think that claims are inevitable and simply pay out repetitively. Such organizations are not acting with the common sense shown by the average person when checking their credit or charge card accounts. Although some claims are inevitable, many are avoidable. In both cases, the extent of the losses can be reduced by effective cost controls.

According to Warner and Whitehead (1991) all organizations ought to implement a proper loss control programme, i.e. should seek to eliminate the avoidable claims, and reduce the frequency and extent of the inevitable claims. This involves the organization in taking three distinct steps:

- acknowledging that a problem exists when a claim is made;
- investigating the sources of the potential loss; and
- taking preventative steps.

In a sense, this exercise is simply a natural extention of the risk audit outlined above except that we now focus on loss control and cost containment. Thus, the analysis will concentrate on negative events such as the personal injuries suffered by employees, customers and others using the organization's premises and products, whether there have been fires or other events damaging the physical buildings or their contents, car and lorry accidents, vandalism and sabotage etc. The measurement must include both the direct costs and the indirect costs such as loss of production, retraining replacement employees, repairing and replacing damaged machinery etc. This review will also help to establish the base cost of claims against which to measure any subsequent improvement.

11.4.1   The role of senior managers

It is easy to suggest ways in which to correct the identified problems. It is more difficult to make them work. The answer lies in a top-down approach. The most senior managers must issue a document emphasizing the importance of the new procedures. They must be seen to be implementing the procedures themselves and must signal the overall importance of the project by appointing a senior person to the post of security or risk manager, with full authority to ensure that all adopt the measures. Then, all those line managers who are to have responsibilities for implementing the procedures must have proper training and be given the necessary authority to make them effective in their area of responsibility. Once the programme is in being, there should be regular monitoring of performance to verify savings.In the longer term, the aim should be to spend the money saved on claims in improving employee productivity and commitment to quality and in building morale. Thus, if staff have fewer days of reported sickness because a stress management programme helps to reduce absenteeism, costs will be contained and productivity is likely to be improved. Indeed, many organizations are now committing resources to life-cycle benefits such as crèche facilities and child-care programmes, financial planning and debt counselling services, subsidised housing, health care, retirement counselling etc. Employees do not leave their personal problems at home. They take them to work. This often results in reduced productivity and increased costs for the employers. If employers do invest in their human capital, they will make significant steps towards loss reductions and cost containment.However, in the past, improvements in workplace health and safety have tended to be tied more closely to tighter regulations and laws rather than to what were considered the more altruistic concerns of risk managers. That these concerns would have produced cost savings was not recognized. It so happens that, as a result of joining the European Community, Britain now finds itself on the receiving end of a significant body of directives which require improvements in a wide variety of health and safety matters. The risk of significant fines is now giving an incentive to senior managers to adopt the strategies long ago suggested by their risk managers. Jones-Lee (1991) has considered the willingness-to-pay approach to the valuation of safety from a theoretical perspective. Various states of mind are possible although empirical research is required to determine which shades of each state of mind operate in real world decision-making situations:

- pure selfishness would exist when the decision-makers care only about their own well-being;
- safety-focused altruism would exist when altruism relates exclusively to other people's safety;
- pure altruism would exist when decision-makers are concerned about other people's utility.

Research shows that the standard willingness-to-pay result requires that public safety expenditure should be carried out to the point at which the value of statistical life is equal to the marginal cost of saving one life. The conclusion is that,

> values of safety and life should definitely not include a sum reflecting people's willingness to pay for other's safety, in spite of the fact that this sum is strictly positive . . . inclusion of such a sum is appropriate, within a utilitarian framework, if and only if altruism is exclusively focused upon other people's safety. (Jones-Lee, 1991, p. 217)

The reason offered for this perhaps slightly odd result is that to push values of safety beyond the limit implied by people's willingness to pay for their own safety would result in an overprovision of safety relative to the other determinants of their utility. Any increase in the values of safety would therefore be considered desirable only by those who disregard those factors besides safety that contribute to other people's utility.

11.5   SETTING THE LOSS RETENTION LEVEL

In the more general field of risk management and insurance, an organization might try to measure success in controlling costs by using the cost of risk benchmark. According to Blinn *et al.* (1991), this yardstick has the following component elements:

- the sum of net insurance premiums;

- unreimbursed losses (self-insured and self-retained);
- the cost of risk control, loss prevention and administration.

Spread over time, this provides a useful way to analyse costs and to compare the various cost elements. Thus, for example, property risk financing costs would include the insurance premiums and other unreimbursed losses resulting from damage to buildings, contents and other resources such as:

- damage to the structure of buildings or to infrastructure services such as wiring, heating and ventilation systems etc;
- damage to plant and equipment;
- damage to cars, trucks and lorries while on the premises;
- business interruption losses;
- crime and fidelity losses; etc.

In pure economic terms, buying insurance may help to stabilize and perhaps even lower an organization's risk financing costs by allowing it to substitute the cost of a known insurance premium for the unknown costs of highly unpredictable accidental losses. Unfortunately, however, the last few years have seen insurance premiums behave with increased volatility and it may now be more cost-effective for the modern organization to meet claims out of retained profits than to try to predict how much next year's insurance premiums will be. Striking the right balance between self-insurance[1] through loss retention and commercial insurance is difficult. In the real world, managers tend to avoid fixed formulas such as retaining, say, 1% of net worth, and perform some form of cost-benefit analysis with a heavy emphasis on the budget for the immediate financial period. Laborde (1991) suggests a consideration of the following factors:

- The current and anticipated financial position of the organization. Insofar as possible, risk managers must ensure that their activities do not impair the organization's objectives. Indeed, wherever possible, the aim should always be to improve the organization's performance.
- The nature of the businesses carried out by the organization should be evaluated to determine the levels of exposure to risk and vulnerabilities to losses, e.g. in a self-service retailing environment, stock losses through shoplifting should be balanced against the need to encourage large numbers of customers to enter the shops to examine the goods with a view to buying.
- The capacity of the organization to tolerate the level of risk. Thus, if the self-service retailing business is making a good profit on current sales, it may decide to tolerate a present stock loss of 4% through shoplifting because changing the store layout may disturb the legitimate customers' buying patterns.
- The perceptions of the insurance market.

This will involve the organization in answering four basic questions:

1. How much can the organization afford to retain?
2. What are the expected losses?

3. What is the least-cost retention alternative?
4. Are the savings worth the additional risk?

Although these questions may, to some extent, be answered through professional judgement, it is also useful to use some of the standard methodologies as well. The following analysis is partly based on the Self Insurance Retention Analysis Method (SIRAM) developed by Scott and Sathianathan (1991). We start by identifying the constraints that may apply to the organization and look at the probability of loss:

*   *Critical constraint analysis (CCA)* (devised by Davis, 1978) This begins with an analysis of the primary financial constraints which apply to the given organization. These may be set internally, e.g. liquidity or profitability targets, or they may be imposed from outside, e.g. borrowing limits set by banks or other sources of venture capital. To some extent, this data may be supplemented by the main operating objectives. These will tend to be budgetary in nature, although they may also include factors such as agreed limits on loss-making ventures, trade-offs between different ventures etc. This analysis should produce a quantified set of financial standards, critical to the organization's well-being. It is then possible to run a simulation to identify the maximum feasible cost level. This is achieved by establishing cost of risk figures for different eventualities and running them against the standards until one or more of the financial constraints are broken. Cost of risk figures are established by estimating the insurance premiums and the costs of alternative methods of meeting the potential losses, e.g. using existing liquid resources, selling existing assets or borrowing the necessary money. This analysis is fundamental to deciding how much an organization can afford to retain or self-insure as against insuring through the conventional market.

*   *Loss probability analysis* Using CCA, we may have arrived at a set of figures showing the organization's capacity to self-insure against particular losses. However, loss forecasting may be affected by the retention levels, i.e. the organization may act in a more risk averse manner if retention levels and insurance coverage are limited. Thus, some probability analysis should be undertaken to determine the likelihood of each loss given different confidence levels. It may also be possible to exploit some historical data to show trends in likelihood but, in all cases, the most conservative approach is the most prudent given the difficulty in predicting the future.

We now have to determine the required minimum premium discount. This is the break-even premium savings required to compensate the organization for changing its retention level.

*   Net present value (NPV) analysis of the change in expected losses. This form of analysis is useful to measure the least-cost retention level by assessing the alternative combinations of retained losses and excess premiums. The problem to overcome may be stated as follows:

- premiums are either payable as a lump sum before the policy is confirmed or they represent an operating cost on a continuing basis throughout the life of each policy;
- the payment of premiums is always a cost rather than the equivalent of a capital investment in a fund managed by the insurance company;
- if the organization is operating on credit, the necessary effect of carrying insurance is to reduce the ability of the organization either to fund other operating costs or generally to reduce the level of indebtedness;
- whether the organization is operating on credit or has cash in hand, the funds retained can be used for income generating purposes;
- it may be years before a payment of losses has to be made out of retained funds.

The NPV of expected losses is used because the full effect of the increase in expected costs is not felt until payment is made to meet the claims. Therefore the premium savings should at least be equal to the NPV of the change in expected self-insured losses.

Most organizations will have a track record of payments to meet claims or will have access to industry norms from which to calculate the average pattern of payments. In relation to the most probable classes of loss, it is also necessary to calculate a figure for aggregate losses under all the worst-case scenarios. This will give us a measure of the amount of additional capital that the organization has exposed to risk by increasing its level of self-insurance (the risk). The calculations should prefer to use the worst-case figures because although this capital is not being used, it is nevertheless exposed, i.e. once the actual liability to pay is confirmed, say by agreement or court action, the capital must ultimately be made available to finance the losses even though those losses may be above the average. The compensation for assuming this greater risk should be the difference between the organization's return on investment and its cost of capital (the risk premium factor). Because most commercial organizations operate on credit, this payout figure should be discounted by the anticipated net cost of borrowing (i.e. after tax). Remember that the organization may already have a retained fund. If so, the relevant figure is the difference in expected losses between the current and the proposed retention levels. The organization should also have an aggregate figure for the extent of coverage offered by the present portfolio of insurance policies. This should be evaluated in the light of the loss probability analysis and the NPV costs should be ranked by retention and loss level to identify incremental savings.

- Discounted payback analysis. The next step is to evaluate whether the incremental savings (if any) are worth the additional risk incurred as retention levels are increased. The aim is to calculate the number of years the savings must be invested at realistic net investment rates to match expenditure throughout the incremental retention layer.

To summarize, the required minimum premium discount is the sum of:

1. the difference in expected losses between the current (if any) and the proposed retention level, discounted at the cost of capital; and
2. the risk at proposed retention – the risk at current retention x the risk premium factor.

This gives a figure for the minimum premium saving required at the new rention level to balance the trade-off between cost savings and increased risk. We should note, however, that the retention level that is shown to have the greatest savings is not necessarily the best even though it would have the shortest payback period. The decision will always have to be made on which of the alternative projects will represent the best use of the newly saved resources. Thus, a small saving with a high rate of return in one project may be better than a large saving with a marginal rate of return in another. The aim should be to evaluate the loss projections, the anticipated premium savings and the inherent uncertainty of the calculation in the light of budgets and the key financial ratios operated by the organization.

However, before we become too excited by the possibility of self-insurance, managements should ask themselves why they should set aside potentially quite large sums of money, perhaps earning only money market interest rates, when the same money could be used to start a new business that would earn a far larger return. If a large claim does arise, the cost can always be met by the sale of one of the businesses run by the organization. If no large claim arises, the organization will be wealthier than if it had set up a risk retention fund.

11.6 DECISION-MAKING AND UNCERTAINTY

When individuals are faced with a decision that is to be made under conditions of uncertainty, i.e. where precise numerical likelihoods cannot be attributed to the consequences associated with the occurrence or non-occurence of events, there are various ways in which progress may be made. For these purposes, we will assume that the decision-maker is not indifferent between the consequences:

1. The decision-maker will identify the uncertain elements and then make the best possible estimates and guesses based on the available evidence. Once the elements have been quantified, he or she will then proceed with the process as if the uncertainty had not existed.
2. Although the decision-maker will make estimates and guesses, the wiser individual will build in an allowance to allow for the possibility that the estimates or guesses are overly optimistic. In a sense, this devalues the calculations by recognizing that the decision-maker has not properly taken uncertainty into account.
3. The decision-maker can attempt formally to incorporate uncertainty into the models that will aid the decision process. These models will

attempt to quantify the uncertainty and to make it an explicit factor in the decision, e.g. by showing it in a simulation, decision matrix or decision tree.

The likelihood of something happening is usually quantified either as a probability figure or as a set of odds. Although economists often debate the philosophical and psychological foundations of probability (e.g. Savage, 1954), it is somewhat unusual for the debate to employ economic concepts. This is a little odd given the importance of markets as social institutions. It may be that no one set of axioms can provide a foundation of probability, or even of some more general belief system, which will underpin decision-making in all situations, but even specific propositions linked to individually invoked environments can be difficult to find. Munier (1991) attacks the assumption that decision-makers confronted by uncertainty have infinite cognitive capacity and so should be able to reach every decision on the basis of rationality. He asserts as a rule that

> one should not demand from the individual more than he can perform from the cognitive point of view. (p. 235)

As managers develop their skills, they learn about the markets that their organizations seek to exploit. This should give them a basis upon which to construct their beliefs, whether probabilistic or not. If we accept that all individuals have bounded rationality in the sense that there will be limits to their cognitive abilities, (see section 3.2.2) they will tend to build up models as a simplified version of their environment. We suggest an intuitive truth that, given available resouces, most decision-makers faced with uncertainty in their choices would prefer additional information about the likelihood of events, even though this information makes the events neither more nor less likely. This investigation and the externalization of their beliefs about their environments will aid the decision-making by making their assumptions more explicit. The source of these models will in part be factual and in part based upon the individual's perceptions of the apparent evidence. They represent the prevailing market psychology.

11.6.1 The sources of uncertainty

As an amplification to the definition offered in section 5.2.1, the source of uncertainty may either be natural, i.e. subject to random chance, or, in game theory terms, it results from the actions and reactions of people whose goals may partly or wholly conflict. This latter form recognizes that the development and prosperity of modern society depends upon the social and commercial interaction of those who live, work in, and service the market place. Thus, each person's decisions, even though made individually, form a part of a social network of cause and effect which manifests itself in surface phenomena such as market confidence as shown through retail and wholesale indexes, price volatility, interest rates, etc.

As we saw in Chapters 2 and 3, the way in which communications help to form or amplify risk perceptions, or to motivate action or inaction are not wholly 'natural' events in the same sense that rain is a natural event. The macro-economic events that affect markets are the product of all the individual decisions and events. Thus, when we attempt to model uncertainty, we are engaged in an attempt to capture the spirit of all the unknowable individual decisions. In fact, the millions of decisions that we all take every day represent too great a level of complexity to incorporate into any proposed calculation but, with apologies to Mack Reynolds,[2] we can engage in a mild fantasy of what might otherwise be achievable.

In a world of perfect certainty, an analyst might be able to discover that the cause of the loss in market confidence leading to recession was the decision of the notoriously prudent Smith family of Milton Keynes not to buy a new car in 1990. Following a discussion with the Smiths, the dealer who every year had sold them a new car passed on his or her fears of an imminent recession to the manufacturer and when the managers intuitively responded to the news, they fuelled the self-fulfilling prophesy by cutting back on overtime and laying off staff. In a chain reaction, the car manufacturer's suppliers and competitors followed suit and the decline snowballed across the country's economy. The solution adopted by the embattled Chancellor of the Exchequer is to send secret envoys to the Smith family to discuss the state of the market with them. If their confidence can be restored and they can be encouraged to buy a new car, albeit a few months later than usual, the whole process can be reversed and the economy can be restored to its former vigor.

Although this is in many respects an idle fantasy, it is based upon the fundamental truth that the beliefs we form about the performance of the economy are derived from the more or less active roles of individuals within the economy and the way in which the information about their activities is brought to our attention. As we have already observed in section 11.1.2, the beliefs and expectations of the Stock Exchange represent a form of discipline on the decision-making of the quoted companies. As evidence of the power of rumour within the Stock Exchange, it is interesting to study the criminal and civil laws which emerge from cases such as *R* v. *De Berenger* (1814/23). In that case, false news of Napoleon's defeat was circulated to influence share prices. The resulting laws deal with the phenomenon of fraudulently influencing the Stock Exchange's view of either individual companies or market trends, a problem that has become more acute as the news media has become more effective in bringing information to people's attention and electronic systems such as SEAQ have proliferated (for a full discussion, see Marshall, 1987).

11.6.2 A model of market psychology

Munier (1991) suggests a model of market psychology that uses five hypotheses as follows:

1. the way in which we form our beliefs does not result from any one

single calculation, but from a continuous interactive process of observation, consultation and absorption during which the decision-maker deliberates on what the market seems to think and on what perception it seems appropriate to form;

2.   decision-makers do not always trust their sources of belief – the extent of their confidence is likely to depend upon the degree to which information is corroborated or appears credible;

3.   decision-makers will often display qualities of prudence when forming their beliefs and aim to be conservative in their estimation of the reliability and credibility of the data collected – there is, however, a tendency in developing data search parameters only to look for evidence that relates to the already shortlisted management strategies rather than to collect data which will help to devise the optimum strategy;

4.   there will often be a conflict between subjective beliefs and the evidence gathered about the market – it can be quite hard to resist the main flow of the discourse within the market and either the individual will subordinate their own beliefs to the general trend resulting in herd-like behaviour such as the various 'Black' days on the stock exchanges in Britain and America, or the evidence of general beliefs will be distorted to make it consistent with subjective beliefs;

5.   decision-makers will keep their eyes open for things that will confirm their own world view.

Munier (1991) suggests that economics has not developed a proper view of probabilities because it has been concerned only with instrumental rationality and he concludes that

> Instead of ensuring consistency between goals and available means, economic rationality endeavors to ensure consistency between beliefs currently encountered in the social system and the individual's own beliefs, given his information. This is precisely the concept of cognitive rationality that has emerged clearly in recent years and that is opposed in economics to the more traditional instrumental rationality. (p. 248)

It is therefore sensible to conclude that decision-makers build up their probability judgements by balancing their own beliefs against market opinions. By engaging in this often interactive process of deliberation, subjective perceptions of likelihood are formed and are influenced by the individual's needs, aims and intelligence.

11.6.3   A model of cognitive rationality

Billot (1991) offers further confirmation for a model of cognitive rationality standing outside the standard model of probability. He offers the major criticism that in the anticipated utility models and the weighted expected utility models, the probabilistic measure of belief is neutral, i.e.

it does not depend on the agent's behaviour facing risk and is therefore independent of the agent's knowledge. Indeed, it produces the alarming proposition that because

> there is no sensitivity to exogenous agent knowledge, the expert and the idiot behave in the same way. (p. 305)

If a person is totally ignorant, that person is, by definition, unable to attribute a weighting to data offered for consideration because it is not possible to form a conviction that any one element of data is any more correct than any other. A natural, if paradoxical, belief would therefore be that each element of data may be equally correct. This reflects the problem that in modelling complete ignorance, there is no contingent information and no self-generating information and the agent will not modify behaviour when the referential set of choice is modified. But if an agent bases a belief on the occurrence of an event, he or she will sift the data available to look for a precise weighting that will affirm the conviction formed. Let us assume that an agent is aware of several possible future events. If this agent collects information and, as a result, assigns a degree of belief to the occurrence of an event A, he or she will rationally assign degrees of belief to event B deduced from A. Because of the degree of belief in event A, there is now better information about event B, and so the degree of belief in event B is likely to be given a greater value. This is termed monotonicity with respect to set-inclusion.

But the measure of belief when there is uncertainty may be either wise or rash. Billot (1991) postulates that the phenomena we call wisdom and rashness are merely two aspects of the same behaviour (i.e. there is duality), because to each wise measure there corresponds a rash measure. Indeed, we can often only judge the degree of rashness by considering what the wise person would have done in the same situation. Thus, if a decision-maker exaggerates the plausibility of an event A, the plausibility of the contrary event A is necessarily minimized, e.g. if a sales manager is over-optimistic in predicting sales for the new product, the other managers may therefore find the likelihood of reduced revenue from poor sales less plausible. Perhaps we should try to devise a test to determine the degree of confidence felt by each decision-maker that his or her view is correct. The problem and the advantage if we were to have a model with a belief measure built in is that we are placing importance on both the knowledge and the wisdom or rashness of the actor involved. When we compare two people in the real world, we should recognize that even though each person's level of knowledge is important, we may find that one decision-maker may be less wise than the other whose knowledge is less. The test is not whether a person has knowledge and experience but whether that knowledge and experience are applied effectively. This will be expressed by a smaller amplitude of the gap between the degree of wise belief and the degree of rash belief in the given event. It is obvious that the more important the knowledge is, the more important this gap is.

However, at a conceptual level, wisdom and rashness are inextricably bound up with a lack of knowledge. A reasonable level of knowledge may be a source of wisdom. A poor level of knowledge may lead to behaviour that may be characterized as rash. If we have relevant experience and have perfect knowledge of what the outcome is likely to be, we can act in a way that avoids being wise or rash. For example, when a judge sits in court, he or she may hear conflicting evidence from witnesses as to how person A came to injure person B. The judge will use measures of credibility and plausibility to decide who is more likely to be telling the truth. The judge does not have perfect knowledge (that would be reserved to an independent observer present at the time of the alleged events) but will try to act with wisdom in eliciting information from the partisan witnesses that will help to make a judgement in the face of uncertainty. Equally, if a potential investor hears a sales pitch from a business promoter but makes no effort to verify what has been said before making capital available, this would be rash. Finally, if an insider dealer buys shares and makes a killing in the market, the judgement of future share price movement leading to the decision to buy was neither wise nor rash because the available information allowed perfect certainty as to outcome in terms of share price movement. Obviously, if the dealer is caught, we may say that the actual decision to buy was rash.

Billot (1991) does not argue that we should abandon probability-based models. On the contrary, he asserts that when a decision-maker builds a judgement on good evidence (say, of repeatable events) and uses innate capacity and knowledge to attribute probabilities to the different possible outcomes, the model should be expanded to include:

- capacity-belief measures;
- a statement of the knowledge used;
- the nature of the evidence collected and relied upon; and
- information about the decision-maker's own disposition.

This will result in a model of cognitive rationality and probability that will be reasonably compatible with instrumental rationality.

11.6.4 Ambiguity as a factor

Winkler (1991) argues that the existence of ambiguity, i.e. uncertainty about the probabilities,[3] leads to decision-making through preferences rather than probabilities, modifying utilities accordingly,

> If additional information is equated with less uncertainty or less ambiguity, then we may say that many decision makers are ambiguity averse. (Hazen and Lee, 1991, p. 177)

Some of the efforts to modify the probabilities in decision-making have involved decision weights, i.e. non-additive probabilities that do not necessarily obey the rules of probability. Although this may be more accurate in descriptive modelling, modified probabilities are more problematical in normative or prescriptive modelling. It would seem more appealing to avoid trying to redefine probabilities and to focus on preferences, i.e. the consequence side of decision-making and the value or utility function of those consequences. In this way, effort can parallel the more extensive work on nonlinear models for pure risk decisions.

Ambiguity about the probability of an event is a perception that there is an increased risk attaching to a course of action leading to identifiable consequences where there may be feelings of regret or blame if the consequences are poor, and satisfaction or joy if the consequences are good. Such concerns could show themselves through feelings of worry or anxiety, or through excitement and pleasure. These emotional conse-quences are related to the preferences to be made and should be modelled through utilities and not probabilities. Obviously, utility does not have to be monetary. It can attach to any consequence and, in evaluating that consequence, the modeller can take any aspect of the decision situation into account. Thus, if the decision-maker or others will make an evalua-tion of performance depending on success or failure, issues of credit, responsibility, embarrassment and regret are highly salient. Thus, if the strategic decision fails to deliver the promised benefits, the investment analysts point to errors and the share price falls on the Stock Exchange, this will constitute a utility loss. The factors that may be included in an expanded consequence space for the assessment of utilities could include:

- issues affecting the health of the decision-makers, e.g. stress-related conditions, ulcers, heart conditions etc;
- psychological effects for the decision-makers, e.g. increased confidence and a sense of well-being in approaching new situations of ambiguity, or loss of confidence and depression leading to increased ambiguity aversion;
- the non-monetary pay-offs for the decision-makers that may follow success or failure, e.g. the acknowledgement of an increase in status and reputation, the reduction in the chances of promotion etc.;
- the size of the pay-offs;
- the effects and pay-offs for individuals other than the decision-makers, e.g. benefits may accrue for senior managers if junior managers perform well, shareholders may feel increased confidence in the security of their investment, marriages may be affected if there is increased stress etc.

In the real world, strategic decision situations are rarely simple, fre-quently dynamic and usually involve several possible outcomes. As such, the uncertainty cannot be described by just a single probability. Similarly, ambiguity becomes more complex. Thus, there may be particular ambigu-ity associated with one possible outcome and less ambiguity associated with the others (producing different levels of anxiety in relation to each option), or there may be equal ambiguity associated with all possible outcomes. Although there has been work on the idea of manipulating probabilities in decision models by using the calculus of probabilities, there is no such work on ambiguities that could, for example, be applied in decision trees to guide the modification of the utilities at the end of the tree in the light of the ambiguities encountered in the passage through the tree.

Winkler (1991) therefore suggests that decision-makers who are worried about some of the assessed probabilities should use sensitivity analysis to test the robustness of the model as the range of probabilities is examined. Such elicited ranges or second order probabilities may also help to suggest what additional information should be collected to aid the decision. Thus, if different actions appear to have similar expected utilities and certainty equivalents, then ambiguity can be used as a form of tie breaker. But if the differences between expected utilities and certainties appear to be larger, the aim of any analysis should be to produce a good decision rather than a good outcome. By concentrating on the process of decision-making and attempting to introduce wisdom into it, the resulting explicit justifications for the decision will help to reduce blame if the outcome proves poor and may enhance credit if the outcome proves good.

11.6.5 Subjectively Weighted Linear Utility Model

We must admit that the formal treatment of ambiguity in decision models will complicate the analysis for the decision-maker, but there is no reason why, as in the case of risk, we cannot have ambiguity aversion as an objective in the preference-related side of decision-making. Indeed, Hazen and Lee (1991) define an increasingly (or decreasingly or constantly) ambiguity-averse decision-maker as,

> one whose ambiguity premiums increase (or decrease or remain constant) as a function of the mean probability. (p. 180)

Their Subjectively Weighted Linear Utility model (SWLU) has been developed as a prescriptive model of ambiguity aversion. It is subjectivist, i.e. both utility and subjective probability are viewed as manifestations of preference behaviour. Thus, probabilities subjectively assigned to an event partition are allowed to depend not just on the preference ranking of the associated prizes, but on their size as well. At an intuitive level, it would seem sensible that if we were only betting pennies, we might be prepared to back purely subjective estimates. But if the decisions were important, it would be foolish to risk much without getting a reasonable amount of information about the component elements of the decision even though our subjective expectations might be quite favourable. Thus, the larger the potential gain or loss, the greater the potential for ambiguity aversion. However, conventional theory also deals with shifts in ambiguity attitude so that,

> the substantiated tendency for ambiguity aversion for gains, when the mean probability of gain is moderate to large, is matched by a tendency for ambiguity seeking for small mean probabilities of gain. In the loss domain, the observed tendencies are reversed, with ambiguity aversion for small mean probabilities of loss, and increasing degrees of ambiguity seeking as the mean loss probability increases. (pp. 187–8)

This is justified and explained in a second-order SWLU model decribing an event-contingent lottery which generates an underlying continuous pay-off scale for the participants. This will produce a shading of aversion whereby a decision-maker may move from an ambiguity seeking posture, through ambiguity avoiding to ambiguity aversion on an increasing or decreasing scale depending on whether the mean probability of gain or loss is increasing. Hazen and Lee (1991) then define a consequential ambiguity premium which depends on the level of ambiguity, the subjective probabilities and the utility function. The larger the premium required, whether in terms of ambiguity, probability or utility, to trigger a preference for a maximizing strategy, the more likely it is that the decision-maker will be ambiguity averse. So, for example, if two decision-makers are faced by identical levels of ambiguity and have attributed similar subjective probabilities to the possible outcomes, but one decision-maker anticipates or desires a greater change in utility as the outcome of the decision, that decision-maker will be more ambiguity averse than the other, i.e. he or she will make greater efforts to resolve the uncertainty before taking the decision.

11.7 THE TOOLS OF MODELLING

According to Hirst and Schweitzer (1991) whatever approach or methodology is adopted, it must have the following ingredients:

- it must specify the data requirements and the criteria to be applied in making assumptions and judgements on resource alternatives and on external factors;
- it must contain analytical methods to simulate the processes undertaken and the likely consequences in the event of a threat or hazard occurring;
- there must be techniques to combine data and assumptions, and analytical methods to analyse uncertainties and to select suitable resource portfolios;
- there must be a monitoring of events so that subsequent plans and actions can be improved.

At its simplest level, the various ways to deal with uncertainty are the following:

- ignore the uncertainty, i.e. concentrate on short-term strategies, assuming that the longer term problems will resolve themselves;
- put off the decision until additional information is made available to reduce the uncertainty;
- transfer the risk to someone else, e.g. through insurance;
- make highly flexible plans that allow for cheap changes to be made to meet the changing circumstances;
- make careful and detailed plans for all the reasonably probable contingencies so that future decisions are as to which plan to implement

and so of nominal importance only.

11.7.1 Scenario analysis

One possibility would be scenario analysis in which alternative futures are defined, each one containing internally consistent combinations of key uncertain factors. Once plausible scenarios are constructed, suitable combinations of supply- and demand-side can be identified for each one. The aim is to fit resources into the scenarios. The best options can then be combined into a unified contingency plan. This plan should then be subjected to sensitivity analysis, i.e. key factors in the preferred plan are varied to see how the plan would respond. This may lead to the development of a portfolio of plans, each of which is designed to meet different corporate objectives in the event of different levels of disaster. This method allows its users to anticipate a broad range of plausible and internally consistent futures and to understand the nature of the underlying factors that determine which future will actually occur. It is not necessary to rely on computer models for this approach. It may be developed through group work and interdepartmental discussions and, as a result, produces results that are easier to communicate to management than the results from some of the mathematical models.

11.7.2 Decision matrix

A decision matrix is a way of modelling relatively straightforward decisions by making the options open to the decision-maker more explicit, defining the state of nature or scenario relevant to the decision and providing a number of decision rules to select between the options. Thus, for each combination of option and state of nature, there will be a consequence and these can be shown in a two-dimensional matrix. Four decision rules may then be applied as follows:

1. The optimistic rule selects the option which appears to give the best result, usually by choosing the option with the lowest cost or the greatest revenue.
2. The pessimistic rule selects the option that provides the best of the worst outcomes, i.e. if we assume that costs will rise, we choose the option that will limit the rise to the lowest achievable figure or if we assume that revenues will fall, we choose the option that will still give us the highest return.
3. The regret rule asks the question, 'If, with hindsight, we are seen to have made the wrong choice, how much will we regret not having chosen the right option?' If, for example, we select the lowest production cost and sales revenue is not good, then we regret nothing because we chose the lowest cost method for the sales actually achieved. But if we had chosen a high-cost production method and sales revenue falls, we regret the difference between the lowest cost and the actual cost we are paying. There are problems

with this rule because the degree of regret will be determined by the number and the viability of the other options considered.

4. The expected value rule weights each outcome by the likelihood of it occurring, using probabilities to clarify the decision.

11.7.3 Fault tree analysis

Fault tree analysis is one of the most important modelling tools used in risk assessment to analyse a system's reliability. It can be used to identify potential weaknesses in a system, or the most likely causes of a system's failure. When discussing the undesirable possibility of both a major fire and the failure of the automatic fire protection system, Youngblood (1991) defines fault tree analysis as follows,

> A fault tree is a picture of the logical relationships between the primary events (such as particular component failures or 'faults'), the intermediate events (such as failure of one train of a safety system as a function of various component failures), and the top event (such as failure of both trains of automatic fire sprinkling, given a fire in a particular zone). (p. 343)

The approach was comprehensively introduced first by Raiffa (1968) and built upon the work of von Neumann and Morgenstern (1944) and Savage (1954) to create single-objective models. The methodology works by first defining a probable failure event, called the top event. The sequence of events that would most probably lead to the occurrence of the top event is then systematically divided into primary events whose failure probabilities can be estimated. Each node in the tree may either show that a decision is to be made or that the outcome will be a matter of chance, i.e. it is a 'state of nature'. Intermediate events are formed by combinations of primary events and/or other intermediate events. The probability for an intermediate event is calculated according to the relationships among the events constituting it. This process is repeated until the top event is reached. Many software packages have been developed since the mid 1980s to assist in the development and analysis of fault trees. One example called FaultrEASE is reviewed by Youngblood (1991).

Tulsiani *et al.* (1990) begin their examination of the conventional fault tree analysis methods with the statement that the initial estimates affecting the primary events are usually based upon both subjective and objective data and the user relies upon probability distributions to develop an interval of uncertainty for the failure probability of the top event. As to the nature of a probability distribution, they say,

> This concept can be called a 'probability of a probability', since the distribution is a probability of the component failure probability (p. 522)

The quantitative analysis then proceeds through the use of methods such as the Taylor series expansion, variance decomposition and partitioning etc. to identify either the probability distribution of the top event or the relative contribution of the subsystems to the whole. But most of the methods used cannot model the dependencies among components because there are no closed-form solutions available for the products and sums of these distributions, and optimization techniques such as linear programming yield an optimal decision as the end result.

The strengths of conventional fault trees flow from the facts that:

- a graphical representation of a problem helps a decision-maker to understand sometimes complex problems;
- the description of the various outcomes and the estimation of probabilities associated with them will help a decision-maker to make decisions, viz in theory, the rollback technique allows the most favourable pay-off to be calculated for each decision; and
- the model shows a chronology of decisions, allowing the consequences of future decisions to be traced back to assess their influence on the present decision.

But, as Haimes *et al.* (1990) comments,

> an optimum derived from a single-objective mathematical model, including that which is derived from a decision tree, often may be far from representing reality – thereby misleading the analyst(s) as well as the decision-maker(s). The more generalized noninferior solution (also known as the Pareto optimum or the efficient solution) renders the utopian single-objective mathematical optimum meaningless in many actual decision-making situations. (p. 112)

11.7.4 MIDAS and DARE

Haimes *et al.* (1990) advocate that the models should be extended to deal with multiple real-world objectives such as minimizing costs, maximizing utilities (not necessarily monetary but including qualitative objectives such as maximizing quality), minimizing risks of various kinds etc. pointing to software systems like MIDAS (Multiobjective Integrated Decision Analysis System) developed under the sponsorship of the Electric Power Research Institute as an early, if unsatisfactory, step in the right direction.

The methodology presented by Haimes *et al.* (1990) and DARE (Distribution Analyser and Risk Evaluator) described by Tulsiani *et al.* (1990) and under evaluation by NASA make considerable theoretical and practical advances towards a reliable multiobjective system. Haimes *et al.* (1990) propose that at each pairing of decision and state of nature node in the tree, a vector-valued performance measure should be given alongside each of the finite number of alternative possible outcomes. By allowing for the evaluation of the multiple objectives at each decision node, they achieve a significant extension to the average out and rollback technique used in the convention approach. However, as they acknowledge, an efficient algorithm must be developed to eliminate some inferior solutions at an early stage otherwise, even with powerful computers, dimension difficulties become significant.

DARE is based on the Monte Carlo simulation method. It avoids the use of the traditional expected value function where all degrees of loss and probability of occurrence are represented by a single value, and generates conditional risk functions to represent the loss, given that the damage falls within certain specified probability (or damage) ranges. The aim of using numerical simulation rather than analysis is to allow the complete distribution for the top event probability to be calculated as opposed to obtaining just the system's moments through analytic methods. However, a major limitation of fault trees, and therefore of DARE, is the inability to model intermediate system states such as partial failure modes. In the real world, systems may develop degraded modes of operation and more research is required to permit such states to be modelled.

Notes

1. Although many use the term self-insurance, we should note that it actually means having no insurance at all. According to the tax authorities, no tax relief is available on risk financing unless there is a transfer of risk, e.g. to an independent insurance company. Thus, if an organization sets up its own fund to meet anticipated losses, there is no transfer of risk and so no tax relief. This desire to subsidize insurance is somewhat odd because no one has ever shown that it is economically or socially preferable to retention as a method of risk financing. Indeed, there would seem to be no good public policy argument to deny relief to a self-insurance retention scheme so long as it is actuarially sound, well-managed and actually used to make payments against claims. The only danger would be that organizations would try to manipulate their forecasts of losses to ensure that excessive retained sums were tax free. This could be countered by a claw back system if claimed actuarial justifications for retentions proved over-pessimistic and the organization wished to use the funds for some other purposes.

2. Mack Reynolds (1917–83) is the pseudonym of Dallas McCord Reynolds, an American author who specialized in science fiction based on socio-economic projections.

3. Within the realms of the theories of subjective probability, the term ambiguity rather than uncertainty is used.

12 A methodology, conclusions and case studies

INTRODUCTION

The title of this book, *Business Risk Management*, has been chosen with care. There can be no dispute that as all organizations and individuals go forward, they face risk in their everyday lives. Most people, whether they are acting individually or on behalf of an organization, cannot afford to ignore risks. We laugh at the ostrich because it puts its head in the sand and somehow hopes that immediate troubles will disappear or not have any effect. We know that risks may often be threatening to the survival of the individual or the organization and that, in some cases, to ignore the risks may further exacerbate the threat to survival. For example, some business organizations continue to believe that the development of the European Community and other global trading agreements will have no impact on their domestic markets. Consequently, they ignore or dismiss such risks. This merely enhances the threat to their long-term survival. So looking backward, the basic approach of this book is to urge the need for organizations more openly to address and manage the risks they face.

The general style of the early chapters should have alerted you to the fact that this is not a subject that can be addressed in a mechanistic way. It is not acceptable to limit our consideration to the process elements of risk and uncertainty encountered in the decision-making process, i.e. to say that risk and uncertainty are simply a reflection either of the decision context or situation, or of the specific nature of the problem addressed. It has been our clear theme from the outset that the phenomena of risk and uncertainty are as much about the perceptions, attitudes and culture of the organization and its decision-makers as about the decision process and the decision-specific elements of each problem. It is the complexity of this social reality which makes it so difficult to devise universal models, constructs, procedures and techniques. In a highly structured, mechanistic world it would be possible to prescribe a number of panaceas which would be readily available to cure all the main decision problems in all the usual organizational settings. In such a world, the quantitative methodologies which proliferate in the books of economic theory and financial accounting would all work reliably and enable management to optimize their decision-making. But, in the real world at a strategic level, unique decision-makers within unique organizational situations face unique decisions at each point in time and the experience of researchers suggests that the search for generic solutions or methods to resolve risk and uncertainty is likely to be a fruitless pursuit.

This might make it tempting to argue that the effectiveness of decision-making is little more than good luck or that it is based on some elusive and non-transmissible qualities possessed by individual decision-makers to assess and handle risk in particular decisions. While there is no real evidence available to refute such a proposition, we take the optimistic view that a more systematic approach to dealing with risk in decision-making can provide scope for improvements in performance for all decision-makers and organizations. As an indication of our modest ambitions, we have tried to occupy the middle ground of the conceptual debate. Thus, rather than adopt either a wholly generic approach aimed to provide 'off-the-shelf' solutions for all decisions or the other extreme (i.e. the situationalist view) that business decisions are so unique that no general rules or guidelines can offer much assistance, we have proposed a contingency approach. Our expectation is that decision-makers in a variety of strategic decision situations will be able to develop a structured approach or, at the very least, some useful guidelines to assist them in handling elements of risk and uncertainty. The aim in this final chapter is therefore to develop a possible framework which might form the basis of a more structured approach to the management of risk and uncertainty in the general diversity of decision situations. We are also going to abandon the more academic style of the rest of the text and try to address the issues in a plain and direct manner.

12.1 FRAMEWORK FOR RISKS IN STRATEGIC DECISIONS

The earlier discussions in the text have covered the two broad issues:

- the *process* of decision-making and the incorporation of risk and uncertainty within it; and
- the approaches that may be employed to *identify and measure* the risks and uncertainty involved in particular decision situations.

Figure 12.1 illustrates the major stages in the decision-making process. An important point to draw from this representation of the process is that each of the stages shown are likely to take place on a continuous basis as the people and their organization(s) move forward to face new challenges and so each stage will, in effect, operate in parallel. New elements of data are received by the decision-makers throughout the working day. Some of that data will be discarded as irrelevant; other elements will undergo differing degrees of processing, and the resulting processed data will almost certainly influence the decision-makers' perception of the risks involved.

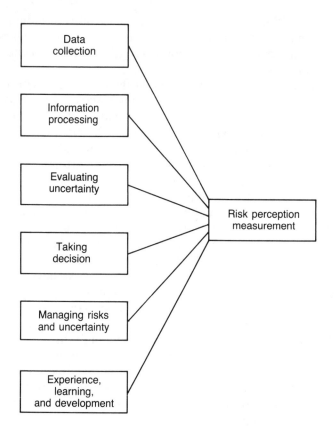

Figure 12.1 Decision framework.

12.2 PLANNED VERSUS RESPONSIVE MANAGEMENT OF RISKS

There are two ways in which organizations may attempt to produce an effective management of risks and uncertainties. These ways may be seen as two different modes of the management process:

- *The planning mode* This depends on the ability of the organization to identify the risks in advance so that the appropriate decisions may be taken to manage the outcomes.

- *The responsive mode* This is more concerned with the ability of the organization to manage the unexpected outcomes or consequences of those risks initially foreseen or to respond to events which were not anticipated.

Each stage in the process shown in Figure 12.1 has an influence on the individual or organizational perception or measurement of risk. It should be obvious that the early stages of data collection, information processing, evaluation and decision-making will have a direct influence on the formation of risk and uncertainty perceptions. Even after the decision has been taken, there are two further elements which can have a significant bearing on the success in handling risks, namely the steps taken both to implement the decision and to manage the resulting activities, and building the knowledge and experience of the organization. If the organization is to be successful, it needs to respond effectively to those risks that materialize during the implementation of the decision whether these risks have been foreseen and evaluated or not.

Although the importance of planning can never be underestimated, the more important survival characteristic for the organization to foster is the ability to make an effective response to the unforeseen event. For example, it is unlikely that the manufacturers of Perrier water anticipated the risks or consequences of the pollution when it was first detected in their processing plant. In fact, the sales of their product were dramatically affected. The management's response was to withdraw all of the product from both the wholesale and retail shelves internationally. Some commentators described this response as brave; others called it a foolhardy decision in the circumstances because there were a number of risks that market position and brand image might be lost. With the benefit of hindsight, we can actually say that the organization managed the risks and uncertainties well. In this instance, the market or brand loyalty on which organizations devote a large proportion of their marketing resources proved to be fairly robust. In other circumstances, that same brand loyalty may prove to be fragile. An off-the-cuff, derogatory comment on the quality of the jewellery products sold in the large national chain of jewellery retailers, Ratners plc by its own managing director had disastrous consequences for market and brand image. Subsequently, the sales and profit performance of the business went into steep decline and the director has now lost his position in the company. It is most unlikely that any member of the organization would have identified let alone predicted the risks associated with the giving of a public lecture. Despite numerous attempts to recover the situation, the company has continued to suffer the adverse consequences for some eighteen months. It may therefore be seen that the effective management of the unexpected, or risk management, is a crucial ingredient in the success of any organization.

The final feature in the process illustrated in Figure 12.1 is the experience, learning and development that ought to take place as a result of the overall process. This should not be limited to the individual or individuals who were directly involved in the process leading to the particular decision, but should apply to all the other individuals or groups in the organization who might benefit from the immediate lessons learned. A significant part of the strategy for producing effective risk management therefore involves the development and diffusion of corporate experience, knowledge and skills. Further, this should be seen as a long-term investment in human, financial and other resources to improve management performance in conditions of risk and uncertainty. This will only pay dividends if the organization as a whole gains this experience, knowledge and skills, but the strategy may pose problems for some decision-makers who may no longer be regarded as indispensable if their knowledge and experience is passed on to others. Thus, if those individuals fear that their status or, indeed, continued employment may be jeopardized, they may seek to retain all or the significant parts of their knowledge, expertise and skills.

12.3 MANAGERIAL RESPONSES TO RISK

As we have shown in earlier chapters, the decision-maker who encounters risks in a decision-making situation may respond to or manage the situation in a number of ways:

- collect more information;
- undertake further analysis, investigation and evaluation of the problem and its associated risks;
- investigate alternative decisions, their alternative outcomes, and associated risks and uncertainties;
- take action to insure the organization or the decision-maker against the worst consequences of potential decision outcomes, both known and unknown;
- seek methods of rationalizing the decision; the decision may have been taken without any formal analysis, or the justification for it depends on criteria other than risk, e.g. the decision solution proposed is either the least-cost solution or provides the best opportunity to increase sales revenues; in risk communications, the decision may also be rationalized on the basis of more publicly acceptable or more apparently rational criteria even though the key criteria actually used were different;
- attempt to widen the responsibility for the decision and its consequences and, hence, reduce the personal consequences for individuals involved in taking the decision;
- delay taking the decision until the situation and consequential risks are clarified, even though this may ultimately defer taking the decision indefinitely;
- delay taking the decision until a clearer picture emerges of the support within the organization for particular solutions and the extent of the likely individual responsibility for the outcomes from the decision.

These responses to risky decision situations are not mutually exclusive. Indeed, it is quite common to see elements of almost all of these responses simultaneously in many decision situations both in business and other fields. It would be fair to say that they are all typical, status-driven managerial responses, i.e. most managers feel the need to present themselves as effective in handling either the individual decision situations or the overall process of managing business risk. These responses will be highlighted in the practical case studies in the following sections of this text.

The proposed framework for a more systematic approach to risk management is intended to make it easier to recognize and understand the key factors which relate to risk in decision situations, i.e:

- the types and sources of risks;
- the complexity of the interactions between the different types or sources of risk;
- the inherently dynamic nature of risk;
- the time dimension of risk;
- the influence of human and organizational factors;
- the role of the individual decision-maker or the composition and functioning of the group responsible for taking the decision; and
- the importance of information in risk management.

The next part of this chapter will develop the framework and the more systematic approach by building on our understanding of these particular elements. We will then demonstrate the application of the framework through the use of a case study which details some of the experiences of a typical manufacturing organization as it encounters a variety of risks and it develops its business strategies. A second case study will then be presented to examine the particular risks of technology development and implementation within a public sector service organization. In both cases, the major issues, risks and uncertainties facing the decision-maker will be identified, the approach taken in the situation will be explained and the benefits that might have been achieved from a more systematic approach examined.

12.4 AN APPROACH TO MANAGING BUSINESS RISKS: SIMULATE

The broad outline of the approach to managing business risks may be summarized as:

S   Structure the problem or decision situation.

I   Identify and Investigate the key elements of the problem, the potential uncertainties and risks.

M   Measure and assess the risks and uncertainties.

U   Understand the mechanics of, and the inter-relationships within, the problem, highlighting why the problem occurred, what caused it, and the future implications if not corrected.

L   Learn from the processes employed in analysing the problem and developing alternative solutions.

A   Analyse and evaluate the problem, the potential solutions and their possible outcomes in terms of risk.

T   Take the decision.

E   Experience. Build and develop the experience and expertise of the organization and its decision-makers on the basis of the decision process and the decisions taken.

Before developing this approach further, we will refresh memories as to the key factors which influence the framework and within which risk management operates. These include:

- the types and sources of risk;
- the nature and degree of the interaction between the organization and its environment;
- time as a constraint;
- the role of information.

12.4.1 The types and sources of risk

For our immediate purposes, we must start with a distinction between endogenous and exogenous risks, i.e. the sources and types of risk may be inherent in the organization itself or may originate in the organization's environment. By making this distinction, we do not wish to suggest that the risks from these two sources are entirely separate. In most practical decision situations, there will be significant interactions between the two types of risk, and the nature of these interactions will be discussed later in this chapter. Figure 12.2 has further subdivided the sources of risk in each category into three broad types.

Each of the six elements shown in Figure 12.2 will be discussed and this will be followed by consideration of the effects of the interaction between these elements both within the organization and its environment, and

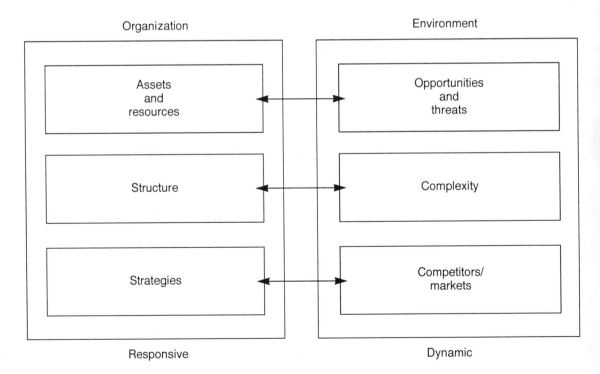

Figure 12.2 Classification of sources of risk.

between the organization and the environment.

12.4.2 Risks inherent in the organization

The risks which are inherent to an organization are likely to originate from four main sources, namely:

- the assets and resources either owned or under the control of the organization;
- the organization's current structure and culture;
- the strategies that are being used;
- the effectiveness of the management of these three elements.

(a) The organization's assets and resources

This heading may be further divided into:

- physical – e.g. the buildings, the plant, the raw materials in hand, the store of finished products etc;
- financial, e.g. the cash and other forms of capital or revenue assets; and
- human resources.

Each of these classes may be an important source of risk in many businesses. The risks may originate from a range of factors relating either to individual resources or to the composite of resources available for exploitation. Thus, physical resource factors such as insufficient quantity, poor quality, excess quantity or lack of potential for development may all generate sources of risk.

Ignoring the effects of recession and other macroeconomic events, the following represent common reasons for business failures:

- the organization lacks the financial resources to maintain their cashflow position;
- the inferior quality of the manufacturing equipment may pose risks to the quality of the output and prejudice the continuing sales performance of the business;
- carrying an excessive number of employees on the payroll may increase the unit costs and reduce the competitiveness of the organization, thereby posing risks to its market share;
- the available human resources may be of poor quality and, consequently, the organization may lack the capacity for further development, improvement or growth; it may also find it difficult to introduce new activities or skills and this may both represent a constraint on the organization's decision-making and enhance the associated risks.

The quantity or quality of individual resources may be a direct source of risk for the organization, but a more important generator of risk is likely to be the interaction between different resources. Indeed, this interaction may have a compounding effect over time and cause increasing levels of risk and uncertainty, prejudicing the ability of the organization to manage the resources effectively. Organizations may be affected by a variety of problems. Some may be outside their immediate ability to control. For example, if an organization is experiencing a shortage of financial resources, this might arise because, in times of general economic hardship, debtors are increasingly slow in paying what is owed, or it might be due to the poor monitoring and control of credit accounts. If we combine this with the fact that the plant is old and of poor quality, this might be due to the fact that management yielded to investor expectations and made generous dividend payments in times of plenty rather than reinvesting in new equipment or, from the outset, the business may have been undercapitalized. Finally, if the staff lack skills this may be due to the poor performance of the education system or the organization may not have made training a high priority. The cumulative effect of the interaction between these three elements might not only pose risks to the survival of the business but might equally represent symptoms of poor management. If the latter, then the chances that the organization will survive can be enhanced if steps are taken to identify and repair management deficiencies. We should therefore conclude that the interaction of the resources and the quality of their management may significantly influence both the nature and severity of the risks faced. Thus, even though an organization might have a poor cashflow position and poor quality equipment, if the staff are well trained and motivated and their efforts are managed effectively, it is likely to face a lower level of risk than the organization with problems in all three resources, or in one which is managed poorly.

(b)   The organization's structure

For these purposes, we define the term 'organization structure' as being no more than the means by which the organization seeks to manage its assets and resources with the intention of achieving its objectives. It is not appropriate to think of the term 'structure' in the rigid sense of ascertainable groups of people whose identity and status can be captured in a formalized chart of the organization. Instead, it should be seen as a series of formal and informal social relationships which are involved in the ongoing processes and operations which comprise the organization (i.e. the organization is nothing but a series of actor networks). These relationships are themselves subject to continuous evolution and change. Viewed in this way, the structure of the organization is an obvious source of risk for the organization both as a whole and for particular decisions.

If the organization structure is inappropriate or inadequate whether as a whole or in relation to individual constituent elements, it may generate risks. Hence, an organization structure may be fuzzy, i.e. perhaps because the initial intention was to encourage greater democracy, it has evolved with no clear identification of responsibility and authority for decision-making and control. Alternatively, the organization may have produced a form which enables it to function but it lacks proper co-ordination, i.e. the way in which the various processes are carried out may not allow information to be communicated effectively between the different groups. In both cases, this may prove a potential source of endogenous risk and it may be a symptom of poor management. Naturally, if component elements or functions within the structure perform inadequately, this may also represent a source of risk. Thus, if the personnel department fails to keep up to date with actual or proposed changes in employment legislation, the organization might, in ignorance, make a number of unlawful strategic human resource decisions and have to face substantial penalties or pay damages to those affected. Similarly, if the organization has not installed effective internal financial control systems, this will increase the likelihood and severity of cashflow or liquidity problems. It may also enhance the risk of falling profitability and, ultimately, cause the failure of the business.

The location, scale and nature of the interface between the organization structure and its environment is a further source of risk. It has been examined extensively in the literature. The work of Burns and Stalker (1961), for example, deals with the issue of how the organization should attempt to design a structure which will allow it to seek congruence with the environment. This may be through the development of more mechanistic structures to match the more stable environments or through more organic structures which may be more suitable for dynamic environments. While it is not appropriate to make a detailed examination of the work of these and similar authors at present, we must emphasize the conclusion that if there are problems in the interaction between the organization's structure and the environment, this will be a potential source of risk to the total organization and to its individual decisions.

(c) The organization's strategies

At this point, the definition becomes cumulative. Strategic management may be defined as the longer term processes through which the organization seeks to achieve its objectives by applying the assets and resources at its disposal within the internal structure to match the opportunities identified in the environment. The bland statement that the strategies of the organization may be a source of risk should not be surprising. The term 'risk' is most commonly associated with the 'bigger' decisions, i.e. with those decisions which deal with the totality of the business activities and commit substantial resources to activities of critical importance to the commercial future of the organization. But this simple acceptance requires some qualification. Although it is true that the risks which are inherent in a strategy may be attributed to the strategy itself, strategies are nothing more than the manipulations proposed for the assets and resources that can be made available for the particular purpose at the relevant time. Further, these assets and resources can only be made available through the prevailing structure of the organization. It is therefore more appropriate to make an initial location of the risk in the assets and resources to be used and in the structural context of that use. All strategies are nothing more than the declared outcome from the decision-making process and they reflect the risk perceptions and judgements of the organization and its members. The next source of risk is therefore located in this decision-making process. Obviously, the appropriateness of the strategy selected can only be judged in relation to the existing and potential environment. Thus, should the managers adopt a strategy which does not match the demands of the environment, this will increase the likelihood of strategic failure and represent a final source of risk for the organization in this definitional sequence.

To clarify the terminology further, although we have been referring to strategic decisions, the decisions at the tactical and operational levels are an essential part of the strategic decision-making and management processes. One view of a strategy is that of a series of tactical and operational decisions united under the broad umbrella of a strategic plan. Thus, a strategy is put into operation by decomposing it into a large number of separate tactical and operational decisions. Individually, each subordinate decision may have relatively minor consequences. But the cumulative effect of the range of tactical and operational decisions may produce a total level of real risk that considerably outweighs the potential risks and consequences that were foreseen when planning the strategic decisions.

(d) Management integration

Before we move on to analyse the external risks which may face the organization, it is important to reiterate the potential effects arising from the integration and interaction of these internal sources of risk. Albeit at a crude and simplistic level, we have asserted that the organization and its operation are made up of the three elements of assets/resources, structure and strategies. The fourth element is the process of integrating these elements and co-ordinating activities through the processes of management. If the organization fails to achieve an effective and efficient integration, this will generate greater risks for the organization. For example, the risks for a manufacturer which are likely to arise from technological developments in the manufacturing processes will be reflected in the:

- resources, e.g. the ability of the organization to make the necessary capital investment in plant and equipment which may leave the organization with dangerously reduced contingency funding or with little scope for further borrowing; having the appropriate amount of space in existing buildings to site the new plant or being faced with the need to find alternative factory premises; and being able to draw on existing levels of skill or having the potential to retrain the relevant employees;
- structure, e.g. the new manufacturing process may call for the combination of previously separate production units and this may have significant cultural implications for those whose traditional working practices and lines of authority may disappear; and

- strategies, e.g. the managers must select their response to the threats and opportunities posed by the technological development.

The capability of the management team to manage these three elements effectively at the strategic, tactical and operational levels will also influence the total exposure to risk. Risk is not simply a phenomenon that confronts management during its decision-making. It is an inherent product of the management process itself.

12.4.3 Risks external to the organization

Most people would identify the environment as the most obvious source of risk to the organization. However, as we have already shown, the internal elements of an organization and the way in which it formulates its responses to the risks perceived in the environment are equally important. This is not to deny the importance of exogenous risks. Indeed, the potential sources of risk to the organization from the environment are probably limitless, though the extent of the impact and the likelihood of occurrence will vary between different external sources. Thus, the threat that a fire may damage the production facilities and stocks may be fairly remote but, should a fire occur, the consequences could be very significant for the organization. The loss of an overseas customer due to delays in the delivery and distribution channels may be quite likely but whether it proves to be disastrous for the organization will be determined by the real value of the orders lost. Figure 12.2 divided the range of potential sources and types of risk which emanate from the environment into three categories, namely opportunities and threats, complexity, and market/competitive forces. These three categories are also interrelated. The interaction between the three dimensions may itself prove to be the source of the more significant and often the more complex forms of risk and uncertainty. We will start with a brief review of the three sources, and return to the discussion of their interaction later.

(a) Opportunities and threats

The term risk is most commonly associated with the idea that threats will emerge from the environment to menace the organization, e.g. the threat of central government action to remove subsidies and controls over the pricing structure of energy sources may pose a threat to organizations like Nuclear Power and the NCB within the supply industry and to all organizations that need to purchase significant quantities of energy. Potential opportunities also pose risks for organizations. When opportunities are identified, it will be rare for the organization to have complete confidence that the event(s) will occur exactly as foreseen and with the nature of the outcomes within the predicted range. Strategies are always designed to be responsive, i.e. different responses will be planned to meet contingencies as and when they arise and, to that extent, the organization will be accepting the inevitable risks in the plan as the price to be paid if the foreseen rewards are to be achieved.

Thus, if an organization is planning the launch of a new range of male toiletries and cosmetics, the management will be making judgements at two different levels. On the one hand, this venture may provide potential profit opportunities. It may equally pose risks for the organization even though the organization's own and other competitors' products have proved successful in the past. Risk management should not simply be viewed as the negative process of avoiding the perceived threats in the environment. More importantly, it is the positive process of seeking and developing commercially viable opportunities. The two activities of avoiding threats and pursuing opportunities both expose the organization to risk but provide differing types of returns or rewards for the taking of such risks. We believe that one of the major weaknesses in modern business is the tendency in risk management to focus on the avoidance of the risks generated by threats in the environment rather than on the management of the risks involved in the exploitation of environmental opportunities.

(b)   Complexity

An increasingly common statement about the economic, social and political environment in which organizations operate is not only that it is very complex already but that the degree of complexity is accelerating each year. While such a statement is undoubtedly true in the objective sense, there is a suspicion that such claims are often made by decision-makers in an attempt to absolve themselves or their organization from liability for the consequences of the decisions taken, or perhaps even as a justification for not taking a decision at all. As a reaction to this negativity, we should argue that the increasing complexity is a potential opportunity in its own right to those organizations capable and willing to tackle the problems and risks created. The manufacturer of electrical components for the automobile industry may perceive a very complex environment of global competition, technological change, market changes, pricing and cost competitiveness etc. If all component manufacturers have similar perceptions of a hostile environment and this tends to breed hesitancy in taking decisions, then it creates an opportunity for the individual organization prepared to cut through this complexity and to take the necessary risks involved in a strategy to increase market share.

The degree of complexity will vary not only between situations but also between different time periods in the same situation. The supplier of a basic commodity such as water to domestic customers who live within a given geographical region may, with some justification, argue that it faces a less complex environment than the manufacturer of fashionable clothing intended to be sold on an international scale. Both organizations may also argue that the environment that they face today is significantly more complex than that faced ten years ago. While we might attempt a more objective assessment to determine which really has the more complex environment, the more important measure probably lies in the subjective perceptions of the individuals and organizations as they interface with their own environments. The scale of risk and the associated factor of complexity are both determined by their perceptions. We frankly admit that these perceptions may be a poor measure of the reality of the situation both as to complexity and the risks. So a perception that the external environment is overly complex may often be associated with perceptions that the risks of operating within this environment are also high. In many cases, this diagnosis of excessive complexity may engender considerable fear in the hearts of some decision-makers. Their responses may vary considerably.

The usual response of managers when complexity is apparent is to research the environment in greater depth with a view to establishing some of the major elements and the nature of their interaction. The reaction of academics who study and research complexity is to resolve the difficulty by developing models, whether empirical or conceptual. These models are designed to distil the key factors or parameters out of the complexity and then to link them back together through appropriate interrelationships to generate a more easily understood version of reality. The major problem in this approach is that the models themselves are invariably inadequate to replicate the complexity of the real situation. This significantly limits the power of the model to identify and measure the risks involved for the individual or the organization. A critical danger from the decision-makers point of view is that they do not fully recognize that such models only reflect part of the real world situation and continue to make decisions as if they were fully comprehensive.

(c) Competitive and market forces

The more evident sources of risk in the environment are the changes in the levels of market demand, and the responses or actions of competitors to such changes. These changes in market demand may arise from a number of different sources, including:

- changing consumer tastes;
- shifts in demographic trends;
- technological changes;
- distribution channel changes; etc.

In some instances, the organizations in the market individually or collectively may have little or no influence on these factors, e.g. changes in the age distribution of the population cannot be affected by organizations. In other cases, the organizations may initiate or sustain particular changes, e.g., the use of advertising and promotional tools to promote the benefits of changes in product technology and to arouse consumer demand for these benefits. These competitive responses by organizations within the market provide further sources of risk to other competitors. In a sense, when each management team examines the market and tries to predict the actions of each competitor organization, the organization is seeking to identify and assess:

- any fundamental changes as they occur in the functioning of the market;
- the actual and likely responses or strategies of competitors to these changes; and
- the likely impact of various strategies that the organization might adopt itself in response to both of these.

(d)   Interaction within the environment

Although it may appear self-evident, it is important to recognize that the three broad environmental elements outlined above are themselves in a continuous process of interaction and change. The development of new and associated technologies may:

- create threats and opportunities;
- change the markets and the competitive structure of those markets; and
- simultaneously, increase the complexity of the environment faced.

The invention of solid-state electronic technology and its application to drive watches and clocks caused interactions across all the dimensions of the environment for organizations involved in the sector. In addition to the obvious threats to the mechanical clockwork technologies, opportunities were created for new products and markets. The previous structure of competition was overturned, all of which resulted in much greater complexity. The examples in other industry sectors may appear less dramatic although, in most cases, the strategic impact caused may be just as significant.

12.4.4   Organization/environment interaction and interdependence

Each of the six broad elements we have discussed, together with the interaction between them, has the potential to generate different types and levels of risk for the organization. But the way in which the organization interacts with its environment will be the crucial factor in determining the extent of the impact that the potential risks may have. Further, as time passes, it is the effectiveness of the processes of strategic control over the significant interactions that will determine the nature of the risks and the consequences experienced by the organization. By this, we mean that the organization must develop effective and efficient management systems and maintain quality in managing not only the individual components within the organization but also the total interface with the environment over time. Almost without exception, the modern organization is required to respond to an increasingly dynamic environment as regional and global markets are formed. The quality of the responses made at this time will help to dictate the nature of the risks, the scale of their impact and, ultimately, the performance of the organization. The organizations most likely to succeed will be those who develop the greatest levels of effectiveness in managing the business risks.

In addition to the major group of elements already addressed, a further two elements need to be considered before we are able to construct a methodology for managing risks. These are time and information. These two elements pervade all dimensions of decision-making at different levels in organizations and, hence, will significantly influence the perceptions of risk by both individuals and groups within organizations.

12.4.5 Time: a luxury or a constraint

When decision-makers take their decisions, they are basing those decisions on the current perceptions of the risks and uncertainties in each particular situation. With the passage of time, many of those risk perceptions and uncertainties will be confirmed or denied by events. Hindsight may be both a blessing and a curse for the decision-maker as the actual nature of the problems, uncertainties and risks become so much clearer when all the cards in that deal have been played! Unfortunately, few decision-makers can afford the luxury either of hindsight or, indeed, of delaying the decision until such time as the uncertainties are clarified and the risks resolved. The rules of the game usually require the players to keep playing even though they are uncertain. Time is therefore a critical factor in its ability to influence perceptions of risk but it may also constrain the ability of the decision-maker to do much about changing those initial perceptions.

It should be apparent that the degree of uncertainty increases with the futurity of the decision situation faced. In Figure 12.3 we represent a range of decision situations. The vertical scale reflects the spread from complete certainty to total uncertainty. It can be seen that this spectrum

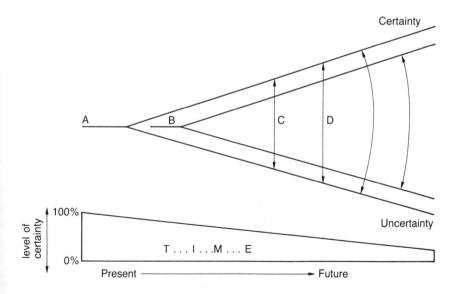

Figure 12.3 Time and its effects on uncertainty.

becomes wider the further the decision-maker is required to look into the future. For example, the degree of risk and uncertainty for a decision that will impact on the organization at point D in the future is considerably wider than that for a decision that will impact at point C. This is true no matter when the decision concerning these two outcomes is being taken. In general terms, we suggest that there is less certainty about those decision outcomes which are more distant. This uncertainty will affect both the likelihood of occurrence and the detail of the consequences.

But as time progresses, the width of this uncertainty will tend to narrow, i.e. the degree of uncertainty reduces as further information is received so long as it resolves some of the previous uncertainties. In terms of the diagram, if the present time period progresses from point A to point B, then the range of uncertainty present will narrow as the particular event or decision draws nearer. The degree of uncertainty at point C reduces from that previously present, as does that for point D. This is a very simplified statement of what may happen in reality. There are no objective grounds on which to assume that the reduction in risk and uncertainty for D will exactly parallel that for C. Thus, the risk perceptions in certain types of decision situation may reduce as time progresses because more information becomes available and better understanding emerges (e.g. because better quality decision-makers join the group, or through investment in better manual search strategies or the introduction of new technologies). In other situations, the assessment of the risk may remain relatively unchanged over a significant period of time (e.g. in situations of relative stability when the commercial assessment is equivalent to assessing the chances of winning first prize in a lottery). Finally, in other situations, the perception may be that the risks have actually increased (e.g. because more international competitors have announced their entry into the organization's domestic market).

For any given decision situation, therefore, we might be tempted to argue that a decision-maker should always delay making the decision for as long as possible. The reason would be that the longer the delay, the greater the degree of certainty achievable as to the nature of the factors affecting the decision and so the better the decision that will be taken. While in principle this would appear to be the more rational approach, there are reasons why this may not represent a feasible, practical or, indeed, an optimal approach.

1. There may be a number of time constraints on the decision including:

    - a deadline for taking the decision has been externally imposed, e.g. a closure time for bids has been set, contractual requirements may stipulate an express time for performance, a superior may have laid down fixed requirements etc.; or
    - a deadline may have been imposed internally, e.g. a target set in terms of personal time management.

2. Delay may pose potential threats or loss of opportunities in a

competitive sense as competitors respond more swiftly to market demands.

3. The passage of time may actually result in greater uncertainty as the nature of the decision and the context within which it is to be taken change.

If we were dealing with an unchanging environment, then some delay might be beneficial. But in a more dynamic environment, the nature of the decision may be constantly changing, so any delays in taking that decision may result in either the emergence of new types of risk or a further enhancement of the existing scale of risks involved in the decision.

12.4.6 The role and importance of information

For our purposes, the availability of information is the final factor which may have a significant impact on the perceptions of risk. Information will always be classified as a resource for an organization. Like any other piece of raw material received by the organization, data may vary in terms of both quantity and quality. This leads us to various myths which wrongly have been perpetuated. Thus, some people apparently continue to believe that:

• simply increasing the quantity of information available to the decision-maker will reduce the level of risk and uncertainty; and
• processing data will produce better quality information and thereby improve the quality of the decision.

Neither belief can be sustained in practice. Not only are there likely to be diminishing returns as the volume of information is increased, but the decision-maker may rapidly approach a situation of information overload. In such circumstances, the decision-maker may form a heightened perception of the risks involved. This may arise because the situation may seem to have become more complex or new parameters, not previously considered, are brought to the decision-maker's attention. It is true that improvements in the quality of the information available may assist in resolving some of the risk issues, but the key factor is which dimensions of quality have been improved. For example, improvements in the accuracy of the information may enhance the quality of the decision taken, but if this is at the expense of timeliness, i.e. it may require significantly more time to produce accurate information, then this may delay the decision and increase the risks.

Some of the studies have shown that the information made available can either support or deny the existing perceptions of a situation including the risks. But there is a general finding that information which appears to challenge or deny the existing perceptions will have a lesser impact than information which is supportive of existing perceptions. This is based on the entirely human proposition that both individual and group decision-makers will be tempted to try to interpret new data inputs as being consistent with their already formulated views or perceptions of the decision situation. The more the situation appears similar to previous situations in which the decision-makers have been proved correct in their analysis, the more decision-makers are seen to be reluctant radically to alter their initial views or perceptions of the immediate decision situation. Sometimes, the need for radical or fundamental changes of view are signalled through the new information, but even in such apparently different cases, some decision-makers cling stubbornly to their past ideas, and may seek reasons to refute the new evidence. For example, despite all the statistical evidence to the contrary, most people still perceive travel by air as carrying a higher risk than travel by road.

The first and most important step in the decision process is for the decision-maker to identify what he or she does not know about the situation. It would be quite appropriate to apply the expression that 'ignorance is bliss when it is folly to be wise' to the decision situation involving risk. If a decision-maker remains blissfully ignorant of a particular dimension of a decision, this may prove comforting as further elements sometimes do little more than add greater layers of complexity and, hence, uncertainty to the situation. If the decision-maker is lucky, this ignorance will not prove fatal. But if this ignorance relates to critical elements in the situation, it may actually invalidate the decision taken and enhance the risks involved even further. Many factors may influence the individual's ability to detect the important elements in a given situation. Among the more important are the following:

- The quality of the decision-makers – they must be able to recognize, receive, analyse and synthesize new information in relation to the decision situation. Naturally, the experience they have gained through their careers, and the training and skills they have received, may prove critical in directing the initial identification of the main elements of the decision and the specification of the information that will be required to analyse those elements. In terms of the decision process, the initial structuring of the problem, the identification of the key or more important variables, and the subsequent focusing of the information search in relation to those elements are all critical factors.
- The effectiveness of the information system – this begins with the quality of the information and communication systems within the organization to capture, process and deliver the necessary and relevant information to the right person at the right time. Even though the decision-maker may have correctly identified and specified the information required, inadequacies in the information system may fail to provide either the necessary information or provide only poor quality information.
- The cost of information collection and processing and the benefits that collection and processing generates for the quality of the decisions. If a decision-maker has a limited budget, he or she may not be able to justify devoting the additional resources necessary to cover the cost of the additional work required to reduce the levels of uncertainty. Even if the resources can be made available, there is no guarantee that the

additional work will produce the benefit of greater certainty, nor that the decision quality will be improved. In boardrooms, it is not uncommon to overhear the suggestion that the costs of acquiring additional information would outweigh the benefits but, as already indicated, the real reason could be that the decision-maker does not want to receive information which contradicts the currently held perceptions or the proposed decision alternative. There is the further possibility that the new information might expose the weakness of the decision already taken, and could undermine the decision-maker's position.

Further, the way in which both the people and the systems work will be conditioned by the organization's structure and culture – they are the key factors that will colour the perception of risk and the consequent responses to such risks. This is not to deny that all organizations operate within the limitations imposed by their capital and assets holdings. Indeed, the strategies formulated by the organization will typically reflect the current and prospective resource situation. However, we should note that the resource profile of the organization will usually be determined by the strategy of the business and the organization structure devised. Moreover, the management style and therefore the responses made by the organization to the opportunities or threats perceived will always be affected by the prevailing culture, no matter what quality of information is available.

Degrees of uncertainty

Any decision situation will comprise a range of potential degrees of uncertainty as shown in Figure 12.4. Most decision situations will fall somewhere within the spectrum between total or complete certainty and complete uncertainty. When managers are designing a decision-making process and the tools that are going to be used to support that process, the usual intention is to move the situation more towards the certainty end of the spectrum.

12.5   A SIMPLE APPROACH: SIMULATE

We hope that the approach we now propose to the task of managing risk effectively is one that is easy to understand, simple to apply and responsive to the issues discussed throughout the book. The SIMULATE approach focuses on the normal decision process that has evolved within the culture of each organization but stresses those areas requiring attention.

Ignoring the detail of the discussion in Chapter 4, we assert the truth that the process of strategy formulation is essentially the process of providing a blueprint for the middle- to long-term management of the organization's resources so that an effective and efficient utilization of

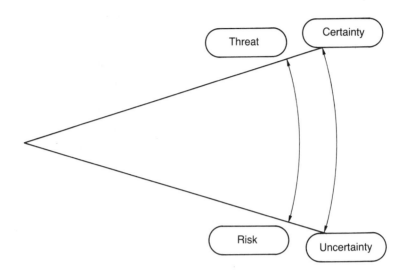

Figure 12.4 Spectrum of certainty–uncertainty.

those resources results. Figure 12.5 demonstrates our view that the strategic management interfaces with the resources of the organization can only be conducted through the various structures and processes within the organization. Naturally, the complex nature of these interactions is belied by the simplicity of the diagram, but we have tried to give an indication of the extent of this complexity in the earlier paragraphs in this chapter.

The methodology we propose has two strands:

- a process strand which we have termed SIMULATE; and
- a content strand based on a structure of the decision.

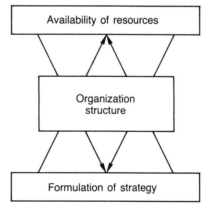

Figure 12.5 Interactions underpinning stategy formulations.

The process strand was outlined in section 12.4. The second element of the methodology is represented by the structured model of the internal and external dimensions of the decision situations or problems encountered by the organization. We will now apply the methodology to two case study situations.

12.6 CASE STUDY ILLUSTRATIONS

The demonstration of the proposed structured approach to risk management will be developed through the two case studies in a number of stages. The first step will be to provide a general background to the organization. This will be followed by a brief historical analysis of the situation that has faced the organization over a period of some three to four years before the case study starts to run. In giving this analysis, we will describe the main sources of risk and uncertainty actually identified and evaluated by the organization in formulating its strategic plans. We will then apply the more structured approach to identify and evaluate the risks and uncertainties that should have been considered by the organization's decision-makers. This will give us two versions of perceived reality – as it *is*, and as it *ought* to be. The strategies implemented by the organization on the basis of their perception of the strategic situation as it is will then be compared with those strategies that might have been more appropriate to the actual situation. We will also describe the impact of the strategies as they are implemented and examine the consequent changes in the nature and scale of the risks and uncertainties. As an afterword, we will suggest the effect of the strategies as they might have been. The point is not to be 'wise after the event'. Rather we hope to show how a more structured approach to the process of identifying and analysing the risks and uncertainties might have improved the quality of the strategic decisions taken.

12.7 HEBLON PLC: RISK MANAGEMENT IN A TRADITIONAL MANUFACTURER

12.7.1 Backround to company

Heblon PLC specializes in the production of high-quality wooden furniture, focusing on the market for the more traditional or reproduction style of product. The business was established in the 1950s on a small scale, relying on the individual craftsmanship of its workers. Since that time, it has developed at only a modest rate. The main reason for this modest level of growth has been the policy of the family who own the business not to expose their investment to any significant risks. In essence, therefore, the growth rate has been dictated by the profits generated by the business after deducting the return required by the owners. Thus, as at the date we start this study, the business employs 250 people and achieves sales of almost £10 million.

Generally, the company's management has avoided the risks associated with entering new markets, developing new products or introducing new technologies. Instead, the managers have preferred to handle the more familiar types of uncertainties and risks which are associated with their current markets, products and technologies. The result is that the company has a small share of the traditional furniture niche within the overall market for wooden furniture products. But its high reputation for quality has assured a steady demand for its products with little pressure from its customers to improve delivery times even though these may often stretch to months rather than weeks for particular products from the range.

Because of the nature of the product, the production processes are still primarily based on individual craftsmanship and are therefore labour intensive. Although developments in manufacturing technology have taken place, those which have been considered acceptable to Heblon's working practices have been introduced on a piecemeal basis rather than as the result of an integrated strategic plan for developing manufacturing technology. The pace of development has also been restricted not only by the shortage of financial resources, but equally by the lack of knowledge, expertise and commitment on the part of the management and owners. Indeed, the traditional nature of the designs, often with hand-chiselled or adzed features has been used as an excuse not to place any emphasis on updating the manufacturing techniques.

A further feature relevant to an understanding of past strategy is the relative insensitivity of the market to product prices. The nature of the niche in which the company operates has enabled it to pass on increases in its costs to the market through increased prices without losing sales volume. As a consequence, the pressure on the business to maintain or improve productivity has been limited.

12.7.2 The developing situation

The previously stable pattern of market demand, minimal technology development, manufacturing productivity and overall business performance has become increasingly disturbed in the last five years for two main reasons:

- there have been a number of developments in the environment which have had a concerted effect, increasing pressure on the revenues from the market and on the internal costs; and
- decisions by the management team have been taken to develop both the product range and markets served.

As we will explain, these two factors have also had a compounding effect on each other and, more importantly, they have significantly increased the exposure of the organization to different types and greater levels of risk than previously experienced.

The developments in the environment have arisen from a number of sources, the most important of which are as follows:

1. The increasingly strong international pressures to restrict deforestation, particularly of rain forests, so that the approach of global warming can be slowed down, has caused:

   - reductions in the supply of the hardwoods used in furniture manufacture;
   - increases in the lead time for the delivery of hardwood raw materials with deliveries becoming less predictable; and
   - escalating wood prices.

   Although market researchers have yet to detect the impact of such green issues on the general level of demand for wood-based products, this may become a significant factor in the future. In anticipation that the conservation pressures will continue to grow, the industry has begun the search for substitute materials and has increased effort to introduce innovation into the manufacturing processes so that a more efficient use of the increasingly scarce hardwood resources can be achieved.

2. Shifts and changes in consumer behaviour towards the purchase of furniture products have begun to manifest themselves. The latest market intelligence suggests that the replacement cycle for furniture products in general is becoming shorter. The consumer is becoming more fashion and design conscious, seeking a greater variety of designs and a range of supporting and complementary products. To date, this has not had a real effect on Heblon's traditional markets but there may be an impact in the future. Overall, it is inevitable that these developments will affect both the price and the cost structure of the business.

3. There have been technology developments which have and ought to have influenced Heblon. Broadly, these developments may be subdivided into two groups:

   - developments in the fields of the basic raw materials, product design, manufacturing processes, and handling and transportation systems should all have some influence on the overall manufacturing system; and
   - developments in production control systems, interfirm communications, quality management techniques, information systems, and the structure and style of management within each organization will influence the total management and control of the business.

   All the developments of this type are increasing the pressures on business in all aspects of the furniture market, including that occupied by Heblon.

4. There have been developments in the pattern of competition in the

furniture market. In the lower priced sectors, there are increasing competitive pressures and the entry of overseas manufacturers to the UK market has intensified pressures on prices and profit margins. This has caused a number of organizations to increase emphasis on non-price factors such as quality, design and delivery as the basis of their competitive advantage.

5.   In the last decade, a concentration of distribution channels has been particularly evident in the UK market. The market share of super-stores and national furniture distribution chains has been growing at the expense of the smaller high-street furniture retailer. This has shifted the bargaining power from the manufacturer to the retailer, with obvious consequences for profit margins and terms of supply.

At a general level, Heblon's management has maintained awareness of these developments in the environment and has recognized that they may create risks in the future. However, no serious attempt has been made to examine whether these risks have become more real nor whether their potential impact on the business has become more likely. (We should perhaps observe that this is a not an untypical situation. The managers of most organizations usually are aware of the general risks facing the business. But, frequently, major problems arise because the understanding or evaluation of these risks never proceeds much beyond this level of general awareness.)

Further, the complexity and interrelated nature of these risks mean that Heblon's management has been unable or unwilling fully to comprehend the precise nature or scale of the aggregate risks facing the business. The management's response to the situation, while having some degree of plausibility in the circumstances, has in fact resulted in the generation of further risks for the organization.

The actions actually taken to address the risks, uncertainties and problems as the managers perceived them have included:

- a more intensive marketing and sales campaign directed at both the multiples and independent retailers; this has required an increase in the number of in-house staff, an investment in consultancy services and an enhancement of the associated overheads;
- an enhancement of the product development and design function by recruiting both a designer and product development engineer;
- a greater emphasis on the improvement of productivity and the control of costs; the latter has depended on the development and implementation of an information system and procedures to facilitate more effective and efficient planning and control;
- a series of tactical decisions which appeared to the management to be integrated but which did not represent an integrated strategy for the future of the business.

12.7.3   A review of the emerging situation

It should be obvious that the response of Heblon's management has failed to address the key risks involved. As we will see later, the responses made not only failed to address these risks but, in themselves, created further risks for the organization.

12.8   HOW SHOULD THE MANAGERS HAVE APPROACHED THE SITUATION?

We now propose to go through the process strand of SIMULATE, indicating how the managers could have achieved a better view of the problem situation. In deciding how much detail to include, we have been influenced by the need not to be distracted too far away from the methodology itself. Obviously, it would have been possible to build up an increasingly detailed view of Heblon, but we have restricted our coverage to the most salient points only. Let us start by reminding ourselves of the SIMULATE structure.

S   Structure the problem or decision situation

I   Identify and Investigate the key elements of the problem, the potential uncertainties and risks

M   Measure and assess the risks and uncertainties

U   Understand the mechanics and interrelationships within the problem, why the problem occurred, what causes it, and the future implications if not corrected

L   Learn from the processes employed in analysing the problem and developing alternative solutions

A   Analysc and evaluate the problem, the potential solutions and their possible outcomes in terms of risk

T   Take the decision

E   Experience. Build and develop the experience and expertise of the organization and its decision-makers on the basis of the decision process and the decisions taken.

12.9   A GUIDE TO THE PROCESS OF STRUCTURING

The organization needs to develop a picture of the decision situation that it faces. One way of achieving this is to produce a KISSAF model – **K**eep **It** **S**imple, **S**trategic **A**nd **F**ocused. To be sufficiently comprehensive, this model should be based on the following guidelines:

- *Simple*   One of the greatest hindrances to effective decision-making is the development of models or views of the situation which are too complex, too detailed and too wide ranging. The key message is to strike a balance:

  the models must be simple but not simplistic!

- *Strategic*   To take a strategic perspective is deliberately to limit the organizational view of the situation. But, if decision-makers attempt to incorporate tactical and operational factors into the model, this tends to result in models that are too comprehensive, over complex and difficult to handle. The tactical and operational issues and risks will still have to be addressed, but the management team should ensure that they are considered within their contextual strategic framework.

- *Focused* The achievement of a simple and effective description or model of the situation is usually through a more focused attention to the key issues. The less focused the approach, the more difficult will be the task of the decision-maker in analysing the risks, taking the decision and implementing the solution.

In the case of Heblon, the organization's management needed to develop a model not only based on these principles, but also featuring the elements developed earlier in the chapter and reproduced as Figure 12.6.

12.9.1 Heblon's environment

(a) Opportunities and threats

In many respects, this stage of the analysis requires the management to do nothing more than pose and seek answers to a variety of questions. For example:

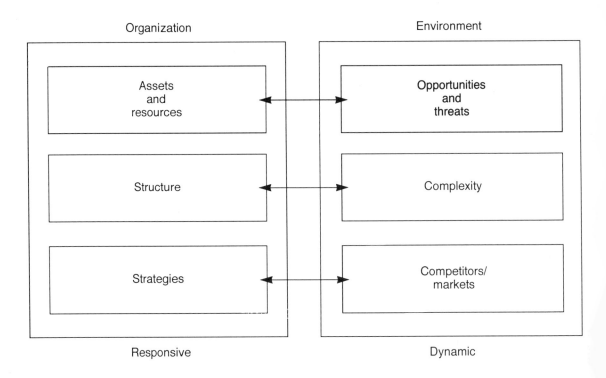

Figure 12.6 Structured approach for Heblon.

- What are the key environmental trends both currently and prospectively?
- Will the political pressures to prevent deforestation prove sufficiently strong to have a significant impact in the next 5–10 years?
- If so, what real effect will this have in strategy terms on the business of Heblon?
- Will customers move to alternative products and, if so, in what proportions?
- What realistic market opportunities does this provide?
- If Heblon was to invest in developing new products based on synthetic materials or, perhaps, other more prevalent types of wood, what would be the realistic time-scale for the product design and manufacture life-cycle and what demand would there be in the market?

A similar set of questions could be posed about all the other elements in the environment including changes in technology, demographic and social trends, or future political events. The foreseeability of the range of the elements that may have some impact on the future of the business is limited only by the intelligence and imagination of the managers, so the scope of the questioning must be constrained within constructive and reasonable boundaries.

(b) Complexity

In our earlier discussion of complexity, we suggested that it is often used in a negative or defensive sense by decision-makers either to justify the characterization of the decision faced as difficult or as a form of insurance against subsequent criticism if the decision outcome(s) prove unfavourable. There is no question that the management of Heblon is faced with a complex environment, but their reaction has fitted the familiar pattern of trying to use this as a shield against potential criticism.

(c) Competitors/markets

Perhaps because it would be expected of them as potential exploiters of a market, commercial organizations always claim to understand this dimension of the environment better than the others. Unfortunately, in practice, this seldom appears to be the case. The reason that the managers make this assumption of understanding is that it is the purpose of organizations to be involved in the market, continuously interfacing with customers, distributors and competitors. It would therefore not be unreasonable to argue that the decisions and activities of the organization will in some way influence or be influenced by the trends and events within the market. But, in all probability, it is this latter point that makes organizations poor at assessing the *strategic* developments and trends within their markets, as the focus of their attention is often too heavily at the level of operational and tactical decisions and activities.

12.9.2 Heblon's organization

(a) Assets and resources

The first of the three internal elements of the decision environment to be considered relates to the assets and resources currently and potentially available to Heblon. In the context of the present discussion on the identification of risks within the decision situation, there are four resources which influence its strategic decisions:

- *Human resources* The key resource for most organizations flows from the exploitation of its human capital. Heblon has always possessed skills appropriate to its current technologies, operations and markets and it has used its reputation for high-quality craftsmanship as the distinctive feature of its product promotion. At a technical level, this would give it sufficient scope to develop, implement and manage new production management and control methods. But the organization lacks the necessary potential at middle and senior management levels to redevelop into new directions of technology and/or markets. In all organizations, the major and often the more intractable risks arise from decisions and strategies which do not take proper account of human resource capabilities. Hence, the decisions to develop new products and particularly the proposal to enter new markets overseas were inherently risky because of the current and potential weakness in the profile of the senior managerial and other human resources available.

- *Finance* The capital structuring of Heblon has been driven not by the internal needs of the company, objectively assessed, but by the selfish requirements of the owners to maintain their return on investment. If the organization is to fund a major change in strategy, it must undertake a fundamental reappraisal of the role of the owners and consider whether additional sources of finance may be made available.

- *Production technology* Although hand crafting has been a distinctive feature of Heblon's products, the managers need to consider whether similar results can be achieved by other means, e.g. by plastic injection moulding the shapes and then laminating the output with wood grain. Naturally, this would involve a major change in the use of human resources and require a major capital injection, but without a willingness to consider radical new possibilities, Heblon may be left behind in a changing market.

- *Raw materials* The availability and reliability of supply is already suspect. Unless the company takes urgent steps to safeguard the short-term situation, it may find itself unable to maintain current production levels. Although the retailers have been tolerant given the quality of the Heblon's product, their attitude may well change as competition in the market becomes more acute. In the medium- to long-term, Heblon must consider the raw material position in line with production technologies to ensure that a coherent and comprehensive survival package emerges from their deliberations.

(b) Organization structure

The structure of any organization directly affects the way in which people are expected or allowed to make their contribution to the success of the business which employs them. It therefore has a significant impact on the organization's capacity to develop strategies for the future and may be an inherent source of risks for the organization. Heblon's structure, as shown in Figure 12.7, represents a typical functional structure. It has developed over the years as a response to both internal and external pressures. This structure produces a number of practical constraints on the options available to the organization in responding to the new challenges, risks and uncertainties which are encountered. The rigidity in the structure and the artificial demarcation of responsibilities between the various functional elements represent a barrier both to new initiatives and to the exploitation of emerging opportunities. For example, the company's wish to develop an effective strategy to increase its share of the multiple retail market should not be based solely on the contributions from, and co-operation of, sales and marketing. The production, stock control, warehousing and management accounting functions can all make an important contribution to the success of such a strategy. Indeed, a failure to consult with all the interested parties may lead to significant difficulties during implementation.

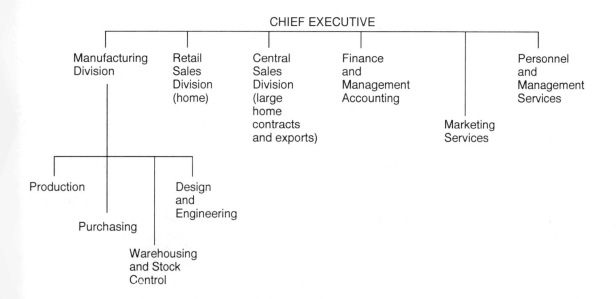

Figure 12.7 Heblon plc: organization chart.

Once the strategy has been formed, Heblon's problems persist because the capacity of the human resources to implement the chosen strategy effectively will continue to be constrained by the limitations in organization structure. These constraints therefore represent a further source of risk and uncertainty. When Heblon was formulating its strategies, the senior management simply presumed that the organization would be sufficiently responsive to ensure effective implementation. In fact, the major problem encountered almost immediately was the implied change in the status or standing of particular functions and the consequences for the management of these functions. Once the strategy document was released for implementation planning, the affected managers saw that the changes required the development of a more generally targeted, market-oriented strategy. This was combined with an increasing emphasis on productivity improvements within the manufacturing processes. Overall, this seemed to pose a threat to the managers and employees in the production-related functions. Their traditional skills, production technologies and control systems were all being threatened with the need for change. The strength of the reaction to this threat was enhanced by the political position of the manufacturing division within the organization's structure and it created additional risks to the success of the strategies developed even before they could be implemented.

(c) Organization strategy

Heblon has had neither a clear nor a coherent strategic development route for the business. Although the organization's management team seems to have been aware of some of the historical/topical trends and developments, it has not taken steps to develop its understanding of these developments nor of the implications for the business. Consequently, no real effort has been made to formulate the broad strands of the strategic response required to meet these developments and changes.

12.10   ACHIEVING AN INTEGRATED MODEL THROUGH SIMULATE

12.10.1   Structure the problem

When the organization is developing its view or model of the decision situation faced, it needs to follow the rule KISSAF – **K**eep **I**t **S**imple, **S**trategic **A**nd **F**ocused. The development of this initial model has critical implications for the remaining stages in the decision process, i.e. data collection and analysis, risk assessment and the formal decision-taking stages. Any substantial failure in the process to develop a KISSAF model is likely to increase the costs and to reduce the effectiveness of the subsequent decision stages. We should also emphasize that the development of a model is not a 'one off' exercise. The process of model building is or should be continuous and, as such, the view or model of the decision situation ought to be evolving dynamically in response to the changing situation. This evolutionary process in itself will pose dangers to the achievement of KISSAF models as there will be a temptation simply to add to the existing view/model rather than to undertake a more fundamental review of the whole model.

12.10.2 Identify and Investigate the decision situation

Once it has established a KISSAF model of the decision situation faced, the organization should undertake a more detailed investigation. We should think of the KISSAF model as a sort of skeleton, showing the outline of the structure that will support and give direction to the necessary research into the basic elements of the decision situation. The aim should then be to go through a disciplined process to put flesh on to the bones by answering questions such as the following:

- What causes each key element in the model to behave as it does or to manifest itself in that way?
- What impact does each key element have on the external environment?
- What impact does each key element have on the business of Heblon itself?

For example in Heblon's case, the increasing concentration of the retail distribution channels should have been viewed as a significant strategic factor. But the management failed to investigate fully or to research the development and its consequences for the business. Closer investigation would have revealed that although the major multiple furniture retailing chains are gaining an increasingly large share of the overall market, this is being achieved through competitive pricing and, hence, significantly reduced profit margins. To achieve further scope for price competition, the retailing chains are reducing all their administrative, corporate financing and stock holding costs to the minimum achievable. At its simplest level, therefore, these retailing organizations are operating on high volume, fast turnover and low margin sales. The profits generated are then being combined with borrowed capital to finance ambitious expansion schemes in terms of new outlets. While growth in the national economy is sustained and these retail businesses are achieving sufficient growth in sales and profits to finance their investment commitments, this pattern could well continue. But if we assume either a decline in the national economic growth rate or in these organization's sales volume (say, because of a slow-down in the housing market), this could be sufficient to cause problems for these organizations and, more importantly, for other retailers and manufacturers in the industry.

Naturally, Heblon's management has been aware of the growing importance of the large multiple chains, recognizing that they were becoming the major distribution outlets within the retail market. They did perceive a risk to the future sales potential of Heblon if they failed to respond to this development. The difficulty is that the managers were unduly pessimistic and negatively characterized the risk scenario primarily as a loss of opportunity. As a result, they failed to investigate more fully other possible implications using differing 'what if?' scenarios. Indeed, a closer investigation might have revealed alternative opportunities by focusing attention on particular niches within the overall market. For example, different opportunities might have been detected if Heblon were to concentrate on supplying the smaller independent high-street retailers, or concentrated efforts on developing within the commercial furniture sector, including office furniture or the hotel furnishing business.

12.10.3   Measure the risks and uncertainties

Once the company has identified the major sources of risk, it should consider how to develop approaches to their measurement. As we discussed in earlier chapters, there are no foolproof methods for the measurement of risks likely to be involved in the majority of organizational situations. Indeed, it is interesting to note that in 1993 the Monopolies and Mergers Commission will be required to referee the dispute between British Gas and Ofgas, the industrial regulator, as to the rate of return the fuel company is allowed to earn on its pipeline business. Both sides use the Capital Asset Pricing Model and the Weighted Average Cost of Capital but each side's estimates of risk-free returns, equity risk premiums and debt costs are wildly at variance, demonstrating the clear subjectivity of both methodologies (see Dobie, 1992).

The measurement process always involves a number of interrelated assessments. To some extent, these assessments may be based on certain elements of objective data but, more typically, they will rely on either a subjective interpretation of the available quantitative data or, in other less favourable cases, on pure guesswork, hunch or intuition. In taking decisions about measurement methodologies, the organization will need to:

- identify the range of possible outcomes to the decision situation, given two alternative responses;
- the organization feels that it cannot affect the continuing market trends and so proposes to do nothing proactive; or
- the organization proposes to implement explicit strategies;
- measure the likelihood of each of the outcomes actually occurring;
- measure the consequences of each possible outcome; and
- estimate the margin of error inherent in the measurement methodologies adopted.

Heblon, for example, should be able to identify the possible outcomes of the continuing trend in the concentration of distribution channels for furniture products. Very briefly, these may be identified as:

- no change on the current situation which shows 75 per cent of industry sales through the large superstore chains;
- a further increase in the proportion of sales through the superstore chains;

- a reversal of the previous trend with independent retailers playing a more significant role in the retail distribution of furniture.

The fact that Heblon does not hold a concentration of market power does not mean that it should decline to act positively. The success of the larger superstores is only maintained through high volume sales at lower prices. In manufacturing terms, this can only be achieved either by sacrificing design and quality standards or by radically achieving cost savings through the exploitation of new materials and new production technologies. At present, the result tends to be that consumer choice is reduced because all the superstore outlets stock the same rather bland range of furniture at highly comparable prices. If Heblon and the other smaller specialist manufacturers were to concentrate their efforts on supplying the needs of the independent retail outlets, maintaining distinctiveness of style and high-quality craftsmanship, this might assist the independents to retain or improve their market share. Heblon should therefore consider discussing strategy with both competing smaller manufacturers and representatives of the independent retailers. Possible outcomes might include the formation of a small manufacturers' marketing consortium where the member companies could achieve economies of scale in promoting their products or the design of a new range of products, better suited to the needs of the independent customers, with better guarantees of sales stability in the future.

The management team would then be required to measure the likelihood that each of these outcomes might actually occur at some time in the future. Clearly, the further into the future the team tries to look, the more speculative the measurement of these likelihoods and so the more uncertain the managers are likely to become. If Heblon were seeking to assess the likelihood that the independents might retain or improve their market share in the next two years only, the managers might feel quite certain that there would be no significant revival. But, over a period of five to ten years this may be much less certain as a number of possible influencing factors may become significant in the longer run, e.g:

- changes in the structure of the market may be forced either by new legislation governing competition or by rulings from the Monopolies and Mergers Commission;
- economic forces may necessitate structural change, say, arising from more favourable tax treatment being given to smaller businesses; or
- changes in consumer attitudes towards more personalized service and a better differentiated product range may favour the independents.

Finally, the assessment of the consequences to Heblon for each of the nominated outcomes is further complicated by the range of other factors which might influence them. Thus, assessing the changes in profits as a consequence of a further concentration of market share by the large multiple retailers requires an assessment of:

- the additional pressure the retailers may be able, or wish, to exert on the company's profit margins through negotiations;

- the rate of growth of the total market;
- the nature of the competition (i.e. other suppliers competing on the basis of price, quality, design etc.); and
- pressures from other sources both internal and external to Heblon.

In many respects, the way we have described this process implies a fairly rational, structured and objective approach to decision-making. Indeed, we could model this process in a number of ways (e.g. construct a decision tree) and apply a battery of analytical tools (e.g. spreadsheets employing sensitivity analysis) to produce further information to assist the decision-maker. But, in reality, the approach is likely to be far less structured; far more complex given the almost infinite range of possible outcomes and the interaction between different factors; and, typically, more highly subjective than this short summary might suggest. As a parting warning, if Heblon is to take better quality decisions, it should have some idea of the likely margin of error built into the measurement and estimation methods that the managers are using. At least the managers will then have an indication of the extent of the risk that their measurements are unreliable and so will not place undue reliance on them in their search for a rational decision.

12.10.4 Understand the mechanics of the problem

A frequently diagnosed (and, perhaps, surprising) fundamental weakness in the decision-making process is the failure of managers to reach a complete understanding of the problem or situation being addressed. We would take it as an obvious truth that if the risks and uncertainties are to be more correctly identified and measured, the managers must achieve improved levels of understanding of the underlying mechanisms which produce the more visible aspects of the problem. By this, we are suggesting something more than the managers simply making themselves aware of the parameters involved and their relative importance. The most significant step is to study the nature of the interaction between these variables in the specific context of the actual problem situation. It is not sufficient to build up knowledge as to the operation of individual variables as each variable may prove more significant and operate in a different manner in other situations.

In this case study, Heblon's management have been aware of the inadequate status of their manufacturing technology, but the managers have not properly understood the reasons for this. The usual explanations offered in board meetings have either been the lack of capital investment or the lack of appropriate technical knowledge and skills. But the major underlying factor actually appears to be the reluctance and lack of commitment by management at all levels towards introducing new technologies and the fear of change. Behavioural factors relating to organizational change are often the most difficult for managers to understand because they are so deeply rooted in the organization's culture and therefore only visible to those with the will to see. Where the organization has a rigid functional structure and the management style does not encourage or permit criticism of the existing hierarchy, the true problems are likely to remain invisible to those with the power to make the organization take a different path.

12.10.5 Learn from the processes employed and build experience

If the organization is to move towards taking better quality decisions, this stage of the process is of fundamental importance. The managers have reached an interim stage in their assessment of the problem situation. If they do not have open minds at this point, all the good work will be wasted. If the evidence to date suggests that previous perceptions were wrong, the managers must have the confidence to admit error and be prepared to learn from the evidence collected. If this means that individual manager's reputations may be damaged, then that is the price to be paid if the organization is to build the quality of experience necessary to aspire towards optimizing decision-making. The willingness to question existing perceptions is an essential survival trait for the organization to encourage. At the very least, the reaction of a senior manager to information suggesting that a previous perception is no longer valid should be to specify new information search requirements which will clarify the reality of the situation. The aim should always be to have the best quality of information available to support the next stage of the process. If it is known that the available information is not of the best quality, the limitations should be made explicit.

12.10.6 Analyse and evaluate the problem situation

The processes of problem analysis and evaluation inevitably combine both the quantitative and the qualitative, i.e. both the objective and the subjective elements. The decision-makers must therefore make themselves aware of the limitations in the methods used to measure the elements identified as constituting the particular problem, and then assess which techniques will give the best support as the data is processed prior to taking the decision. Those responsible must not blindly assume that because quantitative data has been made available by others within the organization, it can be processed in such as way as to permit a rational decision to be taken.

12.10.7 Take the decision

As we observed in Chapter 3, the taking of a decision where a choice has to be made between alternative solutions can rarely be established as an identifiable event or point in the decision process. The choice or selection may have been made before the decision actually arises, taken during the earlier stages in the decision process, emerge gradually through a consideration of the data or it may be postponed indefinitely.

12.10.8 Experience

One might have expected the management of Heblon to gain from their previous experiences and decisions taken within the broad industry/ market sector. The optimists often argue that we learn from the mistakes made in our decision-making. While this may be true of the more frequent and highly programmable decisions encountered, it seems less likely for the less routine decisions. This is particularly true in an organizational setting where the individual may learn and gain experience from a particular decision situation but, unless there are good lines of communication, other colleagues involved in the organization will not benefit from this experience. Further and more importantly, the ability to learn is dependent on the willingness to learn. All organizations must encourage the constructive review of both the decision-making processes and the outcomes so that the organization can benefit from the experience gained and gradually improve their performance over time. This depends upon having the confidence to engage in egoless, self-criticism at all levels. It is a sad fact of human nature that the ambitious male executive is often more concerned with protecting image than engaging in a co-operative venture to improve team performance.

12.11   MEDIWELL HOSPITAL: RISK MANAGEMENT IN A PROFESSIONAL PUBLIC SERVICE

12.11.1   Background to organization and situation

Mediwell Hospital is a major hospital. It supplies a range of general medical and specialist surgical services and provides central medical services for a rural population of 300,000. The hospital has also established a national reputation in the field of neonatal services and therefore offers specialist services on a national basis. The organization was created fifty-five years ago. Until ten years ago, it enjoyed considerable stability, with growth driven purely by demographic trends in its immediate catchment area. But subsequently, it has experienced considerable growth in patient numbers as several of the smaller hospitals in the area have been closed in a rationalization exercise, with the transfer of the service responsibility for the affected patients to Mediwell. The organization has therefore been required to manage an expanding range of services to an expanding population while experiencing the imposition of increasing constraints on the level of financial resources available. The current budget expenditure is in the region of £30 million. The continuing development of these and a number of other factors relating to health-care provision at the national level has now necessitated a more fundamental strategic change in the organization, its services and operations. The more significant of these factors will be discussed briefly before we begin evaluating the organization's strategic responses to the emerging situation.

12.11.2   The developing situation

The level of commitment by central government to support the services of social benevolence such as medicine, education and welfare, has long been a major debating point in both the national and local political arenas in most of the Western nations. This has been particularly true in the UK. During the 1980s and early 1990s, we have witnessed two fundamental and interrelated changes to the provision of medical services in Britain, namely, the introduction of a general management structure and the increasing financial independence of the hospitals. General managers have been introduced into the system with two short-term objectives, i.e:

- of introducing more effective practices of financial and management control; and
- of improving the efficiency of the service.

The medium-term purpose has been to introduce into the public sector organizations those management practices of the private sector which are deemed to be the best. The opportunity for each hospital to increase the level of financial independence has been created through the development of the concept of trust status. Effectively this means that, for those hospitals that are granted trust status, the source of funding is no longer a regional organization but rather the central government. The principal justification asserted for such a change is that hospitals like Mediwell would have greater autonomy in deciding how to use their resources within the overall budget allocated. In theory, with the use of the private sector's management style, trust hospitals will be able to develop more effective service provision.

A further feature of the new national policy on the health services has been the principle of an open market system for health and medical services. The development of this open market principle has allowed each hospital in the market to offer its specialist services and resources to the other hospitals and, if necessary, to purchase services from the others. It has been argued that new opportunities will arise for a hospital to develop specialist expertise or to invest in specialist facilities and then to sell these to the market, i.e. to other hospitals, general practitioners and private fee-paying patients. Equally, those other existing services which are found to be too expensive to operate, are inefficient or lack the appropriate quality of specialist staff can be closed down and the necessary services purchased from another hospital supplier. In the case of Mediwell, the opportunity would be available to capitalize on its outstanding reputation in the field of neonatal medical services.

Recent technological developments have provided important challenges for both the management of Mediwell and the other suppliers of medical services. The technological developments may be grouped under two headings, namely, medical and administrative. The pace of innovation in health technologies has been as rapid and significant as those in the fields of electronics and computers, and include developments in diagnostic and surgical techniques (sometimes non-invasive),

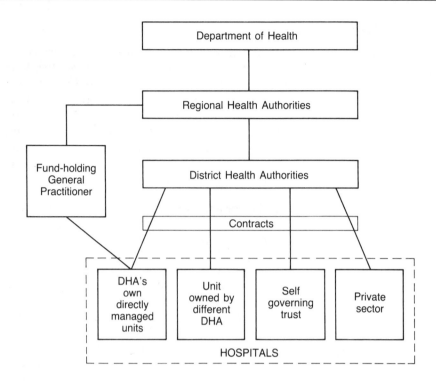

Figure 12.8 Overall hierarchy of the Health Service.

nursing practices, preventative health care, medicine and pharmacy. Developments in other areas of scientific endeavour, such as lasers, magnetic resonance etc, have contributed to this progress in new applications for eye surgery, diagnostic scanning etc. The advances in administrative support technologies, i.e. electronic communications, centralized database systems, have also had a major impact on the potential for improving management performance and for achieving nursing and general operational efficiencies.

In developing its strategies for the future, Mediwell has been obliged to address these and several other issues, some of which have been primarily externally related and others internal. For example, the balance of the demographic age profile of the nation has been shifting towards an older population. This will not only increase the demands on the organization's services as older persons require greater health care, but it will also change the nature of the services required. One feature of demographic trends in terms of age distribution is that they have a high degree of predictability and may be detected well in advance, i.e. uncertainty levels are low for such factors.

An implicit feature of the increased delegation of authority to the hospitals themselves has been the creation of a system of a free market for the provision of health services. The public-sector health and care providers will now be expected to compete on broadly equal terms both with the privately owned providers and with other publicly owned providers. In itself, this has introduced a significant new source of risk and uncertainty, i.e. market forces, which previously had been outside the experience of Mediwell or the other publicly owned health providers.

A necessary consequence of the requirement to become more patient- or market-oriented in terms of service provision is that the hospitals should become more conscious of the quality of the services provided. Suggested measures of this improvement in quality of service have included the shortening of waiting times for operations, reducing the delays in outpatient clinics, or simply providing a friendlier image to the client/customer. All these criteria pose risks for the organization. The main source of the risks lies not only in the need to change the structure of the health service and the lines of accountability within it, but also to change individual attitudes, systems and methods of operation. Both types of change generate uncertainties at all levels in the organization. Indeed, in this instance, the scale of the uncertainties in themselves may pose significant risks for the management and the organization as a whole if the result is that progress towards achieving the changes is slowed.

A fundamental objective underlying the changes instituted in the health service has been the desire to increase the efficiency of the service as a whole and therefore to reduce the burden on central government resources. The management in all the relevant parts of the service has been strongly encouraged to improve the efficiency of all aspects of their operations from the surgical level through to the support services such as catering and cleaning. The introduction of a compulsory system of competitive tendering for the full range of central services has been a further complication for the managers to contend with. Improving productivity while simultaneously seeking to improve the levels of service, handling increasing numbers of patients and responding effectively to changes in technologies, provides a scenario full of uncertainties and risks.

12.11.3 The strategic approach developed

The first phase in the Mediwell strategic plan calls for change in the organization's structure, the management structures and the decision-making processes. The continuing intention is that this should apply not only to the higher corporate levels, but equally at ward level. The justification for the scale of this reorganization is to improve the degree of delegated authority and responsibility lower down the chain of command. The outcome of the reorganization has been the creation of a range of smaller units, each with clearly defined responsibilities for the management of their operational activities and services within the broad parameters and objectives set by the organization as a whole.

At an early point, the managers recognized a number of problems as implicit in proposing such substantial changes in the culture, structures and processes of the hospital. The first and most serious difficulty has been that simply making the proposal proved a significant barrier to effecting change and hence generated risks and uncertainties. Within

Mediwell, as in other hospitals, this barrier has been most apparent in the reactions of the senior medical staff, the consultants and the doctors. For example, the consultants' negative reaction has been based on the perception that this reorganization is a gratuitous attack on their existing power and influence. Previously, their role in major decisions affecting the hospital has been very significant and, not unnaturally, they wish to retain the status and authority which has given justification and progression to their career structure.

Similarly, the clash of objectives and styles between the professional medical staff and the professional management staff is one that was predictable but difficult to measure in terms of the consequences. A new wave of professional managers have been appointed to take responsibility for the resources in the hospital, whether financial, human or other. An immediate consequence is that a new layer has been added to the decision-making process. Whereas the major resource allocation decisions had been made primarily on medical grounds and were strongly influenced by the views of the specialist consultants, those decisions are now being subjected to a further set of parameters which are predominantly financial in nature. To that extent, the performance objectives which have emerged for Mediwell require it to pursue a strategy that addresses not only the quality of service objectives but, equally, the efficiency of resource utilization.

As indicated earlier, the situation as it develops requires the involvement of staff at all levels. Staff at the ward level are now required to take more responsibility for the day-to-day expenditures in operating the units. As a part of this downwards migration of responsibility, the development and implementation of new IT technologies has represented a significant dimension of the strategic plan. The creation of central patient databases, computer-based internal communications and the provision of financial and other performance data has become a central plank of the organization's approach to achieving the necessary changes. In retrospect, the management have devoted too much attention to the more tangible or 'harder' issues in the strategic plan and not sufficient time to the less tangible, human or 'softer' issues. The consequences are that the debate has focused on the technical requirements and operation of systems, and the current training is aimed mainly at the development of IT skills. The more significant issues of managing change, developing teams, enhancing human resources management skills or seeking solutions to professional conflicts have been given secondary priority. The failure to address issues of this type is a major contribution to the failure of the strategic development of the IT system and operations within the hospital.

The structure of the organization developed by Mediwell is shown in Figure 12.9.

12.11.4 Identification of risks and uncertainties

It would not be wholly fair to say that the senior management at Mediwell has failed to identify the particular risks and uncertainties likely to be

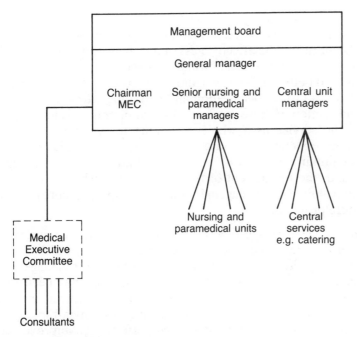

Figure 12.9 Traditional organization structure (adapted from Pandey, 1991).

faced. But it is clear that the managers have completely underestimated the scale and degree of interaction between the different risks, and the range of their potential consequences. The major risks and uncertainties have included the following:

- *Political uncertainties*   The importance of health as a national political issue, and discrepancies between the policies of the different political parties, mean that a change in result at the next general election would almost certainly reverse the changes undertaken by the present government. Changes in policy would have significant consequences for both the organization as a whole and for the continued employment of some individual managers.

- *Future funding*   The future funding of the health service as a whole and the basis on which such total funds will be allocated between competing hospitals provides a significant source of uncertainty. The extent to which hospitals, such as Mediwell, may require to become self-funding in the future provides a further dimension of uncertainty on funding.

- *Responsiveness to change*   The responsiveness of the senior consultants and doctors to changes in their role, responsibilities and status represents the most significant source of risk to the strategic development of Mediwell. These staff are in a particularly influential position and they have the power to frustrate the implementation of any strategies that may be pursued. The responsiveness of the nursing and other staff to the changes and the preparedness of particular individuals to assume the increased levels of responsibilities represent other significant risks. The effectiveness of the changes proposed will depend on the adjustment of relationships between the staff working on the wards, and between the wards and other groupings within the hospital. Until issues of job specification and regrading have been addressed to the satisfaction of those involved, little co-operation is likely. At a time when the service as a whole is looking for economies, finding the additional revenue to fund an expansion in the duties of lower and middle ranking staff will be very hard to find. But, if the money cannot be found, the resentment of the affected staff who see themselves as being exploited as 'management on the cheap' will represent a barrier to future progress.

- *Future efficiency performance* The level of efficiency improvements that can be achieved by the Mediwell and the rate at which these can be achieved represent a major source of uncertainty for management. The difficulties faced by the new management team has been increased because pressure has been exerted from the political environment. With much media attention, ministers and other high-ranking officials have promised that certain quantified performance improvements will be achieved by identified deadlines, e.g. reductions in waiting lists.

- *Quality of service* The launch of the Patient's Charter and the public discussion of the quality of treatment given to some individual patients, has had a real impact on the levels or quality of service provided to patients. Given the willingness of the news media and politicians to highlight individual cases, no matter how untypical they may be of the general standard of care, any significant deterioration in any part of the range of health services could cause significant embarrassment to Mediwell and its management.

12.11.5 A review of the emerging situation

The primary problem has not been the failure to identify the potential sources of risk and uncertainty but the failure of the management to appreciate the magnitude of these risks and, particularly, of the impact of the changes required in the organization's structure, political infrastructure and total culture. As we will be showing, the responses made not only failed to address these issues and associated risks but created further risks for the organization.

12.12   HOW SHOULD THE MANAGERS HAVE APPROACHED THE SITUATION?

We now return to the process of SIMULATE and, as in the case of Heblon, we will build up a picture only of those factual elements that will demonstrate the working of the methodology.

S   Structure the problem or decision situation.
I   Identify and Investigate the key elements of the problem, the potential uncertainties and risks.
M   Measure and assess the risks and uncertainties.
U   Understand the mechanics and interrelationships within the problem, why the problem occurred, what causes it, and the future implications if not corrected.
L   Learn from the processes employed in analysing the problem and developing alternative solutions.
A   Analyse and evaluate the problem, the potential solutions and their possible outcomes in terms of risk.
T   Take the decision.
E   Experience. Build and develop the experience and expertise of the organization and its decision-makers on the basis of the decision process and the decisions taken.

12.13   A GUIDE TO THE PROCESS OF STRUCTURING

Mediwell should develop a KISSAF model as a clearer statement of the situation faced. The model would concentrate on the following factors:

- *Simple*   Developing simple, though not simplistic models, will help the decision-makers to identify more clearly which of the more critical issues ought to be addressed. Mediwell has recognized that government funding of the service will be a key issue in the future. It should have developed unambiguous models outlining the likely scenarios and the possible implications.

- *Strategic*   The temptation in any decision situation involving radical changes to an organization's structure, processes and systems is to manage the more immediate problems. This is particularly true in service sectors such as the health service where people represent the major resource. Mediwell's senior management ought to be spending more effort on the strategic issues relating to the situation over the next 5–10 years.

- *Focused*   A greater degree of clarity in the identification of the key issues to be addressed is achieved through focusing attention. The management at Mediwell, including the senior consultants, have perceived a wide range of existing and potential issues to be addressed. The list would include medical standards, patient care, efficiency, future resourcing, technological change, organizational change, skill development etc. The decision-makers need to focus their attention more clearly on whatever are perceived to be the key issues. While recognizing that all the other issues will have some degree of importance and deserve attention, the resources of the management will be used best in concentrating collectively on the key strategic issues.

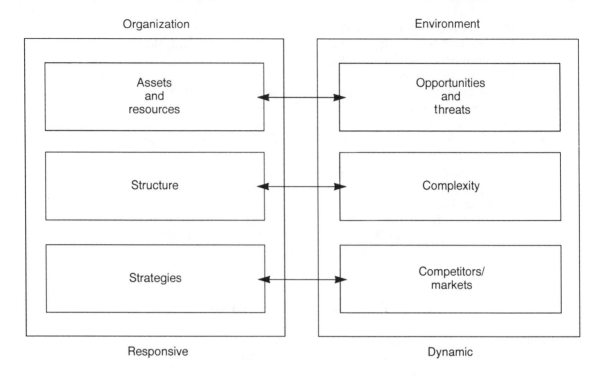

Figure 12.10 Structured approach for Mediwell.

12.13.1 Mediwell's environment

(a) Opportunities and threats

Mediwell operates in an environment which is undergoing fundamental changes. These changes are being inspired by the primary funding agency, the national government. This means that there is a certain compulsion about the changes and, while threats and opportunities may arise, the extent to which Mediwell can respond to them is limited. The more significant threats and opportunities which the organization needs to address in its decision-making include the following:

- Further changes in national health service policies which either result from a change in national government or through forced changes in existing government policies to respond to other political pressures.
- Increased privatization of some or all services may relieve financial pressures on overheads and allow a greater percentage of the funding resource to be devoted to care provision.
- The growth in the health-care sector and the associated services, and the forecasts that such growth will continue in the future, provide a source of opportunities. Associated with this is the strong underlying support of the general public for the health sector. This will tend to reduce the potential impact of threats both to the sector as a whole and

to the local providers such as Mediwell.

- The enforced objective to achieve improved performance poses the most significant threat to organizations in the health services. One of the more threatening of the requirements is the need to increase cost efficiency in service delivery. The criteria formulated to determine budget allocations are based on standard costs for the delivery of particular services. These cost figures exploit the performance data derived from the most efficient deliverers of each service. This device will force costs and budgets downwards. There are also opportunities for the more efficient deliverers of either general services or specialist services to sell their services to other hospitals or health service organizations. If Mediwell is able to reduce its costs significantly for a particular medical service or operation, it could sell this service to other potentially higher cost providers in the region.

- The other dimension of performance improvement being sought is that of service quality to the patients or clients. Each hospital is required to determine target performance levels for each of its major services and to develop approaches to achieving them. The development and publication of a Patients' Charter is also part of the approach to encourage the development of performance standards and targets. The quantification of service performance generates particular problems for each of the 'caring professions' which make up the hospital services. The ethos of these professions is to provide professional medical care and the suggestion that this may be measured in terms of what may be seen as non-medical criteria such as the time a patient is kept waiting in the clinic prior to receiving attention represents a fundamental challenge to the conventional beliefs and objectives of the staff involved.

- The developments imposed throughout the service have provided an important opportunity for many of the staff in the organization. A significant opportunity is being offered to staff:

  - to improve their working conditions;
  - to improve the nature of their work;
  - to assume greater responsibility for the decisions directly affecting their work environment; and
  - to generate greater opportunities for career development.

(b) Complexity

Historically, it is difficult to judge whether the level of complexity in the environment facing hospitals such as Mediwell has been substantially greater than that facing commercial organizations such as Heblon, the traditional furniture manufacturer discussed in the previous case study. The nature of the environments faced by both organizations has been very different but, in their own ways, each was probably no less complex than the other. This does not deny the existence of a reasonably convincing argument that the environment facing Mediwell and similar organizations is more complex than that facing strictly commercial organizations. It derives its force from the novelty of the competitive and market forces that have just been introduced into the operating environment. The culture of organizations in commercial environments can draw on a substantial period of history and experience in the operation of their markets. Whereas the hospitals' experience is not only relatively short-lived but also in an environment where the rules of competition have been progressively released by central government. Like their parallel organizations in other sectors, the hospitals are exposed to environmental pressures and forces at all levels in the organization, e.g. at the operational level through interfaces with patients and at the strategic level through interfaces with regional officers or central government representatives who provide the financial resources. The technology interface has provided significant challenges and risks to the organization. The hospital needs to respond to technological changes which affect not only the medical aspects of the organization's operation, but also administrative efficiency and effectiveness. The scale of the financial and human resources required to develop and implement such changes in technology successfully is usually so great that it poses substantial risks for the organization, so easy is it to make incorrect decisions in the field of technology developments.

The one underlying factor which contributes most to the complexity of the decision situation is the human factor. The major change which the management of Mediwell and other health-care organizations are being asked to achieve is a fundamental change in culture. This involves:

- the breaking down of the barriers both between different strata within the professions and between the professions themselves;
- the recognition that each element in the service provides an equally valuable contribution;
- the introduction of performance criteria other than those directly related to medical well-being; and
- the delegation of authority for the management of the service.

These are all major changes requiring a significant shift in the total culture and style of operation for the organization.

(c) Competitors and markets

The competitive threat faced by Mediwell in the future may come from both local and national institutions and may have an effect across all the services currently delivered. This competition is being generated not only for the provision of services to patients but also for the provision of services to internal customers. For example, internal service units within Mediwell would be able to contract with a neighbouring hospital for that hospital to provide identified medical services to Mediwell. That would be possible even though those services might already be available within Mediwell. The sole criterion would be service provision at the lowest cost. The significant strategic risk facing Mediwell in this scenario is the decision setting the range of services it wishes to provide internally and then ensuring the appropriate mechanisms to protect the demand for those services. As time passes and the new breed of health service managers become acclimatized to the greater competitiveness and market principles within the health service, there is likely to be an escalation in the amount of uncertainty and risk faced by managers. One obvious effect will be the increased tensions within the organization structure and in the employees.

12.13.2 Mediwell's organization

(a) Assets and resources

The previous paragraphs describing the nature of Mediwell and its environment lead to the conclusion that the key resource within the organization is its people. But the number and quality of those employed is constrained by the level of financial resource available, and there must be suitable equipment for them to use, housed in appropriate accommodation:

- *Human resources* The clinical, nursing and general medical knowledge, skills and experience of the staff, both individually and collectively, are the major asset on which the organization relies. A number of changes are beginning to affect the role of staff and, hence, the structure of the organization. The two most important are:

  - the Project 2000 courses for the training of nurses are changing the educational emphasis away from the practical routines of care towards providing a set of skills that will enable the nursing staff to be more involved in the diagnosis and treatment of the patients; and
  - the concessions won by the junior doctors on hours has necessitated changes to working patterns and the recruitment of additional staff.

- *Finance* Mediwell has deferred the decision whether to apply for trust status. One justification for this delay is that Mediwell is a comparatively small hospital, albeit one that is beginning to grow in importance. The funding therefore still comes through the appropriate regional health authority. Tentative plans have been drawn up which could form the basis of a third wave application for trust status or which could form the basis of an operational plan should trust status be imposed by the abolition of the present national administrative and funding hierarchy.

- *Technology* This is relevant in two very different spheres of activity and has very different consequences as follows:

  - The practice of medicine is increasingly reliant on technology. Although some of the new developments involve cost-savings on present labour-intensive alternatives, most involve considerable capital expenditure. The publicity given to the more spectacular successes in other hospitals puts considerable political pressure on Mediwell's managers to make the latest diagnostic and surgical equipment available for local patients. That this will involve reallocating scarce financial resources both to acquire the equipment and to train the staff in its use, is not appreciated by the public whose only expectation is that health care provision will continue to improve.

- The development of in-house information systems is considered a vital strategic step forward. The cost of this exercise has been significantly underestimated and the continuing expenditure represents an embarrassment because funds earmarked for other equally high-profile projects have had to be diverted to help fund the implementation of the information system.

- *Physical resources* The physical resources of the hospital are in various conditions ranging from the more modern facilities to those facilities that have not been modernized in any substantial way for over thirty years. The capital available for new building and renovation has been severely limited in the past, preventing nothing more than a piecemeal approach to upgrading work. An increasing strategic problem for the organization derives from the constraints stemming from the continued use of older buildings, e.g:

  - It becomes more difficult to achieve improvements in efficiency. Modern buildings can be constructed with energy efficient materials and to the best design standards, whereas the energy savings achievable in older buildings are always marginal. Similarly, it can be difficult to reduce staffing levels given the inefficient way in which older buildings were laid out.
  - It can be difficult or, indeed, impossible to introduce new technologies given the inappropriate structure of the building itself, e.g. the new machinery cannot physically be housed, say, because the floor will not carry the load.
  - The constraints in the potential to restructure the organization and to locate similar units within reasonable proximity for management and control purposes. Thus, if it would be convenient to relocate several departments, all of which could share some common facilities, there might not be a suitable single building or group of buildings in which to house them all.

(b) Organization structure

The original structure of the organization was provided earlier in Figure 12.9. The key differentiating features of this structure and its operation were as follows:

- *A very hierarchical structure* The role of the general management committee was very dominant with control over not only the key strategic decisions, but also the major operational (i.e. day-to-day operational) decisions. The sense of hierarchy permeated the whole structure with everyone made very aware of their position and role. This had the effect of making each individual who achieved some status, zealous in the protection of the power and authority that went with the office.

- *The decision-making process* The views of the senior medical practitioners, usually the consultants, dominated throughout the hierarchy. This group not only possessed a high degree of authority in the day-to-day decisions on individual patient treatment but it was able to influence the tactical and strategic policies equally effectively.

The introduction of the hospital general managers has disrupted the traditional lines of authority and responsibility. The fact that they have been given responsibility for, and formal authority to promote, the general efficiency of the organization's operations, has created substantial problems for most hospitals. There has been an immediate clash of professional objectives as areas of responsibility traditionally occupied by the consultants have been taken over with the direct challenge to medical authority made highly visible to all those employed in the service. The problem is one of culture shock. The whole ethos of the decision-making structure and process has been medical. All those involved in the practical provision of health care must now move from a management regime dominated by professional medical considerations and influenced by medical practitioners to one that focuses more on professional management performance criteria and is dominated by individuals with general management experience who need not have any medical background or training. This represents a formidable change for the organization not only because it undermines the traditional authority of the consultants, but also because it encourages other staff to consider what their role should be in the newly emerging hospital organization.

One of the explicit objectives in the central government's reorganization plans has been to match the changes in the decision-making structure at senior levels with a reshaping of the organization structure to accommodate greater decentralization and devolution of decision-making authority in all areas including the operational and the tactical. This has required Mediwell to begin planning a new organization structure. The present version of the revised structure is shown in Figure 12.11. The significant feature of this structure is the creation of units which are to be responsible for the delivery of particular services.

(c) Organization strategy

The main distinguishing feature of the strategy developed by Mediwell is its short-term focus. This decision, consciously taken, is a response to the attention of national and local politicians which tends to concentrate on the performance of the revised organizations both in terms of financial efficiency and the measurable quality of service. Thus, the new managers at Mediwell also concentrate their efforts and resources in resolving the

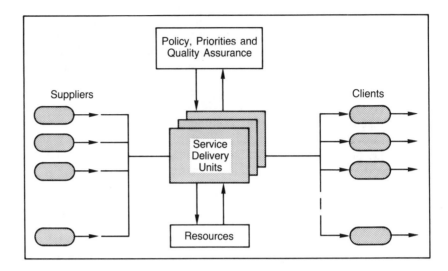

Figure 12.11 Mediwell: revised organization structure (adapted from Pandey, 1991).

short-term problems. On a human level, this would appear perfectly rational because the performance of the managers is to be measured on short-term criteria in their annual appraisal system. Survival in the immediate post and the prospects of promotion may therefore be dependent on the ability to meet short-term performance measures. This is not to suggest that these managers do not recognize the need for longer-term strategic decisions and the additional risks that are created by not addressing these strategic issues effectively. The organization does develop certain strategic plans but these are dictated primarily by the more immediate short-term factors.

A second feature of the strategy has been the focus on what might be termed the harder or more tangible elements. Considerable effort has been expended in developing detailed forecasts about the future levels of service required and, consequently, the future human, fixed asset and financial resources necessary to provide this. Little attention has been devoted to identifying and analysing the potential uncertainties and risks associated with a more open-market system of providing health care services. The strategy has also concentrated on the development of IT within the organization and the technical detail of how the entire organization should be networked and the consequential developments in systems and software development.

The third feature which has absorbed the majority of the senior managers' time in these early years is the development and implementation of the new organization structure. The major criticism of the approach adopted is the concentration on the structural issues and formal relationships, responsibilities and authority rather than on the development of a more effective organization. Little attention has been given to how the changes in culture, management style and mode of operation will be achieved other than by considering the design of the structure and the roles within it. This has probably been the greatest omission from the strategic debate and, rather than reducing levels of risk for the whole organization, it has been the cause of increasing levels of risk. As a priority, more will have to be done to reduce the resistance of employees at all levels in all areas of the organization to the changes which have become increasingly inevitable.

12.14 ACHIEVING AN INTEGRATED MODEL THROUGH SIMULATE

12.14.1 Structure the decision

The management ought to have taken a more strategic approach to their decision-making if they are to reduce the exposure of the organization to risks in the future. A KISSAF approach which stresses a simple model, related to strategic considerations and focused on the objectives of the organization would be the most appropriate first step to resolve future risks. A simple model should be developed which incorporates the major elements of the external environment, recognizing the potential risks and their consequences for the organization, and detailing their possible interaction with the significant dimensions of the internal environment. A more focused approach on the key resource within the organization would concentrate on the human resource element. Unfortunately, although it is probable that this approach will produce strategic solutions that will aid the resolution of future risks and uncertainties, the solutions are unlikely to be wholly acceptable to the management. The reason is that these solutions will certainly involve more direct action on changing the culture, attitudes and working practices.

12.14.2 Identify, Investigate and research the situation

The second stage in the risk management process proposed is the need to research the strategic situation and clearly identify and investigate the sources of uncertainty or risk. Mediwell's senior management have displayed a sound ability to identify the potential risks facing the organization. They have, however, failed to address them constructively within their decision-making process. A number of the risks have already been discussed in the preceding paragraphs. The major sources of risk and uncertainty include:

- changes in the future organizational and funding arrangements at the national level;
- developments in the 'market forces' principles which might result in more unconstrained competition;
- reactions by staff at all levels to the changing nature of the organization, its structure, operations and objectives;

- failure to achieve the necessary level of cultural change or support necessary to implement the developments required;
- failure to achieve the short- to medium-term performance criteria established for both financial/efficiency performance and quality of service performance.

That there is resistance to the proposed changes should be taken as a symptom of organizational disease. By studying the situation, it should be possible to identify a set of factors which form the basis of the actual or potential conflict between the managers and the managed. Once the diagnosis has been made, it should then be possible to begin steering the discourse towards a more constructive than obstructive course. Self-evidently, some of the resistance will be anticipatory. Thus, it is a natural human response to be apprehensive when faced by the unknown. Equally, the experiences we have may trigger resistance. Whatever the cause, the loss of motivation or active prejudices which result may represent real barriers to the success of whatever project is in hand.

Given the reality of the resistance to change at Mediwell, it is clear that progress cannot be made through an increase in the pressure to change. This will serve only to demoralize the staff further or to stiffen their resistance and, in any event, the use of force will be an unreasonable tactic. To understand how better to proceed, let us take one aspect of the information system as an example. The hospital is moving towards a unit structure. Each unit will be responsible for providing identified services and will be a cost centre. As such, the unit staff will be required to assume responsibility for ensuring that the central patient database is kept up to date and that the accounting procedures are followed to guarantee that all items relevant to the calculation of unit income and expenditure are properly recorded. Thus, whereas the staff would previously have approached many of their tasks as being clerical and highly routine, even the most lowly employee must now accept direct responsibility for ensuring the accuracy of their own work. If the staff are to respond positively to this change, proper attention must be paid to their psychology.

The significance of the tasks that they will be instructed to perform has become more critical. Indeed, some aspects of the tasks will become judgemental. Thus, not only is the skill level required likely to be higher, but staff will be expected to demonstrate greater competence. If the staff are to respond constructively, several steps are essential as follows:

- Staff must understand the purpose of the changes and be allowed to make a real contribution to the design of the new systems.
- More meaningful job specifications must be written to reflect the new responsibilities.
- In line with the rewriting of individual job specifications, the structure of each unit should be reconsidered; if people are to assume new responsibilities and form new working relationships, a supportive

environment must be created in which all may contribute to the formation of a culture in which all may work effectively.

- In appropriate cases, technical training must be given to improve skill levels, and time to practise and refine those skills must be given before any appraisal or assessment is made.
- More general training must be offered to enhance talents and abilities in those employees whose jobs will now involve the exercise of judgement and the acceptance of greater responsibility.
- Proper funding must be made available to regrade staff in line with their acceptance of more demanding duties.

To date, Mediwell has approached the design and implementation of an information system through the use of the in-house computer services unit, acting with the advice of external consultants. Their primary focus has been on the hardware and the functional aspects of the proposed system. There has been little or no consultation with those whose responsibility it will be to make the system work. The new tactic should be to give the affected staff a sense of ownership of the project. This will come through real consultation on design matters and on implementation strategy. Once the redefined jobs come into being, the work must be a more meaningful experience for each employee. In part, this will be based on giving the staff more responsibility for the quality of their output, with fair, reasonable and supportive feedback on performance and a proper structure of rewards for those whose performance meets the targets. The moral should be that happy and contented people who feel that they have some ownership over the substance of their jobs, make more effective workers.

12.14.3 Measure the risks and uncertainties

Once the organization has identified the major sources of risk, it will need to decide which measurement methodologies to apply. As we have shown, there are neither foolproof nor objective methods available for the measurement of the risks involved in most organizational situations. The measurement process involves a number of interrelated assessments. These assessments may be supported by different types of historical or objective data but, more usually, they rely on a subjective interpretation of the available quantitative data or, in other cases, on pure guesswork, hunches or intuition. Mediwell needs to:

- identify the range of possible outcomes;
- measure the likelihood of each of these outcomes actually occurring;
- measure the consequences of each possible outcome.

Mediwell's managers should be able to identify the range of possible outcomes at all levels of operation. At a national level, for example, the two extremes of possibility are that the existing trend towards market-oriented policies will be accelerated, or that central government will abandon competition-based policies and revert to those that existed previously. In fairness, we should recognize that the latter possibility is not as simple as it might first appear. Once changes have begun to take root in any organization, it would be unusual if it proved possible to reverse a decision completely. It is necessary to recognize the changes in the situation as a result of the earlier decision and to plan the next changes taking account of the new reality. Once the managers have established the possible outcomes, they would then be required to measure the likelihood of each of these scenarios actually occurring at some time in the future. As we explained earlier, the further into the future you try to look, the less certain you are likely to become. The managers must therefore always try to work within the known limitations of their measurement methodologies. In fact, Mediwell's management has identified the broad range of outcomes, but it has failed to assess the likelihood of their occurrence. The managers have preferred to retain a much shorter planning horizon, apparently hoping to reduce some of the uncertainty involved and certainly aiming to meet the short-term performance criteria imposed by government.

12.14.4 Understand the mechanics of the problem

To comprehend the nature of the risks facing the organization fully, the managers need to understand the nature of the major influencing factors and how they interrelate. The generic model articulated earlier in this section provides a useful basis on which to develop this understanding. Recognition of the external factors and the internal organizational issues would assist in defining the nature of the risks, the scale of their consequences and the likelihood of their occurrence.

Following on the identification of the cultural factors that underlie the present resistance to the proposed information system, the management must try to understand the processes at work. If a human being was to feel pain, he or she would stop and consider the situation. Pain is a signal that all is not well. If we were to feel a muscle begin to pull and this set up a sense of resistance to the possibility of further movement, only the rash continue to force movement. The human body is a self-monitoring system and, if we wish to remain fit and healthy, we ignore the signals at our peril. Organizations should also learn to recognize internally generated pain and to stop what they are doing until they understand the cause of the problem. If the working of the organization is impaired through resistance to proposed change, this should be a signal that dialogue with those affected should begin immediately. These people have vital information about the system as it is and about the effectiveness of the proposals for change. After all, they are the people who are being asked to change and their knowledge and beliefs are critical to the success of the project. That they are slow to make the change is a sign that they are unhappy about the proposals. By understanding why they are slow to change, the organization can learn more about the detailed working of its existing systems and so make better decisions about which changes are really desirable.

12.14.5 Learn from the processes employed and build experience

Wisdom is not only the strength to admit that you can make mistakes, but also the willingness to learn from those mistakes. Mediwell should admit error in having taken a hard approach to its automation proposals and should move towards a human-centred decision-making approach. People need time to adjust to new situations and they tend to react adversely when they are reduced to mere cyphers in a management plan. Indeed, the more distant the managers from the social reality of the systems they are trying to design, the more likely it is that they will make mistakes about what the current systems are and how they may be changed for the better. Resistance should be a stimulus for the experts in the current systems (i.e. the workers) to give feedback to the managers before and during the process of change. Viewed in this way, resistance may be turned into a positive part of the process of change because it should help the planners to identify any unintended consequences of their plans and to spot and cure problems before they become acute. It will also help employees at all levels to feel that they are involved in directing the changes, albeit at the margin as individuals. But if they do feel that they have some control over the nature and direction of their careers, they are likely to be better motivated and work more effectively for the benefit of the organization.

12.14.6 Analyse and evaluate the problem situation

Once Mediwell takes the step of listening to and learning from their staff on all questions involving cultural change, it will be able to make a better analysis and evaluation of its present position. At present, the new administrators are too wrapped up in their jurisdictional disputes with the consultants, and the consultants are too defensive of their previous power base to pay proper attention to the longer term issues affecting the running of the hospital. If the senior decision-makers cannot heal their relationships, this will send signals down the system. So as nurses enter the hospital service from the Project 2000 courses with training that will enable them to perform many of the more routine tasks now performed by doctors, who will have the standing to arbitrate on disputes as to who should now do what? The management must become a team with the wisdom to look beyond the superficial short-term indicators of performance set by the politicians. Pursuing our analogy of the organization as a human body capable of experiencing pain, the doctors and psychiatrists who make up the medical staff should bring their own diagnostic skills to bear on the internal constitution of the problem. If they are capable of producing dispassionate evaluations of the conditions afflicting their human patients, they should be able to prescribe appropriate remedies for their own problems.

12.14.7 Take the decision

Once an appropriate prescription has been drawn up, and it appears to meet both the needs of the health services providers and the tests of cost-effectiveness devised by the general managers, the senior decision-makers should have the strength to take the decision to proceed with the major changes required.

12.14.8 Experience

In a sense, the lessons should be learned both within Mediwell as an organization and within the central government hierarchy because both managements have sought to impose major structural change without considering the cultural implications. But, given the political commitment of the present government to pursue these changes, the short-term need is for Mediwell to adapt itself to the new environment. Indeed, it should take this opportunity to undertake a major review of its structure and processes, and be prepared to take bold decisions, say, on whether to apply for trust status if the staff as a whole are behind it. At this final point in the book, perhaps we should identify a potential paradox. We often take it as a sign of youthfulness and enthusiasm if a person keeps the thirst for knowledge alive. We attribute the labels of maturity and wisdom to those who have built up a significant body of useful experience. Yet we tend to equate youthfulness with inexperience. In our view, anyone who retains an open mind and a willingness to learn from experience is, by definition, wise. Naturally, there can never be any guarantee that, at a strategic level, individuals will always be able to make what prove, in retrospect, to have been the right decisions. But if their method has been built upon SIMULATE or a methodology with a similar spirit, the decisions will always have a number of significant characteristics, i.e:

- because the basis of the decision has, at each point, been made explicit there is a greater chance that the decision will have features of rationality;
- because the decision elements should be seen in their environmental context, the rationality should be relatively unbounded;
- because the process calls for the decision elements to be reviewed at an intermediate stage before the decision itself is taken, there is a reasonable opportunity for the final decision to be taken on the basis of the most timely and the best available information;
- because the process calls for understanding, there is a better chance that proper consultation will have taken place and that the decision will be consistent with the culture of the organization; and
- because the process calls for continuously developing (or, if necessary, recapturing) the ability to learn, it should help to promote wisdom in those who retain their youthful enthusiasms for life.

Let us try to finish on a note that avoids both rash arrogance and that sort of preachy enthusiasm often affected by those who ambitiously aspire to guru status. We have been bold enough to offer a methodology and we claim certain advantages for those prepared to follow it. But we are not so lacking in wisdom that we would claim SIMULATE as anything more than a theme to follow when taking strategic decisions. We cannot talk blithely of improving human wisdom and not acknowledge the difficulty in what we propose. But, if we are modest enough to recognize the limitations in our own thoughts, can this not be the final lesson to be taken away from this text. There is no other book on risk that we know that can provide any more reliable method for taking decisions under conditions of risk and uncertainty. If common sense tells us that the best way is for decision-makers to decompose complexity into a KISSAF model and then to struggle through a SIMULATE process, i.e. to reduce things to a level that is simple without being simplistic and then to think things through to a decision, keeping a sense of humility to hand, should we not take that thought firmly in hand and take the necessary steps to improve the quality of the decisions that we make.

Bibliography

Abell, D.F. (1980) *Defining the Business: The Starting Point of Strategic Planning*, Prentice Hall, Englewood Cliffs, NJ.

Abelson, R.P. *et al.* (1968) *Theories of Cognitive Consistency: A Source Book*, Rand McNally & Co; Chicago.

Abraham, K.S. (1991). The once and future crisis. *Journal of Risk and Uncertainty*, **4** (4), December, 353–71.

Ackerman, R.W. (1975) *The Social Challenge to Business*, Harvard University Press, Cambridge, Mass.

Ackoff, R.L. (1967) Management misinformation systems. *Management Science*, **14**, B14–B156.

Ackoff, R.L. (1970) *A Concept of Corporate Planning*, Wiley Interscience, New York.

Ackoff, R.L. (1981) On the use of models in corporate planning. *Strategic Management Journal*, **2**, 353–9.

Ackoff, R.L. (1990) Strategy. *Systems Practice*, **3** (6), 523–4.

Aguilar, F.J. (1967) *Scanning the Business Environment*, Macmillan, New York.

Aharoni, Y., Maimon, Z. and Segev, E. (1978) Performance and autonomy in organizations: determining dominant environmental components. *Management Science*, **24** (9), May, 949–59.

Al-Bazzaz, S. and Grinyer, P.H. (1980) How planning works in practice – a survey of 48 UK companies. *Long Range Planning*, **13**, Aug., 30–42.

Alderfer, C.P. and Bierman, H. (1970) Choices with risk: beyond the mean and variance. *Journal of Business*, **43** (3), July, 341–53.

Allison, G.T. (1969) Conceptual models and the Cuban Missile Crisis. *American Political Science Review*, **63** (3), Sept., 345–74.

Anderson, C.R. and Paine, F.T. (1975) Managerial perceptions and strategic behaviour. *Academy of Management Journal*, **18** (4) Dec., 811–23.

Anderson, C.R. and Paine, F.T. (1977) Contingencies affecting strategy formulation and effectiveness: an empirical study. *The Journal of Management Studies*, May, 147–58.

Anderson, C.R. and Paine, F.T. (1978) PIMS: a re-examination. *Academy of Management Review*, July, 602–12.

Anderson, C.R. and Zeithaml, C.P. (1984) Stage of the product life cycle, business strategy, and business performance. *Academy of Management Journal*, **27** (1) 5–24.

Anderson, N.H. and Shanteau, J.C. (1970) Information integration in risky decision making. *Journal of Experimental Psychology*, **84** (3), 441–51.

Andrews, D. (1982) PADIS-ODE: the exigence to evaluate policy decisions. *Management Research News*, **5** (1), 18–21.

Andrews, D. (1982) Assurance technology: the philosophy of risk management. *Management Research News*, **5** (3), 1–5.

Andrews, K.R. (1971) *The Concept of Strategy*, Dow Jones-Irwin, Homewood, Ill.

Ang, J.S. and Chua, J.H. (1979) Long-range planning in large United States corporations – a survey. *Long Range Planning*, **12**, 99–102.

Anshen, M. and Guth, W.D. (1973) Strategies for research in policy formulation. *Journal of Business*, Oct., 499–511.

Ansoff, H.I. (1965) *Corporate Strategy*, McGraw-Hill, New York.

Ansoff, H.I. (1969) *Business Strategy*, Penguin, Baltimore.

Ansoff, H.I. (1975) Managing strategic surprise by response to weak signals. *California Management Review*, **43** (2), Winter, 21–3.

Ansoff, H.I. (1977) Strategy formulation as a learning process: an applied managerial theory of strategic behaviour. *International Studies of Management and Organization*, **7** (2), Summer, 58–77.

Ansoff, H.I. (1978) Strategy and strategic management: the changing shape of the strategic problem, in *Strategy Formulation: Analytical Concepts* (eds C.W. Hofer and D.E. Schendel), West Publishing, St Paul.

Ansoff, H.I. (1983) Societal strategy for the business firm. *Advances in Strategic Management*, **1**, 3–29.

Ansoff, H.I. (1983) Corporate capability for managing change. *Advances in Strategic Management*, **2**, 1–30.

Ansoff, H.I., Declerk, R.P. and Hayes, R.L. (1976) *From Strategic Planning to Strategic Management*, Wiley, New York.

Ansoff, H.I. and Leontiades, J. (1976) Strategic portfolio management, *Journal of General Management*, **4** (1), 13–29.

Ansoff, H.I. and Stewart, J. (1967) Strategies for a technology-based business. *Harvard Business Review*, **45** (6), 71–83.

Anthony, R.N. (1965) *Planning and Control Systems, A Framework for Analysis*. Harvard University Graduate School of Business Administration, Division of Research, Boston.

Argenti, J. (1968) *Corporate Planning: A Practical Guide*, George Allen & Unwin, London.

Argenti, J. (1974) *Systematic Corporate Planning*, Thomas Nelson & Sons, London.

Argenti, J. (1980) *Practical Corporate Planning*, George Allen & Unwin, London.

Argenti, J. (1976) *Corporate Collapse: The Causes and Symptoms*, Wiley, New York.

Argyris, C. (1970) Resistance to rational management systems. *Innovation*, **10**, 28–34.

Argyris, C. (1977) Organisational learning and management information systems. *Accounting, Organisations and Society*, **2** (2), 113–23.

Armour, D.H. and Teece, D.J. (1978) Organizational structure and economic performance: a test of the multidivisional hypothesis. *The Bell Journal of Economics*, Spring, 106–22.

Armstrong, J.S. (1982) The value of formal planning for strategic decisions: review of empirical research. *Strategic Management Journal*, **3**, 197–211.

Arrow, K.J. (1971) *Essays in the Theory of Risk Bearing*, North-Holland, Chicago.

Astley, W.G. *et al.* (1982) Complexity and cleavage: dual explanations of strategic decision making. *Journal of Management Studies*, **19** (4), Oct. 357–75.

Astley, W.G. and Fombrun, C.J. (1983) Technological innovation and industrial structure: the case of telecommunications. *Advances in Strategic Management*, **1**, 205–29.

Atkin, R.H. (1980) The methodology of Q/analysis. *Management Decision*, **1**, 205–29.

Avriel, M. and Williams, A.C. (1970) The value of information and stochastic programming. *Operations Research*, **18** (5), Sept./Oct., 947–54.

Axelsson, R. and Rosenberg, L. (1978) Decision-making and organizational turbulence. *Acta Sociologica*, **22**, 45/62.

Baird, I.S. and Thomas, H. (1985) Toward a contingency model of strategic risk taking. *Academy of Management Review*, **10** (2), 230–43.

Bajgier, S.M. *et al.* (1978) Multiattribute risk-benefit analysis of citizen attitudes towards societal issues involving technology, in *Multiple Criterion Problem Solving (ed. S. Zionts)*, Proceedings of a Conference in Buffalo, NY (USA), 22–6 Aug. 1977, Springer Verlag, pp. 424–47.

Bales, C.F. (1977) Strategic control: the president's paradox. *Business Horizons*, Aug., 146–61.

Barkin, S.R and Dickson, G.W. (1977) An investigation of information system utilization. *Information and Management*, **1**, Nov., 33–45.

Barnard, C. (1938) *The Function of the Executive*, Harvard University Press, Cambridge, Mass.

Barnes, J.H. (1984) Cognitive biases and their impact on strategic planning. *Strategic Management Journal*, **5**, 129–37.

Bariff, M.L. and Galbraith, J.R. (1978) Intraorganizational power considerations for designing information systems. *Accounting, Organizations and Society*, **3** (1), 15–28.

Barron, F.H. (1974) Behavioural decision theory: a topical bibliography for management scientists. *Interfaces*, **5** (1), Nov., 56–62.

Bassler, J.F. *et al.* (1978) Multiple criterion dominance models: an empirical study of investment preferences, in *Multiple Criterion Problem Solving* (ed. S. Zionts), Proceedings of a Conference in Buffalo, NY, USA, 22–6 Aug. 1977, Springer Verlag, pp. 494–508.

Bazerman, M.H. and Samuelson, W.F. (1983) I won the auction but don't want the prize. *Journal of Conflict Resolution*, **27**, 618–34.

Beach, L.R. and Mitchell, T.R. (1978) A contingency model for the selection of decision strategies. *Academy of Management Review*, **3**(3), July, 439–49.

Beach, L.R. *et al.* (1978) Information relevance, content, and source credibility in the revision of opinions. *Organizational Behaviour and Human Performance*, **21**, 1–16.

Beard, D.W. (1978) The structure of organizational environments: a factor analytical approach. *Organization and Administrative Science*, **8**(4), 85–105.

Beard, D.W and Dess, G.S. (1981) Corporate-level strategy, business-level strategy, and firm performance. *Academy of Management Journal*, **24** (4), 663–88.

Beaver, W.H., Kettler, P. and Scholes, M. (1970) The association between market determined and accounting determined risk measures. *The Accounting Review*, Oct., 654–82.

Beccaria (1785) *An Essay on Crimes and Punishments*, 4th edn, E. Newberry, London, p. 42.

Beer, S. (1966) *Decision and Control*, Wiley, New York.

Beer, S. (1980) *Preface to Autopoiesis and Cognition: The Realisation of the Living* (eds H.M. Maturana and F.G. Varela), Reidel, Dordrecht.

Bethlehem, D.W. (1985) *A Social Psychology of Prejudice*, Croom Helm, Beckenham, Kent.

Bettis, R.A. (1981) Performance differences in related and unrelated diversified firms. *Strategic Management Journal*, **2**, Oct./Dec., 379–94.

Bettis, R.A. (1982) Risk considerations in modelling corporate strategy. *Academy of Management Proceedings*, 22–5.

Bettis, R.A. (1983) Modern financial theory, corporate strategy, and public policy: three conundrums. *Academy of Management Review*, **8**, 406–16.

Bettis, R.A. and Hall, W.K. (1982) Diversification strategy, accounting determined risk and accounting determined return. *Academy of Management Journal*, **25** (2), June, 254–64.

Bettman, J.R. (1980) Information processing models of consumer behaviour. *Journal of Marketing Research*, **7**, Aug., 370–6.

Bettman, J.R. and Jacoby, J. (1976) Patterns in processing consumer information acquisition. *Advances in Consumer Research*, Chicago Association for Consumer Research, **3**, 315–20.

Biggadike, R. (1979) The risky business of diversification. *Harvard Business Review*, May/June, 103–11.

Billot, A. (1991) Cognitive rationality and alternative belief measures. *Journal of Risk and Uncertainty*, **4**, 299–324.

Blandin, J.S., Brown, W.B. and Koch, J.L. (1974) Uncertainty and information gathering behaviour: an empirical investigation. Paper presented at the 34th Annual Meeting, Academy of Management.

Blinn, J.D., Duncan, S.R. and Goodwin, B. (1991) 1990 cost of risk survey: a yardstick for managers. *Risk Management*, **38**, (2), Feb., 46–50.

Blume, M.E. (1971) On the assessment of risk. *Journal of Finance*, **26** (1), Mar., 1–10.

Blume, M.E. (1975) Betas and their regression tendencies. *Journal of Finance*, 30 (3), June, 785–95.

Bogdan, R. and Taylor, J.S. (1975) *Introduction to Qualitative Research*, John Wiley & Sons, London.

Boland, R.J. (1979) Control, causality and information system requirements. *Accounting, Organisations and Society*, **4** (4).

Borch, K. and Mossin, J. (eds) (1968) *Risk and Uncertainty*. Proceedings of a Conference held by the International Economic Association, Macmillan, London.

Boulton, W.R. *et al.* (1982) How are companies planning now? – a survey. *Long Range Planning*, **15** (1), 82–6.

Bourgeois, L.J. (1985) Strategic goals, perceived uncertainty, and economic performance in volatile environments. *Academy of Management Journal*, **28** (3), Sept., 548–73.

Bower, J.L. (1967) Strategy as a problem solving theory of business planning. *Intercollegiate Case Clearing House*, Boston, Mass., **9**, 368–439.

Bower, J.L., and Doz, Y. (1978) Strategy formulation: a social and political process, in *Strategy Formulation: Analytical Concepts* (eds C.W. Hofer and D.E. Schendel), West Publishing, St Paul.

Bowman, E.H. (1974) Epistemology, corporate strategy, and academe. *Sloan Management Review*, Winter, 35–50.

Bowman, E.H. (1980) A risk/return paradox for strategic management. *Sloan Management Review*, **21** (3), 17–31.

Bowman, E.H. (1982) Risk seeking by troubled firms. *Sloan Management Review*, Summer, 33–42.

Brealey, R.A. (1983) *An Introduction to Risk and Return from Common Stocks*, 2nd edn, Basil Blackwell, London.

Breznitz, S., and Lieblich, A. (1972) How to simulate if you must: simulating the dream/work, in *Simulation and Gaming in Social Science* (eds M. Inbar and C.S. Stoll), Free Press, New York, pp. 69/91.

Brimm, O.G and Hoff, D.B. (1957) Individual and situational differences in desire for certainty. *Journal of Abnormal and Social Psychology*, **54**, 225–29.

Brown, J.S. (1970) Risk propensity in decision making: a comparison of business and public school administrators. *Administrative Science Quarterly*, **15**, 473–81.

Brown, R.V., Kahn, A.S. and Peterson, C.R. (1974) *Decision Analysis: An Overview*, Rinehart & Winston, New York.

Brunsson, N. (1982) The irrationality of action and action rationality: decisions, ideologies and organizational actions. *Journal of Management Studies*, **19** (1), 29–44.

Brunswick, E. (1952) *The Conceptual Framework of Psychology*, Chicago University Press, Chicago.

Brunswick, E. (1955) Representative design and probabilistic theory in a functional psychology. *Psychological Review*, May, 193–217.

Burns, T. and Stalker, G.M. (1961) *The Management of Innovation*, Tavistock Publications, London.

Butler, R.J. *et al.* (1979) Strategic decision making: concepts of content and process. *International Studies of Management and Organization*, **4**, 5–36.

Cairns, D. and Marshall, D. (1991) How long is a piece of string? Exploring the hidden agenda of rule-based systems in *Computers, Artificial Intelligence* and the *Law* (ed. M.E. Bennun), Ellis Horwood, Chichester, pp. 77–94.

Camillus, J.C. (1982) Reconciling logical incrementalism and synoptic formalism – an integrated approach to designing strategic planning processes. *Strategic Management Journal*, **3**, 277–83.

Campbell, D.T. and Stanley, J.C. (1963) *Experimental and Quasi-Experimental Designs for Research*, Rand McNally, Chicago.

Carlisle, H.M. (1968) Measuring the situational nature of management. *California Management Review*, **11** (2), 45–52.

Carlisle, H.M. (1973) *Situational Management*, AMACOM, New York.

Carroll, J.S. (1980) Analyzing decision behaviour: the magician's audience, in *Cognitive Processes in Choice and Decision Behaviour* (ed. T.S. Wallsten), Lawrence Erlbaum, Hillside, NJ pp. 69–76.

Carter, E.E. (1971) The behavioural theory of the firm and top-level corporate decisions. *Administrative Science Quarterly*, **16** (4), 413–28.

Cartland, R.E. (1991) Emerging RM concerns for directors and officers. *Risk Management*, **38** (2), Feb., 24–9.

Chaffee, E.E. (1985) Three models of strategy. *Academy of Management Review*, **10** (1), 89–98.

Chandler, A.D. (1962) *Strategy and Structure: Chapters in the History of the American Industrial Enterprise*, MIT Press, Cambridge, Mass.

Channon, D.F. (1973) *The Strategy and Structure of British Enterprise*, Graduate School of Business Administration, Harvard University, Boston.

Channon, D.F. (1977) Strategy formulation as an analytical process. *International Studies of Management and Organization*, **7** (2), Summer, 41–57.

Charajedaghi, J. (1985) *Towards a Systems Theory of Organisation*, Intersystems, Seaside.

Child, J. (1972) Organization structure, environment, and performance – the role of strategic choice. *Sociology*, **6** (1), Jan., 1–22.

Child, J. (1974a) Managerial and organisational factors associated with company performance – part I. *Journal of Management Studies*, **2**, (3), 175–89.

Child, J. (1974b) What determines organizational performance? – the universals v's the it-all-depends. *Organizational Dynamics*, Summer, 2–18.

Child, J. (1975) Managerial factors associated with company performance – part II: a contingency analysis. *Journal of Management Studies*, **12** (1), 12–27.

Child, J. (1978) Commentary on a paper by Bower, J.L. and Doz, Y, strategy formulation: a social and political process, in *Strategy Formulation: Analytical Concepts* (eds C.W. Hofer and D.E. Schendel), West Publishing, St Paul.

Child, J. and Francis, A. (1977) Strategy formulation as a structured process. *International Studies of Management and Organizations*, **7** (2), Summer, 110–26.

Choffray, J.M. and Johnston, P.E. (1979) Measuring perceived pre-purchase risk for a new industrial product. *Industrial Marketing Management*, **8** (4), 333–4.

Christensen, C.R., Andrews, K.R. and Bower, J.L. (1973) *Business Policy: Text and Cases*, Richard D. Irwin, Homewood, Ill.

Christensen-Szalanski, J.J. (1978) Problem solving strategies: a selection mechanism, some implications and some data. *Organizational Behaviour and Human Performance*, **22**, 307–23.

Churchman, C.W. (1971) *The Design of Inquiring Systems*, Basic Books, New York.

Clark, R.D. (1971) Group induced shift toward risk: a critical appraisal. *Psychological Bulletin*, **76** (4), 251–70.

Clifford, D.K. (1973) *Managing the Threshold Company: The Making of Tomorrow's Leaders*, McKinsey & Co, New York.

Cohen, J. (1972) *Psychological Probability or the Art of Doubt*, George Allen & Unwin, London.

Cohen, J. and Christensen, I. (1970) *Information and Choice*, Oliver & Boyd, Edinburgh.

Cohen, M.D., March, J.G. and Olson, J.P. (1972) A garbage can model of organizational choice. *Administrative Science Quarterly*, **17** (1), Mar., 1–25.

Connolly, T. (1977) Information processing and decision making in organizations, in *New Directions in Organizational Behaviour*, (eds B.M. Staw and G.R. Salancik), St Clair Press, Chicago, pp. 205–34.

Conrad, G.R. and Plotkin, I.H. (1968) Risk-return: US industry pattern. *Harvard Business Review*, Mar./Apr.

Conrath, D.W. (1967) Organizational decision making behaviour under varying conditions of uncertainty. *Management Science*, **13**, B487–B500.

Conrath, D.W. (1973) From statistical decision theory to practice: some problems with the transition. *Management Science (Applications Series)*, **19** (8), Apr., 873–83.

Cook, C.W. (1975) *Corporate Strategy Change Contingencies*. Academy of Management Proceedings, Aug., 52–54.

Cooke, S. and Slack, N.R. (1984) *Making Management Decisions*, Prentice–Hall International, London.

Coombs, C.H. and Huang, L.C. (1970) Tests of a portfolio theory of risk preference. *Journal of Experimental Psychology*, **85**, 23–9.

Coombs, C.H. and Pruitt, D.G. (1960) Components of risk in decision making. *Journal of Experimental Psychology*, **60**, (5) 265–77.

Cooper, R. (1992) Systems and organisations: distal and proximal thinking. *Systems Practice*, **5**, (4), Aug., 373–7.

Cootner, P.H. and Holland, D.M. (1970) Rate of return and business risk. *The Bell Journal of Economics and Management Science*, Autumn, 211–26.

Corbin, R.M. (1980) Decisions that might not get made, in *Cognitive Processes in Choice and Decision Behaviour*, (ed. T.S. Wallsten) Lawrence Erlbaum, Hillside, NJ, pp 47–67.

Cosier, R.A. (1978) The effects of three potential aids for making strategic decision on prediction accuracy. *Organizational Behaviour and Human Performance*, **22**, 295–306.

Cosier, R.A. and Alpin, J.C. (1980) A critical view of dialectical inquiry as a tool in strategic planning. *Strategic Management Journal*, **1**, 343–56.

Covello, V.T., Sandman, P.M. and Slovic, P. (1988) *Risk Communication, Risk Statistics, and Risk Comparisons: A Manual for Plant Managers*, Chemical Manufacturers Association, Washington DC.

Cox, D.F. (ed.) (1967) *Risk Taking and Information Handling in Consumer Behaviour*, Graduate School of Business Administration, Harvard University, Boston.

Cox, D.F. and Rich, S. (1964) Perceived risk and consumer decision making. *Journal of Marketing Research*, **1** (4), 32–9.

Cunningham, S.M. (1967) The major dimensions of perceived risk, in *Risk Taking and Information Handling in Consumer Behaviour* (ed. D.F. Cox), Graduate School of Business Administration, Harvard University, Boston.

Cyert, R.M. and March, J.G. (1963) *A Behavioural Theory of the Firm*, Prentice Hall, Englewood Cliffs, NJ.

Cyert, R.M and March, J.G. (1992). *A Behavioral Theory of the Firm*, 2nd edn, Blackwell, Oxford.

Cyert, R.M., Simon, H.A. and Trow, D.B. (1956) Observation of a business decision. *Journal of Business*, **29**, 237–48.

Datta, Y. (1980) New directions for research in business strategy. *Journal of General Management*, **6** (1) 48–60.

Davis, J.V. (1978) Determining a firm's loss retention level. *Risk Management*, Nov. 48–9.

Dessler, G. (1976) *Organization and Management: A Contingency Approach*, Prentice Hall, Englewood Cliffs, NJ.

Diffenbach, J. (1982) Influence diagrams for complex strategic decisions. *Strategic Management Journal*, **3**, 33–46

Dillard, J.F. (1984) Cognitive science and decision making research in accounting. *Accounting, Organisations and Society*. **9**, (3/4), 343–54.

Dobie, C. (1992) A small matter of methodology. *Independent*, Tuesday, 8 December, 23.

Doherty, N.A. (1985) *Corporate Risk Management: A Financial Exposition*, McGraw-Hill, New York.

Donaldson, G. and Lorsch, J.W. (1983) *Decision Making at the Top: The Shaping of Strategic Direction*, Basic Books, New York.

Doucouliagos, C. (1992) Worker entrepreneurship. *Entrepreneurship, Innovation and Change*, **1** (1), 109–26.

Downey, H.K., Hellriegel, D. and Slocum, J.W. (1975) Environmental uncertainty: the construct and its application. *Administrative Science Quarterly*, **20**, 613–29.

Downey, H.K., Hellriegel, D. and Slocum, J.W. (1977) Individual characteristics as sources of perceived uncertainty variability. *Human Relation*, **30**, 161–74.

Downey, H.K. and Slocum, J.W. (1975). Uncertainty measures, research, and sources of variation. *Academy of Management Journal*, **18** (3), Sept., 562–78.

Downey, H.K. and Slocum, J.W. (1982) Managerial uncertainty and performance. *Social Science Quarterly*, **63** (2), June, 195–207.

Driscoll, J. and Lanzetta, J. (1965) Effects of two sources of uncertainty in decision making. *Psychological Reports*, **17** (2), 635–48.

Driver, M.J. (1974) *Decision style and its management*. Working Paper Graduate School of Business Administration, University of Southern California, Los Angeles, Cal.

Driver, M.J. and Hunsacker, P. (1972) The Luna 1 Moon Colony: a programmed simulation for the analysis of individual and group decision making. *Psychological Reports*, **31**, 879–88.

Driver, M.J. and Lintott, L. (1973) *Managerial Decision Diagnostics*, Graduate School of Business Administration, University of Southern California, Los Angeles, Cal.

Driver, M.J. and Mock, T.J. (1975) Human information processing, decision style theory and accounting information systems. *The Accounting Review*, **50**, 490–508.

Drucker, P.F. (1974) *Management: Tasks, Responsibilities, Practices*, Harper & Row, New York.

Durbin, R. (1969) *Theory Building*, The Free Press, New York.

Duhaime, I.M. and Schwenk, C.R. (1985). Conjectures on cognitive simplification in acquisition and divestment decision making. *Academy of Management Review*, **10**, (2), Apr., 287–95.

Dukes, R. (1973) *Symbolic Models and Simulation Games for Theory Construction*. Paper presented to Annual Meetings of the American Sociological Association.

Duncan, C.A. (1991) Risk management audits set directors minds at ease. *Risk Management*, **38** (8), Aug., 48–54.

Duncan, R.B. (1972) Characteristics of organizational environments and perceived environmental uncertainty. *Administrative Science Quarterly*, **17** (3), Sept., 313–27.

Duncan, R.B. (1974) Modifications in decision structure in adapting to the environment: some implications for organizational learning. *Decision Sciences*, **5**, Oct., 705–25.

Duncan, R.B. (1979) Qualitative research methods in strategic management, in *Strategic Management* (eds D.E. Schendel and C. Hofer), Little, Brown & Co, Boston, pp. 424–47.

Eardley, A., Marshall, D.V. and Ritchie, R.L. (1991) *Management Information Systems*, 2nd edn, Longman, London.

Earl, M.J. and Hopwood, A.G. (1980) From management information to information management, in *The Information Systems Environment* (eds. Lucas; Land, Lincoln and Supper). North-Holland, NY, pp. 3–13.

Ebbesen, E.B. and Konecni, V.J. (1980) On the external validity of decision making research: what do we know about decisions in the real world?, in *Cognitive Processes in Choice and Decision Behaviour* (ed. T.S. Wallsten), Lawrence Erlbaum, Hillside, NJ, pp. 21–45.

Ebbesen, E.B. Parker, S. and Konecni, V.J. (1977) Laboratory and field analysis of decisions involving risk. *Journal of Experimental Psychology, Human Perceptions and Performance* **3** (4), 576–89.

Edwards, J.P. (1977) Strategy formulation as a stylistic process. *International Studies of Management and Organizations* **7** (2), 13–27.

Edwards, W. (1971) Bayesian and regression models of human information processing – a myopic perspective. *Organizational Behaviour and Human Performance* **6** (6), 639–48.

Edwards, W. and Slovic, P. (1965) Seeking information to reduce the risk of decisions. *American Journal of Psychology*, **78**, 188–97.

Einhorn, H.J. (1980) Learning from experience and suboptimal rules in decision making, in *Cognitive Processes in Choice and Decision Behaviour* (ed. T.S. Wallsten), Lawrence Erlbaum, Hillside, NJ, pp. 1–20.

Ellsberg, D. (1961) Risk, ambiguity and the savage axioms. *Quarterly Journal of Economics*, **75**, 643–69.

Estes, W.K. (1980) Comments on directions and limitations of current efforts towards theories of decision making, in *Cognitive Processes in Choice and Decision Behaviour* (ed. T.S. Wallsten), Lawrence Erlbaum, Hillside, NJ, pp. 263–74.

Ewing, D.W. (1969) *The Human Side of Planning*, Macmillan, New York.

Fahey, L. (1981) On strategic management decision processes. *Strategic Management Journal*, **2** (1), Jan./Mar., 43–60.

Farmer, R.N. and Richman, B.M. (1965) *Comparative Management and Economic Progress*, Richard D Irwin, Homewood, Ill.

Farris, G.F. (1979) The informal organization in strategic decision making. *International Studies of Management and Organizations*. **9** (4), 37–62.

Fayol, H. (1949) *General and Industrial Management*, Sir Isaac Pitman & Sons, London.

Feldt, A. (1972) *Operational Games as Educational Devices, Community Land Use Game: Player's Manual*, Free Press, New York.

Ferguson, K.E. (1984) *The Feminist Case against Hierarchy*, Temple University Press, Philadelphia.

Ferguson, R.L. and Jones, C.H. (1969) A computer aided decision system. *Management Science*, **15** (10), June, B550–561.

Fiedler, F.E. (1971) Validation and extension of the contingency model of leadership effectiveness: a review of empirical findings. *Psychological Bulletin*, **76** (2), 123–48.

Fiedler, F.E. (1974) The contingency model – new directions for leadership utilization. *Journal of Contemporary Business*, **3** (4), Autumn, 65–80.

Fisher, I.N. and Hall, G.R. (1969) Risk and corporate rates of return. *Quarterly Journal of Economics*, Feb., 79–92.

Fischoff, B. and Beyth-Marom, R. (1983) Hypothesis evaluation from a

Bayesian perspective. *Psychological Review*, **90**, 239–60.

Fischoff, B., Slovic, P. and Lichtenstein, S. (1980) Knowing what you want: measuring labile values, in *Cognitive Processes in Choice and Decision Behaviour* (ed. T.S. Wallsler), Lawrence Erlbaum, Hillside, NJ, pp. 117–41.

Fischoff, B., Slovic, P. and Lichtenstein, S. (1978) Fault trees: sensitivity of estimated failure probabilities to problem representation. *Journal of Experimental Psychology, Human Perception and Performance*, **4** (2), 330–44.

Fishburn, P.C. (1974) Lexicographic orders, utilities and decision rules: a survey. *Management Sciences*, **20** (11), July, 1442–71.

Fishburn, P.C. (1977) Mean-risk analysis with risk associated with below-target returns. *American Economic Review*, **67** (2), 116–26.

Fishburn, P. (1988) *Nonlinear Preference and Utility Theory*, Johns Hopkins University Press, Baltimore.

Fitzpatrick, M. (1983) The definition and assessment of political risk in international business: a review of the literature. *Academy of Management Review*, **8**, (2), 249–54.

Flood, R.L. and Jackson, M.C. (1991) *Creative Problem Solving: Total Systems Intervention*, Wiley, Chichester.

Flood, R.L. (1992) Entrepreneurship, intrapreneurship and innovativeness. *Entrepreneurship, Innovation and Change*, **1** (1), 13–25.

Foucault, M. (1975) *Discipline and Punish* (English edn. 1977), Allen Lane, London.

Foucault, M. (1976) *The History of Sexuality* Vol. 1. (transl. Robert Hurley, 1978), Penguin, Harmondsworth.

Foucault, M. (1980) *Power-Knowledge: Selected Interviews and Other Writings 1972–77.* (Ed. C. Gordon), Harvester Press, Hemel Hempstead.

Frederick, C.B. and Wilson, A.G.E. (1991) Comments on incorporating mechanistic data into quantitative risk assessment. *Risk Analysis*, **11** (4), 581.

Frederickson, J.W. and Mitchell, T.R. (1984) Strategic decision processes: comprehensiveness and performance in an industry with an unstable environment. *Academy of Management Journal*, **27** (2), June, 399–423.

Friedel, W. (1991) A changing world inspires new definitions of risk. *Risk Management*, **38** (10), Oct., 22–30.

Fulmer, R.M. and Rue, L.W. (1974) The practice and profitability of long/range planning. *Managerial Planning*, **22**, May/June, 1–7.

Funk, S.G., Rapoport, A. and Jones, L.V. (1979) Investing capital on safe and risky alternatives: an experimental study. *Journal of Experimental Psychology – General*, **108**, 415–550.

Galbraith, C. and Schendel, D. (1983) An empirical analysis of strategy types. *Strategic Management Journal*, **4** 153–73.

Galbraith, J. (1973) *Designing Complex Organisations*, Addison-Wesley, Reading, MA.

Galbraith, J.R. (1974) Organization design: an information processing view. *Interfaces*, **4** (3), May, 28–36.

Gastelaars, M. (1992) Morality materialised: notes on public prevention as a policy system. *Systems Practice*, **5**, (4), Aug., 411–23.

Gibson, K.R. (1991) Making risk management happen in your organisation. *Risk Management*, **38**, (4), 71–5.

Gifford, W.E., Bobbitt, H.R. and Slocum, F.W. (1979) Message characteristics and perceptions of uncertainty. *Academy of Management Journal*, **22**, (3), 458–81.

Ginsberg, A. (1984) Operationalizing organizational strategy: toward an integrative framework. *Academy of Management Review*. **9**, (3), 548–57.

Ginsberg, A. and Venkatraman, N. (1985) Contingency perspectives of organisational strategy: a critical review of the empirical research. *Academy of Management Review*, **10**, (3), July, 421–34.

Glaser, B.G. and Strauss, A.L. (1967) *The Discovery of Grounded Theory: Strategies for Qualitative Research*, Aldine, Chicago.

Glueck, W.F. (1972) *Business Policy: Reality and Promise*. Proceedings of the National Meetings of the Academy of Management, pp. 108–11.

Glueck, W.F. (1976) *Business Policy: Strategy, Formulation and Management Action*, 2nd ed, McGraw-Hill, Tokyo.

Grant, J.H. and King, W.R. (1978) Strategy formulation: analytical and normative models, in *Strategy Formulation: Analytical Concepts* (eds (W. Hofer and D.E. Schendel), West Publishing, St Paul.

Graen, G. *et al.* (1970) Contingency model of leadership effectiveness: antecedent and evidential results. *Psychological Bulletin*, **74**, (4), 285–96.

Greenblat, C.S. and Duke, R.D. (1975) *Gaming-Simulation: Rationale, Design, and Applications*, Sage Publications Inc, New York.

Greenblat, C.S. (1975a) Basic concepts and linkages, in *Gaming-Simulation: Rationale, Design, and Applications* (eds C.S. Greenblat and R.D. Duke), Sage Publications Inc, NY, pp. 10–14.

Greenblat, C.S. (1975b) Gaming-simulation as a tool for social research, in *Gaming-Simulation: Rationale, Design, and Applications* (eds C.S. Greenblat and R.D. Duke), Sage Publications Inc., NY, pp. 320–33.

Greer, W.R. (1974) Theory versus practice in risk analysis: an empirical study. *Accounting Review*, **49** (3), July, 496–505.

Greer, W.R. and Skelel, T.D. (1975) Theory versus practice in risk analysis: a reply. *Accounting Review*, **50** (4), Oct., 839–43.

Guth, W.D. and Tagiuri, R. (1965) Personal values and corporate strategy. *Harvard Business Review*, **43**, (5), Sept./Oct., 123–32.

Guttentag, M. (1971) Models and methods in evaluation research. *Journal of Theory and Social Behaviour*, **10**, 75–95.

Habermas, J. (1984) *The Theory of Communicative Action, Vol. 1*, Heinemann, London.

Habermas, J. (1987) *The Theory of Communicative Action, Vol. 2*, Polity Press, Cambridge.

Haimes, Y.Y. Li, D. and Tulsiani, V. (1990) Multiobjective decision tree analysis. *Risk Analysis*, **10** (1), 111–29.

Haimes, Y.Y. (1991) Total risk management. *Risk Analysis*. **11**, (2), 169–71.

Hambrick, D.C. (1980) Operationalizing the concept of business-level strategy in research. *Academy of Management Review*, **5** (4), 567–75.

Hambrick, D.C. (1982) Environmental scanning and organizational strategy. *Strategic Management Journal*, **3**, 159–74.

Hambrick, D.C. (1983) High profit strategies in mature capital goods industries: a contingency approach. *Academy of Management Journal*, **26**, (4), 687–707.

Hambrick, D.C. (1984) Taxonomic approaches to studying strategy: some conceptual and methodological issues. *Journal of Management*, **10**, (1), 27–41.

Hammitt, J.K. (1990) Risk perceptions and food choice: an exploratory analysis of organic- versus conventional-produce buyers. *Risk Analysis*, **10** (3), 367–74.

Hampton, J.M., Moore, P.G. and Thomas, H. (1973) Subjective probability and its measurement. *Journal of the Royal Statistical Society*, Series A, **136** (1), 22–42.

Handy, C.B. (1978) *Gods of Management: How They Work and Why They Will Fail*, Souvenir Press, London.

Handy, C.B. (1981) *Understanding Organisations*, Penguin, Harmondsworth.

Hardy, C.O. (1923) *Risk and Risk Bearing*, The University of Chicago Press, Chicago.

Harrar, W.S. and Bawden, D.L. (1972) The use of experimentation in policy formulation and evaluation. *Urban Affairs Quarterly*, **7**, 419–30.

Harrigan, K.R. (1983) Research methodologies for contingency approaches to business strategy. *Academy of Management Review*, **8** (3), 398–405.

Harrison, R. (1978) Developing autonomy, initiative and risk-taking through a laboratory study. *International Studies of Management and Organizations*, **8**, 119–41.

Harvey, D.F. (1982) *Strategic Management*, Merrill, Columbus, OH.

Hatten, K.J. (1979) Quantitative research methods in strategic management, in *Strategic Management*, (eds D.E. Schendel and C. Hofer), Little, Brown & Co, Boston, pp. 448–67.

Hatten, K.J. and Schendel, D.E. (1975–76) Strategy's role in policy research. *Journal of Economics and Business*, **28**, 196–202.

Hawkins, C and Lanzetta, J. (1965) Uncertainty, importance and arousal as determinants of predecisional information search. *Psychological Reports*, **17**, 791–800.

Hazen, G.B. and Lee, J. (1991) Ambiguity aversion in the small and in the large for weighted linear utility. *Journal of Risk and Uncertainty*, **4**, 177–212.

Heath, C. and Tversky, A. (1991) Preference and belief: ambiguity and competence in choice under uncertainty. *Journal of Risk and Uncertainty*, **4** (1), Jan., 5–28.

Hedberg, B. and Jonsson, S. (1977) Strategy formulation as a discontinuous process. *International Studies of Management and Organizations*. **7**, (2), Summer, 88–109.

Hedberg, B. and Jonsson, S. (1978) Designing semi-confusing information systems for organizations in changing environments. *Accounting, Organizations and Society*, **3** (1), 47–64.

Hegarty, W.H. (1979) Policy and planning research: teaching implications, in *Strategic Management*. (eds D. E. Schendel and C. Hofer) Little, Brown & Co, Boston., pp. 493–501.

Hellriegel, D. and Slocum, J.W. (1973) *Management: A Contingency Approach*, Addison-Wesley, Reading, Mass.

Hellriegel, D. and Slocum, J.W. (1973) Organization design: a contingency approach. *Business Horizons* **16**, (2), Apr. 59–68.

Henderson, D.B. (1979) *Henderson on Corporate Strategy*, Abt Books, Cambridge, Mass.

Herold, D.M. House, R.J. and Thune, S.S. (1972) Long-range planning and organizational performance: a cross-validation study. *Academy of Management Journal*, **15** (1), 91–104.

Hertz, D.B. (1979) Risk analysis in capital investment. *Harvard Business Review*, Sept./Oct., 169–81.

Hertz, D.B. and Thomas, H. (1983) Decision and risk analysis in a new product and facilities planning problem. *Sloan Management Review*, **24**, (2) 17–31.

Hertz, D.B. and Thomas, H. (1983) *Risk Analysis and its Applications*, Wiley, Chichester.

Hertz, D.B. and Thomas, H. (1983) Risk analysis approaches to strategic management, *Advances in Strategic Management*, **1**, 145–58.

Hertz, D.B. and Thomas, H. (1984) *Practical Risk Analysis – An Approach through Case Studies*, Wiley, Chichester.

Hester, G. *et al.* (1990) Small group studies of regulatory decision-making for power-frequency electric and magnetic fields. *Risk Analysis*, **10**, (2), 213–27.

Hicks, J.R. (1946) *Value and Capital*, 2nd edn, Oxford University Press, Oxford.

Hickson, D.J. *et al.* (1971). A strategic contingencies theory of intra-organizational power. *Administrative Science Quarterly*, 216–29.

Hirst, E. and Schweitzer, M. (1991) Electric-utility resource planning and decision–making: the importance of uncertainty. *Risk Analysis*, **10**, (1), 137–46.

Hofer, C.W. (1975) Toward a contingency theory of business strategy. *Academy of Management Journal*, **18**, (4), Dec., 784–810.

Hofer, C.W. (1976) Research on strategic planning: a survey of past studies and suggestions for future efforts. *Journal of Economics and Business*, **28**, Spring/Summer, 261–86.

Hofer, C.W. (1983) ROVA: a new measure for assessing organizational performance. *Advances in Strategic Management*. **2**, 43–55.

Hofer, C.W. and Schendel, D.E. (1978) *Strategy Formulation: Analytical Concepts*, West Publishing, St Paul.

Hoffman, P.J. (1968) Cue consistency and configurality in human judgement, in *Formal Representation of Human Judgement* (ed. B. Kleinmetz), Wiley, New York.

Hogarth, R.M. and Kunreuther, H. (1989) Risk, ambiguity and insurance. *Journal of Risk and Uncertainty*, **2**, 5–35.

Hoggatt, A.C. and Balderston, F.E. (Eds) (1963) *Symposium on simulation models: Methodology and Applications to the Behavioural Sciences*, South-Western Publishing Co, Cincinnati, Ohio.

Horvath, D. and McMillan, C.J. (1979) Strategic choice and the structure of decision processes. *International Studies of Management and Organizations* **9**(3), 87–112.

Huber, G.P., O'Connell, M.J. and Cummings, L.L. (1975) Perceived environmental uncertainty: effects of information and structure. *Academy of Management Journal*, **18**,(4) 725–40.

Hulbert, J., Farley, J.U. and Howard, J.A. (1972) Information processing and decision making in marketing organizations. *Journal of Marketing Research*, **9**, 75–7.

Hull, J.C. (1980) *The Evaluation of Risk in Business Investment*, Pergamon Press Ltd, London.

Hunger, J.D., Snyder, N. and Wheelen, T. (1981) *The Management Theory Jungle: A Proposed Integration of Koontz and Mintzberg*. Working Paper Series (81–4), McIntyre School of Commerce, University of Virginia.

Hunsacker, P. (1975) Incongruity, adaptation, capability and risk preference in turbulent decision making environments. *Organizational Behaviour and Human Performance*, **14**, 173–85.

Hussey, D. (1979) *Introducing Corporate Planning*, 2nd edn, Pergamon Press, Oxford.

Hussey, D. (1982) *Corporate Planning: Theory and Practice*, 2nd edn, Pergamon Press, New York.

Hussey, D. (1983) *The Truth About Corporate Planning*, Pergamon Press, Oxford.

Inbar, M. and Stoll, C.S. (1972) *Stimulation and Gaming in Social Science*, Free Press, New York.

Irwin, F.W. and Smith, W.A.S. (1957) Value, cost and information as determiners of decision. *Journal of Experimental Psychology*, **54**, 229–32.

Jacobi, J. and Chestnut, R.W. (1976) Pre-purchase information acquisition: description of a process methodology, research paradigm and pilot investigation. *Advances in Consumer Research*, Chicago Association for Consumer Research, **3**, 306–14.

Janis, I.L. and Mann, L. (1977) *Decision Making: A Psychological Analysis of Conflict, Choice and Commitment*, The Free Press, New York.

Jauch, L.R. (1983) An inventory of selected academic research on strategic management. *Advances in Strategic Management*. **2**, 141–75.

Jaunch, L.R., Osborn, R.N. and Martin, T.N. (1980) Structured content analysis of cases: a complementary method for organizational research. *Academy of Management Review*, **5**, (4), 517–25.

Jauss, H.R. (1982) Literary history as a challenge to literary theory, in *Towards an Aesthetic of Reception* (transl. T. Bahti), Harvester Press, Brighton, pp. 3–45.

Javidan, M. (1984) The impact of environmental uncertainty on long-range planning practices of the U.S. savings and loan industry. *Strategic Management Journal*, **5**, 381–92.

Jemison, D.B. (1981) Organizational v environmental sources of influence in strategic decision making. *Strategic Management Journal*, **2**, (1) Jan./Mar., 77–89.

Jemison, D.B. (1981) The importance of an integrative approach to strategic management research. *Academy of Management Review*, **6**, 601–8.

Jick, T.D. (1979) Mixing qualitative and quantitative methods: triangulation in action. *Administrative Science Quarterly*, **24**, 602–11.

Johnson, G. (1985) Strategic management in action, in *Current Research in Management*. (ed. V. Hammond), Francis Pinter, London, pp. 21–38.

Jones, C.S. (1985) An empirical study of the evidence for contingency theories. *Accounting, Organizations and Society*, **10**, (3), 303–28.

Jones-Lee, M.W. (1991) Altruism and the value of other people's safety. *Journal of Risk and Uncertainty*, **4**, 213–19.

Kahneman, D. and Tversky, A. (1979) Prospect theory: an analysis of decision under risk. *Econometrica*. **47**(2), Mar., 263–91.

Kaplow, L. (1991) Incentives and government relief for risk. *Journal of Risk and Uncertainty*, **4**, 167–74.

Kasperson, R.E. *et al.* (1988) The social amplification of risk: a conceptual framework. *Risk Analysis* **8**, 177–87.

Kast, F.E. and Rosenzweig, J.E. (1972) General systems theory: applications for organization and management. *Academy of Management Journal*, **15**, Dec., 447–65.

Kast, F.E. and Rosenzweig, J.E. (1973) *Contingency views of Organization and Management*, Science Research Associates, Chicago.

Kast, F.E. and Rosenzweig, J.E. (1974) *Organization and Management: A Systems Approach*, 2nd ed., McGraw-Hill, New York.

Kates, R.W. (1977) *Managing Technological Hazard*, Institute of Behavioural Science, University of Colorado, Boulder.

Katz, R.L. (1970) *Cases and Concepts in Corporate Strategy*, Prentice Hall, Englewood Cliffs, NJ.

Keegan, W.J. (1974) Multinational scanning: a study of the information sources utilized by headquarters executives in multinational companies. *Administrative Science Quarterly*, **19**, 411–21.

Kerr, S. (1974) *Contingency Theories and Alternatives*. Paper presented to the Midwest Division, Academy of Management.

Keynes, J.M. (1937) *The General Theory of Employment, Interest and Money*, Macmillan, London.

King, W.R. (1983) Evaluating strategic planning systems. *Strategic Management Journal*, **4**, 263–77

Kirchoff, B.A. and Kirchoff, J.J. (1980) Empirical assessment of the strategy tactics dilemma. *Academy of Management Proceedings*, 7–11.

Knight, F.H. (1921) *Risk, Uncertainty, and Profit*, Houghton Mifflin Company, Boston and New York.

Kogan, N. and Wallach, M.A. (1964) *Risk Taking: A Study in Cognition and Personality*, Holt, Rinehart & Winston, New York.

Kogan, N. and Wallach, M.A. (1967) Risk taking as a function of the situation, the person and the group in *New Directions in Psychology III* (ed. G. Mander), Holt, Rinehart & Winston, New York, pp. 111/278.

Koontz, H. (1961) The management theory jungle. *Academy of Management Journal*, Dec., 174–88.

Koontz, H. (1980) The management theory jungle revisited. *Academy of Management Review*, **2**, 175–87.

Korman, A.K. (1972) *Applications of Management Theory: A Review of the Empirical Literature and a New Direction*. Proceedings of the 32nd Annual Meeting of the Academy of Management, pp. 170–3.

Krimsky, S. and Plough, A. (1988) *Environmental Hazards: Communicating Risks as a Social Process*, Auburn House, Dover, Massachusetts.

Kudla, R.J. (1981) Strategic planning and risk. *Review of Business and Economic Research*, **17**, Fall, 1–14.

Kunreuther, H. (1989) The role of actuaries and underwriters in insuring ambiguous risks. *Risk Analysis*, **9**, 319–28.

Laborde, L.P. (1991) Optimising a company's loss retention level. *Risk Management*, **38**, (2), Feb., 54–9.

Laird, F.N. (1989) The decline of deference: the political context of risk communication. *Risk Analysis*, **9**, 543–50.

Lamm, H. (1967) Will an observor advise higher risk-taking after hearing a discussion of the decision problem? *Journal of Personality and Social Psychology*, **6**, 467–71.

Lang, J., Dittrich, J. and White, S. (1978) Managerial problem solving models: a review and a proposal. *Academy of Management Review*, **3**, 854–66.

Lanzetta, J.T. and Driscoll, J.M. (1968) Effects of uncertainty and importance on information search in decision making. *Journal of Personality and Social Psychology*, **10**, 479–86.

Lanzetta, J.T. and Kanareff, V.T. (1962) Information cost, amount of payoff and level of aspiration as determinants of information seeking in decision making. *Behavioural Science*, **7**, 459–73.

Lawrence, P.R. and Lorsch, J.W. (1967) *Organization and Environment: Managing Differentiation and Integration*. Graduate School of Business Administration, Harvard University.

Layfield, Frank (1986) *Sizewell B Public Inquiry Report*. HMSO, London.

Learned, E.P. *et al.* (1965) *Business Policy: Text and Cases*, Irwin, Homewood, Ill.

Leifer, R. and Huber, G.P. (1977) Relations among perceived environmental uncertainty, organization structure and boundary spanning behaviour. *Administrative Science Quarterly*, **22**, 235–47.

Levy, H. and Sarnat, M. (1984) *Portfolio and Investment Selection: Theory and Practice*, Prentice Hall International Inc, Englewood Cliffs, NJ.

Libby, R. and Fishburn, P.C. (1977) Behavioural models of risk taking in business decisions: a survey and evaluation. *Journal of Accounting Research*, **15**, 272–92.

Libby, R. and Lewis, B.L. (1982) Human information processing research in accounting: the state of the art in 1982. *Accounting, Organizations and Society*, **7** (3), 231–85.

Lindblom, C.E. (1959) The science of muddling through. *Public Administration Review*, **19**(2), 79–88.

Lindblom, C.E. (1968) *The Policy-Making Process*, Prentice Hall, Englewood Cliffs, NJ.

Lindblom, C.E. (1979). Still muddling, not yet through. *Public Administration Review*, **39**, 517–26.

Lindsay, W.M. and Rue, L.W. (1976) *Environmental Complexity in Long-Range Planning*, Planning Executives Institute, Oxford, Ohio.

Lindsay, W.M. and Rue, L.W. (1980). Impact of the organization environment on the long-range planning process: a contingency view. *Academy of Management Journal*, **23**, 385–404.

Linnerooth-Bayer, J. and Wahlstrom, B. (1991) Application of probabilistic risk assessments: the selection of appropriate tools. *Risk Analysis*, **11** (2), 239–48.

Lintner, J.V. (1965) The valuation of risk assets and the selection of risky investments in stock portfolios and capital budgets. *Review of Economics and Statistics*, **47**, Feb., 13–37.

Loomes, G. (1991) Evidence of a new violation of the independence axiom. *Journal of Risk and Uncertainty*, **4** (1), Jan., 91–108.

Lowrance, W.W (1976) *Of Acceptable Risk: Science and the Determination of Safety*, William Kaufmann, Los Altos, California.

Lucas, W. (1974) *The Case Survey Method: Aggregating Case Experience*, Rand, Santa Monica, Calif.

Luthans, F. (1973) The contingency theory of management: a path out of the jungle. *Business Horizons*, **16** (3), 67–72.

Luthans, F. (1976) *Introduction to Management: A Contingency Approach*, McGraw-Hill, New York.

Luthans, F. and Stewart, T.I. (1977) A general contingency theory of management. *Academy of Management Review*, **2**, 181–95.

Lyles, M.A. (1981) Formulating strategic problems: empirical analysis and model development. *Strategic Management Journal*, **2**, 61–75.

Lyles, M.A. and Lenz, R.T. (1982) Managing the planning process: a field study of the human side of planning. *Strategic Management Journal*, **3**, 105–18.

MacCrimmon, K.R. (1968) Descriptive and normative implications of the decision theory postulates, in *Risk and Uncertainty*, (eds K. Borch and J. Mossin), Macmillan, London.

MacCrimmon, K.R. (1970) Elements of decision making, in *Behavioural Approaches to Modern Management* (ed. W. Goldberg), Vol. I. BAS, Gothenburg, Sweden. pp. 15–44.

MacCrimon, K.R. (1973) Decision making and problem solving, in *Handbook of Industrial and Organizational Psychology*, (ed. M.D. Dunnette), Rand McNally, Chicago.

MacCrimmon, K.R. (1974) Managerial decision making, in *Contemporary Management: Issues and Viewpoints* (ed. J.W. McGuire), Prentice Hall, Englewood Cliffs, NJ, pp. 445–95.

MacCrimmon, K.R., Stanbury, W.T. and Wehrung, D.A. (1980) Real money lotteries: a study of ideal risk, context effects and simple processes, in *Cognitive Processes in Choice and Decision Behaviour* (ed. T.S. Wallsten), Lawrence Erlbaum, Hillside, NJ, pp. 155–77.

MacCrimmon, K.R. and Taylor, R.N. (1976) Decision making and problem solving, in *Handbook of Industrial and Organizational Psychology* (ed. M.D. Dunnette), Rand McNally, Chicago. pp. 1397–1454.

MacCrimmon, K.R. and Wehrung, D.A. (1985) *Taking Risks*, Mac-Millan, London.

MacGregor, D. (1991) Worry over technological activities and life concerns. *Risk Analysis*, **11**, (2), 315–24.

Machlis, G.E. and Rosa, E.A. (1990) Desired risk: broadening the social amplification of risk framework. *Risk Analysis*, **10**, (1), 161–8.

McFarlane, P. (1971) Simulation games as social psychological research sites: methodological advantages. *Simulation and Games*, **2**, (7) 149–61.

McGhee, W., Shields, M.D. and Birnberg, J.G. (1978) The effects of personality on a subject's information processing. *Accounting Review*, **53** (3), 681–97.

McGill, S.M. (1987) *The Politics of Anxiety*, Pion, London.

McGrath, J. (1964) Toward a theory of method for research in organizations, in *New Perspectives in Organizational Research*, (eds W.W. Cooper, H.J. Leavitt and M. Shelly.) Wiley, NY, pp. 157–88.

McGuire, M., Pratt, J. and Zeckhauser, R. (1991) Paying to improve your chances: gambling or insurance? *Journal of Risk and Uncertainty*. **4**, (4), 329–38.

McKone, T.E. (1991) Human exposure to chemicals from multiple media and through multiple pathways: research overview and comments. *Risk Analysis*, **11** (1), 5–10.

McNichols, T.J. (1977) *Policy Making and Executive Action*, McGraw-Hill, New York.

MacIntosh, N.B. (1981) A contextual model of information systems. *Accounting, Organizations and Society*, **6**(1), 39–53.

Mack, R.P. (1971) *Planning on Uncertainty*, Wiley, New York.

Mallory, G.R. and Wilson, D.C. (1981) Strategic decision making in British organisations. *Management Research News*, **4**, (1), 13–15.

March, J.G. (1979) Ambiguity and the engineering of choice. *International Studies of Management and Organizations*, **9**(3), 9–39.

March, J.G. Cohen, M.D. and Olsen, J.P. (1972) A Garbage can model of organizational choice. *Administrative Science Quarterly*, **17**(1), 319–43.

March, J.G. and Olsen, J.P. (1976) *Ambiguity and Choice in Organizations*, Universitet Sforlaget, Oslo.

March, J.G. and Simon, H.A. (1958) *Organizations*, Wiley, New York.

Markowitz, H. (1952) Portfolio selection. *Journal of Finance*, Mar., 77–91.

Markowitz, H. (1959) *Portfolio Selection*, Wiley, New York.

Marshall, D.V. (1987) Expert systems in the Stock Exchange (1).

Computer Law and Security Report, **3**, (1), 21–3.

Marshall, D.V. (1987) Expert systems in the Stock Exchange (2). *Computer Law and Security Report*, **3**, (2), 18–9.

Marshall, D.V. (1987) Expert systems in the Stock Exchange (3). *Computer Law and Security Report*, **3**, (4), 17–18.

Mason, R.O. and Mitroff, I.I. (1973) A program for research on management information systems. *Management Science (Theory Series)* **19**, (5) 475–87.

Mason, R.O. and Mitroff, I.I. (1981) *Challenging Strategic Planning Assumptions*, Wiley, New York.

Mason, R.O. and Mitroff, I.I. (1983) A teleological power-oriented theory of strategy. *Advances in Strategic Management*, **2**, 31–41.

Maturana, H.M. and Varela, F.G. (1980) *Autopoiesis and Cognition: The Realisation of the Living*, Reidel, Dordrecht.

Melcher, A.J. and Melcher, B. (1980) Toward a systems theory of policy analysis: static versus dynamic analysis. *Academy of Management Review*, **5**, (2), 235/47.

Miles, R.E. and Snow, C.C. (1978) *Organization Strategy, Structure and Process*, McGraw-Hill, New York.

Miles, R.H. (1982) *Coffin Nails and Corporate Strategies*, Prentice Hall, Englewood Cliffs, NJ.

Miller, D. (1975) Towards a contingency theory of strategy formulation. *Proceedings of the Academy of Management*, 64–6.

Miller, D. (1981) Toward a contingency approach: the search for organizational gestalts. *Journal of Management Studies*, **18**, (1), 1–26.

Miller, D. and Friesen, P.H. (1977) Strategy making in context, *Journal of Management Studies*, **14**, 253–80.

Miller, D. and Friesen, P.H. (1978) Archetypes of strategy formulation. *Management Science*, **24** (9), 921–33.

Miller, D. and Friesen, P.H. (1983) Strategy making and the environment: the third link. *Strategic Management Journal*, **4**, 221–35.

Miller, G.A. (1956) The magical number seven, plus or minus two: some limits on our capacity for processing information. *Psychological Review*, **63**, 81–97.

Mingers, J. (1989) An introduction to autopoiesis – implication and applications. *Systems Practice*, **2**, (2), 159–80.

Mintzberg, H. (1973a) Strategy making in three modes. *California Management Review*, **16**, (2), 44–53.

Mintzberg, H. (1973b) *The Nature of Managerial Work*, Prentice Hall, New York.

Mintzberg, H. (1975) The manager's job: folklore and fact. *Harvard Business Review*, July/Aug., 49–61.

Mintzberg, H. (1977) Policy as a field of management theory. *Academy of Management Review*, **2**, 88–103.

Mintzberg, H. (1977) Strategy formulation as a historical process. *International Studies of Management and Organizations*, **7**, (2), 28–40.

Mintzberg, H. (1978) Patterns in strategy formation. *Management Science*, **24**, (9), 934–48.

Mintzberg, H. (1979) An emerging strategy of 'direct' research. *Administrative Science Quarterly*, **24**, 582–9.

Mintzberg, H., Raisinghani, D. and Theoret, A. (1976). The structure of 'unstructured' decision processes. *Administrative Science Quarterly*, **21**, 246–75.

Mitroff, I.I., Barabba, V.P. and Kilmann, R.H. (1977) The application of behavioural and philosophical technologies to strategic planning: a case study of a large federal agency. *Management Science*, **24**,(1), 44–58.

Mitroff, I.I. and Mason, R.O. (1980) Structuring ill-structured policy issues: further explorations in a methodology for messy problems. *Strategic Management Journal*, **1**, 331–42.

Moberg, D.J. and Koch, J.L. (1975) A critical appraisal of integrated treatments of contingency findings. *Academy of Management Journal*, **18**,(1), 109–24.

Mock, T.J., Estrin, T.L. and Vasarhelyi, M.A. (1972) Learning patterns, decision style and value of information. *Journal of Accounting Research*, Spring.

Mockler, R.J. (1971) Situational theory of management. *Harvard Business Review*, **49**(3), 146–54.

Montanari, J.R., Moorhead, G. and Montanari, E.O. (1980). A laboratory study of a strategic decision making methodology. *Proceedings of American Institute for Decision Science*, Nov., 472–4.

Montgomery, C.A. and Singh, H. (1984) Diversification strategy and systematic risk. *Strategic Management Journal*, **5**, 181–91.

Moore, P.G. and Thomas, H. (1975) Measuring uncertainty. *Omega*, **3**,(6) 657–72.

Moore, P.G. and Thomas, H. (1976) *Anatomy of Decisions*, Penguin, London.

Moore, P.G. (1983) *The Business of Risk*, Cambridge University Press, Cambridge.

Morgan, M. and Lave, L. (1990) Ethical considerations in risk communication practice and research. *Risk Analysis*, **10**(3), 355–8.

Munier, B.R. (1991) Market uncertainty and the process of belief formation. *Journal of Risk and Uncertainty*, **4**,(4), 233–50.

Murray, E.A. (1978) Strategic choice as a negotiated outcome. *Management Science*, **24**,(9), 960–72.

Murray, J.A. (1978/9) Toward a contingency model of strategic decision. *International Studies of Management and Organizations*, **8**(4), Winter, 7–34.

Nachmias, D. and Nachmias, C. (1976) *Research Methods in Social Sciences*, St Martin's Press, New York.

NATO Office of Information and Press (1991) *The Alliance's Strategic Concept*. Agreed by the Heads of States and Government in Rome on 7–8 November 1991. Document 1215/91.

Naylor, T.A. (1980) *Strategic Planning Management*, Planning Executives Institute, Oxford, Ohio.

Nebeker, D.M. (1975) Situational favorability and perceived uncertainty: an integrative approach. *Administrative Science Quarterly*, **20**, 281–94.

Nees, D.B. (1978/9) The divestment decision process in large and medium-sized diversified companies: a descriptive model based on clinical studies. *International Studies of Management and Organization*, 8(4), 67–95.

Nees, D.B. (1983) Simulation: a complementary method for research on strategic decision-making processes. *Strategic Management Journal*, **4**, 175–85.

Newell, A. and Simon, H.A. (1972) *Human Problem Solving*, Prentice Hall, Englewood Cliffs, NJ.

Newman, W.H. (1967) Shaping the master strategy of your firm. *California Management Review*, **9**(3), 77–88.

Newman, W.H. (1971) Strategy and management structure. *Academy of Management Review*, Aug., 8–24.

Nickerson, R.N. and Feehrer, C.E. (1975) *Decision Making and Training: A Review of Theoretical and Empirical Studies of Decision Making and their Implications for the Training of Decision Makers*, Bolt, Beranok & Newman, Cambridge, MA.

Nutt, P.C. (1976) Field experiments which compared the effectiveness of design methods. *Decision Sciences*, **7**, 739–58.

Nutt, P.C. (1976) Models for decision making in organizations and some contextual variables which stipulate optimal use. *Academy of Management Review*, **1**, 84–98.

Nutt, P.C. (1977) An experimental comparison of the effectiveness of three planning methods. *Management Science*, **23**, 499–511.

Nystrom, H. (1974) Uncertainty, information and organizational decision making: a cognitive approach. *Swedish Journal of Economics*, 131–9.

Otley, D.T. (1980) The contingency theory of management accounting: achievement and prognosis. *Accounting, Organization and Society*, **5**(4), 413–28.

Otway, H.J. (1972) The quantification of social values. Paper presented at the Symposium on Risk versus Benefit, Solution or Dream. Los Alamos, N.M. Ref. LA 4860 – MS.

Paine, F.T. (1979) Commentary on paper by G.A. Steiner, in *Strategic Management: A New View of Business Policy and Planning* (eds D. E. Schendel and C.W. Hofer), Little, Brown & Co, Boston, 417–23.

Paine, F.T. and Anderson, C.R. (1977) Contingencies affecting strategy formulation and effectiveness: an empirical study. *Journal of Management Studies*, **14**, 147–58.

Paine, F.T. and Naumes, W. (1974) *Strategy and Policy Formation: An Integrative Approach*, W.B. Saunders, Philadelphia.

Pandey, V. (1991) *The effective management of organisation development with reference to the National Health Service*, Staffordshire University Business School.

Pavis, P. (1982) The aesthetics of theatrical reception, in *Languages of the Stage: Essays in the Semiology of the Theatre*, Performing Arts Journal Publications, New York.

Payne, J.W. (1973) Alternative approaches to decision making under risk: moments versus risk dimensions. *Psychological Bulletin*, **80**, 439–53.

Payne, J.W. (1976) Task complexity and contingent processing in decision making: an information search and protocol analysis. *Organizational Behaviour and Human Performance*, **16**, 366–87.

Payne, J.W. (1980) Information processing theory: some concepts and methods applied to decision research, in *Cognitive Processes in Choice and Decision Behaviour* (ed. T.S. Wallsen), Lawrence Erlbaum, Hillside, NJ.

Payne, J.W. and Braunstein, M.L. (1978) Risky choice: an examination of information acquisition behaviour. *Memory and Cognition*, **6**, 554–61.

Pennings, J.M. (1975) The relevance of the structural-contingency model for organizational effectiveness. *Administrative Science Quarterly*, **20**, 393–410.

Pennings, J.M. (ed.) (1985) *Strategic Decision Making in Complex Organizations*, Jossey-Bass.

Perrow, C. (1970) *Organizational Analysis: A Sociological View*, Wadsworth Publishing, Belmont, Calif.

Perrow, C. (1973) The short and glorious history of organizational theory. *Organizational Dynamics*, 3–14.

Perrow, C. (1979) *Complex Organisations* Scott Foresman, Glenview, Illinois.

Pettigrew, A.M. (1973) *The Politics of Decision Making*, Tavistock, London.

Pettigrew, A.M. (1977) Strategy formulation as a political process. *International Studies of Management and Organization*, **7** (2), 78–87.

Pettigrew, A.M. (1985) Culture and politics in strategic decision making and change, in *Strategic Decision Making in Complex Organizations*, (ed. J.M. Pennings) Jossey-Bass.

Pitz, G.F. (1980) The very guide of life: the use of probabilistic information for making decisions, in *Cognitive Processes in Choice and Decision Behaviour* (ed. T.S. Wallster), Lawrence Erlbaum, Hillside, NJ, pp. 79–94.

Porter, R.B and Carey, K. (1974) Stochastic dominance as a risk analysis criterion. *Decision Sciences*, **5** (1), 10–21.

Pounds, W.F. (1969) The process of problem finding. *Industrial Management Review*, **11**, 1–19.

Pratt, J.W., Raiffa, H. and Schlaifer, R. (1964) The foundations of decisions under uncertainty: an elementary exposition. *Journal of American Statistical Association*, 353–75.

Pruitt, D.G. (1961) Informational requirements in making decisions. *American Journal of Psychology*, **74**, 433–9.

Quinn, J.B. (1977) Strategic goals, process and politics. *Sloan Management Review*, **18**, 21–37.

Quinn, J.B. (1978) Strategic change: logical incrementalism. *Sloan Management Review*, **19**, (5), 7–21.

Raiffa, H. (1968) *Decision Analysis, Introductory Lectures on Choice under Uncertainty*, Addison-Wesley, Reading, Mass.

Ramani, S. and Finlay, H.F. (1991) Some models for analysis of hazards and justification for investment. *Risk Analysis*, **11**, (3), 405–8.

Ramsey, F. (1931) Truth and probability, in *The Foundations of Mathematics and Other Logical Essays* (ed. F.P. Ramsey), Harcourt, Brace & Co, New York.

Rappaport, A. (1967) Sensitivity analysis in decision making, *Accounting Review*, July, 441–56.

Raser, J. (1969) *Simulation and Society*, Allyn & Bacon, Boston.

Rawls, J. (1972) *A Theory of Justice*, Clarendon Press, Oxford.

Rice, G.H. (1980) But how do managers make decisions? *Management Decision*, **18**, (4), 194–202.

Richards, M.D. (1974) Managerial decision making: a review, in *Contemporary Management: Issues and Viewpoints*, (ed. J.W. McGuire), Prentice Hall, Englewood Cliffs, NJ, pp. 495–9.

Richman, B.M. (1964) *Achieving Corporate Objectives*: *Significance of Cultural Variables*. Academy of Management Proceedings.

Riker, W. and Allison, G. (1971) *Essence of Decisions*, Little Brown, Boston.

Robb, F.F. (1989) Cybernetics and suprahuman autopoietic systems. *Systems Practice*, **2**, (3), 343–8.

Robb, F.F. (1991) Accounting – a virtual autopoietic system? *Systems Practice*, **4** (3), 215–35.

Ronkainen, I.A. (1983) Risk in product development stages. *Industrial Marketing Management*, **12**, 157–63.

Rose, G.L. (1974) Assessing the state of decision making, in *Contemporary Management: Issues and Viewpoints*, (ed. J.W. McGuire), Prentice-Hall, Englewood Cliffs, NJ, pp. 499–506.

Rostopt, J.F. and Aiello, G.M. (1991) Spreading the word about risk management. *Risk Management*, June.

Roth, E. *et al.* (1990). What do we know about making risk comparisons? *Risk Analysis*, **10** (3), 375–87.

Rowe, W.D. (1977) *Anatomy of Risk*, Wiley, New York.

Rumelt, R. (1974) *Strategy, Structure, and Economic Performance in Large American Industrial Corporations*, Harvard University Press.

Rumelt, R. (1979) Evaluation of strategy: theory and models, in *Strategic Management: A New View of Business Policy and Planning*, (eds D. Schendel and C. Hofer), Little Brown & Co, Boston, pp. 189–212.

Salter, M. and Weinhold, W. (1979) *Diversification through Acquisition*, Free Press, New York.

Sarrazin, J. (1981) Top management's role in strategy formulation: a tentative analytical framework. *International Studies of Management and Organization*, **11** (2), 9–23.

Saunders, C.B. and Thompson, J.C. (1980) A survey of the current state of business policy research. *Strategic Management Journal*, **1**, 119–30.

Savage, L.J. (1954) *The Foundation of Statistics*, Wiley, New York.

Savich, R.S. (1977). The use of accounting information in decision making. *Accounting Review*, **52** (3), July, 642–52.

Schendel, D.E. and Hofer, C.W. (1979) *Strategic Management: A New View of Business Policy and Planning*, Little Brown, Boston.

Schendel, D.E. and Patten, R.G. (1978) A simultaneous equation model of corporate strategy. *Management Science*, **24**, 1611–21.

Schoeffler, S., Buzzell, R. and Heaney, D. (1974) Impact of strategic planning on profit performance. *Harvard Business Review*, **52** (2), 137–45.

Schoonhoven, C.B. (1981) Problems with contingency theory: testing assumptions hidden within the language of contingency theory. *Administrative Science Quarterly*, **26**, (1), 349–77.

Schroder, H.M., Driver, M.J. and Struefert, S. (1967) *Human Information Processing*, Holt, Rinehart & Winston, New York.

Schwenk, C.R. (1982) Why sacrifice rigour for relevance? A proposal for combining laboratory and field research in strategic management. *Strategic Management Journal*, **3**, 213–25.

Schwenk, C.R. (1982) Effects of inquiry methods and ambiguity tolerance on prediction performance. *Decision Sciences*, **13**, 207–11.

Schwenk, C.R. (1984) Cognitive simplification processes in strategic decision making. *Strategic Management Journal*, **5**, 111–28.

Schwenk, C.R. and Thomas, H. (1983) Formulating the mess: the role of decision aids in problem formulation. *Omega*, **11**, 239–52.

Scott, B.R. (1973) The industrial estate: old myths and new realities. *Harvard Business Review*, 156–83.

Scott, D. and Sathianathan, R. (1991) How much risk can your company stand? *Risk Management*, **38** (6), June, 85–8.

Shackle, G.L.S. (1961) *Decision, Order and Time in Human Affairs*, Cambridge University Press, London.

Shackle, G.L.S. (1969) *Decision, Order and Time in Human Affairs*, 2nd edn, Cambridge University Press, Cambridge.

Shah, K. and La Placa, P.J. (1981) Assessing risks in strategic planning. *Industrial Marketing Management*, **10** (2), 77–91.

Shalley, C.E. and Oldham, G.R. (1985) The effects of goal difficulty and expected external evaluation on intrinsic motivation: a laboratory study. *Academy of Management Journal*, **28** (3), 628–40.

Shanteau, J. (1974) Component processes in risky decision making. *Journal of Experimental Psychology*, **103**, 680–91.

Shapiro, A.C. (1978). Capital budgeting for the multinational corporation. *Financial Management*, Spring.

Sharpston, E. (1990) Legitimate expectations and economic reality. *European Law Review*, **15**, 103–60.

Sheth, J.N. (1973) A model of industrial buyer behaviour. *Journal of Marketing*, **37**, Oct., 50–6.

Shetty, Y.K. (1978). Management power and organizational effectiveness: a contingency analysis. *Journal of Management Studies*, May, 176–86.

Shields, M.D. (1980) Some effects of information load on search patterns used to analyse performance reports. *Accounting, Organizations and Society*, **5** (4), 429–42.

Shrivasta, P. (1983) Variations in strategic decision making processes.

Advances in Strategic Management, **2**, 177–89.

Shubik, M. (1954) Information, risk, ignorance and indeterminancy. *Quarterly Journal of Economics*, **64** (4), 629–40.

Simon, H.A. (1973) The structure of ill-structured decisions. *Artificial Intelligence*, **4**, 181–202.

Simon, H.A. (1977) *The New Science of Management Decision*. Prentice Hall, Englewood Cliffs, N.J.

Simon, H. (1978) Rationality as a process and as a product of thought. *American Economic Review*; **68**, 1–16.

Simon, H.A. (1979). Rational decision making in business. *American Economic Review*, **69**, (4), 493–513.

Slovic, P. (1966) Cue consistency and cue utilization in judgement. *American Journal of Psychology*, **79**, 427–34.

Slovic, P. (1972) Information processing, situation specificity and the generality of risk-taking behaviour. *Journal of Personality and Social Psychology*, **11**, 128–34.

Slovic, P. Fischoff, B. and Lichtenstein, S. (1977) Behavioural decision theory. *Annual Review of Psychology*, **28**, 1–39.

Slovic, P. Fleissner, D. and Bauman, W.S. (1972) Analyzing the use of information in investment decision making: a methodological proposal. *Journal of Business*, **45** (2), 283–301.

Slovic, P. and Lichtenstein, S. (1968) Relative importance of probabilities and payoffs in risk taking. *Journal of Experimental Psychology*, **78**, (3), 1–18.

Slovic, P. and Lichtenstein, S. (1971) Comparison of Bayesian and regression approaches to the study of information in judgement. *Organizational Behaviour and Human Performance*, **6**, (6), 649–744.

Slovic, P. (1987) Perception of risk. *Science*, **236**, 280–5.

Smith, D. and Nichol, R.T. (1981) Change, standardization and contingency theory. *Journal of Management Studies*, **18** (1), 73–88.

Smith, M.L. and Williams, C.A. (1991) How the corporate risk manager contributes to company value. *Risk Management*, **38** (4), 58–66.

Snow, C.C. (1976) *The role of managerial perceptions in organizational adaptation: an exploratory study*. Academy of Management Proceedings, pp. 249–55.

Snow, C.C. and Hambrick, D.C. (1980) Measuring organizational strategies: some theoretical and methodological problems. *Academy of Management Review*, **5**, 527–38.

Snyder, N. and Wheelen, T. (1981) *Managerial Roles: Mintzberg and the Management Process Theorists*. Academy of Management Proceedings, pp. 249–53.

Soelberg, P.O. (1967) Unprogrammed decision making. *Industrial Management Review*, **3**, 19–29.

Spender, J.C. (1980) Strategy making in business. PhD thesis, Manchester Business School.

Spender, J.C. (1983) The business policy problem and industry recipes, in *Advances in Strategic Management, Vol 2* (ed. R. Lamb) JAI Press, Greenwich, CT, pp. 211–29.

Spetzler, C.S. (1968) The development of a corporate risk policy for capital investment decisions. *IEEE, Transactions on Systems Science and Cybernetics*. **4**, (3), 279–300.

Stagner, R. (1969) Corporate decision making: an empirical study. *Journal of Applied Psychology*, **53**, (1), 1–13.

Stahl, M.J and Zimmer, T.W. (1984) Modeling strategic acquisition policies: a simulation of executives' acquisition decisions. *Academy of Management Journal*, **27** (2), 369–83.

Star, S.L. (1992) The Trojan door: organisations, work, and the open black box. *Systems Practice*, **5** (4), Aug., 395–410.

Steiner, G.A. (1979) Contingency theories of strategy and strategic management, in *Strategic Management: A New View of Business Policy and Planning*, (eds D.E. Schendel and C.W. Hofer), Little Brown & Co, Boston, pp. 405–16.

Steiner, G.A. and Miner, J.B. (1977) *Management Policy and Strategy*, Macmillan, New York.

Streufert, S. *et al.* (1965) A tactical game for the analysis of complex decision making in individuals and groups. *Psychological Reports*, **17**, (3), 723–9.

Streufert, S. and Streufert, S.C. (1970) Effects of failure in a complex decision making task on perceptions of cost, profit and certainty. *Organizational Behaviour and Human Performance*, **5**, 15–32.

Summers, T. and White, D.E. (1976) Creativity and the decision process. *Academy of Management Review* **1**, 99–107.

Swalm, R.O. (1966) Utility theory – insights into risk taking. *Harvard Business Review*, **44**, Nov./Dec., 123–36.

Taback, H. (1991) Preventing a crisis from getting out of hand. *Risk Management* **38** (10), Oct., 64–9.

Taylor, B. and Sparkes, J.R. (1977) *Corporate Strategy and Planning*, William Heinemann, London.

Taylor, R.N. (1975) Psychological determinants of bounded rationality: implications for decision making and strategy. *Decision Sciences* **6**, 409–29.

Thaler, R.H. (1988) The winner's curse. *Journal of Economic Perspectives*, **2**, 191–202.

Thietart, R.A. (1978/9) Introduction: new challenges for strategic management. *International Studies of Management and Organizations* **8** (4), Winter, 3–6.

Thomas, H. (1984) Strategic decision analysis: applied decision analysis and its role in the strategic management process. *Strategic Management Journal*, **5**, (2), 139–56.

Thomas, H. and Schwenk, C.R. (1984) Decision analysis as an aid to strategy. *Management Decision*, **22**, (2), 50–60.

Thompson, A.A. and Strickland, A.J. (1980) *Strategy Formulation and Implementation*, Business Publications, Dallas, Texas.

Thompson, J.D. (1967) *Organizations in Action*, McGraw-Hill, New York.

Thompson, J.D. and Tuden, A. (1959) Strategies, structures and processes of organizational decision, in *Comparative Studies in Administration* (eds J.D. Thompson *et al.*), University of Pittsburg Press.

Thune, S.S. and House, R.J. (1970) Where long range planning pays off. *Business Horizons*, **13** (4), Aug., 81–7.

Tichy, N.M. (1983) *Managing Strategic Change, Technical, Political and Cultural Dynamics*, Wiley, London.

Tobin, J. (1958) Liquidity preference as behaviour towards risk. *Review of Economic Studies*, **25**, (2), 65–85.

Tomassini, L.A. (1976) Behavioural research on human resource accounting: a contingency framework. *Accounting, Organizations and Society*, **1** (3), 239–50.

Tosi, H.L., Aldag, R. and Storey, R. (1973) On the measurement of the environment: an assessment of the Lawrence and Lorsch environmental uncertainty subscale. *Administrative Science Quarterly*, **18** (1), 27–36.

Tosi, H.L. and Carroll, S.J. (1976) *Management Contingencies, Structure and Process*, St Clair, Chicago.

Tosi, H.L. and Hamner, W.C. (1974) *Organizational Behaviour and Management: A Contingency Approach*, St Clair Press, Chicago.

Tosi, H.L. and Slocum, J.W. (1984) Contingency theory: some suggested directions. *Journal of Management*, **10**, (1), 9–26.

Tuffey, T.J. (1991) Technology forecasting as a risk management tool. *Risk Analysis*, **11**, (1), 35–9.

Tulsiani, V., Haimes, Y.Y. and Li, D. (1990) Distribution analyser and risk evaluator (DARE) using fault trees. *Risk Analysis*, **10**, (4), 521–38.

Tversky, A. (1967) Additivity, utility and subjective probability. *Journal of Mathematical Psychology*, **4**, 175–202.

Tversky, A. (1969) Intransitivity of preference. *Psychological Review*, **76**, 31–48.

Tversky, A. (1972) Elimination by aspects: a theory of choice. *Psychological Review*, 79, 281–99.

Tversky, A. (1974) Assessing uncertainty. *Journal of the Royal Statistical Society*. Series B, **36**, 148–59.

Tversky, A. and Kahneman, D. (1974) Judgement under uncertainty: heuristics and biases. *Science*, **185**, Sept., 1124–31.

Vancil, R.C. (1976) Strategy formulation in complex organizations. *Sloan Management Review*. **17** (2), Winter, 2–5.

Versteeg, M.F. (1988) External safety policy in the Netherlands: an approach to risk management. *Journal of Hazardous Materials*, **17**, 215–22.

Von Neumann, J. and Morgenstern, O. (1944) *Theory of Games and Economic Behaviour*, Princeton University press, Princeton, New Jersey.

Walker, R. (1985) *Applied Qualitative Research*, Gower, London.

Wallsten, T.S. (ed.) (1980) *Cognitive Processes in Choice and Decision Behaviour*, Lawrence Erlbaum, Hillside, NJ.

Warner, R.F and Whitehead, W.G. (1991) Using a TPA to control losses. *Risk Management*, **38**, (7), 35–6.

Warren, K.E. (1966) *Long Range Planning: The Executive Viewpoint*, Prentice Hall, Englewood Cliffs, NJ.

Weick, K.E. (1977) Enactment processes in organizations, in *New Directions in Organizational Behavior* (eds B.M. Staw and G.R. Salancik), St Clair Press, Chicago.

Weir, J.E. (1979) Toward the theoretical foundations of contingency policy-making behaviour, in *Academy of Management Proceedings* (ed. R.C. Huseman).

Whitley, R. (1984) The scientific status of management research as a practically-oriented social science. *Journal of Management Science*, **21** (4), 369–90.

Willet, A.H. (1901). *The Economic Theory of Risk and Insurance*, repr. 1951, Irwin, Homewood, Ill.

Wilson, D.C. (1982) Electricity and resistance: a case study of innovation and politics. *Organization Studies*, **3**.

Winkler, R.L. (1967) The quantification of judgement: some methodological suggestions. *Journal of the American Statistical Association*, **34**, 1105–20.

Winkler, R.L. (1968) The consensus of subjective probability estimates. *Management Science*, **15** (2), B61–B75.

Winkler, R.L. (1991) Ambiguity, probability, preference, and decision analysis. *Journal of Risk and Uncertainty*, **4**, 285–97.

Wissema, J.G, Van Der Pol, H.W. and Messer, H.M. (1980) Strategic management archetypes. *Strategic Management Journal*, **1**, 37–47.

Witte, E. (1972) Field research on complex decision making processes – the phase theorem. *International Studies of Management and Organizations*, **2**, 156–82.

Wood, S. (1979) A reappraisal of the contingency approach to organization. *Journal of Management Studies*, Oct., 334–54.

Woodward, J. (1965) *Industrial Organization: Theory and Practice*, Oxford University Press, London.

Yaprak, A. and Sheldon, K.T. (1984) Political risk management in multinational firms: an integrative report. *Management Decision*, **22**, (6), 53–67.

Yin, R.K. (1981) The case study crisis: some answers. *Administrative Science Quarterly*, **26**, 58–65.

Yin, R.K. and Heald, K.A. (1975) Using the case study method to analyse policy studies. *Administrative Science Quarterly*, **20**, 371–81.

Youngblood, R.W. (1991) A review of faultrEASE version 1.0. *Risk Analysis*, **11** (2), 343–48.

Zadeh L.A. (1973) Outline of a new approach to the analysis of complex systems and decision processes. *IEEE Transactions on Systems, Man, and Cybernetics*, **3**, (1), 28–44.

Zelemy, M. (1976) Multidimensional measure of risk: prospect rating vector. Working Paper, Graduate School of Business, Columbia University.

Zeleny, M. and Pierre, N. (1975) *Simulation Models of Autopoietic Systems*. Proceedings 1975 Summer Computer Conference, San Francisco.

Index